T0361102

Routledge Handbook of the Economics of Knowledge

The *Routledge Handbook of the Economics of Knowledge* provides a comprehensive framework to integrate the advancements over the last 20 years in the analysis of technological knowledge as an economic good, and in the static and dynamic characteristics of its generation process.

There is a growing consensus in the field of economics that knowledge, technological knowledge in particular, is one of the most relevant resources of wealth, yet it is one of the most difficult and complex activities to understand or even to conceptualize. The economics of knowledge is an emerging field that explores the generation, exploitation, and dissemination of technological knowledge. Technological knowledge can no longer be regarded as a homogenous good that stems from standardized generation processes. Quite the opposite, technological knowledge appears more and more to be a basket of heterogeneous items, resources, and even experiences. All of these sources, which are both internal and external to the firm, are complementary, as is the interplay between bottom-up and top-down generation processes. In this context, the interactions between the public research system, private research laboratories, and various networks of learning processes, within and among firms, play a major role in the creation of technological knowledge.

In this *Handbook* special attention is given to the relationship between technological knowledge and both upstream scientific knowledge and related downstream resources. By addressing the antecedents and consequences of technological knowledge from both an upstream and downstream perspective, this *Handbook* will become an indispensable tool for scholars and practitioners aiming to master the generation and the use of technological knowledge.

Cristiano Antonelli is Professor of Economics at the University of Torino where he is the President of the School of Economics and Statistics and a Fellow of the Collegio Carlo Alberto, Italy.

Albert N. Link is Professor of Economics at the University of North Carolina at Greensboro, USA.

Routledge Handbook of the Economics of Knowledge

Edited by Cristiano Antonelli and Albert N. Link

LONDON AND NEW YORK

First published 2015
by Routledge

2 Park Square, Milton Park, Abingdon, Oxfordshire OX14 4RN
52 Vanderbilt Avenue, New York, NY 10017

Routledge is an imprint of the Taylor & Francis Group, an informa business

First issued in paperback 2019

Copyright © 2015 selection and editorial material, Cristiano Antonelli and
Albert N. Link; individual chapters, the contributors

The right of the editors to be identified as the authors of the editorial
material, and of the authors for their individual chapters, has been
asserted in accordance with sections 77 and 78 of the Copyright,
Designs and Patents Act 1988.

All rights reserved. No part of this book may be reprinted or reproduced or
utilised in any form or by any electronic, mechanical, or other means, now
known or hereafter invented, including photocopying and recording, or in
any information storage or retrieval system, without permission in writing
from the publishers.

Notice:
Product or corporate names may be trademarks or registered trademarks,
and are used only for identification and explanation without intent to
infringe.

British Library Cataloguing in Publication Data
A catalogue record for this book is available from the British Library

Library of Congress Cataloging-in-Publication Data
Antonelli, Cristiano.
Routledge handbook of the economics of knowledge / Cristiano
Antonelli, Albert N. Link. – First Edition.
pages cm
Includes bibliographical references and index.
1. Knowledge management–Economic aspects. 2. Information
technology–Economic aspects. 3. Technological innovations–Economic
aspects. I. Link, Albert N. II. Title.
HD30.2.A5793 2014
658.4'038–dc23
2014018440

ISBN: 978-0-415-64099-2 (hbk)
ISBN: 978-0-367-86758-4 (pbk)

Typeset in Bembo
by Cenveo Publisher Services

Contents

Contents

Figures

Tables

Contributors

Cristiano Antonelli, University of Torino and Collegio Carlo Alberto, Italy.

David B. Audretsch, Indiana University, USA.

Barry Bozeman, Arizona State University, USA.

Phil Cooke, University of Cardiff, Wales.

Francesco Crespi, University of Rome III and Collegio Carlo Alberto, Italy.

Benoît Godin, INRS (Montréal), Canada.

Rajeev K. Goel, Illinois State University, USA.

Devrim Göktepe-Hultén, Lund University, Sweden.

Christopher S. Hayter, Arizona State University, USA.

Joshua Hinger, Indiana University, USA.

Börje Johansson, Jönköping International Business School, Jönköping, Sweden.

Rodrigo Kataishi, University of Torino, Italy.

Erik E. Lehmann, University of Augsburg, Germany.

Albert N. Link, University of North Carolina at Greensboro, USA.

Hans Lööf, Royal Institute of Stockholm, Sweden.

Fabio Montobbio, University of Torino, Italy.

Müge Özman, Telecom Ecole de Management, France.

Contributors

Rati Ram, Illinois State University, USA.

Heather Rimes, University of Georgia, USA.

Giuseppe Scellato, Politecnico di Torino and Collegio Carlo Alberto, Italy.

Gregory Tassey, University of Washington, USA.

Jennie Welch, University of Georgia, USA.

Yet another measure of ignorance

Albert N. Link

> Since we know little about the causes of productivity increase, the indicated importance of this element may be taken to be some sort of measure of our ignorance about the causes of economic growth in the United States and some sort of indication of where we need to concentrate our attention.
>
> *Moses Abramovitz (1956, p. 11)*

The Abramovitz (1956) paper, from which the above epigram came, and the seminal work by Solow (1957) are heralded by many as foundational reading for what Antonelli and Link (2014) have referred to as the area of investigation known as "the economics of technological change." Antonelli and Link (2014, p. xiii) write:

> The analysis of the causes and consequences of the increase of the general efficiency of labor and the associated changes in production, consumption, and distribution brought about by the introduction of new technologies in economic systems is a field of economic investigation of growing interest and widening activity both in research and teaching. This field has evolved over time, partly in response to the changing focus of economic analysis. This area of investigation was identified as "the economics of technical progress" for a large part of the 20th century. In the 1960s and 1970s, it was referred to as "the economics of technological change," and through the 1980s and 1990s it became known as "the economics of innovation." Since then a new shift occurred to bring to the attention of scholars "the economics of knowledge" as a crucial crossing between the economics of science and the innovation. …
> The discovery of the so-called residual, along with an appreciation of its size, pushed economics to investigate more deeply the characteristics of the new technologies in terms of factor intensity, elasticity of substitution, output elasticity, and technology diffusion. This phase of academic understanding coincides with "the economics of technological change."

The residual mentioned by Antonelli and Link (2014) refers to the residual calculated by Solow (1957). Implicit in the Solow model is a Cobb-Douglas production function written in terms of output (Q), capital (K), labor (L), and time (t):

$$Q = F(K, L; t) \tag{1}$$

And if technical change, that is "*any kind of shift* in the production function" (Solow 1957, p. 312), is neutral then equation (1) becomes:

$$Q = A(t) f(K, L) \tag{2}$$

Mathematically it follows that:

$$Q'/Q - \alpha K'/K - \beta L'/L = A'/A \tag{3}$$

where Q', K', and L' are time derivatives and α and β are relative shares. The residual, A'/A, represents the percentage growth in output that is not attributable to the percentage growth of inputs K and L. Following Solow (1957, p. 320):

> Gross output [Q] per man hour doubled over the interval [1909–1949], with 87½ per cent of the increase attributable to technical change and the remaining 12½ per cent to increased use of capital.

Conventionally interpreted, the lion's share of the changes in output from 1909 to 1949 cannot be explained in terms of changes in K and L inputs; thus, residually measured growth is for the most part unexplained.

Decades of research by able scholars have been devoted to explaining the residual, that is explaining what had previously been viewed to be merely a measure of ignorance. They have accomplished this by identifying empirical correlates with either A' or A'/A. What has evolved is an empirical as well as conceptual understanding that research and development (R&D) investment spending is a driver of so-measured technological change (Griliches, 1996; Hall *et al.*, 2010).

However, another measure of ignorance has, in my opinion, arisen, and it relates to the effectiveness of public policies, be they U.S. policies or not, initiated with the intent of actually stimulating R&D spending.

Consider Figure 1.1. It shows the movement over time in the total factor productivity (TFP) index for the private business sector in the United States from 1948 through 2011. Simply, and with reference to equation (1) above, the TFP index is calculated as $Q/F(K, L, M, E, S)$, where M refers to material inputs, E to energy inputs, and S to purchased business services.[1]

Two time periods are noteworthy in the figure; they are associated with two periods of productivity slowdown that are particularly important for understanding the evolution of U.S. technology and innovation policies. The first time period is from 1973 through 1974, and the second time period is from 1978 through 1982.

The slowdown in measured productivity in 1973 and 1974 was presumed by many economists, and likely many policy makers, to be a result of non-recurring and periodic events, such as the energy crisis of 1973. Many economists and policy makers in the United States thought at the time that such events were normal, one-time cyclical shocks to the economy, and movement in the TFP index was accordingly a normal cyclical response around a more stable, long-term growth in productivity.

More important, however, from both an economic and a policy perspective, was the productivity slowdown that began in 1978 and ended in 1982. In fact, in 1978 the Bureau of Labor Statistics' TFP index was 78.906, the highest it had been in the post-World War II

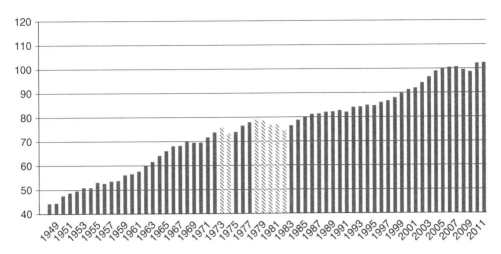

Figure 1.1 U.S. Total Factor Productivity Index, 1948–2011 (2005 = 100)

period. By the end of 1982, the TFP index was 74.401, only slightly higher that it had been a decade earlier.

Many explanations have been offered for this precipitous and unprecedented decline in productivity, or technological advancement, from 1978 through 1982 as summarized in Link (1987). For example, Link and Siegel (2003, p. 58), reflecting the concern that the slowdown was not a response to cyclical, one-time, and temporary shocks but rather due to a more fundamental and enduring change in long-term growth prospects, wrote:

> In the early 1980s there was great concern among economists and policymakers in the United States regarding the pervasive slowdown in productivity growth and the concomitant decline in the global competitiveness of American firms in key high-technology industries. One of the alleged culprits of this productivity slowdown was a decline in the rate of technological innovation, which is a reflection of declining entrepreneurship.

In response to these productivity declines, the U.S. Congress passed five major initiatives, as shown in Table 1.1 and described in more detail in Table 1.2. Each of the initiatives was intended to have a direct and/or indirect impact on private R&D activity under the implicit assumption that investments in R&D drive technological advancement.

As an aside, it is interesting to point out that while the foundation for U.S. technology and innovation policy has been traced by some to the five initiatives in Table 1.1 and Table 1.2, it was not until 1990 that there was a formal technology policy statement for the United States. Many point to President George H.W. Bush's 1990 *U.S. Technology Policy* as the nation's first formal domestic technology policy statement. Albeit important as an initial formal policy statement, it failed to articulate a foundation for government's role in innovation and technology. Rather, it implicitly assumed that government had a role, and then set forth the general statement (Executive Office of the President, 1990, p. 2):

> The goal of U.S. technology policy is to make the best use of technology in achieving the national goals of improved quality of life for all Americans, continued economic growth, and national security.

Table 1.1 U.S. technology- and innovation-related policies initiated in the post-productivity slowdown period

Legislation	Targeted party(s)	Direct impact on R&D	Indirect impact on R&D
University and Small Business Patent Procedure Act of 1980 (known as the Bayh-Dole Act of 1980)	Universities Private-sector firms		Yes
Stevenson-Wydler Technology Innovation Act of 1980 (known as the Stevenson-Wydler Act of 1980)	National laboratories and other research organizations Private-sector firms		Yes
Economic Recovery Tax Act (ERTA) of 1981 (relevant portion known as the R&E Tax Credit of 1981)	Firms conducting R&D	Yes	
Small Business Innovation Development Act of 1982	Small firms (< 500 employees)	Yes	
National Cooperative Research Act of 1984	Firms of all sizes and their research partners		Yes

Table 1.2 Description of U.S. post-productivity slowdown period technology and innovation policies

Legislation	Description
Bayh-Dole Act of 1980 (Public Law 96-517)	The Act redefined property rights that facilitated the transfer of existing knowledge resulting from public-sector support from universities to the private sector.
Stevenson-Wydler Technology Innovation Act of 1980 (Public Law 96-480)	The Act called for federal laboratories to actively promote technology transfer to the private sector for commercial exploitation. Each national laboratory was mandated to establish an Office of Research and Technology Applications to facilitate this technology transfer.
R&E Tax Credit of 1981 (Public Law 97-34)[a]	The Act provided a 25 percent marginal tax credit, that is a 25 percent tax credit for qualified R&E expenditures in excess of the average amount spent during the previous three taxable years, in an effort to increase private-sector R&D spending. The marginal rate was later lowered to 20 percent.
Small Business Innovation Development Act of 1982 (Public Law 97-219)	The Act created the Small Business Innovation Research (SBIR) program to provide research grants to small firms for the purposes of stimulating technology development and its subsequent commercialization.
National Cooperative Research Act of 1984 (Public Law 98-462)	The Act created a registration process under which joint research and development ventures, or more simply research joint ventures (RJVs), can voluntarily disclose their research intentions to the U.S. Department of Justice and thereby gain partial indemnification from antitrust laws and penalties.

Note: [a]Research and experimentation (R&E) expenditures are more narrowly defined than R&D expenditures, which include all costs incident to development. R&E does not include ordinary testing or inspection of materials or products for quality control of those for efficiency studies, etc. R&E, in a sense, is the experimental portion of R&D.

A question that has yet to be investigated is: How effective were these U.S. post-productivity slowdown technology and innovation policies? Our lack of information about how to answer this question is what I call yet another measure of ignorance.

I investigate this question in this chapter, and I offer suggestive evidence that these initiatives were indeed effective. Building on equation (3), scholars have quantified the relationship between R&D investments and residually measured growth as:

$$A'/A = \lambda + \rho\left(T'/Q\right) \tag{4}$$

where T represents the stock of technical capital, $\rho = \partial Q/\partial T$, and $T' = \partial T/\partial t$. Interpreting T' as private investments in the stock of technical capital, as approximated by investments in private R&D, then ρ can be interpreted as an estimate of the rate of return to R&D (RD) from:[2]

$$A'/A = \lambda + \rho\left(RD/Q\right) \tag{5}$$

Based on the TFP index data that underlie Figure 1.1, data on aggregate U.S. private R&D (RD), and data on Gross Domestic Product (to approximate Q), estimates from equation (5) yield a rate of return to investments to R&D over the period of available R&D data, 1953 through 2009, ρ, of 21.5 percent. However, on re-estimation by dividing the sample of data into two time periods: (1) before 1980 and (2) 1980 forward, the period when the first of the five policies in Table 1.1 was initiated, the rate of return to R&D was only 7.1 percent in the pre-public sector technology and innovation policy period, and it was 32.8 percent in the subsequent period.[3]

Although measuring the efficacy of any public-sector policies that are in effect in an uncertain economic environment is fraught with difficulties that suggest caution, these initial findings provide a remarkable first judgment on the performance of U.S. public-sector technology and innovation policies over the past three decades. As such, they begin to inform the gap in our knowledge about our ignorance about the effectiveness of U.S. technology and innovation policies.

In a broader sense, this chapter, like all of those in this Handbook, is a part of a search for understanding new dimensions of what is called the economics of knowledge. By using the term economics of knowledge, I am referring herein to the analysis of the determinants of knowledge that is requisite for a meaningful investigation into the variety of actors involved in identifying the vagaries of productivity growth in an economy. A desired outcome of such an analysis is a step forward toward an improved understanding of the effects of the generation, dissemination, exploitation, valorization, and utilization of knowledge in an economy.

Notes

1 See <http://www.bls.gov/mfp/mprtech.htm>. The U.S. Bureau of Labor Statistics refers to this as a multi-factor productivity (MFP) index.
2 See Hall *et al.* (2010, 2014) for a review of findings from estimating the model in equation (4).
3 Held constant in this regression model is a binary variable to account for the productivity slowdown periods in the 1970s. These empirical results are described in detail in Leyden and Link (2015, forthcoming).

References

Abramovitz, Moses (1956). "Resource and Output Trends in the United States since 1870," *American Economic Review* 46: 5–23.
Antonelli, Cristiano and Albert N. Link (2014). "Building the Economics of Knowledge: A Roadmap," in A.N. Link and C. Antonelli (eds.), *Recent Developments in the Economics of Science and Innovation*, pp. xiii–xx, New York: Edward Elgar.

Executive Office of the President (1990). *U.S. Technology Policy*, Washington, DC: Office of Science and Technology Policy.

Griliches, Zvi (1996). "The Discovery of the Residual," *Journal of Economic Literature* 34: 1324–1330.

Hall, Bronwyn H., Jacques Mairesse, and Pierre Mohnen (2010). "Measuring the Returns to R&D," in B.H. Hall and N. Rosenberg (eds.), *Handbook of the Economics of Innovation*, pp. 1033–1082, Amsterdam: North Holland.

Hall, Michael J., Stephen K. Layson, and Albert N. Link (2014). "The Returns to R&D: Division of Policy Research and Analysis at the National Science Foundation," *Science and Public Policy*, 41: 458–463.

Leyden, Dennis P. and Albert N. Link (2015). *Public Sector Entrepreneurship*, New York: Oxford University Press, forthcoming.

Link, Albert N. (1987). *Technological Change and Productivity Growth*, Chur, Switzerland: Harwood Academic Publishers.

Link, Albert N. and Donald S. Siegel (2003). *Technological Change and Economic Performance*, London: Routledge.

Solow, Robert M. (1957). "Technical Change and the Aggregate Production Function," *Review of Economics and Statistics* 39: 312–320.

2

Innovation and creativity

A slogan, nothing but a slogan

Benoît Godin

1. Introduction[1]

If there is one basic idea that defines research and development (R&D) and technological innovation today, it is certainly that of creativity. But what is creativity? In a review article on the study of technological innovation among economists, Dominique Foray, the researcher responsible for the re-awakening of interest in the concept of a knowledge economy in the 2000s, states his intention to enlighten us on what economics ignores, in particular creativity. However, Foray is nothing if not frugal when it comes to providing a definition and analysis of what creativity is, except to state briefly that it is "l'aptitude à engendrer de la nouveauté, des nouvelles idées" (the aptitude to engender novelty, new ideas) (Foray, 2004: 246). To Foray, creativity is the "fruit du hasard … et de la nécessité" (fruit of chance and necessity). It remains a mystery. In addition, Foray makes reference to two metaphors, including the Scrabble metaphor, to explain the combination and chance inherent in creativity. Furthermore, in a reminder of Schumpeter's famous metaphor on "creative destruction" (Foray, 2004: 242), Foray discusses one half of the metaphor (destruction), but the second (creativity) not at all. Foray concludes: "jusqu'à présent, l'analyse économique de l'innovation n'a pas porté très loin"; the study of creativity is "un domaine encore en friche" (up to the present, the economic analysis of innovation has not led very far; the study of creativity is a realm still fallow) (Foray, 2004: 272). Foray's analysis is itself a perfect example of state of the art.

Such a cloud surrounding the idea of creativity is also found with the economic historian Joel Mokyr, incidentally also author of a book on the knowledge economy (Mokyr, 2004). In *The Lever of Riches*, which bears the subtitle *Technological Creativity and Economic Progress*, Mokyr defines "technological creativity" as "the application of new ideas to production" in industry (Mokyr, 1990: 263).[2] As with Foray, we find in Mokyr a reference to Schumpeter's metaphor. However, the author also concentrates his analysis on the destructive dimension of innovation without discussing creativity (Mokyr, 1990: 261–69). Having defined creativity as he does, Mokyr could reply that creativity constitutes the subject of the book as a whole. However, the definition of creativity that Mokyr provides is what others simply call innovation – and what others again, including Mokyr, discuss as *technological change*. Without further analysis of creativity itself, we must conclude that there is a circularity in the concepts.

Let's end this reflective introduction with a third author. I choose and critique Norbert Alter on this point because *L'innovation ordinaire* (Alter, 2000) is, I believe, an example to be followed when it comes to analyzing innovation. It includes an analysis of innovation that is empirical rather than strictly conceptual. "Creative" is a recurring term in Alter, and also appears in a chapter title (*Les processus créateurs*).[3] However, Alter never defines the concept. We find a distinction between invention and innovation (Alter, 2000: 8), another between innovation and change (Alter, 2000: 119), but no definition of what creativity is. We understand that Alter uses the concept for "emergence of newness", but we find no analysis of creativity.

In brief, creativity is more postulated than studied, at least in science, technology and innovation studies. Creativity is simply a synonym for change and newness. The concept possesses a mythic value. When you have said the word, you have said it all. The above three stories are an exact copy of Joseph Schumpeter in *The Creative Response in Economic Theory*:

> Whenever the economy or an industry or some firms in an industry do something else, something that is outside of the range of existing practice, we may speak of *creative response* [Schumpeter's italics] ... A study of creative response becomes coterminous with a study of entrepreneurship ...
>
> *(Schumpeter, 1947: 222)[4]*

This chapter presents a contribution to the intellectual history of innovation, or the history of the concept of innovation. It attempts to explain how the concept of creativity came to be associated with the idea of innovation, creativity coming to define, to some, what innovation is. This chapter differs from what I have written in recent years on innovation. I conduct no archaeology nor genealogy of the concept of innovation in order to study its construction, the associated ideas or concepts and the authors who have contributed to the development of the representations. Space does not permit. This chapter attempts rather to provide an essay that draws freely on my current research into the intellectual history of innovation. In addition, I offer in conclusion some critical thoughts that I am not in the habit of including in historiographical writings.

2. A few words on history[5]

Innovation is everywhere, in the world of things – novelties of all sorts emerged continuously – but also in language, whether scientific or ordinary speech. Discussions on innovation occur every day, turning the concept into a cliché. The scientific literature is full of writing about innovation. In every country, public policies make innovation an instrument (a panacea) of economic policy.

But what is innovation? What is the origin of the concept, and could this origin have had an impact on our current representations and the uses that are made of the concept? The concept of innovation has its origins in antiquity. It goes back to the metaphoric use of a Greek term (*kainotomia*), which means literally to make new cuts, such as opening new galleries in the mines (Xenophon). Thereafter, innovation was used by philosophers within the framework of discussions on governments and changes of political constitutions. Innovation was then understood as the introduction of a change into the established order (Plato, Aristotle, Polybius). The Romans made a similar use of the concept (*novare*).

Innovatio entered the everyday vocabulary in the context of the Reformation (*in* + *novare*). In the sixteenth and seventeenth centuries, the English Puritans were responsible for one of the first controversies regarding innovation, using the term abundantly against their opponents. Bishops were accused of innovating in wishing to subtly integrate elements of Catholicism into

Protestant doctrine. Then in the eighteenth century, the concept came to be associated with political revolutions and, incidentally, with violence. Starting in the 1830s, it was the socialists' and social reformers' turn to be treated as (social) innovators because they overthrew the social and economic order. Innovation's pejorative connotation would endure until the twentieth century. The innovator is a deviant, and that includes innovators in the fields of science and industry (technology).

It is in the aftermath of the French Revolution, and of that period called *Sattelzeit* (1750–1850) by Reinhart Koselleck, that the concept gradually acquired a positive connotation. However, it is in the last 50 years that the concept was transformed into an ideology, and by the same group that had previously contested it: governments. Since the sixteenth century, governments have prohibited innovation by royal decree. Today, to governments, and supported in this by theorists, innovation, understood as technological innovation, has become an instrument of economic policy. Innovation is everywhere valued. The scientific literature is no exception: the vocabulary on technology is becoming that of technological innovation; biologists talk of animal innovation; sociologists resurrect the concept of social innovation, a concept that had appeared at the beginning of the nineteenth century.

Innovation's rehabilitation, and the related change in meaning, makes use of a rhetoric that replaces that relating to deviance (heresy, revolution). Two arguments have developed to this end during the past two centuries. The first relates to economics, in the broad utilitarian sense: innovation, provided it is "useful", is from then on not only welcomed but even sought after. The second argument relates to creativity: innovation is a creative activity, creative (in the productive sense) of economic value certainly, but creative also in the sense given to it in the arts (originality).

I suggest that it is by means of the idea of composition or combination that creativity made its entry into the vocabulary of innovation, beginning in the late nineteenth century. Innovation is the combination of existing elements with the goal of producing something new. In turn, the idea of combination, and this is the second contribution of this chapter, owes its origins to philosophical theories relating to the association of ideas in the eighteenth century.

If, however, as I mentioned above, there are two logics that contributed to the rehabilitation of the idea of innovation, it is the economic one that has prevailed over the "cultural" logic. This is the central idea of this chapter. For this reason, creativity, a concept with a "cultural" connotation *par excellence*, remains a word, nothing but a word – at least with regard to analyzing technological innovation. Creativity has become a metaphor, and the association between creativity and innovation has become a slogan.

3. The association of ideas

The epistemological question is at the heart of philosophical discussions of knowledge in the seventeenth and eighteenth centuries. How do we explain knowledge? If our senses trick us so often, and the mind, due to its capacity for imagination, falsifies our representation of reality, what is true knowledge? The doctrine of the association of ideas is the (or one) answer to that question.

In his *Essay Concerning Human Understanding* (1690), John Locke suggests that the mind constructs ideas from simpler ideas. The mind actively associates simple ideas (arising from perception) to produce complex ideas, and this, according to Locke, *ad infinitum*. This is the theory that would become known as the doctrine of the association of ideas. The expression does come from Locke.

To Locke, however, but also to Thomas Hobbes before him and David Hume after him, the association of ideas is pure fantasy. It is too often a source of error, particularly if the associations are not "natural" (necessary). Associations are the fruit of education and of habit. Among the associationists there is no question of creative imagination, with few exceptions. The association is automatic: it occurs unconsciously. It is the memory that does the work. The imagination is only a passive faculty.

In fact, at the time, imagination is contrasted to reason. The imagination certainly produces newness, but it must do so according to strict rules. Association must be under the control of reason. A consistency should guide the association: similarity, proximity or succession (in time and space) and causality. Between simple ideas (sensation) and complex ideas, there must exist reasoning.

The psychological doctrine of the association of ideas had many followers in the eighteenth century among philosophers and other thinkers who were trying to explain knowledge (Warren, 1921; Kallich, 1970; Rapaport, 1974). "Associate, compose, combine, merge, unite", these are just some of the terms regularly used to explain knowledge. The analogy with physics and chemistry (matter is a compound of elements) and with linguistics (words are the components of sentences) is also frequently heard among the associationists. However, it is as a result of literary criticism that association acquired a real legitimacy. From then on, the imagination (of the artist) was defined in a positive way. The imagination uses association or combination to create something new.

4. Combination

Imagination as a category remained fundamentally pejorative in the eighteenth century, and to many, long after that. The imagination is spoken of using synonyms like fantasy and fancy: the imagination invents (fictions). When philosophers have a good word to say about imagination, it is that it is said to be "active" – but still not creative. The imagination makes the required associations or plays a transcendental role (in the Kantian sense) that reflects the distinction or dichotomy between fantasy and imagination.[6]

Then, beginning at the end of the eighteenth century, the imagination acquired its stamp of nobility. The imagination produces newness, that is, it is creative. What had previously been a distortion of reality became embellishment of nature, deepening of things, interior truth revealed, creation. From then on there is postulated a distinction between reproductive imagination (memory) and productive imagination. This story has long been known (Bundy, 1927; Bowra, 1950; Abrams, 1953; Rossky, 1958; Engell, 1981). What I would like to emphasize here is the relationship between the idea of the imagination understood as creativity and the doctrine on the association of ideas (Mednick, 1962; Engell, 1981). To Locke, we have said, the mind associates or combines simple ideas to produce more complex ideas. Similarly, the imagination combines ideas and facts for producing something new. This combination is often described by analogy with the doctrine on the association of ideas.

The *Encyclopédie* of Diderot and d'Alembert (1751) is a good example of a conception of the imagination understood as combination. In the article on the imagination, Voltaire distinguishes passive imagination and active imagination, a dichotomy very popular at the time. The former is a simple reproduction (memory) of what the senses perceive, while the active imagination arranges: it "rapproche plusieurs objets distants, elle sépare ceux qui se mêlent, les compose & les change" (it brings together several distant objects, it separates those that go together, arranges them and changes them). Pour Voltaire, les "perceptions entre par les sens, la mémoire les retient, l'imagination les compose" (the perceptions enter via the senses, the memory retains them, the imagination arranges them).

Diderot, Condillac, Helvétius and several others espouse a similar conception. Even those to whom the imagination is not a positive faculty discuss it in terms of combination. Francis Bacon, for example, suggests in *The Advancement of Learning* (1605) "The imagination, being not tied to the laws of matter, may at pleasure join that which nature hath severed and sever that which nature had joined, and so make useful matches and divorces of things".

But let us be clear. Imagination is not yet a question of "creativity". To Voltaire, the imagination does not create; it only arranges "car il n'est pas donné à l'homme de se faire des idées, il ne peut que les modifier" (as it is not given to man to make ideas, he can only modify them). Rather, we owe the connotation of the imagination taken as creative production or combination to literary criticism (Romanticism) – Addison, Wordsworth and Coleridge to speak only of the English, as it is in England (and Germany) that Romanticism is most productive on this topic – and to Kant and German idealism (Fichte, Schelling).[7] To Coleridge, the imagination is a force or power of composition (a "synthetic power"). The imagination creates more than it associates. To idealism the imagination produces a transcendental synthesis of perceptions and consciousness. Alexander Gerard, in his *Essay on Genius* published in 1756, is a good example of the conception of imagination as combination too. To Gerard, genius is imagination, and the latter is essentially a matter of combination (association).

The conception of the imagination understood as combination has been influential: it developed in the eighteenth and nineteenth centuries and remains present in the literature of the twentieth century. This conception is found in particular in psychological theories or theories of a psychological nature. To Théodore Ribot, in *L'imagination créatrice*, imagination is a matter of association (Ribot, 1900). To the psychologist Robert Woodworth, who doesn't hesitate to refer to the doctrine on the association of ideas, the imagination is a mental "manipulation" that combines previously perceived facts into a new product (artistic, technological, social). The imagination rearranges in order to produce newness (Woodworth, 1929). Some decades later, Arthur Koestler invented the concept of "bisociation": "combining two hitherto unrelated cognitive matrices in such a way that a new level is added to the hierarchy, which contains the previously separated structures as its members" (Koestler, 1967: 213–15).

The conception of the imagination seen as combination is also that of invention. In fact, the two concepts have often been a pair since the eighteenth century. Invention as genius or ingenuity (*ingenium*) is a highly creative ability that gathers, collects, rediscovers and borrows from what exists in order to produce something new. The concept of invention, of rhetorical origin, thus takes on a connotation related to originality and to (free) creation (Smith, 1925; Nahm, 1973–74).[8] In every field, invention would thereafter refer to a creation and would be discussed in terms of combination. In the article on Art in the *l'Encyclopédie*, inspired by Bacon, Diderot suggests that complex machines are the combination of simpler machines. The idea is present as well in Adam Smith, Jean-Baptiste Say and Charles Babbage: "Improvements in machinery … have been made by the ingenuity of the makers of the machines … and some by that of those who are called philosophers or men of speculation, whose trade is not to do anything, but to observe everything; and who, upon that account, are often capable of combining together the powers of the most distant and dissimilar objects" (*Wealth of Nations*, 1776, Book 1, Chapter 1).

From the end of the nineteenth century, several writings appeared with titles explicitly suggesting a theory of invention, often from a psychological perspective (see box). Almost all of the theorizing defined invention in terms of combination, whether from scientists (Ernst Mach, Henri Poincaré, Albert Einstein, Jacques Hadamard) or from researchers in social sciences. The idea of combination also became multiple and "total" (covering everything). It appears from then on under various terms and the meanings are extensive: the result of the exchanges among the people from different cultures (anthropology), the contribution by accumulation or combination of several individuals to an invention (sociology), the functions or activities of an organization interacting together with the goal of producing an invention (management)

(Miettinen, 2006). Already in the nineteenth century, to many philosophers and literary critics, the imagination was a total faculty (*organic unity*) that unifies opposites: objectivity and subjectivity, mind and matter, man and nature, reason and emotion (Engell, 1981). Over the twentieth century, Gestalt psychology continued the tradition: invention is the reorganization and redefinition of organized wholes.

Theories of invention

- P. Souriau, *Théorie de l'invention*, 1881.
- O. T. Mason, *The Origins of Invention*, 1895.
- F. Paulhan, *Psychologie de l'invention*, 1901.
- A. P. Usher, *A History of Mechanical Invention*, 1929.
- J. Rossman, *The Psychology of the Inventor*, 1931.
- J.-M. Montmasson, *Invention and the Unconscious*, 1932.
- S. C. Gilfillan, *The Sociology of Invention*, 1935.
- J. Hadamard, *The Psychology of Invention in the Mathematical Field*, 1945.

---

5. Innovation

Among the theoreticians on the imagination in the nineteenth century, there is one named Victor Egger of the *Collège de France*. In *La parole intérieure: essai de psychologie descriptive*, published in 1881, Egger defines the imagination by introducing the concept of innovation. He distinguishes the reproductive imagination from the imagination *per se*. To Egger, only the latter is a matter of innovation: it combines and "makes" a new ensemble from old elements, while the reproductive imagination is only a memory of sensations. This is one of the rare acceptations of the term innovation in the theoretical writings of the time. Innovation is a contested term right up to the twentieth century. In consequence, innovation is discussed in terms of and with the more positive term combination among the earliest theoreticians on innovation. In fact, combination is really a precursor term to innovation.

Many trace the origin of theoretical interest in innovation to Joseph Schumpeter.[9] It is rarely mentioned, however, that Schumpeter himself spoke of combination and not innovation, at least until the publication of *Business Cycles* (Schumpeter, 1939). The first edition (in German) of *The Theory of Economic Development* (1912) does not make use of the concept. The second edition (1926), as well as the translation into English (Schumpeter, 1934), introduces the term innovation in the sense of newness. Innovation remained a secondary idea. It is rather combination that is defined explicitly in terms of what would become innovation in 1939: a new combination of factors of production (labour and capital). That said, Schumpeter introduces at least four different definitions of innovation in this 1939 book.

The omission of the term innovation by economists in the first half of the twentieth century is symptomatic of the denial that innovation was still subjected to in the vocabulary, but it is also witness to a step in the construction of a representation of innovation. Basically, before coming to be defined in fundamentally economic terms as it is today, innovation was a matter of combination. Schumpeter is not the only one to talk about innovation in these terms. The sociologist Gabriel Tarde preceded him at the end of the nineteenth century (Tarde, 1890), as did the American sociologist Lester Ward (Ward, 1903). Vilfredo Pareto also speaks of innovation in terms of combination. In his *Traité de sociologie générale* (1917), the sociologist explains society in terms of psychological categories, two of which are fundamental. A first class of individuals is distinguished by its spirit of innovation, called combination, and a second by its conservatism. To Pareto, combination unites disparate elements to create a new entity. This is the principal factor that explains the political, economic and cultural systems as well as social change.

Today, the literature on innovation does not study innovation as combination. Theoreticians on technological (invention and) innovation, from the very earliest (e.g.: Abbot P. Usher, Colum S. Gilfillan, Josef A. Schumpeter, Simon Kuznets, Everett M. Rogers, Chris Freeman) up to today (Basalla, 1988; Arthur, 2009) regularly define or rather briefly mention innovation using the idea of combination, but without studying the phenomenon.[10] There is also a research tradition (*technological change*) that defines innovation in terms of a new combination of factors of production. But combination here has no connotation at all relating to creativity. It is essentially economic: the substitution of labour and capital in a new way (or combination). In addition, the idea of combination in economics is very frequently associated pejoratively with imitation or a minor (incremental) innovation. Not novel (revolutionary) enough. It is *bricolage*, in the Claude Lévi-Strauss sense (*The Savage Mind*, 1962: 16–36): a *bricoleur* combines bits and pieces, remains and remnants of previous activities in a contingent way. Except for some occasional articles (such as Kogut and Zander, 1992; Weitzman, 1998; Fleming, 2001; Faucheux and Forest, 2012), the only analytical writing on combination worth mentioning is that of the American anthropologist Homer G. Barnett: *Innovation: The Basis of Cultural Change* (1953). In fact, over the twentieth century the representation of innovation as a faculty of combination gave way to an economic representation that became dominant and even hegemonic: innovation is the commercialization of an invention.

6. Creative innovation

However, there remains a residue of the idea of combination in that of creativity. The idea of creativity is very old (Nahm, 1973–74; Tatarkiewicz, 1980; Kristeller, 1983; Mason, 2003) and the theoretical explanations are many: anthropological, historical, social, psychological, metaphysical (mystery), accidental (chance) (MacKinnon *et al.*, 1968; Miettinen, 1996; Simonton; 2004; Kronfeldner, 2009). In the twentieth century, the idea of creativity is ubiquitous among anthropologists trying to explain invention in all its forms. The philosopher John Dewey applies the concept of creativity to all forms of human activity and experience. A significant quantity of writing also comes from psychology: different groups of selected professionals are studied (artists, scientists, inventors) in order to identify (measure) the source and the conditions for the emergence of creativity. The researchers Morris Stein, Calvin Taylor and Anne Roe are among the most prolific authors. Well-known authors such as Robert Merton and Thomas Kuhn have produced papers on creativity too (Kuhn, 1959; Merton, 1965).

The historical development of societies (civilization) is also explained in terms of creativity. There are the creative man of Florian Znaniecki (1918–20), the creative minority of Arnold Toynbee (1957), and the creative eras of Reinhold Niebuhr (1941) and Alfred Kroeber (1944). Today, we speak of "creative classes", "creative industries", "creative economy", "creative culture", expressions that strive to be all-encompassing and creativity covers almost everything that is not manual (and much more). Organizations (European Commission) decreed 2008 to be the year of creativity … and innovation.

In the twentieth century, the idea of technological innovation is closely linked to that of creativity too, starting with economic historian A. P. Usher (1929). Among the many definitions that Schumpeter gives of innovation, one makes reference to creativity, itself defined in terms of "energy", as Thorstein Veblen and Lester Ward had done before him – and as Coleridge and many others had said of the imagination: innovation requires a "surplus of energy".[11] We also owe to Schumpeter the "popularization" of an expression that has become a cliché to many: capitalism is "creative destruction" (Schumpeter, 1942). Innovation destroys old things to create new ones. However, the idea of creative destruction (and often the expression) can be found prior and simultaneously to Schumpeter: Friedrich Nietzsche, Werner Sombart, Paul Tillich and Fritz Redlich.

Despite the fad for creativity today, the idea of creative innovation remains more often than not a cliché. This is particularly the case with the literature on management of technology and organizational innovation, which made abundant use of the idea of creativity starting in the 1950s, but also with the literature on technological innovation in general. Early such titles include *Creativity and Innovation* by John Haefele (1962) and *The Creative Organization* by Gary Steiner (1965). Another testimony to this wave of interest in creativity is the re-edition of the classic work by Joseph Rossman, *The Psychology of the Inventor* (1931), the title of which became *Industrial Creativity: The Psychology of the Inventor* in 1964. However, the reader would be hard put to find in these writings an analysis of what creativity is – if it is not just a synonym for "productivity".[12] The same is true of recent writings, as I mentioned in the introduction.

The concept of creativity has been relegated to a metamorphic role in recent decades, at least with regard to analyzing technological innovation. Creativity, or rather analyzing creativity, has shifted to what is conventionally called innovation, and to the study of innovation as *process*. Psychological analysis has been replaced by social and economic analysis. With analogies, however. Innovation is a process that takes place according to steps analogous to the stages of cognitive development and/or of the life cycle of an organism. In spite all of this, the concept of – or rather the word – creativity remains in the vocabulary. It is used, in this case, as a label to name the process of innovation. The historian of technology John Staudenmaier for example, in a chapter of his otherwise-excellent study on the history of technology as seen through articles published in the journal *Technology and Culture*, a chapter titled *Emerging Technology and the Mystery of Creativity*, discusses creativity in terms of the process of innovation by stages, or rather substitutes for a psychological analysis of creativity an analysis in terms of socio-economic stages – because invention remains of a "mysterious nature" to historians who "rarely approach the topic of the individual creative process" (Staudenmaier, 1985: 41). By the end of the chapter, creativity has become a socio-economic process of invention, development and innovation.

7. Science, R&D and innovation

Yet, the idea of creativity has led to a specific representation of innovation over the twentieth century: that of research and development (R&D). To understand this, one has to remember that, for several decades now, technological innovation has been postulated as intimately linked to science or invention. As a matter of fact, the concept of innovation entered into science in the nineteenth century as the "introduction of the scientific method into the useful arts" (Godin, 2014). Over the next century, theorists on innovation extended this understanding to the "application of science to industry".[13] Industrial R&D laboratories hold a special place here, and they have been studied precisely for their central role, so it is said, in the generation of technological innovation.

This phrase or concept of R&D has contaminated innovation and transmitted its connotation of creativity to innovation in the following way. First, from the early theoretical thoughts on technological invention to the first world-wide standardized definition of R&D for survey purposes (OECD, 1962; 1970), R&D is defined as innovation and creativity:

The guiding line to distinguish R. and D. activity from non-research activity is the presence or absence of an element of **novelty** or **innovation**. Insofar as the activity follows an established routine pattern it is not R. and D.

(OECD, 1962: 16)

Research and experimental development may be defined as **creative** work undertaken on a systematic basis to increase the stock of scientific and technical knowledge and to use this stock of knowledge to devise new applications.

(OECD, 1970: 8)

Second, R&D so defined has been imagined as the source or first step in the process of innovation. The first theory of technological innovation, known as the linear model of innovation, states that innovation starts from basic research, then moves on to applied research then to development – despite the oft-repeated distinction drawn between invention and innovation.

Third, in statistical and econometric matters – a whole "industry" or business by the way – R&D is used as a proxy for innovation. And today, R&D remains the main official statistics on innovation, or at least the first and central one that is discussed when talking about innovation in statistical scoreboards, for example.

In spite of all this, our main conclusion remains true. Although creativity defines innovation, through science or R&D, there is no study of creativity *per se* in the literature. The idea of creativity is in the background, namely it defines related concepts associated with innovation, but it is not theorized upon.

8. Conclusion

Innovation has become a cliché that, to many, there is no need to define or analyze. The term is applied at every opportunity, some even going so far as to be amazed not to find it in the arts (Oakley *et al.*, 2008) – an innovative field it may be, but one that has its own vocabulary (creation) without any need for the concept of innovation.

To limit ourselves to saying that knowledge and innovation are synonymous with creativity and vice versa is not enough. The association (the combination!) of the two ideas has become a slogan.[14] Creativity says nothing more here than change and/or newness. As if the thinking is already done and the "mystery" explained. This pseudo-thinking is now embodied in the word in an impressive and allusive form. But if one wishes to add substance to the analysis of innovation in its relationships to creativity, one must necessarily at some point explicitly study the creative act. For decades, the issue of creativity is treated more felicitously in the literature on invention. Yet, in that on technological innovation, creativity is too often taken as a given. Creativity is a word, nothing but a word, at best a metaphor. A metaphor, since only the individual innovates – it is an anthropocentric conception that attributes the power of creation to God, to Nature (Bergson, 1907) … or to animals (Reader and Laland, 2003). It is also in a metaphoric sense that we say, *ad nauseam*, that a society or that the economy is creative. Society changes; it does not innovate.[15]

The psychological explanation, no matter which psychological explanation, is no longer in favour, except among psychologists (but few of them take an interest in innovation). Perhaps it is that we have retained from the psychological explanation of creativity a discredited conception, that of mystery and genius. But besides this more-than-century-old conception, there is combination, which may be studied empirically: machines come apart in order to study the combination; new theories analyze themselves in order to count up borrowings and interdisciplinary activity. Innovation is indeed a combination. But the study of combination no longer takes place. Certainly social researchers mention regularly the idea that innovation is a combination, but only in passing. The study of combination and creativity necessitates empirical and historical research, like looking at different versions of an idea or thing over time.

Innovation has acquired a dominant connotation that today is under the wing of economics. Beyond the economic dimension, it appears extremely difficult, even for "alternative" researchers (such as the so-called evolutionary economists), to study the cultural (creative) dimension of innovation.

Notes

1 I sincerely thank Reijo Miettinen for comments on a first draft of the paper.
2 A more inclusive definition is provided implicitly in the introduction: "the tale of technological creativity requires citing who first came up with an idea [invention] and who made the critical revisions and improvements necessary for the idea to work" (Mokyr, 1990: 12).
3 Like Foray and Mokyr, Alter makes use of the Schumpeter metaphor too.
4 In this paper from 1947, Schumpeter proceeds as our authors do, or rather our authors proceed exactly as Schumpeter does. First, Schumpeter suggests that "economic change" is a "sadly neglected area" of study. Second, he brings a definition of creativity (as a synonym to economic change, as cited above). Third, Schumpeter discusses the mysterious characteristics of creativity: it "cannot be predicted", but it has enormous effects ("shapes the whole course of subsequent events"); it has something to do with the "quality of the personnel" and with "individual decisions, actions". Fourth, Schumpeter defines economics (the entrepreneur) in terms of innovation (a subset of creativity): "the doing of new things or the doing of things that are already being done in a new way".
5 The reader is invited to consult the following site for precise archival references to this section: www.csiic.ca.
6 In the seventeenth and eighteenth centuries, we find a few (rare) mentions among philosophers of the fact that the imagination produces something entirely new or original, something different from its group of components, for example among certain English associationists such as Alexander Bain (Warren, 1921) and Franz von Baader in Germany (Faivre, 1981). The idea of the creative imagination is also present in Kant and the post-Kantians (Warnock, 1976; Kearney, 1988).
7 On the creative imagination in philosophy and religion before that date, seen as power to act upon the world (magical and demiurgical power), see Faivre (1981).
8 In the field of literature and the arts, however, the concept of creation has come to have precedence over that of invention. Basically, after Francis Bacon, invention acquired a "technological" connotation. On the history of the concept of invention, see Sergeant (1923), Watson (2001) and Langer (2008).
9 Wrongly, because: 1. Schumpeter was not the only one to produce writings on innovation at the time – others preceded him (Gabriel Tarde in 1890, Thorstein Veblen in 1899, Lester Ward in 1903), or were writing at the same time he was (Vilfredo Pareto in 1917), and from a much broader perspective than his – I should mention, however, that the first edition of *The Theory of Economic Development* contained a chapter of a "sociological" nature that was abandoned in subsequent editions; also, an article was recently unearthed titled *Development*, never published, that dealt with innovation in a general way; 2. Schumpeter's "theory" comes down to some ten pages, no more and no less than others before him had produced, with the exception of Tarde; 3. Schumpeter's theory concentrates on the economy only and is indistinguishable from the writings on technological change, from which it also espouses the conception of innovation. In short, Schumpeter is a symbolic figure to economists. It was rather the (many) followers of Schumpeter who developed his ideas after his death, such as Rupert W. Maclaurin and Fritz Redlich. However, these two are completely forgotten today, at least in the literature from "innovation studies" (Godin, 2008).
10 For example, the British economist Chris Freeman's combination makes analogies with Abbott P. Usher's "Gestalt" theory of an "imaginative process of 'matching' ideas". "All theories of discovery and creativity stress the concept of imaginative association or combination of ideas", states Freeman: "coupling first takes place in the minds of imaginative people" (Freeman, 1982: 111–12). Then Freeman expands, without further analysis, the theory of the mind to "the whole of the experimental

development work and the introduction of the new product" – "linking and coordinating different sections, departments and individuals", "communication within the firm and between the firm and its prospective customer" (Freeman, 1982: 112) – and the entrepreneur: "the crucial contribution of the entrepreneur is to *link* the novel ideas and the market" (Freeman, 1982: 110).

11 "Power" and "energy" are two key terms of the vocabulary of imagination in the eighteenth and nineteenth century. In *The Theory of Economic Development* (1934), Schumpeter talks of the entrepreneur as innovator in these terms too. The terms used (and opposed to routine) are energy – "exercising one's energy and ingenuity" – motive power, effort, strength, great surplus force (Schumpeter, 1934: 81–94).

12 At the time it was a matter of increasing the number of inventions or productivity within enterprises. Conditions were therefore studied that were likely to encourage "creativity". Researchers as consultants to organizations are well represented in this type of literature.

13 The results of scientific research – inventions – as well as the scientific method.

14 As J. H. McPherson, manager, Psychology Department, Dow Chemical Company, puts it in his paper on "creative engineers": "engineers expect to carry their brain children on out to maturity – through pilot plant and production plant on out to the marketplace … to carry an idea out through the verification stages, reduction to practice … to get ideas off the ground" (McPherson, 1965: 33–35).

15 Certainly metaphor is a source of knowledge. However, to some researchers the metaphor replaces knowledge. On uses of the idea of creativity in social sciences, see Joas (1996).

References

Abrams, M. H. (1953), *The Mirror and the Lamp: Romantic Theory and the Critical Tradition*, Oxford: Oxford University Press.

Alter, N. (2000), *L'innovation ordinaire*, Paris: La Découverte.

Arthur, W. B. (2009), *The Nature of Technology*, New York: Free Press.

Bacon, F. (1605), *The Advancement of Learning*, London: Printed for Henrie Temes.

Barnett, H. G. (1953), *Innovation: The Basis of Cultural Change*, New York: McGraw Hill.

Basalla, G. (1988), *The Evolution of Technology*, Cambridge: Cambridge University Press.

Bergson, H. (1907), *L'évolution créatrice*, Paris: Presses universitaires de France.

Bowra, C. M. (1950), *The Romantic Imagination*, London: Oxford University Press.

Bundy, M. W. (1927), The Theory of Imagination in Classical and Medieval Thought, *University of Illinois Studies in Language and Literature*, 12: 183–289.

Diderot, D. and d'Alembert, J. (1751), *Encyclopédie of Diderot and d'Alembert*, Paris: Briasson.

Egger, V. (1881), *La parole intérieure: essai de psychologie descriptive*, Paris: Germer Baillière et Co.

Engell, J. (1981), *The Creative Imagination: Enlightenment to Romanticism*, Cambridge (Mass.): Harvard University Press.

Faivre, A. (1981), L'imagination créatrice (fonction magique et fondement mythique de l'image), *Revue d'Allemagne et des pays de langue allemande*, 13: 355–90.

Faucheux, M., and J. Forest (2012), Reflections on Technology: A Science of Creative Rationality?, in M. Faucheux and J. Forest (eds), *New Elements of Technology*, Belfort: Université de technologie de Belfort-Montbéliard, pp. 49–62.

Fleming, L. (2001), Recombinant Uncertainty in Technological Search, *Management Science*, 47 (1): 117–32.

Foray, D. (2004), Ce que l'économie néglige ou ignore en matière d'analyse de l'innovation, in N. Alter (ed.), *Les logiques de l'innovation: approche pluridisciplinaire*, Paris: La Découverte: 241–74.

Freeman, C. (1982), *The Economics of Industrial Innovation*, 2nd edition, Cambridge (Mass.): MIT Press.

Godin, B. (2008), In the Shadow of Schumpeter: W. Rupert Maclaurin and the Study of Technological Innovation, *Minerva*, 46 (3): 343–60.

Godin, B. (2014), *Innovation and Science: When Science Has Nothing to Do with Innovation, and Vice Versa*, Project on the Intellectual History of Innovation, INRS: Montreal.

Haefele, J. (1962), *Creativity and Innovation*, New York: Reinhold Publishing Corporation.

Joas, H. (1996), *The Creativity of Action*, Chicago: University of Chicago Press.

Kallich, M. (1970), *The Association of Ideas and Critical Theory in Eighteenth-Century England*, The Hague: Mouton.

Kearney, R. (1988), *The Wake of Imagination: Ideas of Creativity in Western Culture*, London: Century Hutchinson.

Koestler, A. (1967), *The Ghost in the Machine*, London: Pan Edition.

Kogut, B., and U. Zander (1992), Knowledge of the Firm, Combination Capabilities, and the Replication of Technology, *Organization Science*, 3 (3): 383–97.

Kristeller, P. O. (1983), Creativity and Tradition, *Journal of the History of Ideas*, 44 (1): 105–13.

Kroeber, A. (1944), *Configurations of Culture Growth*, Berkeley: University of California Press.

Kronfeldner, M. E. (2009), Creativity Naturalized, *The Philosophical Quarterly*, 59 (237): 577–92.

Kuhn, T. S. (1959), Innovation and Tradition, in M. Taylor and F. Barron (eds), *Scientific Creativity*, London: Wiley, pp. 162–74.

Langer, U. (2008), Invention, in G. P. Norton (ed.), *The Cambridge History of Literary Criticism, volume 3: Renaissance*, Cambridge: Cambridge University Press, pp. 136–44.

Lévi-Strauss, C. (1962), *The Savage Mind*, London: Garden City Press pp. 50–65.

Locke, J. (1690), *Essay Concerning Human Understanding*, London: Church Yard.

MacKinnon, D. W., J. M. B. Edwards and R. E. L. Faris (1968), Creativity, in D. Shills (ed.), *International Encyclopedia of the Social Sciences*, London: Collin-Macmillan, pp. 434–61.

McPherson, J. H. (1965), How to Manage Creative Engineers, *Mechanical Engineering*, 87 (2): 32–36.

Mason, J. H. (2003), *The Value of Creativity*, Aldershot: Ashgate.

Mednick, S. A. (1962), The Associative Basis of the Creative Process, *Psychological Review*, 69 (3): 220–32.

Merton, R. K. (1965), The Environment of the Innovating Organization: Some Conjectures and Proposals, in G. A. Steiner (ed.), *The Creative Organization*, Chicago: University of Chicago Press, pp. 50–65.

Miettinen, R. (1996), Theories of Invention and Industrial Innovation, *Science Studies*, 2: 34–48.

Miettinen, R. (2006), The Sources of Novelty: A Cultural and Systematic View of Distributed Creativity, *Creativity and Innovation Management*, 15 (2): 173–81.

Mokyr, J. (1990), *The Lever of Riches: Technological Creativity and Economic Progress*, Oxford: Oxford University Press.

Mokyr, J. (2004), *The Gifts of Athena: Historical Origins of the Knowledge Economy*, Princeton: Princeton University Press.

Nahm, M. C. (1973–74), Creativity in Art, in P. P. Wiener (ed.), *Dictionary of the History of Ideas*, New York: Scriber, pp. 577–89.

Niebuhr, R. (1941), *The Nature and Destiny of Man*, New York: Charles Scribner's Sons.

Oakley, K., B. Sperry and A. Patt (2008), *The Art of Innovation: How Fine Arts Graduates Contribute to Innovation*, London: National Endowment for Science, Technology and the Arts (NESTA).

OECD (1962), *The Measurement of Scientific and Technical Activities: Proposed Standard Practice for Surveys of Research and Development*, Paris: OECD.

OECD (1970), *The Measurement of Scientific and Technical Activities: Proposed Standard Practice for Surveys of Research and Experimental Development*, Paris: OECD.

Pareto, V. (1917), *Traité de sociologie générale*, Paris-Genève: Droz [1968].

Rapaport, D. (1974), *The History of the Concept of Association of Ideas*, New York: International Universities Press.

Reader, S. M. and K. N. Laland (2003), *Animal Innovation*, Oxford: Oxford University Press.

Ribot, T. (1900), *L'imagination créatrice*, Paris: Félix Alcan.

Rossky, W. (1958), Imagination in the English Renaissance: Psychology and Poetic, *Studies in the Renaissance*, 5: 49–73.

Rossman, J. (1931), *The Psychology of the Inventor*, Washington: The Inventors Publishing.

Schumpeter, J. A. (1934), *The Theory of Economic Development: An Inquiry into Profits, Capital, Credit, Interest, and the Business Cycle*, Cambridge, Mass. Harvard University Press.

Schumpeter, J. A. (1939), *Business Cycles: A Theoretical, Historical, and Statistical Analysis of the Capitalist Process*, Volume 1, New York: McGraw Hill.

Schumpeter, J. A. (1942), *Capitalism, Socialism and Democracy*, New York: Harper [1962].

Schumpeter, J. A. (1947), The Creative Response in Economic History, reprinted in *Essays on Entrepreneurs, Innovations, Business Cycles, and the Evolution of Capitalism*, R.V. Clemence (ed.), New Brunswick: Transaction Books [1989], pp. 221–31.

Sergeant, A. M. (1923), *The History of the Term "Invention" in English Criticism*, Thesis, University of Illinois: Urbana (Ill.).

Simonton, D. K. (2004), *Creativity in Science: Chance, Logic, Genius and Zeitgeist*, Cambridge: Cambridge University Press.

Smith, A. (1776), *Wealth of Nations*, Book 1, Chapter 1, London: W. Strahan.

Smith, L. P. (1925), Four Romantic Words, in L. P. Smith, *Words and Idioms: Studies in the English Language*, London: Constable and Co.

Staudenmaier, J. M. (1985), *Technology's Storytellers: Reweaving the Human Fabric*, Cambridge (Mass.): MIT Press.

Steiner, G. (1965) *The Creative Organization*, Chicago: University of Chicago Press.

Tarde, G. (1890), *Les lois de l'imitation*, Paris: Seuil [2001].

Tatarkiewicz, W. (1980), Creativity: History of the Concept, in W. Tatarkiewicz (ed.), *A History of Six Ideas: An Essay in Aesthetic*, Boston: Kluwer, pp. 245–65.

Toynbee, A. (1957), *A Study of History*, Oxford: Oxford University Press.

Usher, A. P. (1929), *A History of Mechanical Inventions*, New York: Dover [1954].

Ward, L. F. (1903), *Pure Sociology: A Treatise on the Origin and Spontaneous Development of Society*, New York: Macmillan.

Warnock, M. (1976), *Imagination*, Berkeley: University of California Press.

Warren, H. C. (1921), *A History of the Association Psychology*, New York: Charles Scribner's Sons.

Watson, W. (2001), Invention, in T. O. Sloane (ed.), *Encyclopedia of Rhetoric*, London: Oxford University Press, pp. 389–404.

Weitzman, M. L. (1998), Recombinant Growth, *Quarterly Journal of Economics*, 113 (2): 331–60.

Woodworth, R. S. (1929), Imagination, in R. S. Woodworth (ed.), *Psychology*, New York: Holt, pp. 463–500.

Znaniecki, F. (1918–20), *The Polish Peasant*, New York: Alfred A. Knopf.

3

From knowledge to innovation
The role of knowledge spillover entrepreneurship

David B. Audretsch, Erik E. Lehmann, and Joshua Hinger

1. Introduction

Knowledge is generally considered to be the essential ingredient for innovative activity. However, knowledge is not equivalent to innovation. The purpose of this chapter is to explain the role of entrepreneurship in facilitating the spillover of knowledge from an organization where that knowledge is created to a new organization where it is used for innovative activity. The body of the chapter is organized in three primary sections. The first section discusses the knowledge production and the emergence of the knowledge production function, which was primarily cited in the academic literature between 1983 and 1997. Additionally, this section highlights the model's strengths and weaknesses in regards to various levels of analysis, as well as the three stages of the innovation process and its variable measurement constraints. The second section then discusses knowledge spillover theory, the distinctions between information and knowledge, and highlights how the impacts of knowledge spillover can be estimated within the framework of the knowledge production function. The third section discusses the theoretical links between entrepreneurial activity and knowledge spillover, and how these links assist in explaining the heterogeneity that is observed among different levels of analysis.

2. Knowledge production

Along with the emergence of the Endogenous Growth Theory in the mid-1980s (see Romer, 1986, 1990), interest in innovative activity began to increase, and the literature responded by fitting the innovative process into the well-known production function model (Solow, 1956). The production function model in economics connects inputs in the production process to outputs. As Milton Friedman (1975) famously quipped, "There is no such thing as a free lunch," implying that inputs in the production process are a requisite to producing outputs. Ample theoretical models and evidence providing empirical validation of the production function model exist in the economics literature.

Consequently, as the focus on innovation as an output began to emerge in the economic literature, one prevalent approach was to embed innovation into the more general production function model. As for production, the unit of analysis is typically at the firm level, while levels of innovation are examined as the output. The inputs are generally considered to be knowledge, or some proxy measurement of knowledge-related input, such as research and development, human capital, or academic research (see Audretsch, Keilbach, and Lehmann, 2006).

The theoretical specification Griliches (1990) termed the *knowledge production function* typically specifies knowledge inputs as exogenous to the model and influencing the dependent variable – innovative activity. The empirical estimation of the knowledge production function has been influenced by measurement problems. Both the independent variables and dependent variables that are used to estimate the knowledge production function are not easily measured. Concepts such as knowledge and innovative activity do not lend themselves to obvious quantification. Paul Krugman (2013) commented in reference to the decline of the New Growth Theory, "too much of it involved making assumptions about how unmeasurable things affected other unmeasurable things." Similarly, the empirical literature on estimating the knowledge production function has been limited in its ability to measure both the knowledge inputs as well as the innovative outputs.

Attempts to measure innovative activity have revolved around three stages of the innovative process. The first stage involves production inputs. Measures of inputs into the innovative process, such as research and development (R&D) expenditures, or the share of employment devoted to research and development, have been used as proxy measurements for innovative activity. A clear limitation of using R&D activity as a proxy measurement for technological change is that R&D reflects only the resources devoted to producing innovative output, but not the amount of innovative activity actually realized. That is, R&D is an input in the innovation process, not an output. As Mansfield (1984) points out, not all efforts within a formal R&D laboratory are directed towards generating innovative output in any case. Rather, other types of output, such as imitation and technology transfer, are also common goals in R&D laboratories.

The second stage involves an intermediate output, which exceeds that of a pure input in the production process, but has not yet reached the level of final output. The most prevalent measure of an intermediate output is the number of inventions with patents. In fact, inventions granted patent protection seem to be the most common measure used as a proxy for innovative activity. Scholars have typically interpreted this new measure not only as being superior to R&D but also as representing a *bona fide* measure of innovative output. However, it should be emphasized that inventions that have received legal patent protection are not, in fact, a direct measure of innovative output, but rather they reflect an intermediate stage of the innovation process. While the granting of a patent for an invention does reflect that a certain level of new technical knowledge has been attained, there is absolutely no guarantee that new technical knowledge has a positive economic value, other than the fact that someone is willing to incur the cost of obtaining that patent. While innovations and inventions are related, they are not identical.

Therefore, many inventions that are granted a patent do not necessarily generate innovative activity, in that they do not result in an innovation, or a positive revenue stream. Although this is not to suggest that innovations are mutually exclusive with positive revenue streams. Additionally, several valuable and historically significant innovations stemmed from inventions that were never patented. Benjamin Franklin, one of history's most notable inventors, did not patent his innovations, such as the lightening rod, the Franklin stove, the odometer, or bifocal glasses. He stated "As we benefit from the inventions of others, we should be glad to share our own … freely and gladly" (Lobel, 2013, p. 121).

The rather striking gaps between patented inventions on the one hand and realized innovations on the other led Scherer (1983) to observe that the "propensity to patent" is not constant across specific technologies, firms, or industries. Rather, just as certain firms, technologies, and industries have a greater propensity to patent inventions, others exhibit a lower propensity to patent inventions. Similarly, the propensity of those patented inventions to result in innovations also varies systematically across technologies, firms, and industries. As Scherer (1983, pp. 107–108) explains,

> The quantity and quality of industry patenting may depend upon chance, how readily a technology lends itself to patent protection, and business decision-makers' varying perceptions of how much advantage they will derive from patent rights. Not much of a systematic nature is known about these phenomena, which can be characterized as differences in the propensity to patent.

A similar view about the reliability of patents as a measure of innovative activity is expressed by Mansfield (1984, p. 462),

> The value and cost of individual patents vary enormously within and across industries … Many inventions are not patented. And in some industries, such as electronics, there is considerable speculation that the current patent system is being bypassed to a greater extent than in the past. Some types of technologies are more likely to be patented than others.

The varying propensities to patent across technologies, industries, and firms indicate that inferences about innovative activity based on patent data are inherently erroneous. As Pakes and Griliches (1980, p. 378) conclude, "patents are a flawed measure [of innovative output]; particularly since not all new innovations are patented and since patents differ greatly in their economic impact." Similarly, Griliches (1990, p. 1669) poses the question, "Patents as indicators of what?" To which he answers:

> Ideally, we might hope that patent statistics would provide a measure of the [innovative] output … The reality, however, is very far from it. The dream of getting hold of an output indicator of inventive activity is one of the strong motivating forces for economic research in this area.

While the first two stages attempting to measure innovative activity involve measures of inputs and intermediate outputs, the third stage provides direct measures of innovative activity. Direct measures of innovative activity have ranged from new products and processes introduced into the market, to the share of sales accounted for by new products. Such direct measures attempt to identify new products and processes introduced into the market, and therefore enable the observation of innovative outputs, not just production inputs.

The knowledge production function has been found to hold most strongly at broader levels of aggregation. The most innovative countries are those with the greatest investments to R&D. Little innovative output is associated with less developed countries, which are characterized by a paucity of new economic knowledge production. Similarly, the most innovative industries also tend to be characterized by considerable investments in R&D and new economic knowledge. Not only are industries such as computers, pharmaceuticals, and instruments high in R&D inputs that generate new economic knowledge, but also in terms of innovative outputs (Audretsch, 1995). By contrast, industries with little need for R&D, such as wood products, textiles, and paper, also tend to produce lower amounts of innovative output. Therefore, the knowledge production model linking knowledge-generating inputs to innovative outputs certainly holds at the more aggregated levels of economic activity.

The relationship between knowledge-generating inputs and outputs becomes less compelling at the disaggregated microeconomic level of the enterprise, establishment, or even line-of-business. For example, while Acs and Audretsch (1990) found that the simple correlation between R&D inputs and innovative output was 0.84 for four-digit standard industrial classification (SIC) manufacturing industries in the United States, it was less than half, 0.40, among the largest U.S. corporations. The knowledge production function model becomes even less compelling in view of the recent wave of studies revealing that small enterprises serve as the engine of innovative activity in certain industries. These results are startling, because as Scherer (1991) observes, the bulk of industrial R&D is undertaken in the largest corporations; small enterprises account only for a minor share of R&D inputs.

3. Knowledge spillovers

Kenneth Arrow's classic 1962 article remains one of the most cited in the field of economics because he explained that information is inherently characterized as a public good in some cases, and by positive externalities in other cases. This is because multiple economic agents are able to reuse information. For example, opportunistic entrepreneurs are able to use information that has been previously utilized by a firm, organization, or individual, in order to produce additional value that was otherwise unrealized in the market. Much of the ensuing literature responding to Arrow's insights, at least from the perspective of the firm, was based on concerns for the under-investment in the creation of information, because the ability to fully accrue the returns from such investments is limited. As Charles Ferguson (1988, p. 61) argues,

> Fragmentation, instability, and entrepreneurialism are not signs of well-being. In fact, they are symptoms of the larger structural problems that afflict U.S. industry. In semiconductors, a combination of personnel mobility, ineffective property protection, risk aversion in large companies, and tax subsidies for the formation of new companies contribute to a fragmented "chronically entrepreneurial" industry. U.S. semiconductor companies are unable to sustain the large, long-term investments required for continued U.S. competitiveness.

Companies avoid long-term R&D, personnel training, and long-term cooperative relation-ships because these are presumed, often correctly, to yield no benefit to the original inves-tors. Economies of scale are not sufficiently developed. An elaborate infrastructure of small subcontractors has arisen in Silicon Valley. Personnel turnover in the American merchant semiconductor industry has risen to 20 percent compared with less than 5 percent in IBM and Japanese corporations. Fragmentation discouraged necessary coordinated action – to develop technology and also to demand improved government support.

However, Arrow's characterization of information became increasingly re-characterized as knowledge. The main distinction between information and knowledge involves three funda-mental characteristics. The first is the extent of uncertainty. Information is relatively certain and based on fact. By contrast, knowledge is inherently uncertainty. While the economic value of information is relatively certain, the economic value of knowledge is uncertain.

The second characteristic distinguishing knowledge from information is its high degree of asymmetry across economic agents. This means that the economic valuation of knowledge assigned by any particular agent differs significantly from the assigned economic valuation of that same knowledge by a different economic agent. Not only is the outcome, or economic value of knowledge, uncertain but the expected value of that knowledge differs significantly across economic agents. This is a contrast to information, which is not only associated with less uncertainty but also by a low degree of asymmetries across economic agents. Thus, the economic valuation of information tends to be relatively homogeneous while the economic valuation of knowledge is heterogeneous.

The third characteristic involves the cost of transacting information versus knowledge across economic agents. While the cost of transacting information across economic agents is trivial, especially in the internet-era, the cost of transacting knowledge is not trivial. Information consists largely of codified facts, but knowledge has a considerably greater component of tacit understanding. To transact tacit knowledge is costly and typically requires face-to-face communication. Due to the importance of face-to-face communication in transacting knowledge, the geographic range of such knowledge spillovers plays an important role.

A rich and growing literature has found compelling empirical evidence confirming that knowledge investments create significant externalities in that they contribute to the innovative activity of other firms (Audretsch and Feldman, 1996; Jaffe, 1989; Audretsch and Stephan, 1996; Anselin, Varga, and Acs, 1997, 2000; Acs, Anselin, and Varga, 2002; Acs et al., 2009, 2012; Braunerhjelm et al. 2010; and Jaffe, Trajtenberg, and Henderson, 1993). An important finding of this literature is that knowledge spillovers tend to be geographically concentrated within close spatial proximity to the knowledge source. Studies show that while knowledge has a high propensity to spill over, such knowledge spillovers are geographically bounded (Audretsch and Lehmann, 2005; Audretsch and Keilbach, 2007).

Krugman (1991, p. 53) expressed skepticism that knowledge spillovers could actually be measured and analyzed, because, "knowledge flows are invisible, they leave no paper trail by which they may be measured and tracked." However, the ensuing studies, in many ways responding to Krugman's implied challenge, have argued otherwise. For example, Jaffe, Trajtenberg and Henderson (1993, p. 578) conclude that, "knowledge flows do sometimes leave a paper trail, in the form of citations in patents."

One prevalent approach to estimate the impact and extent of knowledge spillovers is based on the knowledge production function. According to Jaffe (1989), knowledge spillovers can be modeled within the context and framework of the knowledge production function:

$$I_{si} = IRD^{\beta_1} * UR_{si}^{\beta_2} * \left(UR_{si} * GC_{si}^{\beta_3} \right) * \varepsilon_{si} \tag{1}$$

where I refers to the output of innovative activity, IRD represents R&D investment by private companies and organizations, UR reflects investments by universities on the research expenditures undertaken at universities, and GC measures the geographic coincidence of university and corporate research. The unit of observation for estimation was at the spatial level, s, a state, and industry level, i. Estimation of equation (1) essentially shifted the knowledge production function from the unit of observation of a firm to that of a geographic unit.

Implicitly contained within the knowledge production function model is the assumption that innovative activity should take place in those regions, s, where the direct knowledge-generating inputs are the greatest, and where knowledge spillovers are the most prevalent. Audretsch and Feldman (1996), Anselin, Varga, and Acs (1997, 2000), and Audretsch and Stephan (1996) link the propensity for innovative activity to cluster together to industry specific characteristics, most notably the relative importance of knowledge spillovers.

4. Knowledge spillover entrepreneurship

More recently, a different approach has suggested that there may be alternative perspectives shedding a different light, not just on why some people choose to become entrepreneurs while others do not, but also how and why entrepreneurship is a critical issue in regards to improving economic performance (see Acs and Audretsch, 2010; in particular Alvarez, Barney, and Young, 2010). According to the knowledge spillover theory of entrepreneurship, the context in which decision-making is derived can influence one's determination to become an entrepreneur. In particular, a context that is rich in knowledge generates entrepreneurial opportunities from those ideas created but not commercialized by incumbent organizations. By commercializing those ideas, which evolved from an incumbent organization but commercialized with the creation of a new firm, the entrepreneurs not only serve as a conduit for the spillover of knowledge, but also for the ensuing innovative activity and enhanced economic performance (Audretsch and Lehmann, 2005; Leyden and Link, 2013).

The knowledge spillover theory of entrepreneurship brings together contemporary theories and thoughts of entrepreneurship with prevailing theories of economic growth (see Acs, Audretsch, and Lehmann, 2013). In particular, this approach advances the microeconomic foundation of the endogenous growth theory by providing a new framework explaining the unobserved heterogeneity of growth rates between regions and nations. While keeping constant the primary research question involving intrinsic motivation among entrepreneurs, the knowledge spillover theory is concerned with the contextual variables that shape entrepreneurship. Considering that entrepreneurship and new venture creations are not a recent phenomenon, and by keeping the intrinsic motivations of entrepreneurs constant, the observed increase in the rate of startups and entrepreneurial activities should reflect a change in the benefits and costs of creating a new venture based on changes in the benefits and costs of the operating context. Knowledge created by incumbent firms and research organizations, which is underexploited and not fully commercialized for purposes of economic gain, then spills over to other economic agents – entrepreneurs – and is identified as the primary factor in shifting benefits and costs. To this end, we propose the concept of the *Knowledge Incubator* – a government, university, private firm, or research institution that has, through its own labor and resources, developed new knowledge with potential in the commercial markets but has, for various reasons such as uncertainty or disinterest, instead opted not to commercialize and exploit said knowledge, therefore allowing the knowledge to be spilled over to other willing economic agents. The knowledge incubator is unique specifically due to its decision not to enter the market with its new endogenously developed knowledge.

Economic agents, which are able to absorb knowledge spillovers and convert them into economic knowledge, are not required to bear the full costs of the knowledge development. This specific type of entrepreneur, one who utilizes knowledge spillovers, and does not bear the full costs of the newly developed knowledge, is referred to as an *opportunistic entrepreneur*. This individual, or group of individuals, is unique from other entrepreneurs in the sense that they are utilizing the spillover from the knowledge incubator, commercializing this knowledge by founding a new firm, entering the marketplace, and converting the new knowledge into economic knowledge. Consequently, the expected benefits increase via exploitation of the knowledge spillovers, which is ideally converted into economic knowledge and ultimately fosters economic growth.

Knowledge spillover theory of entrepreneurship contributes to the existing body of knowledge by explaining how and why knowledge spills over, and in what manner entrepreneurship acts as the mechanism by which knowledge evolves into economic knowledge within a given framework. While new ventures in the tech-sectors have led to the well-known erosion of previously existing industries (Schumpeter, 1934), such as Facebook, technological change and progress have been considered drivers of economic growth since the first industrial revolution. Since then, new venture creation and technological change were considered to be almost entirely exogenous. The most influential factors in the last few decades can be characterized by a shift in

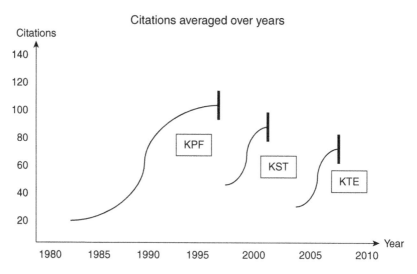

Figure 3.1 Emergence and diffusion of the knowledge spillover theory of entrepreneurship

the benefits and costs of the contextual factors, which have led to innovations and new venture creation far beyond exogenous factors. Not only innovations, but new ventures and entrepreneurial firms also often fall like manna from heaven.

The knowledge spillover theory of entrepreneurship thus shifts the unit of analysis away from firms and knowledge endowments assumed to be exogenous, and focuses attention on individual agents, specifically *opportunistic entrepreneurs*, who possess new knowledge endowments characterized as knowledge that has been captured from spillovers. This suggests a strong relationship between knowledge spillovers on the one end of the spectrum, and entrepreneurial activities on the other, while both have influence on the growth rates of regions and countries. Unobserved heterogeneity between regions and countries is based on differences in the knowledge spillover endowment and the ability to foster entrepreneurship (entrepreneurship capital), or in other words, unobserved heterogeneity in growth rates is due to differences in the benefits and costs of the knowledge endowments.

Figure 3.1 depicts the evolution of studies analyzing the knowledge production function, knowledge spillovers, and the knowledge spillover theory of entrepreneurship. The number of citations for each literature is measured on the vertical axis, against the year on the horizontal axis. There are two important and observable trends from Figure 3.1. The first is the temporal sequencing of these three strands of literature. The literature on the knowledge production function developed first. The literature on knowledge spillovers developed subsequently. The strand of literature focusing on the knowledge spillover theory of entrepreneurship is in its incipiency.

The second notable observation from Figure 3.1 is that the strands of literature on the knowledge production function and knowledge spillovers have peaked and are producing diminishing returns. By contrast, the strand of literature on the knowledge spillover theory of entrepreneurship is still growing.

5. Conclusions

There are both compelling theoretical reasons and empirical evidence suggesting that knowledge is not the equivalent of innovation. Rather, a gap exists between knowledge and innovation.

The knowledge spillover theory of entrepreneurship explains the important role that entrepreneurship plays in spanning this gap. By taking ideas that have been developed in one organizational context and transforming them into innovations in the form of a new firm or organization, entrepreneurship plays an important role in transforming knowledge into innovation.

References

Acs, Z. J. and Audretsch D. B. (1990). *Innovation and Small Firms*. Cambridge, MA: MIT Press.

Acs, Z. J. and Audretsch, D. B. (Eds.). (2010). *Handbook of Entrepreneurship*. New York, NY: Springer.

Acs, Z. J., Anselin, L., and Varga, A. (2002). Patents and innovation counts as measures of regional production of new knowledge. *Research Policy*, 31(7), 1069–1085.

Acs, Z. J., Audretsch, D. B., and Lehmann, E. E. (2013). The knowledge spillover theory of entrepreneurship, *Small Business Economics*, 41(4), 757–774.

Acs, Z. J., Audretsch, D. B., Braunerhjelm, P., and Carlsson, B. (2009). The knowledge spillover theory of entrepreneurship, *Small Business Economics*, 32(1), 15–30.

Acs, Z. J., Audretsch, D. B., Braunerhjelm, P., and Carlsson, B. (2012). Growth and entrepreneurship. *Small Business Economics*, 39(2), 289–300.

Alvarez, S. A., Barney, J. B., and Young, S. L. (2010). Debates in entrepreneurship: opportunity formation and implications for the field of entrepreneurship. In Z. J. Acs and D. B. Audretsch (Eds.), *Handbook of Entrepreneurship* (pp. 23–46). New York, NY: Springer.

Anselin, L., Varga, A., and Acs, Z. (1997). Local geographic spillovers between university research and high technology innovators. *Journal of Urban Economics*, 42(3), 422–448.

Anselin, L., Varga, A., and Acs, Z. (2000). Geographic and sectoral characteristics of academic knowledge externalities. *Papers in Regional Science*, 79(4), 435–443.

Arrow, K. J. (1962). Economic welfare and the allocation of resources for invention. In R. R. Nelson (ed.), *The Rate and Direction of Inventive Activity* (pp. 609–626). Princeton, NJ: Princeton University Press.

Audretsch, D. B. (1995). Innovation, growth and survival. *International Journal of Industrial Organization*, 13(4), 441–457.

Audretsch, D. B. and Feldman, M. P. (1996). R&D spillovers and the geography of innovation and production. *American Economic Review*, 86(3), 630–640.

Audretsch, D. B. and Keilbach, M. (2007) The theory of knowledge spillover entrepreneurship. *Journal of Management Studies*, 44(7), 1242–1254.

Audretsch, D. B. and Lehmann, E. E. (2005). Does the knowledge spillover theory of entrepreneurship hold for regions?, *Research Policy*, 34, 1191–1202

Audretsch, D. B., and Stephan, P. E. (1996). Company-scientist locational links: the case of biotechnology. *American Economic Review*, 86(3), 641–652.

Audretsch, D. B., Keilbach, M., and Lehmann, E. (2006). *Entrepreneurship and Economic Growth*. Oxford, UK: Oxford University Press.

Braunerhjelm, P., Acs, Z. J., Audretsch, D. B., and Carlsson, B. (2010). The missing link: knowledge diffusion and entrepreneurship in endogenous growth. *Small Business Economics*, 34(2), 105–125.

Ferguson, Charles H. (1988). From the people who brought you voodoo economics. *Harvard Business Review*, 66(3), 55–62.

Friedman, M. (1975). *There is No Such Thing as a Free Lunch*, La Salle, Il, Open Court, p. iii.

Gerard, A. (1756). *Essay on Genius*, London: W. Strahan.

Griliches, Z. (1990). Patent statistics as economic indicators: a survey. *Journal of Economic Literature*, 18(4), 1661–1707.

Jaffe, A. B. (1989). Real effects of academic research. *American Economic Review*, 79(5), 957–970.

Jaffe A., Trajtenberg, M., and Henderson, R. (1993). Geographic localization of knowledge spillovers as evidenced by patent citations. *Quarterly Journal of Economics*, 108(3), 577–598.

Krugman, P. (1991). *Geography and Trade*, Cambridge: MIT Press.

Krugman, P. (2013). The new growth fizzle. *The New York Times*, August 18. Retrieved from http://krugman.blogs.nytimes.com/2013/08/18/the-new-growth-fizzle/?_r=0 (accessed: July 6, 2014).

Leyden, D. P. and Link, A. N. (2013). Knowledge spillovers, collective entrepreneurship, and economic growth: the role of universities, *Small Business Economics*, 41(4), 797–817.

Lobel, O. (2013). *Talent Wants to Be Free*, New Haven, CT: Yale University Press.

Mansfield, E. (1984). Comment on using linked patent and R&D data to measure interindustry technology flows. In Z. Griliches (ed.), *R&D, Patents, and Productivity* (pp. 462–464). Chicago, IL: University of Chicago Press.

Pakes, A. and Griliches, Z. (1980). Patents and R&D at the firm level. *Economic Letters*, 5(4), 377–381.

Romer, P. (1986). Increasing returns and long-run growth. *Journal of Political Economy*, 94(5), 1002–1037.

Romer, P. (1990). Endogenous technological change. *Journal of Political Economy*, 98(5), S71–S102.

Scherer, F. M. (1983). The propensity to patent. *International Journal of Industrial Organization*, 1(1), 107–128.

Scherer, F. M. (1991). Changing perspectives on the firm size problem. In Z. Acs and D. Audretsch (Eds.), *Innovation and Technological Change: An International Comparison* (pp. 24–38). Ann Arbor, MI: University of Michigan Press.

Schumpeter, J. A. (1934). *The Theory of Economic Development: An Inquiry into Profits, Capital, Credit, Interest, and the Business Cycle*. Cambridge, MA: Harvard University Press.

Solow, R. (1956). A contribution to the theory of economic growth. *Quarterly Journal of Economics*, 70(1), 65–94.

4

Innovation strategies combining internal and external knowledge

Börje Johansson and Hans Lööf

1. Introduction

Economists' recognition of innovation and technology is often ascribed to the contribution of Schumpeter (1934), spelled out in *The Theory of Economic Development*, conveying the message that without innovations the market economy would settle in a stationary Walrasian equilibrium. Precisely the same message was delivered by Solow (1957), declaring that in equilibrium GDP per capita of a competitive economy will grow only to the extent that technology improves over time. A novel element was that the Solow model prescribed a way to calculate the size of the yearly change of technology.

In the Solow perception of the economy, knowledge improvements drive the annual increase of the productivity of the representative (average) firm, and hence there are no questions asked about the distribution of productivity across firms in the same industry. The Schumpeter perception is quite different by focusing on how individual firms in an industry develop innovation ideas that improve their productivity relative to the average firm in the same industry. This implies that, at any point in time, we should expect heterogeneity such that some firms are clearly superior to the average, whereas others are inferior.

The Schumpeter view incorporates a second dynamic phenomenon that is strongly associated with innovations. This additional factor may be termed adoption and considers the opportunity of other firms to imitate and get inspired to catch up with those firms that have reached a higher productivity level, reflecting the reward associated with innovation efforts. This reward erodes as other firms adopt the same or a similar solution as the initial innovation, a view that remains a basic perception of innovation adjustment processes (Cefis and Cicarelli, 2005). Adoption processes of this kind work against and reduce heterogeneity. In the following presentation, the analysis will rely on numerous observations that heterogeneity is a generic feature of firms in an industry or firms that supply product varieties belonging to the same product group.

The observations to which we will refer cover differences between firms with regard to variables such as size, internal knowledge resources, productivity and profitability, market extension, output prices. Thus, differences are present for both inputs and outputs; in fact, differences are present in all dimensions that can be observed (Dosi and Nelson, 2010). In view of this we suggest that firm differentials to a large extent are caused by the innovation and adoption strategy of each firm. Given that the innovative and renewal behavior of most firms remains unchanged over time, then this is consistent with observations saying that productivity and other performance differentials remain approximately unchanged over fairly long sequences of years (Geroski, 1998). Our ambition is to examine the idea that firm performance differentials are generated by knowledge differences across the same firms.

How should we conceive the notion of a firm's innovation strategy, and should it be labeled "innovation strategy"? A major element in a pro-active strategy of an innovating firm is its plans to build up renewal capabilities and maintain a resource that includes renewal skills of employees, routines for orchestration of R&D and efforts to access external knowledge. Firm capabilities also include links to other actors for knowledge accession and collaboration (Andersson, *et al.* 2012). In line with these thoughts the presentation will structure the analysis of innovation strategy to concern a firm's development of its (i) internal knowledge, (ii) access to local knowledge sources, and (iii) access to global knowledge sources. Such a strategy comprises both innovation and adoption activities.

In the framework for characterizing, classifying and analyzing innovation strategies of firms, we claim that a firm's knowledge should be divided into two categories, namely *capabilities* and *technical solutions*, where the latter have broad Schumpeterian interpretations and include product attributes, production processes and routines, and interaction approaches vis-à-vis input suppliers and customers. Capabilities refer to a firm's capacity and skills with regard to adjusting, developing and adopting its "library" of technical solutions.

A major message from the presentation is that firm capabilities differentiate firms. They take time to develop, require recurrent maintenance, and they are difficult and costly to imitate (Teece, 2010). Compared to the costs of replicating technical solutions of other firms, the costs of adopting the capability of another firm may appear as prohibitively high. Thus, differences in firms' capabilities form a candidate for explaining remaining heterogeneity among firms. In view of this, the following presentation suggest ways along which this issue can be researched.

2. Literature on knowledge of the innovating firm

2.1 Innovation and adoption efforts

Innovation is about change and hence requires a temporal setting, where the analysis has to recognize that the development of the novelty takes time and that performance effects may be delayed. Novelty is also a temporal distinction and the literature distinguishes between novelties that are new to the firm, new to a separate market, new to an industry, and new in a global context. Obviously, something that is new to a firm may be the outcome of product or process design that has been adopted from an innovation made by another firm, belonging to another industry, or operating in other geographical markets. We will use this as a first indication that innovation and adoption activities are overlapping and in this sense similar processes. The two phenomena belong to the class of firm renewal processes.

Renewal processes comprise a firm's change of product attributes and portfolio of product varieties, processes and routines, links to customer markets, patenting, and recruitment of employees. The effects of those processes can be identified by means of both direct and indirect observations. As an example of direct observations we will consider statistics that reveal entry and exit of product varieties in a firm's output mix, patent applications, grated patents, etc. The second type of observables includes both unobserved fixed effects captured in econometric models and firm performance. Hall (2011) suggests productivity growth as an innovation indicator.

Following an extensive survey by Cohen (2010), one may argue that innovation is identified when productivity can be associated with R&D efforts, the latter being a subcategory of renewal efforts. The identification relies on a coupling of efforts and performance effects. Cohen shows that a considerable amount of empirical research has been devoted to investigating two phenomena: (i) the size of the firm and (ii) the market structure. A first conclusion is that one cannot reject the hypothesis that R&D is proportional to size. A second conclusion is that both firm size and market structure are rather consequences of innovation activities, such that firms that grow to become large do that by developing many product varieties and by arranging destination links to many alternative markets (Andersson and Johansson, 2012).

In the context of market structure, Sutton (1991) observes that the presence of upfront sunk costs associated with long-term R&D investments implies that there will be barriers to entry into and exit from the group of innovating firms in an industry. Moreover, as argued by Aghion *et al.* (2005) and Antonelli, Crespi and Scellato (2012), Schumpeterian rivalry drives firms to innovate in a persistent way, and this gives rise to a twofold effect. First, a higher profitability facilitates the funding of renewal efforts. Second, large margins indicate barriers to entry and associated market power, which in turn can lower the incentives to exercise persistent innovation efforts.

A major part of Cohen's review focuses on the association between firms' innovation activity and their individual characteristics. In that context it is vital to carefully identify characteristics that remain approximately unchanged for periods of several years. Only such characteristics can be meaningfully employed to predict future innovation activity. Keeping this in mind, we consider that Cohen structures the possible firm characteristics into (i) cash flow, (ii) R&D capabilities and internal knowledge resources, and (iii) external knowledge sources.

Cash flow as a determinant of a firm's renewal effort has received much attention over many decades (Antonelli, 1989; Hall, 2002). There is evidence in favor of an association between variation in cash flow and variation in R&D efforts (Martinsson and Lööf, 2013). The intuition behind this finding is that when cash flow wanes, firms tend to refrain from innovation which, by some stochastic probability, only stands to generate cash flow sometime in the future. However, Martinsson and Lööf (2013) suggest that equity capital is a more crucial determinant for sustained renewal efforts. Firms with a large equity-to-total-assets ratio have a better capacity to maintain a smooth innovation profile through time.

Thus, it is evident that cash flow is questionable if we are looking for a slowly changing characteristic of a firm, although it might reflect firm size, while also indicating returns to innovation efforts in the past. R&D capabilities and renewal capacities in general, on the other hand, may be classified as a slowly changing property of a firm, developing as a consequence of collecting experiences in the firm's process of renewal efforts. This form of renewal capacity comprises in a diffuse way both knowledge production and absorption of knowledge flows.

Consider that the above picture describes how differences in firms' renewal capabilities affect their R&D and other renewal expenditures, as well as their size. Then we might also contemplate that a firm's diversification is correlated with renewal capacity and internal knowledge (MacDonald, 1985; Montgomery and Hariharan, 1991). In such a perspective we place the driving force with the slowly changing internal knowledge of the firm. However, this is not where we want to stop. Our ambition is to widen the perspective and consider the external knowledge sources of the firm, and to suggest that firm capabilities also include knowledge about how to access external knowledge and absorb knowledge flows through links for collaboration and knowledge transfer.

Issues of knowledge sources outside the firm bring additional aspects such as a firm's proximity and links to university research as well as commercial knowledge providers (Stephan, 2002).

They also bring to the forefront knowledge links between firms belonging to the same company group (Johansson and Lööf, 2008). In particular, external knowledge flows can be associated with the presence of agglomeration economies of the type related to urbanization economies as suggested by Jacobs (1969, 1984), and more generally to the geography of innovation (Feldman and Kogler, 2010).

2.2 Transitory and lasting performance advantages

Dividing a firm's R&D expenditures by its value added provides a means to control for firm size. This normalization procedure gives us the measure R&D intensity for each firm, and a large share of the variance in this intensity can be explained by fixed firm effects, indicating strong heterogeneity in firms' innovative behavior (Cohen, 2010). This observation leads to the temporal question: do some of the firms in a population within a given industry continue to have a high R&D intensity over a series of years, and do other firms engage in R&D efforts only occasionally or not at all?

The question asked is vital according to the collection of views presented in the introductory section with reference to Schumpeter and Solow as well as to endogenous growth models (Romer, 1990); productivity is augmented by renewal activities, including R&D and knowledge accession efforts. A follow up issue is how the productivity gains unfold across firms and along time. The Schumpeter-Solow model perspective is that firms that manage to adopt and develop new solutions can gain an advantage over other firms, for example in the form of above average productivity, and thereby they represent best practice solutions. This advantage may be interpreted as a temporary monopoly profit or as an economic rent, based on knowledge that is not available to competitors. Advantages of this kind are considered as transitory, which means that the economic rent of an adopter/innovator erodes as other firms strive to adjust their routines and output attributes towards the best practice.

The idea that other firms respond to successful novelties developed by competitors is a fundamental property that economists refer to when arguing in favor of market mechanisms, resembling various versions of Darwinian adjustments, such as replicator dynamics (Vega-Redondo, 2003). Given this, how can this conclusion be reconciled with observations saying that lasting differences in firm characteristics and performance represent a generic phenomenon, which we cannot avoid to observe? Before answers to this question are suggested in sections 3–5, we will dwell on the rigidity of firms' heterogeneity.

Firms in the same industry or firms supplying product varieties belonging to the same product group have as a rule heterogeneous characteristics and display different performance in terms of productivity, profitability or growth, and they differ in their R&D and innovation efforts. In established microeconomic theory such differences are predicted to vanish over time, based on the argument that only the best practice can survive. Empirical observations do not support this view (Dosi and Nelson, 2010). To a large extent, inter-firm differences remain over long time sequences.

Differences between firms in a given industry (or group of industries) may be identified for a panel of firm observations over time. Such a panel will contain differences for each individual firm at different points in time as well as differences between firms that remain basically unchanged along time. We may then, with reference to Geroski (1998), calculate the total variance for a performance variable like value added or gross profit per employee, and then in a second step determine how much of the variance is due to the variation between years for each individual firm, referred to as *within variance*. The remaining variance can then be conceived as a persistent difference between firms, referred to as *between variance*. This between variance is

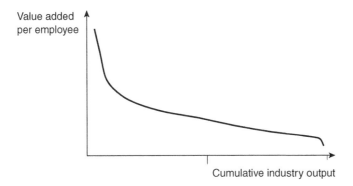

Figure 4.1 Labour productivity cross-tabulated against output of firms in an industry in productivity-descending order

Source: Johansson (2014)

typically 3–4 times larger than the within variance (Andersson *et al.*, 2012). Such observations demonstrate heterogeneity among firms in most industries, while at the same time showing that differences between firms persist over time (Peters, 2009; Antonelli *et al.*, 2012).

Figure 4.1 provides a picture of the labor productivity 2006 in an industry supplying differentiated products, based on Swedish data. The horizontal axis measures the cumulative output from firms in the sector when firms are ordered according to descending productivity. The figure illustrates how the quartile with the highest productivity has a productivity level which is 3–4 times as large as the level in lowest quartile. Such performance differences provide a strong incentive to examine firm characteristics when assessing performance. Among such characteristics the literature has considered firms' behavior with regard to efforts to innovate and to adopt new technology developed by other firms. The first aspect associates with the process of generating innovation and the second with diffusion in the form of commercial transfers and spillovers.

The performance distribution illustrated in Figure 4.1 was discussed early by Heckscher (1918), and from this he could derive the Heckscher cost curve (Johansson, 1991). Hotelling (1932) argued that the cumulative distribution in the figure reflects a bell-shaped frequency distribution and derived an industry supply curve, claiming that the distribution properties can be considered as generic. The diagram in the figure is also related to what is labeled Salter diagrams (Salter, 1960). The intriguing thing with the kind of productivity distributions illustrated in Figure 4.1 is that their shape remains invariant over time and corresponds to a persistent ranking of firms' relative productivity.

2.3 Classifying knowledge

Griliches and Mairesse (1995) discuss the limited understanding we have about why firms are different in a set of essential variables, including the knowledge profile of the firms' employees, the technologies they apply, and the customer markets that they serve. Their conclusion is that research on these issues should be given high priority. Firms also differ with regard to knowledge assets and the ability to exploit such assets. In addition we recognize that firm knowledge has several dimensions as illustrated in Figure 4.2.

Throughout his contributions to the theory of technological change, Mansfield (1987) was careful to make a clear distinction between technology and techniques, stressing that technology has the status of knowledge about techniques. However, the concept of technology has evolved

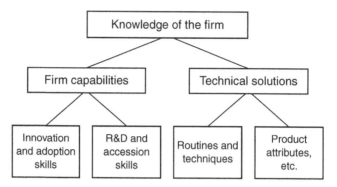

Figure 4.2 The two basic types of firm knowledge

to allow formulations such as "technological knowledge". In Figure 4.2 we introduce another basic distinction which separates firm knowledge into (i) technical solutions and (ii) capabilities, where the latter associates with know-how and the former with specific designs of firm operations such as administrative and logistical routines, product attributes and production techniques in the narrow sense. There are two fundamental aspects of these two forms of knowledge: know-how and technical solutions are characterized by different development processes and by different probabilities of diffusing to other firms.

As will be elaborated further in this presentation, firm capabilities include experiences, skills and organization routines for development and accession of knowledge about technical solutions and for associated renewal activities aiming at innovation and adoption of new technical solutions. This view implies that capabilities partly develop as a side effect of renewal activities, including phenomena like learning-by-doing (Nelson and Winter, 1982; Cohen and Levinthal, 1990; Phene and Almeida, 2008). The outcome of the renewal activities is expanded capabilities and enlargement of the firm's library of technical solutions.

Firm knowledge in the form of capabilities determines the firm's capacity and likelihood to succeed in its efforts to expand and sharpen knowledge about technical solutions. We suggest that capability knowledge shares many properties with other types of know-how. In particular, there are limited possibilities to codify capability knowledge and as a consequence it is difficult to transfer. The skills and abilities associated with capability knowledge also require maintenance which may be an integral part of a firm's intention to repetitively continue its research and renewal activities. A firm with such intentions will behave as if it followed a capability strategy, aiming at a continuous effort to maintain and develop its various renewal skills.

We suggest that the possibilities to codify capability knowledge are limited in concordance with assumptions in the literature about difficulties to codify all forms of know-how, arguing that capabilities are complex (Beckmann, 2000) and tacit in nature and therefore have to be transferred between persons (Polanyi, 1966) in interactive learning processes. This also includes recruitment of new employees who embody renewal experiences, as well as new startups by persons with experiences from their previous employment in innovative firms.

The second type of knowledge in Figure 4.2 comprises technical solutions in a broad sense, subdivided into routines and product attributes, where routines refer to a firm's production, administrative and logistical processes. The second category of technical solutions relates to knowledge about product design (composition of attributes) and customer preferences with regard to attributes, including adjustments of deliveries. The firm may develop and access such knowledge, which still has to be transformed to innovation and/or adoption as an additional creative step.

Following suggestions by Teece (2010), Dosi and Nelson (2010), Almeida and Phene (2012) and Cantwell and Zhang (2012), we conclude that remaining differences between the performance of firms should be associated with remaining differences in firm capabilities. Such differences will allow groups of firms to maintain productivity advantages as well as a more frequent introduction of new product varieties. It then remains to create indicators that can empirically reveal capability advantages.

3. Internal knowledge

In the preceding section the presentation finds two basic notions of knowledge. The first one refers to a firm's knowledge about *technical solutions* and its implemented technology level. The second notion, *capability*, intends to reflect dynamics by considering a firm's know-how with regard to creation and accession of new knowledge that can be transformed to innovation and adoption.

3.1 Applying and creating knowledge

In this subsection, which focuses on firms' internal knowledge, we collect modeling perspectives that distinguish between (i) knowledge creation and accession activities, (ii) innovation and adoption of new technical solutions, and (iii) effects of novelties on firm performance. We also refer to contributions that consider accumulation of firms' internal knowledge and make firm capabilities a key concept.

Creation and accumulation of knowledge

In recent decades we can observe how the theory of the firm has developed to focus on the firm's management of knowledge. For a long while firm-level analysis had been concerned with extending the firm's production function to include technology (knowledge about techniques) as a shift factor augmenting the firm's output per input factors, implying productivity growth. In such a setting the firm output, Y, is modeled as a function of capital, K, ordinary labor, L, knowledge workers, H, and a technology shift factor, A.

In this kind of formulation (Johansson and Lööf, 2008) the H-variable reflects the firm's internal capacity to develop its performance, which may be measured by the productivity of ordinary labor, calculated as Y/L, by productivity growth, $\Delta Y/L$ or by total factor productivity growth. In turn, the A-variable would reflect the performance effect of implementing new technical solutions such as improved product attributes and routines, where new routines save costs and improved attributes can augment output prices and sales value. The empirical literature reveals that the knowledge intensity, $H/(H + L)$, correlates with firm performance as reflected by the productivity level.

It is obvious that the formulation we have presented contains a structural confusion in the sense that the internal knowledge, as given by H, is an indicator of knowledge input (innovation input), whereas the A-component rather refers to consequences of innovation or adoption. We may illustrate this phenomenon by adding an equation for the A-factor, showing how the A-level increases as an effect of past renewal efforts with the help of knowledge workers, H, who participate in R&D work, knowledge accession activities, and efforts to adopt existing technical solutions.

In this widened formulation there are two parallel processes: One cumulates knowledge and the second applies the knowledge by implementing it as technology that improves output performance. The described renewal efforts may take place over time, to become useful at subsequent points in time. We may refer to endogenous growth theory and consider the concept R&D capital, which represents accumulated R&D or renewal efforts over a sequence of years (Hall, 2011). With this approach the R&D capital corresponds to the technology shift factor. Obviously, introducing accumulation of knowledge capital also brings new questions about depreciation of the same capital. Such depreciation, reflecting creative destruction, would primarily affect the firm's "library of technical solutions", whereas renewal capabilities represent a more durable type of knowledge in the sense that it is difficult to copy.

The CDM-model distinctions

Subsection 3.1 presents a structured picture of how innovation and adoption are generated. Observing this phenomenon, Crépon, Duguet and Mairesse (1998) suggested a structural model, labeled the CDM-model, which is composed of three steps where the first step is knowledge creation (R&D efforts), the second is innovation outcome, and the third step is productivity consequences of the innovation. In our discussion we stress the similarities rather than the differences between adoption and innovation, and then the three steps can be labeled as follows:

(i) R&D and other renewal efforts
(ii) Innovation and adoption of novelties
(iii) Firm performance

The basic distinction in the CDM-model is between creation and accession of new knowledge, and the use of this knowledge in improving the firm's performance in terms of productivity, productivity growth or export indicators such as new export varieties, export prices and quantities, etc. In Mairesse and Robin (2012) the three steps presented above are extended to four steps explaining in sequence (i) the probability that a firm engages in continuous or recurrent R&D efforts, (ii) a firm's R&D intensity, contingent on making recurrent R&D, (iii) a firm's innovation output, and (iv) a firm's labor productivity.

An important finding in the Mairesse-Robin study is that the relevant innovation variable is overall innovation, incorporating process and/or product renewal. Table 4.1 presents factors that are shown to positively influence the probability of recurrent R&D and the R&D intensity. As can be seen, three significant factors are the same in both equations. However, among firms doing R&D the intensity is increasing for firms that make use of external knowledge sources (cooperation).

The CDM-approach as applied in Table 4.1 detects a significant influence from knowledge created in cooperation with external actors. What about internal knowledge? In the subsequent analysis we will emphasize that the variable that indicates recurrent R&D efforts also expresses

Table 4.1 Explaining the R&D engagements of firms

Probability of recurrent R&D efforts is explained by	R&D intensity, contingent on making R&D efforts is explained by
International sales are larger than domestic	International sales are larger than domestic
Appropriability protection	Appropriability protection
Firm size	Firm size
	Cooperation with external actors

Source: Adapted from Mairesse and Robin (2012)

the presence of internal knowledge in the form of renewal capabilities that are generated as a learning effect.

3.2 Developing firm capabilities

In what ways can we claim that firms follow strategies for coping with an uncertain future? Can such a strategy be thought of as a conscious planning approach of a firm or is it a reconstruction of each firm's past behavior? Without resolving these questions we suggest that firms' innovation behavior can be described and analyzed by means of the concept innovation strategy, describing pro-active decisions about building up a firm's resource base (Barney, 1991; Teece, 2010). The resource base comprises the firm's renewal capabilities and its ability to apply these skills and competences in the process of developing technical solutions. In view of this, we may suggest the label *capability strategy*.

Figure 4.3 outlines the basic interdependencies between capability objectives of a firm and its efforts to find applicable technical solutions. A fundamental feature in this process is that the capabilities have to be maintained and improved through repetitive efforts to develop new technical solutions. In particular, the figure stresses that renewal efforts have a two-pronged outcome, as they bring about technical solutions and at the same time maintain and refine the renewal capability.

A central suggestion in our presentation is that renewal capabilities are the core of a firm's internal knowledge. This part of firms' internal knowledge can have long-term consequences in separating the performance level of different firms. We will elaborate on this phenomenon with two basic performance variables: the export of firms and the productivity of firms. While we do this, firm capabilities are indirectly observed as persistent sequences of (i) new product varieties, (ii) patent applications, and (iii) R&D efforts – all proxies for persistent renewal efforts. The "size" of the internal capability knowledge is indicated by the degree of persistent recurrence of the phenomena (i)–(iii) and similar indicators.

Capabilities revealed by arrival rate of new product ideas

Our major case recognizes a firm's number of export varieties as the result of its past innovation or adoption activities. This approach to identify capabilities of a firm is elaborated in a study by Andersson and Johansson (2012), who present a model with monopolistic competition, where each exported product variety is a unique combination of an export code, an export destination and a firm. Ideas that can lead to new varieties are generated by a Poisson process which is unique for each firm, such that the arrival rate for firm i, denoted by λ_i, measures the frequency of novel varieties per time period. Observing and estimating λ_i for each firm i provide us with a measurement of firm i's product renewal capability.

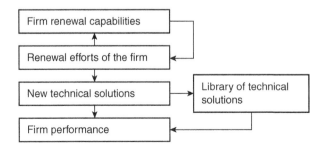

Figure 4.3 Renewal efforts generating new solutions and adding to firm capabilities

Table 4.2 State transitions between years, 1998–2004

State in period t	q_{ii}	$q_{ii} + q_{i,i-1} + q_{i,i+1}$
No export variety	81.8 %	97.2 %
1 variety	31.6 %	81.8 %
2 varieties	23.2 %	71.6 %
3–4 varieties	32.3 %	74.9 %
5–8 varieties	44.7 %	82.5 %
9–12 varieties	35.8 %	81.9 %
13–16 varieties	33.1 %	89.9 %
More than 16 varieties	92.9 %	97.2 %

Source: Adapted from Andersson and Johansson (2012)

In a temporal setting it is possible to study the number of varieties of each firm over a sequence of years. For each year a firm's stock of varieties is a measure of its past innovative behavior, and this is assumed to influence the firm's current capability. A firm's number of varieties changes between years according to a variety-entry and a variety-exit process. Given this, we have two results that shed light on the idea that the size of each firm's stock of varieties informs us about its capabilities. The first observation is based on arranging firms into groups, j, where j indicates the number of varieties for firms in that group. In Table 4.2 for example, $j = 1$ indicates 0 varieties and $j = 4$ indicates 3–4 varieties.

Having classified firms into size groups (in terms of the number of export varieties), we can for each pair of years calculate transition probabilities, q_{ij}, showing the share of firms that shift from class i to class j between two subsequent years. The probability q_{ii} shows the likelihood to remain in class i for two years in sequence. From the table we can see that the probability of remaining a non-exporter is greater than 80 percent, while the probability of staying in the group 5–8 varieties is 44.7 percent.

Table 4.2 illustrates that firms increase and decrease their number of varieties. However, the table also reflects that the stock of varieties changes slowly from year to year, and a large fraction of the firms change at most one interval up or down in the hierarchy, which is recorded by the probability $q_{ii} + q_{i,i-1} + q_{i,i+1}$. For example, more than 97 percent of the firms in the group with more than 16 varieties continue to export more than 16 varieties or drop to the group with 13–16 varieties. Thus, there is a clear feature of inertia in the innovation/adoption variable, and each firm's capability level develops on a slow time scale: firms with no export variety rarely introduce any variety, whereas firms with many varieties continue to have many varieties by persistently introducing new ones as old ones exit.

Consider now that firms with a small number of export varieties also can be expected to have a low arrival rate with regard to innovation/adoption ideas (variety ideas), whereas firms with large stocks of varieties have a high arrival rate. For the latter this is reflected by a high λ_{ii}-value, indicating a large capability. Thus, when λ_i is large a new-variety idea is a frequent event and the variety-renewal activities are persistent. When λ_i is small the renewal capability is small and novelties are rare. This leads to the question: what factors influence the renewal capacity? In a regression analysis by Andersson and Johansson (2012) the following set of factors is shown to influence positively firm i's value of the new-variety arrival parameter λ_i:

- the firm's variety stock
- the firm is an exporter (dummy)

- the firm is an importer (dummy)
- the firm size measured by employment
- the firm's share of knowledge-intensive labor
- export intensity of the firm
- labor productivity of the firm
- the firm belongs to a multinational company group
- number of persistent exporters in the region hosting the firm.

The described regression result is based on entry of varieties between 1998 and 2004 with Swedish data. The regression is conditioned on initial values (explanatory variables observed for the initial year 1998). We should emphasize that the econometric result is obtained from a model, where the historically given variety stock at date t affects the arrival rate (renewal capability) during a subsequent period up to $t + \tau$. This may be interpreted as path dependence. At the same time we conclude from the regression results that firm capabilities also rely on established export and import networks as well as knowledge networks inside a multinational company group. All these factors are also represented in the list of explanatory variables above.

The logic of the findings runs as follows. A high capability in the past (high arrival rate) results in a large variety stock, which stimulates a continued high introduction of new varieties. This is supported by a large share of knowledge-intensive labor in the firm, by potential global knowledge flows for firms belonging to a multinational company group, by knowledge spillovers related to the firm's export and import activities, and a regional milieu of persistent exporters.

4. External knowledge sources

The concept *knowledge accession strategy* is introduced in Cantwell and Zhang (2012), where we are told that the generation of new knowledge has the form of a process which combines and recombines current and acquired knowledge. The external knowledge can be accessed in a firm's local milieu or in a global environment. Section 4 examines the importance of the local milieu.

4.1 Potentials for knowledge interaction

A firm can access external knowledge in different ways. The knowledge may be purchased or transferred according to a license contract, it can move into the firm through new employees who bring with them know-how and knowledge about technical solutions from places where they have worked earlier in their career, and it can spill over from collaborative efforts with other firms and research organizations like universities.

Krugman (1991) suggests that spillovers cannot easily be measured and tracked because knowledge flows are invisible to a large extent. However, more recent research has made important progress in the attempt to open the black box. For instance, a range of empirical studies show that the social rate of return differs across locations and that knowledge flows diminish in volume and intensity as the distance between origin and destination grows.

In case studies one may find out actual channels for knowledge flows and ask questions about the importance of proximity when citing patents, when establishing cooperation links with other actors, and when searching for new employees who embody attractive knowledge. An alternative way is to introduce a potential measure that defines a field of influence which affects knowledge flows in a relevant geography. Jaffe *et al.* (1993) and Feldman and Audretsch (1999) examine how aggregate knowledge sources and R&D activities inside an urban region generate spillovers and affect innovation activities and outcome of firms located in the region. Different studies of this type conclude that knowledge flows and spillovers are spatially bounded.

As an alternative to the approach above, we consider a finer spatial resolution for which information is available about location of firms and location of knowledge sources. In such a setting the following model formulation can be applied. The model identifies locations i and j, and the time distance, t_{ij}, between each such pair of locations. The next step is to collect information about the size of a selected type of knowledge source, G_j, in location j. For any firm in location i we define the firm's distance-discounted knowledge potential with regard to G_j as

$$M_{ij} = \exp\left\{-\lambda t_{ij}\right\} G_j \tag{4.1}$$

where λ is an estimated parameter expressing time sensitivity for making face-to-face contacts between two locations, observing that contacts inside a location also have a time distance, signified by t_{ii}. Using formula (4.1) we can calculate the entire external knowledge potential that firms in location i have as $M_i = \sum_j \exp\left\{-\lambda t_{ij}\right\} G_j$. Moreover, the knowledge of the very local milieu is given by $M_{ii} = \exp\left\{-\lambda t_{ii}\right\} G_i$. We may remark that the knowledge-potential measures (M-values) can be given a probability interpretation so that (4.1) provides a measure of expected knowledge contacts between actors in location i and knowledge sources in location j, based on random-choice behavior or accessibility calculations (Johansson and Klaesson, 2011; Weibull, 1976).

Now it remains to discuss which knowledge resources may be reflected by the G-variable. We shall do that briefly by listing alternatives that span a small universe of candidates. A general observation is that the value of (4.1) with different definitions of G will often be highly correlated. The G-value in a given location can be a measure of any of the following values in the selected location:

(i)   The size of university R&D (spending or man-years)
(ii) The size of R&D efforts made by private industry
(iii) The number of knowledge-intensive workers in the entire economy of the location
(iv) The number of patent applications and/or patents granted
(v)   The supply of knowledge-intensive producer services (employment or economic value of the supply).

Other candidates can be a measurement of export experiences or import experiences, recording the number of exporters and importers. The two alternatives (i)–(ii) are employed in a study by Andersson and Gråsjö (2009) where the time-discounted values manage to capture most of the spatial interdependencies. The authors find that industry R&D is a more powerful knowledge source than university R&D, although locations with much industry R&D tend to host university R&D too. Alternative (iii) which captures the overall knowledge intensity in locations is applied by Andersson and Johansson (2010), who name their G-value external human capital, subdivided into human capital in neighboring locations and human capital in other industries.

Alternative (v) has recently been applied in Johansson, Johansson and Wallin (2014) in a study that compares the influence on export-product renewal from the internal and external knowledge sources accessible to local industries, in a paper by Lööf et al. (2014) that examines the role of the local knowledge milieu in determining firms' propensity to be persistent exporters and their TFP growth rate, and in Lööf, Nabavi and Johansson (2012) illuminating how firms can benefit from access to knowledge-intensive producer services. In the following subsection these recent contributions are examined with the intention to clarify the coupling between local knowledge milieu and firm performance indicators.

The strength of the distance decay of the market potential has important implications for analyzing knowledge flows, diffusion and spillover phenomena, and it should be seriously investigated to find out if different types of knowledge flows have the same time-distance sensitivity or not. A related issue is the precise delineation of local and regional knowledge potentials, respectively.

4.2 Local milieu and global networks

There is a growing amount of evidence that knowledge sources in the local and regional environment of firms generate knowledge transactions and spillovers that affect firm performance. We have noted that a knowledge potential may represent the possible renewal influences that a given firm may get. This idea may be further enriched by adding information about the technology relatedness in the local knowledge milieu. In this way it might become possible to extend our deliberations on spatial factor proportions in the context of renewal activities.

Another strand of analysis stresses that attempts to access external knowledge can be appreciated as a strategy-driven process, in which the firm actively searches for knowledge inputs to the firm's ambition of building up its internal knowledge. In this context the firm is assumed to find new information for knowledge building by establishing formal and informal links to other actors such as its input suppliers, its customers, universities and other knowledge providers. This means that a firm can influence both its local and global environment of knowledge-flows. Network development of this kind is less costly to carry out inside an urban region, and the advantage of being in a region that offers a large knowledge potential lies in the fact that the number of potential contacts is larger and more diversified than elsewhere (Simmie, 2003).

Consider now that the size of an urban region is a characteristic of the local milieu of firms in the urban region. We observe that large urban regions have large labor markets with a rich variety of specialist competence structures and more inter-firm job mobility. Having said this, we also recognize that labor mobility is a process which allows knowledge to spill over from a firm's environment, affecting its knowledge formation. This form of embodied knowledge flows can in addition be part of a firm's recruitment strategy (Andersson and Thulin, 2013).

Besides knowledge flows from the local milieu, the literature also considers knowledge flows that materialize in long-distance links of international networks. The firm may have established links for imports from input suppliers abroad as well as links for export to customers abroad. Moreover, firms may build trans-national links for R&D collaboration with firms abroad. In Swedish data a major indicator of the presence of international knowledge flows seems to be that a firm is part of a multinational company group (Lööf and Nabavi, 2014).

4.3 The conjunction hypothesis

When introducing the present chapter we have referred to challenging contributions by Almeida and Phene (2012) and Cantwell and Zhang (2012). In both cases the focus is primarily on large corporations with links to knowledge sources in both the local milieus and international networks. The two contributions emphasize that knowledge management of such firms concerns the possibilities of combining internal and external knowledge components, and the capacity to

Table 4.3 Construction of nine conjunction-variable categories

Renewal strategy	Low external knowledge potential	Medium-sized external knowledge potential	High external knowledge potential
No efforts	C1	C2	C3
Occasional engagement	C4	C5	C6
Persistent engagement	C7	C8	C9

access external knowledge and integrate it in the in-house renewal efforts. In this presentation we suggest that this conjunction idea is relevant for firms of different sizes and with different ownership structures.

The contribution that we claim to do is to introduce a conjunction variable that informs about how and in what proportions a firm's internal and external local knowledge are combined. One approach to formulate a conjunction variable is to make use of information about each firm's renewal strategy and its local knowledge potential, grouping firms into nine categories as specified in Table 4.3. In this classification C1 represents an extreme category where firms make infrequent or no renewal efforts, whereas category C9 consists of firms that are persistently engaged in renewal efforts. Once the categories have been arranged, one may examine to what extent each category associates with firm performance.

The approach illustrated in Table 4.3 is related to the assumption that a firm's renewal strategy can be used to indicate the size of the firm's internal knowledge. The argument is that persistent renewal efforts in the past reflect formation and maintenance of renewal capabilities of the firm. In the examples presented in Section 5, we apply alternative indicators to determine which renewal strategy a firm follows. One such indicator is based on measuring how often a firm makes patent applications. Another indicator is a firm's statement in the CIS surveys about its engagement in R&D efforts in the past.

A second way to form a conjunction variable is represented by the following specification, C_{ij} for a firm i (or a local industry i) in local economy j:

$$C_{ij} = \Lambda_i \ln M_j \tag{4.2}$$

where Λ_i equals one if i has internal knowledge above average and zero otherwise, and where M_j provides a measure of the external knowledge potential associated with location j. In the example presented in the next section, the internal knowledge is calculated as the sum of university-education years among the employees of i. A similar measure is the number of knowledge-intensive employees (with at least three years of university studies).

A third option to form a conjunction indicator makes use of a distinction between firms located in a metropolitan region with reference to non-metropolitan locations, and firms located in a metropolitan city with reference to non-metropolitan locations, where a metropolitan city is the largest city in a metropolitan region. The classification that obtains in this case refers to the assumption that the local knowledge potential is greater for a metropolitan location than for other locations.

As an additional external knowledge indicator we may also consider if a firm is a member of a company group or not. The distinctions in this case are non-affiliated firms, firms that belong to a uninational, a domestic multinational group, and a foreign multinational group. This classification corresponds to the suggestion that members in a multinational group can make use of internal interaction links to transmit knowledge from global knowledge sources. Such an advantage requires that the individual members of a group are fit for absorbing knowledge flows in their respective local milieu.

The conjunction hypothesis can be applied to investigate a series of questions, such as:

(i)   Can a firm with limited internal knowledge compensate for this by being located in a place with a large knowledge potential?
(ii) To what extent can a firm carry out its renewal activities, relying solely on its internal knowledge?
(iii) Does the amount of internal knowledge determine how successful the firm is in its knowledge accession activities?
(iv) Are internal and external knowledge substitutes or complements in a firm's renewal activities?

5. Empirical evidence in favor of the conjunction hypothesis

Section 5 provides three examples of attempts to capture the effects on firm performance that results from a firm's capability of combining internal and external knowledge. The three examples vary the way performance is measured, the way internal knowledge is identified, and the way external knowledge is reflected.

5.1 Productivity effects of combined internal and external knowledge

In this subsection we provide a detailed example of an attempt to illuminate how the combination of a firm's internal and external knowledge affect firm performance. The presentation makes use of findings in Lööf, Nabavi and Johansson (2012). As a measure of each firm's external knowledge the study relies on information about the firm's knowledge potential as introduced in subsection 4.1. Given this, the empirical analysis applies two alternative measures of each firm's internal knowledge, where the first measure is based on reports from firms in three consecutive CIS waves covering the period 2000–2008 – with 40 percent of the firms observed in all three surveys and 60 percent in two surveys. The second measure is based on firms' patent applications during the period 1997–2008.

Based on information about firms' patenting behavior and on information from the CIS surveys, firms are assumed to have a large internal knowledge base when they have a long history of persistent renewal efforts, to have medium-sized internal knowledge when they have a history of occasional renewal efforts, and to have a small internal knowledge when they have a history of no renewal efforts. The criteria applied are reported in Table 4.4.

It is quite clear that the two types of indicators in Table 4.4 are not conveying identical information about a firm's internal knowledge. In spite of this, they still sort firms in three groups where each pair of groups has similar impacts on firm performance. In the study referred to here, performance is also recorded in two alternative ways. The first performance variable is labor

Table 4.4 Classification of firms with regard to size of internal knowledge

Size of internal knowledge	CIS-based renewal efforts	Number of years with patent applications
Large	All years that are observed	At least 6 out of twelve years
Medium	Less than all years	1–5 out of twelve years
Small	No years	0 out of twelve years

productivity of each individual firm, which is a measure in level, whereas the second variable records firms' TFP growth.

Knowledge conjunction effects on value added

According to Table 4.3 the conjunction variable, C, associates each firm with one of the indicators C1–C9. A basic question is how these indicators affect three firms' output, measured by value added in a regression with a panel using capital, labor, ownership, knowledge intensity, lagged value added and time dummies as regressors, applying the Blundell and Bond (1998) two-step system GMM estimator allowing for a distinction between endogenous, pre-determined and exogenous right-hand side variables. This is presented in Lööf, Nabavi and Johansson (2012) with two alternative ways of classifying firms into persistent, occasional and inactive innovators.

For each firm i the conjunction variable shows the conjunction impact via a regression parameter $\beta(i) = \beta_K$ as i belongs to $K = \{C1, C2, ..., C9\}$, and we can write $\beta_K = \beta(Ck)$, with $k = 1, ..., 9$. The category parameter is ordered according to size of impact for two alternative regressions. In the first column internal knowledge is reflected by patent application frequency, and in the second CIS data are used as indicator of internal knowledge.

The result in the left column of Table 4.5 is salient in the sense that the β-parameter is influenced by both the internal and external knowledge of the firm and that value added is a strictly increasing function of the combination of internal knowledge generation and external knowledge proximity. Another observation is that $\beta(C2)$ is smaller than 1 per cent, whereas $\beta(C9)$ is larger than 20 percent. When internal knowledge instead is identified in the CIS panel (which corresponds to a broader concept of knowledge activity in the firm) a similar but less strict result obtains, where we observe that two of the β-parameters are not significantly different from zero.

The results reported in Table 4.5 appear in settings where the impact of belonging to a multinational company group is statistically significant and large, informing us that such company groups are likely to have considerable advantages in accessing global knowledge that is external to the individual firm.

Knowledge conjunction effects on TFP growth

For the case where firm performance is recorded as TFP growth, the total factor productivity change is measured in two steps, following the approach of Levinsohn and Petrin (2003). In the first step TFP is computed as the residual of a Cobb-Douglas production function where a firm's value added is the dependent variable, and where the determinants are inputs of ordinary labor, university-educated labor and physical capital. In the second step the growth of TFP is

Table 4.5 Impact of the conjunction variable on a firm's output (value added)

Order of impact size as patent applications are used as indicator of internal knowledge	Order of impact size as CIS information is used as indicator of internal knowledge
$\beta(C9) > \beta(C8) > \beta(C7) >$ $\beta(C6) > \beta(C5) > \beta(C4) >$ $\beta(C3) > \beta(C2) > \beta(C1) = 0$	$\beta(C9) > \beta(C8) > \beta(C7) >$ $\beta(C6) > \beta(C5) > \beta(C3)$ $\beta(C4)$ and $\beta(C2)$ are insignificant $\beta(C1) = 0$

Table 4.6 Impact of the conjunction variable on a firm's TFP growth

Order of impact size as patent applications are used as indicator of internal knowledge	Order of impact size as CIS information is used as indicator of internal knowledge
$\beta(C9) > \beta(C8) > \beta(C7) >$	$\beta(C9) > \beta(C8) > \beta(C7) >$
$\beta(C6) > \beta(C4) > \beta(C5)$	$\beta(C6)$ is insignificant on the 5% level
$\beta(C3)$ and $\beta(C2)$ are small in value with a low significance level	$\beta(C5) – \beta(C2)$ are insignificant
$\beta(C1) = 0$	$\beta(C1) = 0$

estimated with a technique that applies a dynamic panel model with error component decomposition (Lööf, Nabavi and Johansson, 2012).

As shown in Table 4.6 the impact of the conjunction variable on TFP growth follows theoretical predictions in the left-hand column (for the first six categories) when the internal knowledge is reflected by patent application frequency. In the right-hand column we can see that the ordering of the β-parameters follows theory predictions only for the first three categories, indicating that CIS information on R&D persistence may not be fully adequate.

The empirical results presented in subsection 5.1 sum up to the conclusion that firms have a superior performance when they manage to combine internal knowledge based on persistent innovation efforts with an environment offering a high knowledge potential. Even when the knowledge environment is poor, firms with high internal knowledge outperform occasional innovators in environments with a high knowledge potential.

5.2 Export varieties and combined internal and external knowledge

In this subsection we consider an alternative type of indicator to reflect firm performance, while also recognizing that a firm's renewal efforts can be based on adoption as well as innovation activities. The short story to be told is based on Johansson, Johansson and Wallin (2014). The focus is the export performance of local industries, where each local industry is identified as a 2-digit industry located in one out of 290 urban areas (municipalities). For each such local industry the study identifies its (i) internal knowledge reflected by the education of employees, (ii) its external knowledge in the form of supply of knowledge-intensive producer services, and (iii) a conjunction variable that reflects the combination of internal and external knowledge.

Variables that reflect export performance of local industries

Export performance of a local industry is identified in five dimensions, comprising (i) total export value, (ii) number of exporting firms, (iii) average number of code-destination specific varieties per exporting firm, (iv) average unit price of code-destination specific varieties per firm, and (v) average export quantity of code-destination specific varieties per firm. A code-destination variety is an 8-digit product code and a destination country, which means that an export variety is a triplet, identified by a unique combination of firm, code and destination. Thus, the study examines how local industries have introduced export triplets reflected by total export value, V, number of exporting firms, F, number of code-destination varieties, N, price, P, and quantity, Q, so that $V = F \times N \times P \times Q$, with the following specification:

V_{js} = Export value for industry s in location j
F_{js} = Number of exporting firms for industry s in location j

N_{js} = Average number of code-destination varieties per firm in local industry (j, s)
P_{js} = Average price of code-destination varieties in local industry (j, s)
Q_{js} = Average quantity of code-destination varieties in local industry (j, s)

Since $V = F \times N \times P \times Q$, the five variables above satisfy the condition $\ln V_{js} = \ln F_{js} + \ln N_{js} + \ln P_{js} + \ln Q_{js}$, and it is possible to determine how each variable contributes to the total export value. In the sequel the discussion concentrates on the four variables V, F, N and P as candidates for performance variables that are positively associated with internal and external knowledge as well as the interaction between internal and external knowledge (conjunction variable). Central questions are: does the conjunction variable have a positive effect on (i) the export price, (ii) the number of triplets, and (iii) the number of firms? Moreover, how is the total export value influenced by the conjunction variable?

Knowledge and knowledge conjunction effects on export performance

Sections 3 and 4 provide a broad outline of how internal and external knowledge of firms and industries can stimulate firm renewal activities that in turn can have positive effects on firm performance, including export performance. The renewal activities bring about new export firms, new export variety triplets, and may elevate the unit price of export flows, based on both adoption and innovation, which are both activities that require knowledge sources. In view of this, performance of a local industry is recorded by the number of export firms, the number of export varieties, the price of export varieties, and the total export value. In the study reported here (Johansson, Johansson and Wallin, 2014) these performance variables are regressed against knowledge sources 2002 and 2006. In addition the study also conducts the same type of regressions for export variety triplets that are introduced in the interval 2002–2006 (and hence new), conditioned on knowledge sources in 2002.

The log-linear regression employs industry dummies and the following regressors:

(i)   The internal knowledge of a local industry, measured by the total number of university-education years among employees
(ii) The external knowledge, captured by the knowledge potential $M_i = \sum_j \exp\{-\lambda t_{ij}\} G_j$ in location i as presented in subsection 4.1
(iii) The conjunction variable $C_{sj} = \Lambda_{sj} \ln M_j$ where M_j is the knowledge potential of location j, and where Λ_{sj} equals unity if the internal knowledge of local industry (j, s) is above average and zero otherwise
(iv) The size of a local industry measured by the number of employees.

Table 4.7 provides an overview of regression results for the four export performance indicators. The first observation is that the number of exporting firms and the export value are positively associated with the three sources internal knowledge, external knowledge and knowledge conjunction. The number of variety triplets per firm is influenced by the conjunction variable and the internal knowledge. The results in the table also indicate internal and external knowledge have a positive price effect.

Table 4.7 suggests that the conjunction of internal and external knowledge sources adds to the knowledge milieu of local industries. A similar exercise for the introduction of new variety triplets generates similar results, although the conjunction variable deviates in this case – with positive influence on the number of export firms and average export quantity. It may be observed that the variables external knowledge and knowledge conjunction reflect

Table 4.7 Knowledge sources and export performance of local industries 2002 and 2006

Explanatory variables	(F) Number of firms	(N) Variety triplets per firm	(P) Average variety price	(V) Export value
Internal knowledge	+	+	+	+
External knowledge	+	–	+	+
Knowledge conjunction	+	+	0	+
Size of local industry	+	+	–	+

Notes: (+) denotes positive and significant, (0) denotes insignificant, and (–) denotes negative and significant, where the significance level is one percent.

both technology externalities and pecuniary externalities associated with the economic milieu of the localized exporting industries (Antonelli, 2013). Moreover, the knowledge-potential variable attempts to capture accumulated knowledge in local economies and its influence on the export performance indicators.

5.3 Productivity and metropolitan milieus

In this subsection we provide a third empirical example of how a firm's innovation strategy and its external knowledge potential combine to a composite variable that explains firm performance, which in this case is a labor productivity measure. The example is based on Lööf and Johansson (2012) in a setting where metropolitan location is assumed to offer a knowledge milieu that brings innovation advantages that are superior to the milieu afforded in other locations. This form of advantage is cross-classified with each firm's innovation strategy that is characterized by one of the following three alternatives: (i) no R&D, (ii) occasional R&D, and (iii) persistent R&D efforts.

Knowledge milieu of metropolitan locations

The approach presented here is special in two ways. First, we assume (as argued in previous sections) that a firm's innovation strategy can be used as a reflection of its internal knowledge. Second, it assumes that the knowledge sources are richer in a metropolitan location than in other locations. The set of non-metro locations is kept constant while varying a metro location to be (i) Sweden's three metropolitan regions, (ii) the largest region of these three, (iii) the three metropolitan cities that are centers of the three metropolitan regions, and (iv) the largest metropolitan city. In the sequel we summarize the literature that suggests that metropolitan milieus provide richer and more diversified knowledge-flow opportunities than other locations.

A firm can influence its knowledge-flow environment by establishing formal and informal links to other actors such as its input suppliers, its customers, universities and other knowledge providers. Network development of this kind is less costly to carry out inside an urban region, and the advantage of a metropolitan region lies in the fact that the number of potential contacts is much larger and more diversified than elsewhere (Simmie, 2003). Large urban regions have also large labor markets with a rich variety of specialist competence structures and a more intense inter-firm job mobility, particularly among knowledge-intensive workers (Cohen and Levinthal, 1990; Almeida and Kogut, 1999; Andersson and Thulin, 2008).

Moretti (2004) suggests that plant productivity is an increasing function of external human capital in the local milieu, while Lychagin *et al.* (2010) finds that geographical markets are very local, which is in line with Lamorgese and Ottaviano (2006) and others who recognize that spillovers rapidly fade away with distance. Crespi *et al.* (2007) report that nearby suppliers and competitors (though less so customers) are primary sources of external knowledge. They also find that much of this information, particularly from competitors, is free, but not given freely, and that the presence of multinational firms makes these flows more intense. Goolsbee and Klenow (2002) report that larger regions and cities may have greater availability of complementary services which reduce the costs of adopting and implementing complex technologies.

Productivity premium for six combinations of internal and external knowledge

The paper by Lööf and Johansson (2012) examines the importance of the local and regional environment for firms that employ one of the following three categories of innovation strategy: (S1) no R&D efforts, (S2) occasional R&D efforts, and (S3) persistent R&D efforts. For each of these three categories, we assess the importance of firm location, classified into the following five types: the entire group of metropolitan regions, the largest metropolitan region, the group of metropolitan cities, where such a city is the urban center of a metropolitan region, the largest metropolitan city, and the entire group of non-metropolitan locations. To reveal how different combinations of strategy and location affect firm performance, we use the Community Innovation Survey (CIS) on Swedish manufacturing and service firms observed 2002–2004, and combine that information with register data for the observed CIS firms over the period 1997–2006. Due to the lag structure of the applied dynamic GMM model (Blundell and Bond 1998), the panel estimates refer to firm characteristics over the period 2000–2006. The majority of firms, almost 60 percent, have no R&D activities.

Table 4. 8 cross-classifies firms with regard to innovation strategy and type of location, which yields six different categories of firms. The strategy labeled S3 represents the largest amount of internal knowledge and S1 the smallest. In the regression analysis the set of non-metro firms is invariant, whereas metro location is varied so that four distinct regressions obtain.

The empirical analysis consists of four regression equations, where each is based on a production function specified as follows for each point in time:

$$Y_i = A_i F\left(H_i, K_i, L_i\right)$$

where Y_i denotes output of firm I in terms of value added, H_i denotes the number of employees with at least three years of university education, K_i denotes the input of physical capital, and L_i the input of ordinary labor. The variable A_i is a shift factor that indicates which of the six categories MR1,…, MR6 that firm i belongs to. The labor productivity is calculated as $y_i = Y_i/L_i$. Adding a dynamic specification and identifying ownership and sector, while allowing for a lag structure of the regressors, the exercise yields the results presented in Table 4.9.

The results in Table 4.9 can be summarized in the following three statements. First, we observe that the productivity premium that follows from persistent R&D efforts is around 8 percent in

Table 4.8 Definition of six category variables

	S1 = No R&D	S2 = Occasional R&D	S3 = Persistent R&D
Non-metro	MR1	MR3	MR5
Metro	MR2	MR4	MR6

Table 4.9 Productivity premium in percent associated with the six category variables

	Group of 3 metro regions	Largest metro region	Group of 3 metro cities	Largest metro city
MR1	Reference	Reference	Reference	Reference
MR2	Insignificant	Insignificant	Insignificant	Insignificant
MR3	Insignificant	Insignificant	Insignificant	Insignificant
MR4	Insignificant	Insignificant	Insignificant	Insignificant
MR5	7.6	6.9	7.4	6.2
MR6	9.7	9.8	12.5	13.3

Table 4.10 Year-to-year persistence in the same classification

Variable	Definition	0/0	1/1
$MR1_{it}$	Non-metro × Non-R&D	99.65	99.40
$MR2_{it}$	Metro × Non-R&D	99.68	99.53
$MR3_{it}$	Non-metro × Occasional R&D	99.90	99.40
$MR4_{it}$	Metro × Occasional R&D	99.91	97.22
$MR5_{it}$	Non-metro × Persistent R&D	99.82	99.17
$MR6_{it}$	Metro × Persistent R&D	99.84	97.12

Notes: 0/0: The proportion of firms that did not belong to this group in one year
that also did not belong to this group the next year.
1/1: The proportion of firms that belonged to this group in one year that also
belonged to this group the next year.

non-metropolitan locations and about 14 percent in the largest metropolitan city. Second, no productivity premium is associated with occasional R&D efforts, regardless of the firm's location. Third, firms with no R&D engagements do not benefit from the external milieu in metropolitan areas. In summary, Table 4.9 signals that metropolitan cities in Sweden provide a superior milieu of knowledge sources and, as emphasized in Antonelli (2013), lower accession costs of external knowledge.

To put the result in Table 4.9 in perspective, we may ask: how invariant is the classification of firms into six categories. An answer is provided in Table 4.10, which reports for each category the proportion of firms that did not belong to the category two years in sequence, signified by 0/0, and the proportion of firms that did belong to the same category two years in sequence, signified by 1/1. A high degree of invariance is observed for the entire period 1997–2006. The persistency covers the type of location and the type of innovation strategy.

6. Concluding remarks

The story told in this chapter has several motivations, ranging from consistency requirement and empirical regularities. First, observations on firms over time reveal that they are heterogenous both with regard to inputs and outputs. Second, the firm heterogeneity displays time invariance with lasting performance differences, with little evidence in favor of convergence to best practice conditions in each industry. Is there a theoretical framework that can host these observations? The presentation in this chapter represents a first attempt to sketch such a framework.

The outline in this chapter associates firm performance differences with the type of innovation strategy applied by each firm, ordered into S1 signifying negligible innovation efforts, S2 signifying occasional efforts, and S3 indicating persistent efforts. The presentation assembles evidence that implies that with the S3-strategy a firm can generate new technical solutions, while at the same time cumulating in-house knowledge that determines the firm's capability of continuing to remain innovative, a capability that is difficult to imitate. In this way persisting differences between innovation strategies can shed light on time-invariant firm performance differentials.

Given the above conclusions, innovation and capability strategies are used as indicators of how large a firm's internal knowledge is. Then the chapter adds the question: how much do a firm's opportunities to access external knowledge influence its innovation capability? Is the usefulness of a generous knowledge milieu the same for firms with strategies S1, S2 and S3? In order to assess this additional issue, the analysis introduces the concept of knowledge potential for each location where a firm is established. From this we are able to conclude two things. First, the knowledge potential captures the probability and cost of integration of external and internal knowledge. Second, such a conjunction of internal and external knowledge sources shifts a firm's innovation and economic performance upwards.

In summary, this chapter has consulted existing literature to find convincing arguments and empirical findings that support the suggestion that adoption and innovation activities are similar in their reliance on skills in combining and integrating internal and external knowledge. The presentation adds to this knowledge by suggesting alternative ways of identifying a firm's internal and external knowledge, and ways of observing phenomena that reveal the conjunction of internal and external knowledge sources. The paper also provides examples of how to define and empirically measure firm performance.

One major suggestion is that a firm's persistent renewal efforts is a reliable indicator of the firm's internal knowledge, including innovation and adoption know-how. Combining this variable with a firm's external knowledge potential, the paper offers an explanation to the observed phenomenon that in each industry an almost invariant set of firms perform far above the average firm in terms TFP growth, labor productivity and export performance.

Bibliography

Aghion, P., Bloom, N., Blundell, R., Griffith, R., and Howitt, P. (2005), Competition and innovation: an inverted relationship, *Quarterly Journal of Economics* May 2005: 701–728.

Almeida, P. and Kogut, B. (1999), Localization of knowledge and the mobility of engineers in regional networks, *Management Science* 45(7): 905–917.

Almeida, P. and Phene, A. (2012), Managing knowledge within and outside the multinational corporation. In M. Andersson, B. Johansson, C. Karlsson and H. Lööf (eds) *Innovation and Growth, From R&D Strategies of Innovating Firms to Economy Wide Technological Change*. Oxford University Press, Oxford, UK.

Andersson, M. and Gråsjö, U. (2009), Spatial dependence and the representation of space in empirical models, *The Annals of Regional Science* 43(1): 159–180.

Andersson, M. and Johansson, B. (2012), Heterogenous distributions of firms sustained by innovation dynamics – a model with empirical illustrations and analysis, *Journal of Industry, Competition and Trade* 12: 239–263.

Andersson, M. and Johansson, S. (2010), Human capital and the structure of regional export flows, *Technology in Society* 32(3): 230–240.

Andersson, M. and Thulin, P. (2008), Labor mobility and spatial density, *CESIS Working Paper Series No 248*, Centre of Excellence for Science and Innovation Studies, Royal Institute of Technology, Stockholm.

Andersson, M. and Thulin, P. (2013), Does spatial employment density spur inter-firm job switching? *The Annals of Regional Science* 51(1): 245–272.

Andersson, M., Johansson, B., Karlsson, C., and Lööf, H. (2012), *Innovation and Growth – From R&D Strategies of Innovating Firms to Economy-wide Technological Change*, Oxford University Press, Oxford, UK.

Antonelli, C. (1989), A failure-inducement model of research and development expenditure, *Journal of Economic Behavior and Organization* 12: 159–180.

Antonelli, C. (2013), Knowledge governance, pecuniary knowledge externalities and total factor productivity growth, *Economic Development Quarterly* 27: 62–70.

Antonelli, C., Crespi, F., and Scellato, G. (2012), Inside innovation persistence: new evidence from Italian micro-data, *Structural Change and Economic Dynamics* 23: 341–353.

Antonelli, C., Crespi, F., and Scellato, G. (2013), Internal and external factors in innovation persistence, *Economics of Innovation and New Technology* 22: 256–280.

Barney, J. (1991), Firm resources and sustained competitive advantage, *Journal of Management* 17: 99–120.

Beckmann, M.J. (2000), Interurban knowledge networks. In D. Batten (ed.), *Learning, Innovation and Urban Evolution*, Kluwer Academic, London, pp. 127–135.

Blundell, R. and Bond, S. (1998), Initial conditions and moment restrictions in dynamic panel data models, *Journal of Econometrics* 87: 115–143.

Cantwell, J. and Zhang, F. (2012), Knowledge accession strategies and the spatial organization of R&D. In M. Andersson, B. Johansson, C. Karlsson, and H. Lööf (eds), *Innovation and Growth, From R&D Strategies of Innovating Firms to Economy Wide Technological Change.* Oxford University Press, Oxford, UK.

Cefis, E. and Cicarelli, M. (2005), Profit differential and innovation, *Economics of Innovation and New Technology* 14: 43–61.

Cohen, W.M. (2010), Fifty years of empirical studies of innovative activity and performance. In B.H. Hall and N. Rosenberg (eds), *Handbook of the Economics of Innovation*, North-Holland, Elsevier, Amsterdam, pp. 129–213.

Cohen, W. and Levinthal, D. (1990), Absorptive capacity: a new perspective on learning and innovation, *Administrative Science Quarterly* 35(1): 128–158.

Crépon, B., Duguet, E., and Mairesse, J. (1998), Research, innovation and productivity: an econometric analysis at the firm level, *Economics of Innovation and New Technology* 7(2): 115–158.

Crespi, G., Criscuolo, C., Haskel, J., and Slaughter, M. (2007), *Productivity Growth, Knowledge Flows and Spillovers.* CEP Discussion Papers dp0785.

Dosi, G. and Nelson, R.R. (2010), Technical change and industrial dynamics as evolutionary processes. In B. Hall and N. Rosenberg (eds) *The Economics of Innovation*, Elsevier, Amsterdam.

Feldman, M. and Audretsch, D.B. (1999), Innovation in cities: science-based diversity, specialization and localized competition, *European Economic Review* 43: 409–429.

Feldman, M. and Kogler, D.F. (2010), Stylized facts in the geography of innovation. In B.H. Hall and N. Rosenberg (eds) *Handbook of the Economics of Innovation*, Elsevier, Amsterdam.

Geroski, P. (1998), An applied econometrician's view on large company performance, *Review of Industrial Organization* 13: 271–294.

Goolsbee, A. and Klenow, P.J. (2002), Evidence on learning and network externalities in the diffusion of home computers, *Journal of Law and Economics* XLV: 317–344.

Griliches, Z. and Mairesse, J. (1995), Production functions: the search for identification, *NBER Working Papers 5067*, National Bureau of Economic Research, Inc.

Hall, B.H. (2002), The financing of research and development, *Oxford Review of Economic Policy* 18: 35–48.

Hall, B.H. (2011), Using productivity growth as an innovation indicator, *Report for the High Level Panel on Measuring Innovation, DG Research, European Commission.* Available at: http://ec.europa.eu/commission_2010-2014/geoghegan-quinn/hlp/documents/20120309-hlp-productivity-innovation_en.pdf (accessed July 10, 2014).

Heckscher, E. (1918), *Svenska produktionsproblem* (Swedish Production Problems), Bonniers, Stockholm.

Hotelling, H. (1932), Edgwort's taxation paradox and the nature of demand and supply functions, *Journal of Political Economy* 40: 577–616.

Jacobs, J. (1969), *The Economy of Cities*, Random House, New York.

Jacobs, J. (1984), *Cities and the Wealth of Nations*, Random House, New York.

Jaffe, A.B., Trajtenberg, M., and Henderson, R. (1993), Geographic localization of knowledge spillovers as evidenced by panel citations, *The Quarterly Journal of Economics* 108: 577–598.

Johansson, B. (1991), Regional industrial analysis and vintage dynamics, *The Annals of Regional Science* 25: 1–18.

Johansson, B. (2014), Generation and diffusion of innovation. In M.M. Fischer and P. Nijkamp (eds) *Handbook of Regional Science.* Springer, Heidelberg, New York, Dordrecht, London, pp. 391–423.

Johansson, B. and Klaesson, J. (2011), Agglomeration dynamics of business services, *Annals of Regional Science* 47, 373–391.

Johansson, B. and Lööf, H. (2008), Innovation activities explained by firm attributes and location, *Economics of Innovation and New Technology* 16: 533–552.

Johansson, B., Johansson, S., and Wallin, T. (2014), Internal and external knowledge and introduction of export varieties, *The World Economy*, doi: 10.1111/twec.12161.

Krugman, P. (1991), Increasing returns and economic geography, *Journal of Political Economy* 99(3): 483–499.

Lamorgese, A.R. and Ottaviano, I.P. (2006), *Intercity Interactions: Evidence from the US*. 2006 Meeting Papers 667. Society for Economic Dynamics.

Levinsohn, J. and Petrin, A. (2003), Estimating production functions using inputs to control for unobservables, *The Review of Economic Studies* 70(2): 317–341.

Lychagin, S., Pinkse, J., Slade, M.E., and Van Reenen, J. (2010), *Spillovers in Space: Does Geography Matter?*, NBER Working Papers 16188, National Bureau of Economic Research.

Lööf, H. and Johansson, B. (2014), R&D strategy, metropolitan externalities and productivity: evidence from Sweden, *Industry and Innovation* 21(2).

Lööf, H. and Nabavi, P. (2014), Joint impact of innovation and knowledge spillovers on productivity and growth for exporting firms, *The World Economy*. Forthcoming.

Lööf, H., Nabavi, P., and Johansson B. (2012), Innovation efforts, spillovers and productivity: how can firms benefit from access to knowledge-intensive producer services? *CESIS Working Papers Series No 283*, Royal Institute of Technology, Stockholm.

Lööf, H., Nabavi, P., Cook, G., and Johansson, B. (2015), Learning-by-exporting and innovation strategies, *Economics of Innovation and New Technology*. Forthcoming.

MacDonald, J.M. (1985), R&D and the direction of diversification, *Review of Economics and Statistics* 47: 583–590.

Mairesse, J. and Robin, S. (2012), The importance of process and product innovation for French manufacturing and service industries. In M. Andersson, B. Johansson, C. Karlsson, and H. Lööf (eds) *Innovation and Growth, From R&D Strategies of Innovating Firms to Economy Wide Technological Change*. Oxford University Press, Oxford, UK.

Mansfield, E. (1987), Price indexes for R and D Inputs 1969–1983, *Management Science* 33(1): 124–129.

Martinsson, G. and Lööf, H. (2013), Financial factors and patents. In Andreas Pyka and Esben Sloth Andersen (eds) *Innovation, Organisation, Sustainability and Crises*. Springer, New York.

Montgomery, C. and Hariharan, S. (1991), Diversified expansion in large established firms, *Journal of Economic Behavior and Organization* 15: 71–89.

Moretti, E. (2004), Workers' education, spillovers, and productivity: evidence from plant-level production functions, *American Economic Review* 94(3): 656–690.

Nelson, R.R. and Winter, S.G. (1982), *An Evolutionary Theory of Economic Change*, Belknap Press, Cambridge, MA.

Peters, B. (2009), Persistence of innovation: stylized fact and panel data evidence, *Journal of Technology Transfer* 34: 226–243.

Phene, A. and Almeida, P. (2008), Innovation in multinational subsidiaries: the role of knowledge assimilation and subsidiary capabilities, *Journal of International Business Studies* 39: 901–919.

Polanyi, M. (1966), *The Tacit Dimension*, Doubleday & Company, New York.

Romer, P.M. (1990), Endogenous technological change, *Journal of Political Economy* 98(5), 71–102.

Salter, W.E.G. (1960), *Productivity and Technical Change*, Cambridge University Press, Cambridge, UK.

Schumpeter, J. (1934), *The Theory of Economic Development*, Harvard University Press, Cambridge, MA.

Simmie, J. (2003), Innovation and urban regions as national and international nodes for transfer and sharing of knowledge, *Regional Studies* 37: 607–620.

Solow, R. (1957), Technical change and the aggregate production function, *Review of Economics and Statistics* 34: 312–320.

Stephan, P. (2002), Using human resource data to illuminate innovation and research utilization. In S. Merrill and M. McGeary (eds), *Using Human Resource Data to Track Innovation*. National Academic Press, Washington DC.

Sutton, J. (1991), *Sunk Cost and Market Structure*, MIT Press, Cambridge, MA.

Teece, D.J. (2010), Technological innovation and the theory of the firm. In B. Hall and N. Rosenberg (eds) *Handbook of the Economics of Innovation*, North-Holland, Amsterdam.

Vega-Redondo, F. (2003), *Economics and the Theory of Games*, Cambridge University Press, Cambridge, UK.

Weibull, J.W. (1976), An axiomatic approach to the measurement of accessibility, *Regional Science and Urban Economics* 6: 357–379.

5

Networks of knowledge
An appraisal of research themes, findings and implications

Müge Özman

1. Introduction

A network is essentially a way of seeing relationships in a system. In the social sciences, the network approach is undertaken to explain how the social structure shapes individual behaviors and performance. The rise of the network approach can be linked to an increasing interest in open systems in many fields of science during the last half century. Open systems emphasize interrelations between parts of a system (Scott and Davis, 2007).

It is possible to trace the roots of the network approach in sociology to Moreno (1934), who first used a sociometric configuration, and Simmel's sociological theory (Simmel, 1950).[1] More recently, the understanding that economic action is embedded in a social context (Granovetter, 1985) has been embraced by an increasing number of subfields in the social sciences. This embeddedness can be represented in different network configurations, and can deepen our understanding about the relation between social connections, and behavior and performance (Smith-Doerr and Powell, 2005). Knowledge networks are particularly important in this context. Consider the role of contacts in knowing about opportunities, or diffusion of an idea, or innovation diffusion through social contagion.

During recent decades industries are increasingly composed of firms that form alliances with each other; universities are becoming more connected through collaborating scientists, and civil societies are becoming more integrated through NGO networks. Firms are giving more and more attention to the social networks between inventors, and the role of intra-firm communities in fostering creativity is frequently emphasized. Moreover, immense improvements in information and communication technologies have also contributed to increased networking between actors, as well as our capabilities to analyze them. In short, networks have become the main means through which public and private knowledge is generated and diffused in the economy at various levels.

Networks both store knowledge, and also diffuse this knowledge. They provide a context in which learning takes place, and depending on their structure, they shape organizational routines that enable (or constrain) knowledge creation. For example, dense networks are efficient in diffusing tacit knowledge as shown empirically in many studies. Networks formed of diverse actors and bridging/brokerage positions are usually associated with novelty and creativity.

In the organization of this chapter, I prioritized the current debates in social network research, so as to highlight those areas which most merit contributions in the future. For this purpose, I categorized the studies according to the following:

1.   Network as a knowledge map, network as a cause, network (or tie) as a consequence;
2.   Secondary network data (archival) and primary network data use;
3.   Inter personal and inter organizational network.

Each of these categories has some implication for the debates in social network research. Consider an example: there is a debate on the structure and agency problem, claiming that network research leaves little space for understanding individual action, since success or failure is explained only through the social structure (Emirbayer and Goodwin, 1994). This debate underlines the importance of studies exploring the role of the individual in network evolution, presented in section 5. Nonetheless, not all studies on network evolution necessarily explain the role of the individual action; data constraints can present important barriers, especially the use of archival data, which is largely ex-post and highly aggregated. Considering similar constraints, the survey is further divided into secondary network data and primary network data, because they contribute to the literature in different ways. In addition, the distinction between inter organizational and inter personal is significant, especially in the following sense: it is possible to collect data on an interpersonal network through surveys and interviews. Then the researcher has access to both the structure of the network (if a sufficient number of interviews are made), and also the qualitative aspects of ties between people (emotional intensity, frequency of meetings, affection, dislike, etc.). This permits understanding links between the structural and the relational. Are bridging positions characterized by ties that "coordinate" the knowledge of people, for example (Obstfeld, 2005)? At the inter organizational level, this is more of a challenge, in terms of data constraints. Qualitative aspects of ties are inferred, or assumed, by large-scale data. For example, the number of times that two inventors have published a paper together is usually taken to imply that they have a strong tie. There is in general no problem with such assumptions, as long as the research questions are designed accordingly. Nonetheless, when the theoretical framing of the study lies in social psychological theories, such inferences may risk undermining the precise mechanisms and causalities in relations.

Overall, such a categorization of research permits seeing how studies are distributed among the three levels above, and highlights the following observations. First, the nature of questions addressed largely depends on the sources of data. Among others, one of the implications of this is to put a divide between the precision in measuring the structural network positions, which is easier with large-scale data (especially for inter organizational networks) and qualitative aspects of ties, which is more readily collected through interviews.

Second, and largely as a result of abundant and accessible large-scale data sources (like patents), some questions are overstudied, leaving other, and possibly more problematic, areas understudied. Third, there is a gap between analytical models on one hand, and empirical ones on the other. The analytical results obtained through simulation studies and models are not reflected in empirical research for more rigorous testing. Fourth, measuring networks in a certain way reflects certain assumptions about how knowledge is taken by the analyst. More studies are needed to establish the links between the epistemological assumptions regarding knowledge, and how it is reflected in network studies. This link should be better understood so as to avoid misalignments between the results of network research, and its contribution to theories of knowledge.

The chapter is organized as follows. In the second section I focus on some important debates in the social network research area. In the third section I focus on knowledge network maps. The fourth section reviews studies that take the network as a cause. The fifth section takes network (or ties) as a consequence. The sixth section presents an overview of simulation models. Some concluding remarks and directions for future research follow.

2. Knowledge networks: definitions, scope, and positioning in network literature in general

What is a knowledge network? It is difficult to find a unique definition in the literature. One of the reasons behind this difficulty is that networks are constructed by analysts, being largely shaped by their own perception of what knowledge constitutes. Nevertheless, a working definition is relevant in a survey article, to clarify the scope of studies covered. In this survey, a knowledge network refers to a structural representation of relationships between individuals, organizations, or artifacts, where these relationships have implications for the way in which our understanding about how knowledge is shared and disseminated (or blocked and retained), its institutional social and cultural context, its nature, cumulativeness, evolution, and its role in innovation is deepened. As such, knowledge networks are closely related with social networks. The social realm is about communications and influences between people, and it is through these that knowledge flows.

I focus on four areas of debate in network research, and review knowledge networks from the lens of these debates. These issues are not exhaustive, for further elaboration, excellent resources exist on social network research referring to recent issues (examples are Kadushin, 2012; Borgatti *et al.*, 2013; Scott and Carrington, 2011). These areas are concerned with theoretical, epistemological, and methodological considerations most frequently mentioned in knowledge network research, and they are presented in Table 5.1. Some of them point to some issues that are most problematic, and/or understudied in the literature.

2.1 Boundaries of research

Is the network research paradigm predominantly a methodology or a theory? (Barnes, 1979). While the social network analysis methodology (SNA) is common in addressing a wide range

Table 5.1 Theoretical and methodological issues in network research

Research axis	Explanation	Implications
Boundaries of research	Does the study utilize social network analysis as a methodology, or as a theory?	Implications for the disciplinary field of contribution.
Causality	Network as a source of (or reason behind) behavior/performance of an organization or individual, or, network as the result of a process, an attribute or a previous state of network.	Implications for the problem of endogeneity in network research.
The role of agency	To what extent can network formation be explained by the deliberate actions of the actors which constitute it, by foreseeing the broader network picture?	Implications for role of structure – agency, strategy and policy.
Tie definition	Is the network constructed by using secondary data sources, or through direct interactions with individuals who constitute it?	Implications for research questions addressed.

of questions in various disciplines, only some of these have a direct impact on the field of social network theory itself. But then, what do we mean by "social network theory"?[2]

Kilduff et al. (2006), define the four core concepts of the network research program, from a Lakatosian perspective (Lakatos, 1970). The first one refers to the primacy of relations, where the focus is "away from the individualist, essentialist, and atomistic explanations, toward more relational, contextual and systematic understandings" (Borgatti and Foster, 2003: p. 992). In other words, the network research program prioritizes relations between actors as a main force behind change and economic action. The second is the "ubiquity of embeddedness", where economic action is taken to be embedded in inter personal relationships and a social context (Granovetter, 1985). The third core concept is taken to be the social utility of connections, which refers to the economic well-being conferred (or the opposite) by network relations. Finally the fourth core concept is "structural patterning of social life", where the apparent complexity of social life can be explained in terms of relationship *patterns*. They state that the hard core of the network research program is largely level free, as it applies to individual as well as organizational networks. In addition, they state that in network research, irrespective of the unit of analysis, it is the *structure* of relations that should be the focus of the organizational research program. In other words, "studies that fail to incorporate structural thinking and analysis are outside the boundaries of network research, even though the term network can be used" (Kilduff et al., 2006). One of the essential features of network perspective is its rejection of "all attempts to explain human behavior or social processes solely in terms of the categorical attributes of actors, whether individual or collective" (Emirbayer and Goodwin, 1994, p. 1414).

In the literature on knowledge networks, it is not uncommon to find studies that take the network as a mathematical object to illustrate, describe, or analyze a knowledge domain and its evolution. In these studies, the use of archival data, like patent documents and publications, is common, which gives the possibility of tracing the long-term developments in a particular knowledge domain, through constructing networks of citations and co-authorship, or through key word analysis. Most of the time, it is *not* the network itself which is the main subject of analysis as a cause, or a consequence, but rather the network representation is used to describe, evaluate, or understand the nature (or the evolution) of a particular knowledge system. This distinction is highlighted in the studies in section 3, which use network analysis as a methodology.

2.2 Direction of causality

Is the network the cause, or is it a consequence? In this review, sections 4 and 5 distinguish between these two broad questions. In the former, the network itself, or the positions of actors in the network, is associated with performance, behavior, or attributes of actors that constitute it. These studies imply some sort of consequence that is conferred by a certain network position. These relations, especially when they are inferred by using large-scale data, point to correlations between positions and performance, rather than direct impact. The latter, on the other hand, explores the mechanisms that give rise to networks. In other words, they are concerned with how and why certain network positions come to be occupied by certain actors, and how a certain network structure emerges. Borgatti and Halgin (2011) call these two broad fields of inquiry *network theory*, and *theory of networks*, respectively. These are covered, respectively, in the fourth and fifth sections of the survey.

It is important to note that network theory and theory of networks are not always easily separable. One of the earliest and most famous studies on intra organizational knowledge flows in an R&D organization, carried out by Allen and Cohen (1969), analyzes both the attributes of inventors who occupy central positions in the network, as well as the impact of such positions on the occupants. In addition, most agent-based simulation studies take network evolution as a dynamic and continuous process, through which agents learn and adapt to a changing network environment, which further modifies their network positions (Özman, 2008; 2010), modeling a feedback mechanism between the individual and the network. Other empirical studies of this nature are rather rare in the literature on knowledge networks (see for example, Stam, 2010 and Zaheer and Soda, 2009).

This causality issue lies at the root of the endogeneity problem in network research. Endogeneity problem refers to the problematic nature of correctly predicting the effect of a network, without investigating how the network got there (Borgatti and Halgin, 2011). To put it differently, those factors which are seen as causing the outcome can themselves be dependent on the outcome.

Endogeneity problem in network research highlights the potential value of studies which examine the dynamics of networks. However, a word of caution here: not all studies which focus on network dynamics necessarily explain network evolution. As Doreian and Stokman (1997) point out, *network evolution refers to understanding the dynamics of the network via some understood process*, so evolution of the network connotes understanding the rules governing the sequence of changes through time.

During recent years there has been an increase in studies on network evolution. In general, three mechanisms are usually referred to explain change. The first one explains the evolution of the knowledge network by the state of the network in the previous periods,[3] emphasizing path dependent processes behind network formation. The second one explains network evolution through common dyadic attributes of network members, being mostly a measure of proximity: geographical, cognitive, technological, organizational, ethnical, gender, etc. These studies are rooted in Festinger's (1964) social comparison theories which underline the importance of social comparisons between people as the main driver of connections. The third approach highlights the role of individual attributes in explaining the network positions that they occupy. Examples are self-monitoring behavior (Sasovova *et al.*, 2010) or scientific success (Luo *et al.*, 2009).

Finally, while these studies may explain network evolution through an *understood mechanism*, this does not mean that they highlight the role of deliberate action (or strategy) of actors in shaping their network positions, giving their decisions initially by overseeing the broader network picture. This question brings forth the third debate in network research. To what extent do actors intentionally manipulate network structure? This dimension is explored in the next subsection.

2.3. Structure, agency, and networks

Historically, network analysis was born as a reaction to the individualistic explanation of social systems which dominated the methodology of sociology in 1950s. As explained by Coleman in this period (cited in Emirbayer and Goodwin, 1994, p. 1416):

> There were no comparable tools of development for analysis of the behavior of interacting systems of individuals or for capturing the interdependencies of individual actions as they combine to produce a system level outcome. The far greater complexity required of tools for these purposes constituted a serious impediment to their development....The end result [was] extraordinarily elaborated methods for analysis of the behavior of a set of independent entities (most often individuals) with little development of methods for characterizing systemic action resulting in the interdependent actions of members of the system.

While the essence of the network approach underlined the effect of relationship structures on performance or behavior of actors, later on it was precisely this aspect of networks that received criticisms. In particular, some authors have criticized structure-oriented explanations, questioning the lack of individual action to guide network evolution or the manipulation of specific positions by individuals who make up the network (Emirbayer and Goodwin, 1994). Consequently, network research, they claim, leaves little space for individual action.

One of the areas which is yet to be developed further in network research is concerned with understanding the deliberate and strategic manipulations of networks by actors who constitute them (Baum and Rowley, 2008). Yet, the literature is developing only slowly in this area (see for example, the works by Baum *et al.*, 2005, and Dantas and Bell, 2009, and for a focus on network strategy Baum and Rowley, 2008). The most likely reason is that organizations rarely have deliberate network strategies, and most network strategy is emergent in nature (cf. deliberate and emergent strategies by Mintzberg and Waters, 1985. Therefore there is a need in the literature to fill this gap by taking an emergent strategy perspective in understanding what factors contribute to organizational decision making mechanisms in organizations occupying certain network positions.

One of the difficulties involved in analyzing the role of deliberate actions of individuals is about collecting network data. The use of archival data, and also large alliance databases which are commonly used to analyze knowledge networks, hardly permits fine-grained information on the specific mechanisms through which actors make decisions. There is too much aggregation, which runs the risk of imprecise generalizations ex-post. For this purpose, surveys, detailed interviews, and long-term anthropological studies in the field of interest are necessary to pinpoint clearer causality mechanisms.

The issues of network data and the boundary specification problem are explored in the next part, as the fourth dimension of network research.

2.4. Knowledge networks, boundary specification, and data gathering

In this section, I focus on two related issues in network studies: the boundary specification problem, and network data collection.

Boundary specification is concerned with specifying the limits of network data to be collected. To illustrate the significance of this issue in network research, one can imagine how the overall network analysis would be rendered meaningless, if only one actor (who forms a bridge, for example) is omitted from the network, which would result in a significantly different network topology. The boundary specification problem is a challenging one, since one can take networks to be endless, unless the limits to inclusion are set by the analyst, or the network members themselves. Laumann *et al.* (1983) distinguish between realist and nominalist approaches to boundary specification. In the realist approach, "the network is treated as a social fact only in that it is consciously experienced as such by the actors composing it" (p. 21). In the nominalist approach, on the other hand, the analyst "self consciously imposes a conceptual framework constructed to serve his own analytic purposes" (pp. 21–22). As such, most of the knowledge network literature, in the economics and management disciplines, adopts a nominalist approach.[4]

The boundary specification problem is also related to the kind of network data to be used. In the case of secondary network data from archival resources, the limits of data depend on either the availability of data or the conceptual interest of the researcher. For example if one studies the evolution of technology for LEDs (light emitting diodes) only the patent classes related to this technology can be included, but this would miss the underlying knowledge which LEDs draw upon, and also the fields which the technology influences. Therefore if the researcher were analyzing knowledge flows, she would include the forward and backward citations of these patents to obtain a network. At which level to stop depends on the analyst and the aim. If the researcher is interested in knowledge diffusion in an R&D lab, network data on the engineers who are part of the lab can be focused upon. But, considering the importance of boundary spanners who carry information from the external to the internal (or vice versa), possibly their external links should be collected as well, especially if the sources of knowledge flows are analyzed. Therefore it is extremely important to have clear and objective criteria to set the limits of network data, especially in knowledge networks considering the highly fluid nature of knowledge.

The second issue is related with the network data. Theories of knowledge are based on two alternative conceptualizations of knowledge. In the first one, knowledge is regarded as an "objective" entity. According to objectivists, knowledge can exist outside the individual, by being embedded in an artifact, for example, or flowing between people and organizations. Accordingly knowledge can be in tacit or explicit form, which implies that it can be fully or partially transferred between actors. This implies that knowledge can be taken separately from the actors who create, diffuse, or process it (Hislop, 2013). The practice based approach to knowledge, on the other hand, emphasizes that knowledge is not unique and it is not independent of interpretations; people have different understandings of it, depending on the context, language, history, or culture. In other words, according to the practice based approach, knowledge is not either "tacit or codified", contrarily, it is both "tacit and codified" (Hislop, 2013).

This distinction is important as far as researchers define and measure ties in a knowledge network. An objectivist perception of knowledge manifests itself clearly when knowledge is assumed to be embodied in a network of artifacts, for example in using bibliometric data, or when it is assumed to flow between actors during an event (like an alliance between two firms). The use of secondary data in studying knowledge networks separates the context within which knowing takes place, and the tangible events and artifacts which accompany the process of knowing by actors. For example, by analyzing the network of artifacts a social tie is *assumed* between actors who create knowledge, although this tie may not be properly defined as a "social tie", but a "proxy for unobserved social ties" (Borgatti and Halgin, 2011).

In addition to the risk of missing important actors in knowledge diffusion who are not included in secondary network data, there is also the risk of omitting multiple relations between the same actors (like geographical proximity and friendship at the same time).[5] Moreover, studies show that there are systematic biases in network perceptions (Kilduff and Krackhardt, 2008), which can limit the extent to which we can compare and harmonize studies based on bibliometric data and interview based studies. It should be noted that some of the problems of secondary data sources are valid as well for primary data collection techniques, especially if some crucial actors do not participate in a field survey (Knoke and Yang, 2008) or are excluded by the researcher. Considering such impacts of data sources, in this review each section is subdivided according to data sources.

Although detailed and long-term observations of members of the network are more suitable to address the majority of these problems, such anthropological studies on networks are relatively few in economics and management studies.[6]

2.5. Overview

Table 5.2 provides a summary of the above debates, and the categorization used in this chapter. A few notes about the rules of inclusion in the study are useful. Unless necessary, the studies since 2005 are covered. In addition, those studies which incorporate network structure explicitly into their analysis are included. Therefore, the review excludes literature on management of dyadic ties (as in alliances), and those that take the network as essentially a group (or agglomeration) of

Table 5.2 Summary of the debates

Section of the survey	Implications for theory	Data and questions/themes commonly addressed
3. Knowledge mapping	•Impact predominantly on science and technology studies	•Evolution of a knowledge domain, critical patents in knowledge flow maps, impact of and source of knowledge flows, comparison of networks in different industries
4. Network as a cause	•Problem of endogeneity	• Analyzes the impact of a network position on performance and/or behavior of actors
4.1. Secondary data	•The risk of omission of important actors in knowledge networks •Objectivist notion of knowledge, higher risk of omitting the context of knowing by distancing the context and artifact •When networks of individuals are derived from network of artifacts (or events), issues like clustering can arise (Lissoni et al., 2013)	•Inventor networks derived from patents (2-mode data) •Strategic alliance networks •Under which conditions do brokerage, centrality, and cohesion influence performance? •What are the moderating factors? Emphasis on past performance, individual attributes, exploration/exploitation, environmental change, strategy, absorptive capacity, heterogeneity
4.2. Field research	•Increased opportunity to take into account actor perceptions in networks •More opportunities for collecting fine-grained information, and multiple relations •Risk of non-participation of important actors •Limited in its capacity for long-term observations, generalizations, static analysis	•What is the nature of ties that bridging actors form? •How does network position and information seeking relate in an organization?
5. Network as a consequence	•Potential to explain the role of intentional manipulation of networks by network members	
5.1. Secondary data	•The risk of omission of important actors and events which derive network change in knowledge networks	•How do patent citation networks evolve? •How do brokers emerge? Emphasis on past performance and past network structure, proximity •What governs overall evolution of networks in different industries?
5.2. Field research	•Contributions in terms of addressing the agency problem, since field research permits a fine-grained analysis of individual/organizational strategy (more so than databases) and additional knowledge that may be difficult to infer by large-scale data •More possibility to take into account actor perceptions in networks	•How do brokers emerge? Emphasis on personal traits that are hard to capture with large databases (self-monitoring, close friendship, social status). How does proximity influence tie formation between organizations? How does past cohesion influence tie formation?
6. Simulation studies	•Permits analyzing co-evolution of networks with actors which constitute them, critical issue of empirical validity	•A wide range of questions on network dynamics and their effects

actors, without an emphasis on structure. Studies that take knowledge as the essential feature of the network are included. The principal aim of the survey is to present a "bird's eye view" of research on knowledge networks. In this sense, the survey is broad in its inclusion of various perspectives rather than being deep and detailed in a particular one. Finally, the research on networks has become a very intensively studied research field and the studies included are obviously far from being exhaustive.

3. Knowledge mapping

The network approach to studying collaborative relations in science and technology has been increasingly used since the 1970s, with a shift of emphasis from "scientific maps" to "networks", which permit long-term and detailed analysis of the development of fields (Maggioni *et al.*, 2013). One of the areas in which the network perspective has been very fruitful is in the analysis of knowledge flows in a geographical context (Breschi and Lissoni, 2009).[7]

The studies covered in this section – by no means exhaustive – take the network as an instrument, which represents relations between entities in a knowledge, technology, or scientific domain, so as to address questions related to its nature and evolution. In this sense, the questions posed are not concerned with networks per se.

The field of medicine is one of the areas which has been studied widely in network studies. Barbera *et al.* (2011) utilize patents in artificial spinal discs and present evidence that patent connectivity analysis (see below) is a promising methodology to study the evolution of science. For example, Mina *et al.* (2007) show the emergence, growth, and transformation of medical knowledge in coronary artery diseases, through network representations of patent citations and complementary interviews. They present evidence of the uneven, uncertain, and often diverging evolution of knowledge domains. Consoli and Ramlogan (2011) carry out a similar study of glaucoma, investigating the evolution of medical knowledge by analyzing scientific publications.

Science and technology studies, social sciences, and innovation are other domains which have been studied intensively by using network analysis. Dolfsma and Leydesdorff (2010) analyze the positioning of the *Journal of Evolutionary Economics* and the interdisciplinary knowledge that it produces using citation network analysis. Bhupatiraju *et al.* (2012) analyze three fields by using social network analysis; they find a cumulative nature of knowledge evolution in science and technology studies, whereas a shift to business oriented research in innovation. In addition, they detect that the three fields have developed in relative isolation from each other, rarely citing each other, with weak links between them. Gossart and Özman (2009) analyze the national and international co-authorship networks in Turkey, and present evidence of segregation among researchers, which inhibits diffusion of knowledge.

In the field of telecommunications, Martinelli (2012) uses patent connectivity analysis to designate the paradigmatic changes in technology in telecommunications switching, from a historical perspective. Connectivity analysis is used to generate knowledge flow maps, which are utilized to see the evolution of a knowledge base (Hummon and Doreian, 1989), by revealing patents which are deemed to be key in the future evolution of the technology (cf. Barbera *et al.*, 2011). Ter Wal (2013) analyzes the evolution of networks in life sciences and information technology in Sophia Antipolis through a patent based network analysis.

Another domain of interest has been environmental technologies. Verspagen (2007) uses patent connectivity analysis to explore the evolution of knowledge in fuel cells. Cecere *et al.* (2014) reveal the evolution of the knowledge bases of green ICTs, by considering the actors involved in their development, as well as the persistence and cumulativeness of underlying knowledge.

Network analysis has also been used to compare different industries in terms of their networks, and how the structure of networks relates to the industries' scientific and knowledge bases. For example, Rosenkopf and Schilling (2007) explain the differences in network structure between industries with respect to modularity and uncertainty characterizing industries. Cantner *et al.* (2010), for the case of three innovation regions in Germany, highlight the association between knowledge base and network structure, underlining that broad knowledge bases are associated with fragmented networks. In a similar vein Broekel and Boschma (2011), by utilizing survey data, compare the differences between aviation and space industry knowledge networks, underlining that although the technological bases are similar, there are marked differences in networks of market knowledge between the two industries. Cassi *et al.* (2012) analyze the differences between the old world and the new world wine producers in terms of the structural closeness between trade networks and scientific collaboration networks. They find that the association between the two is not strong for the case of new world wine producers.

Most of these studies do not directly aim at uncovering a causal mechanism between networks and knowledge domains. In the next section the focus is on those studies in which the network is the independent variable.

4. Network as a cause: implications for knowledge

In this line of inquiry, it is the structural position of the actor in the knowledge network that is presumed to influence his/her performance or behavior. The studies in this section are categorized into two groups, depending on the nature of network data used. In the first section, the networks are constructed through using secondary network data sources. For example, in some cases participation in an event, like an alliance, reveals a relationship between two actors. In a similar way, a relationship between two actors can be inferred by analyzing joint scientific publications or patents, or else by analyzing citations. In the second section, the focus is on studies in which surveys or questionnaires for network construction are used. In both sections, a distinction is made between inter personal and inter organizational networks.

One of the most fruitful areas in this field of research is rooted in the well-known debate on network cohesion and structural holes (Burt, 1992). Briefly, the debate is concerned with what type of network structure is a better source of social capital for an actor. Network cohesion stresses the positive performance impacts of dense and clustered networks (Coleman, 1988), arguing that interactions which are accompanied with intensive exchange of knowledge, which are frequent and face to face, help to build trust among the parties, so that concerns for reputation mitigate possible opportunistic behavior. Such dense networks, in which an actor's partners are themselves connected, are characterized mostly by redundant knowledge flowing in the network, yet they facilitate transfer of tacit knowledge since a common language is developed among the actors, which increases efficiency in terms of time and costs of negotiation (Uzzi, 1997).

On the other hand, proponents of structural holes argue that cohesive networks result in redundancy of knowledge exchange, since the same actors are linked through different intermediaries (Burt, 1992). As the proponents of non-redundant ties claim, actors should fill structural holes in the network, and act as "bridges" connecting otherwise disconnected alters (Burt, 1992). These ties are advantageous in terms of getting access to novel knowledge from diverse sources, thus beneficial for exploration purposes and when the knowledge being transferred is more codified (Rowley *et al.*, 2000).

The debate between proponents of structural holes and cohesive networks has resulted in a very rich stream of research. Earlier on, some authors presented evidence of contingency on external environment (Rowley *et al.*, 2000), and others suggested that these positions are not substitutes, but rather complementary, and a hybrid of both positions is beneficial for performance (Uzzi, 1997). More recent research investigates in detail the contingent nature of this trade-off, highlighting the conditions and the moderating factors which shape the impact of brokerage positions on performance. More on this debate follows in the next sections drawing upon the latest developments in the field.

4.1. Networks from secondary data sources

Inter personal networks

In these studies an inter personal network is usually derived from bibliometric data. For example, a joint patent between two inventors is taken as a link in the network. One of the most commonly addressed questions is related to the performance impacts of brokerage positions. Lissoni (2010) finds that inventors occupying brokerage positions have usually a high number of publications and patents. Although brokerage is usually associated with novelty and scientific success (Allen and Cohen, 1969), more recent studies examine the contexts in which this is so. Moderating factors are considered to be significant in most cases as far as the impact of brokerage is concerned.

Fleming et al. (2007a) use patent data and present evidence that while brokerage is beneficial for generating an idea, it is not good for its subsequent diffusion. In addition, the small world network structure, with high clustering and short path lengths due to brokerage positions in the network, is not found to be significantly associated with increased innovation (Fleming et al., 2007b). According to Lee (2010), it is the actor level variables, like heterogeneity and past performance, that moderate the relation between brokerage and performance. Controlling for past performance of inventors, which enhances brokerage positions, the positive effect of brokerage on performance reduces. Nerkar and Paruchuri (2005) look at the interaction between structural holes and centrality of inventors in determining the citations that they receive. Paruchuri (2010) finds that the impact of intra-firm inventor centrality is moderated by the firm's centrality in the inter-firm network, as well as the firm's span of structural holes. In addition, Soda et al. (2004), for the case of the Italian TV production industry, find that it is the current structural holes, but past closure in networks which influence current performance.

Beaudry and Schiffauerova (2011) find that the effect of central inventors and stars has a positive impact on patent quality and repeated ties have a negative impact for the case of Canadian nanotechnology inventor networks. For the case of the Italian microelectronics sector, Balconi and Laboranti (2006) stress the importance of collaborations between universities and the industry, where they find that strong connections are associated with higher scientific performance and border-crossing relations are driven by cognitive proximity, face-to-face interactions, and personal acquaintances. Stressing the role of knowledge diversity in innovation, Cecere and Özman (2014) find that the impact of strong ties between inventors on technological diversity follows an inverted-u relationship. Cattani and Ferriani (2008) analyze the role of social networks in the individuals' ability for creative outcomes in joint movie production networks. They emphasize the importance of intermediate positions between the core and periphery of networks.

Inter organizational networks

The most commonly used data sources are strategic alliance data (Schilling, 2008) and patent data. While direct effects of certain network positions (like centrality, brokerage, or repeated relations between firms) have been studied intensively, during the recent decade or so attention has shifted to unraveling contingency factors in this relationship.

Shipilov (2009) finds that the performance effect of structural holes depends on firms' capacity to absorb heterogeneous knowledge and bargaining power, and ability to protect against non-cooperation, for the case of mergers and acquisitions. In another study (Shipilov and Li, 2008) the effect of structural holes is found to increase status accumulation, but to dampen market performance of firms. Yang *et al.* (2011) find that joint brokerage and centrality of two firms moderate the relation between learning strategy of the firms and their acquisitions. An exploration strategy is more likely to result in an acquisition, with the joint brokerage with the other firm strengthening this relation. For the case of the steel industry, Koka and Prescott (2008) find that performance effects of different network positions, as entrepreneurial and prominent, depend on environmental change and the strategy of the firm. Strategy of the firm is also found to be a moderating variable between environmental change and network change (Koka and Prescott 2008). Whittington *et al.* (2009) find that the impact of centrality in the local network depends on a firm's connections in the global network. Min and Mitsuhashi (2012) analyze the disappearance of brokerage positions, underlining that their persistence is not good for performance in the airlines industry.

While the use of secondary data can be useful for observing broad patterns, over long periods and involving a large number of actors, there are also potential disadvantages. Firstly, missing relations between actors can pose risks. The constructed knowledge network is confined to what is implied by the artifacts produced or events which analysts have access to, thus running the risk of undermining the social ties, communities, and "silent designers" (Gorb and Dumas, 1987) in understanding the evolution of a knowledge system (see for example, the work by Meyer (2013) on airplane communities), which may not appear in the data. On these issues, Nelson (2009) explains the problems of using patent data, licenses, and publications for the case of DNA recombinant technology. He underlines the importance of using multiple indicators or complementary data sources. Despite these problems, Fleming *et al.* (2007a) present evidence that co-invention patterns found on patent data do reveal technically close interactions between inventors.

A second possible problem is related to deriving "one-mode" data from "two-mode" data (Balconi *et al.*, 2004; Borgatti *et al.*, 2013). In this case, a direct relationship between inventors is assumed, which is derived from a network of patents. More precisely, if three inventor names appear on a patent document, ties between these inventors are constructed. One of the technical issues associated with this process can be unusually high values of clustering, which will mathematically increase the possibility of observing, for example, a small world network (see Lissoni *et al.*, 2013). Another possible problem that may arise with secondary data is to miss possible multiple relations between the same actors. In this case, the use of primary data is statistically more robust (Ter Wal and Boschma, 2009).

4.2. Networks constructed through surveys and interviews

This section reviews research where the network data is collected based on individual interviews and surveys. It is important to note that, as different from secondary data, surveys and questionnaires permit collecting more fine-grained information on the characteristics of the network, to reveal causality mechanisms. In fact we will see that the qualitative aspects of ties are particularly important to consider when knowledge transfer is concerned. Such qualitative aspects cannot be revealed by secondary data sources as effectively as by direct interviews.

Inter personal networks

One of the initial studies on knowledge networks and communication inside organizations belongs to Allen and Cohen (1969). Their research was carried out in two R&D laboratories.

In exploring how technical and scientific knowledge flows within and across the organizational boundaries, they highlighted the critical role of gatekeepers as those who maintain close relations with the outside sources of knowledge, and who are better acquainted with the technical and scientific literature.

More recent research focuses on information seeking in organizations. Borgatti and Cross (2003) address the determinants of probability of seeking information from another. They find that physical proximity and information seeking is mediated by knowing and valuing what the other person knows, as well as ability to access his/her thinking in a timely way. Singh et al. (2010) investigate the effect of network position on individual search behavior. People who are outgroup, because of social status, tenure, or centrality, access people like themselves (homophily) and get further away from knowledge. Another study by Hansen et al. (2005) investigates how existing networks between teams and subsidiaries within a large organization influence the perceived costs of knowledge seeking and transfer.

How do inter personal networks influence knowledge creation? Commonly, the advantages conferred by bridging ties are emphasized, in fostering creativity and innovation, and by enabling access to diversity. While bridging position is a structure-based measure, the qualitative aspects of the bridging ties are also important to understand knowledge transfer. For example, strong ties, as revealed by frequent meetings and emotional intensity, are commonly associated with the transfer of tacit knowledge (Smith et al., 2005), and bridging positions, while beneficial in terms of accessing diversity, can be insufficient when creative ideas are being put to practice (Obstfeld, 2005; Perry-Smith, 2006; see also Fleming et al. (2007a) above for a similar result).

Obstfeld (2005) distinguishes between "tertius iungens" and "tertius gaudens" positions. His case study among the engineers in a large automotive manufacturing plant shows that it is not tertius gaudens but tertius iungens which explains involvement in knowledge exchange. Tertius iungens refers to a brokerage position that prioritizes coordination between the diverse actors connected to rather than obtaining brokering advantages through "playing off" partners as in tertius gaudens (Burt, 1992). In a similar way, Tortoriello and Krackhardt (2010) find that bridging positions have no effect on innovation, unless they are Simmelian. Here a Simmelian tie is taken as a bridging position with ties to a common third party. These studies reveal that mere bridging is not enough for innovative performance; successful bridging positions are usually accompanied by strong ties and coordination capabilities between diverse actors.

Smith et al. (2005) find that strong ties between members are critical in the knowledge creation capabilities of firms, and they find that the number of alters (network range) is not significant. They confirm these findings by studying the management teams and knowledge workers in 72 high tech companies. On the other hand, according to the findings of Perry-Smith (2006) in a university research laboratory, strong ties are neutral, compared to the positive impact of weak ties on creativity. Gargiulo et al. (2009), using data on investment bankers, find that the effects of network closure depend on whether the actor is a knowledge acquirer or a knowledge provider. For the case of managers, Moran (2005) finds that the impact of structural and relational embeddedness in a network depends on the type of task considered; while structural embeddedness is good for routine tasks, it is relational embeddedness which confers advantages when innovative and new tasks are considered.[8] Bjork and Magnusson (2009) find that more connected employees come up with more innovative ideas.

How is the existing local institutional context interwoven with the processes of knowing in a community? Studies in this nature are relatively lacking. An exception is the work by Arora (2012), who carries out a detailed network analysis of the adoption of agro ecological methods by farmers in India. He presents evidence of how the established knowledge networks reflecting the hierarchical status of certain actors restrict the participation of farmers in knowledge circulation networks. Giuliani (2007) analyzes the difference between business networks and knowledge networks in wine clusters in Chile, finding that diffusion on the knowledge network is uneven, owing to the asymmetric knowledge bases between firms.

Inter organization level

Few inter organizational network studies exist which are based on primary data sources (normally, since one cannot survey organizations but people within organizations). One of the most famous case studies was made by Hargadon and Sutton (1997) about the design company IDEO. This work highlights how brokerage positions can bring competitive advantage, when a firm uses the knowledge obtained for one case for other, possibly unrelated, design problems. They mention how being a broker company, which accesses a diverse range of industries, can facilitate such analogous thinking.

In these studies, usually few alliance agreements of a firm are investigated in detail. McEvily and Marcus (2005) look at the qualitative features of ties between firms, and find that it is joint problem solving activities, rather than trust, which explain the transfer of tacit knowledge. Molina-Morales and Martinez-Fernandez (2009) detect an inverted-u relation between the strength of ties between firms and their innovation performance, and Tiwana (2008) highlights the importance of complementarities between strong ties and bridging ties for knowledge integration. Vanhaverbeke *et al.* (2009) find that the impact of partner redundancy on innovation depends on what type of innovation the firm aims for, distinguishing between exploratory and exploitative innovations. In addition, network embeddedness is not only taken in relation to innovation; Echols and Tsai (2005) find that it moderates the relation between offering distinctive products and performance of the firm. Finally, surveys and questionnaires also permit observing the perception and interpretations of actors concerning their networks. Tsai *et al.* (2011) analyze the role of the firm's network in shaping its perception of how rivals prioritize competitors.

One of the weaknesses of studies analyzing the impact of networks on performance or behavior is concerned with the endogeneity problem mentioned in the first section. In short, the endogeneity problem becomes a concern when the factors seen as causing the outcome are in some part dependent on the outcome. For example, if the emergence of networks can be explained by the behavior or intentional actions of actors, can we say that it is the network structure which leads to benefit?

In the next section, we turn to studies in which the network position is taken as the consequence of a mechanism which the study aims to explain. The factors most commonly analyzed are actor attributes, past network structure, and dyadic similarities (or proximity) between actors.

5. Network as a consequence: formation and evolution

While in the earlier phases of network research the attention has been predominantly on performance effects, recent years have witnessed a surge of interest in how networks form and evolve. Before presenting a review of this literature, it is better to note that earlier social psychological theories have been largely influential in the development of this field, especially with regard to the question of how inter personal networks form. Some social psychological theories have been "imported" to the network research program (Kilduff and Tsai, 2003) to address this question. For example, balance theory posits that individuals prefer balanced to unbalanced relations, and focus on two network mechanisms as transitivity and reciprocity (Heider, 1958). The transitivity argument refers to the preference of actors to make their acquaintances friends themselves. In other words, it refers to the preference of actors to form cliquish[9] network structures. Another widely adopted social psychological framework in the network theory is the social comparison theory (Festinger, 1964). It posits that social comparisons with similar others can have important behavioral and attitude effects. In the homophily argument, for example, people like to associate themselves with similar others. Consequently, a range of studies investigate how similarity or difference between actors influences the probability of a tie between them. This framework has been one of the most studied in network research, where similarity can be taken broadly, as proximity in one or more dimensions. However, a largely unresolved problem is related to the network autocorrelation: we tend to form ties with similar others, but at the same time, we become similar to our partners as relations proceed (see Steglich *et al.* (2010) on this).

It is possible to distinguish between three mechanisms that are most commonly employed in the literature, to explain network formation and evolution. The first one is related to individual attributes. In short, can we distinguish individual or organization level factors that shape partner selection? The second one uses a dyadic measure of homophily between two actors, like their similarity/proximity. In this area, a wide range of similarity measures are used, like technological, cognitive, geographical, social, or organizational proximity. Finally, the third one focuses on the overall structure of the past networks as shaping current ones, underlining a path dependent process at work. The second and the third approaches are largely similar, since a path dependent process implies that the network proximity of actors today influences their proximity in the future. The difference is important when we consider the level of analysis, the former focuses on dyads, and the latter on overall network structure.

In the first subsection, the focus is on the studies about the emergence and evolution of knowledge networks that are constructed through secondary data sources. While these studies are valuable in the sense of understanding the mechanisms behind network evolution ex-post, explanation of tie formation through direct interviews about individual motives or intentional actions is lacking in secondary data sources. The second section overviews these studies.

5.1. Network formation and evolution using secondary data sources

Evolution of a network of artifacts and people

What determines the probability that a patent will cite another patent? In other words, how do patent citation networks evolve? These questions have implications not only for understanding the evolution of knowledge domains, but also for exploring the diffusion of knowledge among inventors. According to Singh (2005), inter personal networks between inventors are important in explaining citation patterns and the characteristics of knowledge play an important role (Sorenson *et al.*, 2006; Hansen *et al.*, 2005). Another question of interest is concerned with the emergence of brokers in a network of inventors. Most of the studies in this domain explain brokerage by the past performance or specific attributes of actors. For example, Lissoni (2010) finds that brokers have high numbers of publications and patents, and many of them work with companies (see also Kirkels and Duysters (2010) for a similar result, by using surveys).[10] According to Lee (2010) actor level heterogeneity and past performance enhance brokerage positions. For the case of Italian TV series production networks, Zaheer and Soda (2009) also emphasize the importance of attributes, yet they find a significant impact of past centrality and structural holes spanned by the actors. Stam (2010) also emphasizes the importance of prior career experience, in explaining the antecedents of brokers in the open source software.

Preferential attachment refers to a mechanism in which popular actors attract more ties, which can result in a scale free network structure (Barabasi and Albert, 1999). It has been used to explain a wide range of networks, both at the individual and organizational levels.

Wagner and Leydesdorff (2005), in analyzing international co-authorships, find that preferential attachment explains network formation, but there is no power law distribution, possibly because of institutional context. Another factor which explains network formation has been underlined as labor mobility by Casper (2007), who explores the formation of social networks inside regional clusters for biotech in San Diego.

Some other studies compare the interrelations between two networks, associating the change in one network with changes in the other. For example, Breschi and Catalini (2010) find that for inventors, filling a central position in a scientific network comes at the cost of filling a central position in an inventor network. De Stefano and Zaccarin (2013), on the other hand, find that co-invention and co-authorship tend to occur together to a large extent. D'Amore et al. (2013) detect a similar trade-off between geographical proximity and institutional proximity in inventor networks. They explain this trade-off by the type of knowledge concerned, distinguishing between basic and applied research.

Network of organizations

There is significant evidence about the impact of structural embeddedness on the evolution of networks. The likelihood of collaboration between two firms increases the more they have commonly known third parties (Gulati, 1995, 2007; Gulati and Gargiulo, 1998). In this case the network is a vehicle to carry information among the members about the reliability and capabilities of others (Podolny, 1994). In addition to the existence of common partners in a network, repeated relationships between the same partners help develop trust and information sharing, especially in problem solving activities. Drawing upon the concepts developed within new economic sociology (Granovetter, 1973), proponents of this view stress that firms prefer partners with which they have a previous relationship. Moreover, firms can seldom risk the certainty of continuation with existing partners for the sake of partnering with distant firms (Baum et al., 2005). However, there is a point at which decreasing returns set in to such cohesive relations (Molina-Morales and Martinez-Fernandez, 2009; Uzzi, 1997). Over-embeddedness can be caused by the inability of the firm to change its network portfolio, which is termed to be network inertia by Kim et al. (2006). When firms are excessively embedded in cohesive networks, decreasing returns to performance sets in, whereby their flexibility in adapting to environmental shocks is reduced.

Among the studies which emphasize the role of past networks in explaining current network structure is that of Hanaki et al. (2010) who analyze R&D collaborations in the IT sector. They find that through time the network becomes more clustered, and its growth is explained by preferential attachment. The aim of an alliance between two firms is also an important factor according to Li et al. (2008). When firms aim at radical innovations, they are more likely to partner with those with whom they have frequently collaborated in the past. However, when the past network constrains the current network, peripheral firms can find themselves at sustained disadvantaged positions in the network (Ahuja et al., 2009). These firms are more likely to be involved in ties of social asymmetry rather than ties of structural homophily (Ahuja et al., 2009). In other words, peripheral firms are more likely to be involved in alliances with more central firms, rather than others who occupy similar positions as themselves. Structural embeddedness is found to be another factor which sustains ties between organizations (Polidoro et al., 2011).

Some other studies emphasize a notion of proximity between firms in explaining tie formation. Here proximity refers to the similarity (or distance) between two firms, which can be defined in terms of geography, technology, cognition, organization, or society (Broekel and Boschma, 2012). According to this literature, the impact of proximity largely depends on the type of industry and dimension of proximity considered. For example Cantner and Graf (2006), by analyzing patent data for inventors in Jena, find that it is the technological overlap between firms which predicts network formation. Balland *et al.* (2013) find that as the video games industry evolves, firms are partnering with more cognitively proximate firms. On the other hand, in the global satellite industry, the evolution of project network partnerships is governed by both organizational and geographical proximity, rather than cognitive and social proximity (Balland, 2012). Distinguishing between resources and markets, Mitsuhashi and Greve (2009) find that partnership links are more likely when there is high matching between firms in terms of complementarity in markets and compatibility in resources. Rosenkopf and Padula (2008) for the case of mobile communications, and using strategic alliance data, find that shortcuts in a network are governed by structural homophily.

As far as the third mechanism behind organizational tie formation is concerned, organizational attributes and how they shape partner selection are highlighted. For example, Luo *et al.* (2009) investigate the impact of ratio of scientists in an organization, and find that it increases partner attraction. Rothaermel and Boeker (2008) find that the age of the partner is a factor explaining alliance formation between pharmaceutical and biotech companies.

A more recent theme of inquiry is concerned with the disappearance of certain network positions. In one of these studies, Rowley *et al.* (2005) find that complementarity and inequality predict exits from network cliques better than social cohesion and similarity. They find that role diversity and cohesion reduce exit, while size diversity increases exit. In addition, withdrawal from alliances is influenced by similar factors as initiation of alliances; structural embeddedness tends to increase withdrawal, and relational embeddedness tends to reduce it (Greve *et al.*, 2010). Min and Mitsuhashi (2012) analyze the importance of the disappearance of brokerage positions, underlining that their persistence is not good for performance in the airlines industry.

Although the majority of these studies investigate the formation dynamics of networks, few of them underline the role of organizational strategy, or intentional actions, in driving network change. Exceptions are Baum *et al.* (2003) who find that it is both chance partnering and control partnering by core firms which explain broker and small world characteristics of firms in the banking sector. Dittrich *et al.* (2007) analyze how the alliance network of IBM through time has been governed by changes in its learning strategy from exploitation to exploration learning. They show that this strategy was reflected in IBM's network strategy. Although there is obviously an association between a firm's innovation strategy and its alliances, the evidence does not permit us to conclude that firms have a deliberate network strategy in positioning themselves in a broader network structure. In other words, the extent to which firms are myopic in overseeing the network structure remains understudied.

While statistical analysis of large databases can highlight some broad regularities in network formation mechanisms over the long run, interviews, surveys, and detailed case studies yield more fine-grained insights into the formation of networks, taking into account the participants' viewpoint directly. This is especially valid considering the role of individual/organizational action and strategy, as well as the norms, culture, and values in a certain context, which are difficult to understand by exploring statistical data. In the next section, the focus is on case studies carried out through field work through interviews and surveys.

5.2. Formation and evolution based on case studies

Individual networks

Surveys and case studies permit analyzing the impact of certain individual attributes that are impossible to measure through secondary data sources. For example, Sosovova *et al.* (2010) show that self-monitoring attributes of individuals have been shown to be a significant factor in brokerage. Analyzing the friendship relations, they find that high self-monitors attract new friends, and they are more likely to occupy bridging positions. Singh *et al.* (2010) investigate the effect of network position on individual search behavior. According to their results, people who are outgroup, because of social status, tenure, or centrality, access people like themselves (homophily). Kirkels and Duysters (2010) analyze whether specific attributes are associated with brokers in SMEs, in southeast Netherlands. They find that most influential brokers are in science and non-profit sectors and have a long track record in their field. Jha and Welch (2010) investigate the extent to which homophily influences multifaceted collaborations among scientists and find that close friendship and trust have a positive impact on collaborations in diverse areas. Concerning the network structure in a large project company, Kastelle and Steen (2010) observe that the small world characteristics of the network, accompanied by a largely hierarchical structure, are the result of a network strategy, rather than random occurrence. Network strategies can also reflect the power relations embedded in local formal and informal institutions, giving rise to knowledge networks which can benefit or restrict the participation of some actors (Arora, 2012).

Organizational networks

Case studies using primary network data at the organization level and analyzing network formation are quite rare. Some of these studies are as follows. Broekel and Boschma (2011) analyze the Dutch aviation industry and find that social, organizational, cognitive, and geographical proximity explain network formation. Dantas and Bell (2009) analyze the long-term evolution of a firm's network over 30 years, covering its alliances in 14 technologies. They analyze the objective of collaboration, the kind of knowledge that each partner provided, and how tasks were divided, and present evidence of the relation between the firm's strategy and the evolution of its network. Giuliani (2013), for the case of wine clusters in Chile, finds that a stable hierarchical structure in the informal network is attributable to an asymmetric knowledge base between firms. In this paper, similarity between firms does not significantly influence new knowledge tie formation, but it is the cohesion variables, like reciprocity and transitivity, which contributes to it.

Finally, the next section is allocated to the use of synthetic data, through simulation models in analyzing knowledge networks.

6. Simulation studies

In the social sciences recent decades have witnessed a surge of interest in agent based simulation models (see Heath *et al.*, 2009, for a survey). ABS models permit understanding how aggregate patterns *form*. This modeling exercise is fundamentally different from the top-down approach commonplace in economics, whereby equilibrium conditions are imposed on systems. Rather, complex adaptive systems (CAS) are concerned mostly with out-of-equilibrium conditions, through the self-organization of microstate events into emergent aggregate structures.[11] The essential idea in these models is that, to explain aggregate patterns one has to take into account interactions among heterogeneous agents, how they evolve over time, and how they endogenously shape the choices of individuals in return.

Previously, it was stressed that the network approach in the social sciences is seen as largely structuralist, leaving little scope for individuals' choices, and treating the network as a separate entity which shapes the performance of its members (Emirbayer and Goodwin, 1994). However, the postulate that network position influences the performance and behavior of actors does not imply that networks are independent and autonomous entities separate from the units which make them. This is why computational models are useful; particularly in understanding the gap between the individual attributes and the aggregate patterns which emerge from their interaction. Agent based simulation models enable modeling the feedback between the individual and the network, where the network surrounding the individual actors emerges and evolves as a consequence of actors' decisions, which in turn constrains and shapes their behavior and performance. In some of these studies, a network structure is taken as exogenous, yet there is a significant number of models incorporating this feedback mechanism between the individual and the network. Because the data is generated in a computer environment, the empirical validity of ABS, which is the extent to which the model is an appropriate representation of the real system, has become an extremely important point (Windrum et al., 2007).

Cassi and Zirulia (2008) analyze the impact of network structure on efficiency and equity where they find that small world is not the most efficient network structure. Chang and Harrington (2007) look at how attributes shape networks by exploring an evolving architecture of problem solving networks. They emphasize the dual role of individuals as innovators and imitators.

A range of studies examine the relation between knowledge bases and networks. Özman (2010) models the co-evolution of networks and individuals, where agents learn through networks, which shape future partner selection processes. According to the findings, it is the knowledge base of an industry which impacts network structure, where broad and deep knowledge bases give rise to dense networks between flexible and small organizations. Özman (2008) explores the evolving network structures when firms form alliances for the purpose of exploration and exploitation. The results reveal that, in an exploitation regime, networks are composed more of strong ties, where firms interact repeatedly with geographically close firms. In this regime, high technological opportunities and codified knowledge result in the emergence of locally star firms. As knowledge gets more tacit, local stars become global stars in the network and are more competent than other firms.

Cowan et al. (2006) explain network formation by characteristics of knowledge, taking into account the tension between similarities (common knowledge) and differences (complementarities) between agents. Cowan et al. (2007), in a similar model of network formation based on knowledge complementarities, incorporate the role of subtasks in innovation. Cowan and Jonard (2009) show that it is the knowledge commonality between firms that gives rise to certain network properties like skewed distribution, clustering, and small worlds, rather than the structure of past networks. Llerena and Özman (2013) model how the tacitness of the knowledge base and knowledge relatedness in an industry influence learning, depending on the level of commitment of partners to an alliance. At an intermediate level of knowledge relatedness, knowledge tacitness requires more committed relations, for increased knowledge flows between firms. However, this is not what firms are inclined to do, according to the model results. On the contrary, they change partners frequently. In Arora and Özman (2008), user and producer networks are investigated. How do the co-evolution of these two networks, and the feedbacks between them, shape possible transition patterns to new technologies? The results reveal that the share of early adopters has a strong influence on the resulting producer networks, the total knowledge accumulated in both technologies, and the time period for full transition to a new technology to occur. The SKIN model (Gilbert et al., 2007) is a framework for simulating knowledge and network dynamics, in innovation based industries. Using this modeling framework, Ahrweiler et al. (2011) investigate the impact of university and industry linkages. They find that incorporating collaborations with universities to networks significantly increases the quality and speed of knowledge flows, increases diversity, as well as the knowledge and competence of firms in the population. In an analytical model of tie formation, Letterie et al. (2008) finds that uncertainty increases the propensity to ally and there is reduced incentive to ally when alliance partners are similar.

7. Conclusion

Based on this review, it is possible to make a few observations on the literature on knowledge networks. These observations are made in two spheres: methodological and content related.

One of the methodological issues is that the nature of questions depends on the source of data. While this is not a problem in and of itself, and it is what is expected in any scientific endeavor, in network research it is important in the following senses. The studies using large-scale data sources are very rich in terms of observing multiple industries and long-term developments over a large number of actors. But by focusing on the structure of the network, the precision of tie content is lost. Crude proxies for tie strength can be and are employed, but the problem remains that the theoretical framework that they draw upon is rooted in social psychology. So there is a mismatch between the mechanisms on which theory focuses on one hand, and what the data measures on the other. Given this situation, it is meaningful to come up with tie definitions that are specific to the nature of knowledge and innovation studies. For example, considering the knowledge complementarities between people or organizations is an important step in this regard (Schoenmakers and Duysters, 2006).

Another implication of this mismatch is related to the underlying assumptions about knowledge. Considering the two different conceptualizations of knowledge as objective and practice based approach, network studies have formed a platform in which both perspectives are used in analyzing the diffusion of knowledge. According to objectivists, knowledge can exist outside the individual, by being embedded in an artifact and flowing between people and organizations. Accordingly knowledge can be in tacit or explicit form. An implicit assumption here is that knowledge can be taken separately from the actors who create, diffuse, or process it (Hislop, 2013). According to the practice based approach, on the other hand, knowledge is not unique and it is not independent of interpretations; people have different understandings of it, depending on the context, language, history, and culture. An objectivist perception of knowledge manifests itself clearly when knowledge is assumed to be embodied in a network of artifacts, for example in using bibliometric data, or when it is assumed to flow between actors during an event (like an alliance between two firms). The use of secondary data in studying knowledge networks separates the context within which knowing takes place, and the tangible events and artifacts that accompany the process of knowing by actors. This separation is not necessarily problematic as long as the researcher recognizes the differences in the nature of questions that can comfortably be addressed in either of the approaches. Yet it can pose problems when the two are confused.

Secondly, it is more convenient to collect data through interviews when analyzing inter personal networks. In this case, it is possible to focus on both the structure of the network, as well as the qualitative nature of ties. Moreover, as far as network formation is concerned, the researcher is more flexible to consider different independent variables other than what is available by data, which also leaves more space to uncover the role of individual strategy in network manipulation. Nonetheless, generalizations are more difficult across different organizational contexts. In this sense, it is important to be able to leverage the synergies between the results obtained from these studies and those that utilize large-scale bibliometric data of inventors or scientists.

Above, I focused on some of the methodological issues that can be observed in the research. There are also some observations that can be made regarding the content of studies.

First, certain research questions are overstudied, leaving others understudied. The impact of network structure on performance has been studied from various theoretical and empirical angles, analyzing the impact of moderating factors, as well as the idiosyncrasies between the actors in the network. More recently we are observing the increased importance given to network evolution and formation. In fact, this has been a longstanding field of inquiry within agent based simulation studies, game theoretical approaches, as well as analytical models. Empirical analysis of network evolution is more recent. Nonetheless, the "bridges" between formal models and empirical studies are still weak. There seems to be disciplinary borders between researchers working on networks. Although these borders have subsided to an extent during recent years, a review of the current literature reveals that the borders between physics, sociology, and management and economics hardly disappeared. Efforts to bridge these gaps can be very useful, in terms of addressing many of the challenges facing network research today. This is especially valid for the studies on knowledge networks, considering that knowledge theories transcend disciplinary boundaries.

While the literature on the evolution and formation of knowledge networks has been evolving at full speed recently, the role of strategy and individual manipulations of the actors are hardly studied. There can be two reasons behind this lack of attention. The first is simply that actors do not manipulate their networks by overlooking the whole network structure; therefore this field has achieved less attention in the literature. The second is related to the cost and efforts necessary to collect data in this area. A significant proportion of network studies are based on large-scale data, which do not permit the inference of individual strategic intentions, except when ex-post guesses are made. As far as the first explanation is concerned, this can be only understood by carrying out field studies at the organizational level.

Notes

1 See Freeman (2004) for the history of the field.
2 Borgatti and Halgin (2011) distinguish between social network theory and theory of social networks. The former refers to the impact of social network structure on behavior or performance, the latter refers to the formation and evolution dynamics of networks.
3 See for example the "rich get richer" phenomenon which underlies preferential attachment mechanism (Barabasi and Albert, 1999).
4 I refer the reader to sources such as Carrington, Scott, and Wasserman (2005) and Knoke and Yang (2008) for further reading about these problems.
5 See Ter Wal and Boschma (2009) for a detailed survey of social networks in economic geography, where they discuss the advantages and disadvantages of the use of patent data.
6 An excellent exception is Barley (1990).
7 See Maggioni and Uberti (2011) and Ter Wal and Boschma (2009) for a review of this field.
8 Structural embeddedness emphasizes commonly known parties (and network position), while relational embeddedness emphasizes the qualitative aspects of a relationship.
9 Cliquishness of a network measures the extent to which friends of an actor are friends themselves (as in closure).
10 Note that these studies do not imply a causal relationship, but rather they highlight correlations.
11 In this text, I use the term ABS, but it is important to note that different terms are used which connote this bottom-up approach, for example, self-organizing systems, computational economics, generative social science, and so on.

References

Ahrweiler, P., A. Pyka, and N. Gilbert (2011) A new model for university–industry links in knowledge-based economies. *Journal of Product Innovation Management*, 28(2): 218–235.
Ahuja, G., F. Polidoro, and W. Mitchell (2009) Structural homophily or social asymmetry? The formation of alliances by poorly embedded firms. *Strategic Management Journal*, 30: 941–958.
Allen, T.J. and S.I. Cohen (1969) Information flow in research and development laboratories. *Administrative Science Quarterly*, 14(1): 12–19.
Arora, S. (2012) Farmers' participation in knowledge circulation and the promotion of agroecological methods in South India. *Journal of Sustainable Agriculture*, 36(2): 207–235.

Arora, S. and M. Özman (2008) The adoption of a new technology: The role of niche groups, network effects and learning. *European Journal of Economic and Social Systems*, 20, 2: 187–209.

Balconi, M. and A. Laboranti (2006) University–industry interactions in applied research: The case of microelectronics. *Research Policy*, 35(10): 1616–1630.

Balconi, M., S. Breschi, and F. Lissoni (2004) Networks of inventors and the role of academia: An exploration of Italian patent data. *Research Policy* 33(1): 127.

Balland, P.A. (2012) Proximity and the evolution of collaboration networks: Evidences from R&D projects within the GNSS industry. *Regional Studies*, 46(6): 741–756.

Balland, P.A., M. de Vaan, and R. Boschma (2013) The dynamics of interfirm networks along the industry life cycle: The case of the global video game industry 1987–2007. *Journal of Economic Geography*, doi:10.1093/jeg/lbs023.

Barabasi, A.L. and R. Albert (1999) Emergence of scaling in random networks, *Science*, 286: 509–512.

Barbera, D., F. Jimenez, and I. Castello (2011) Mapping the importance of the real world: The validity of connectivity analysis of patent citations. *Research Policy*, 40: 473–486.

Barley, S. (1990) The alignment of technology and structure through role and networks. *Administrative Science Quarterly*, 35(1): 61–103.

Barnes, J.A. (1979) Network analysis: Orienting notion, rigorous technique, or substantive field of study? In P.W. Holland and S. Leinhardt (eds), *Perspectives on Social Network Research*. New York: Academic, pp. 403–423.

Baum, J. and T. Rowley (2008) Introduction: Evolving webs in network economies. In J. Baum and T. Rowley (eds), *Network Strategy*, Advances in Strategic Management Series. Greenwich, CT: JAI Press.

Baum, J.A., A.V. Shipilov, and T.J. Rowley (2003) Where do small worlds come from? *Industrial and Corporate Change*, 12(4): 697–725.

Baum, J., T. Rowley, A. Shipilov, and A. Chuang (2005) Dancing with strangers: Aspiration performance and the search for underwriting syndicate partners. *Administrative Science Quarterly*, 50: 536–576.

Beaudry, C. and A. Schiffauerova (2011) Impacts of collaboration and network indicators on patent quality: The case of Canadian nanotechnology innovation. *European Management Journal*, 29(5): 362–376.

Bhupatiraju, S., O. Nomaler, G. Triulzi, and B. Verspagen (2012) Knowledge flows – Analyzing the core literature of innovation, entrepreneurship and science and technology studies. *Research Policy*, 41(7): 1205–1218.

Bjork, J. and M. Magnusson (2009) Where do good innovation ideas come from? Exploring the influence of network connectivity on innovation idea quality. *Journal of Product Innovation Management*, 26: 662–670.

Borgatti, S. and R. Cross (2003) A relational view of information seeking and learning in social networks. *Management Science*, 49(4): 432–445.

Borgatti, S.P. and P. Foster (2003) The network paradigm in organizational research: A review and typology. *Journal of Management*, 29(6): 991–1013.

Borgatti, S.P. and D.S. Halgin (2011) On network theory. *Organization Science*, 22(5): 1168–1181.

Borgatti, S., M. Everett, and M. and J. Johnson (2013) *Analyzing Social Networks*. London: Sage Publications.

Breschi, S. and C. Catalini (2010) Tracing the links between science and technology: An exploratory analysis of scientists' and inventors' networks. *Research Policy*, 39(1): 14–26.

Breschi, S. and F. Lissoni (2009) Mobility of skilled workers and co-invention networks: An anatomy of localized knowledge flows. *Journal of Economic Geography*, 9: 439–468.

Broekel, T. and R. Boschma (2011) Aviation, space or aerospace? Exploring the knowledge networks of two industries in the Netherlands. *European Planning Studies*, 19(7): 1205–1227.

Broekel, T. and R. Boschma (2012) Knowledge networks in the Dutch aviation industry: the proximity paradox. *Journal of Economic Geography*, 12: 409–433.

Burt, R.S. (1992) *Structural Holes: The Structure of Competition*. New York: Academic Press.

Cantner, U. and H. Graf (2006) The network of innovators in Jena: An application of social network analysis. *Research Policy*, 35: 463–480.

Cantner, U., A. Meder, and A.L.J., Ter Wal (2010) Innovator networks and regional knowledge base. *Technovation*, 30: 496–507.

Carrington, P., Scott, J., and S. Wasserman (2005) *Models and Methods in Social Network Analysis*. Cambridge: Cambridge University Press.

Casper, S. (2007) How do technology clusters emerge and become sustainable? Social network formation and inter-firm mobility within the San Diego biotechnology cluster. *Research Policy*, 36: 438–455.

Cassi, L. and Zirulia, L. (2008) The opportunity cost of social relations: On the effectiveness of small worlds. *Journal of Evolutionary Economics*, 18: 77–101.

Cassi, L., A. Morrison, and A. Ter Wal (2012) The evolution of trade and scientific collaboration networks in the global wine sector: A longitudinal study using network analysis. *Economic Geography*, 88(3): 311–334.

Cattani, G. and S. Ferriani (2008) A core/periphery perspective on individual creative performance: Social networks and cinematic achievements in the Hollywood film industry. *Organization Science*, 19(6): 824–844.

Cecere, G. and M. Özman (2014) Technological diversity and inventor networks. *Economics of Innovation and New Technology*, 23(2): 161–178.

Cecere, G., N. Corrocher, C. Gossart, and M. Özman (2014) Patterns of innovation in the green ICTs: A patent based analysis, *Research Policy*, forthcoming.

Chang, M.-H. and J. E. Harrington, Jr. (2007) Innovators, imitators, and the evolving architecture of problem-solving networks. *Organization Science*, 18(4): 648–666.

Coleman, J. (1988) Social capital in the creation of human capital. *American Journal of Sociology*, 94: 95–120.

Consoli, D. and R. Ramlogan (2011) Patterns of organization in the development of medical know-how: The case of glaucoma research. *Industrial and Corporate Change*, 21(2): 315–343.

Cowan, R. and N. Jonard (2009) Edge portfolios and the organization of innovation networks. *Academy of Management Review*, 34(2): 320–342.

Cowan, R., N. Jonard, and J.B. Zimmermann (2006) Evolving networks of inventors. *Journal of Evolutionary Economics*, 16: 155–174.

Cowan, R., N. Jonard, and J.B. Zimmermann (2007) Bilateral collaboration and the emergence of networks. *Management Science*, 53(7): 1051–1067.

D'Amore, R., R. Iorio, S. Labory, and A. Stawinoga (2013) Research collaboration networks in biotechnology: Exploring the trade-off between institutional and geographic distances. *Industry and Innovation*, 20(3): 261–276.

Dantas, E. and M. Bell (2009) Latecomer firms and the emergence and development of knowledge networks: The case of Petrobras in Brazil. *Research Policy*, 38(5): 829–844.

De Stefano, D. and S. Zaccarin (2013) Modelling multiple interactions in science and technology networks. *Industry and Innovation*, 20(3): 221–240.

Dittrich, K., G. Duysters, and A.-P. de Man (2007) Strategic repositioning by means of alliance networks: The case of IBM. *Research Policy*, 36(10): 1496–1511.

Dolfsma, W. and L. Leydesdorff (2010) The citation field of evolutionary economics. *Journal of Evolutionary Economics*, 20(5): 645–664.

Doreian, P. and F.N. Stokman (1997) *Evolution of Social Networks*. Amsterdam: Gordon and Breach Publishers.

Echols, A. and W. Tsai (2005) Niche and performance: The moderating role of network embeddedness. *Strategic Management Journal*, 26: 219–238.

Emirbayer, M. and J. Goodwin (1994) Network analysis, culture, and the problem of agency. *American Journal of Sociology*, 99(6): 1411–1452.

Festinger, L. (1964) *Conflict, Decision, and Dissonance*. Stanford, CA: Stanford University Press.

Fleming, L, S. Mingo, and D. Chen (2007a) Collaborative brokerage, generative creativity, and creative success. *Administrative Science Quarterly*, 52(3): 443–475.

Fleming, L., C. King, and A. Juda (2007b) Small worlds and regional innovation. *Organization Science*, 18(2): 938–954.

Freeman, L. (2004) *The Development of Social Network Analysis*. Canada: Empirical Press.

Gargiulo, M., G. Ertug, and C. Galunic (2009) The two faces of control: Network closure and individual performance among knowledge workers. *Administrative Science Quarterly*, 54: 299–333.

Gilbert, N., P. Ahrweiler, and A. Pyka (2007) Learning in innovation networks: Some simulation experiments. *Physica A*, 378: 100–109.

Giuliani, E. (2007) The selective nature of knowledge networks in clusters: Evidence from the wine industry. *J. Econ. Geog.*, 7: 139–168.

Giuliani, E. (2013) Network dynamics in regional clusters: Evidence from Chile. *Research Policy*, 42(8): 1406–1419.

Gorb, P. and A. Dumas (1987) Silent design. *Design Studies*, 8(3): 150–156.

Gossart, C. and M. Özman (2009) Co-authorship networks in the social sciences: The case of Turkey. *Scientometrics*, 78(2): 323.

Granovetter, M.S. (1973) The strength of weak ties. *American Journal of Sociology*, 78(6): 1360–1380.

Granovetter, M. (1985) Economic action and social structure: The problem of embeddedness. *American Journal of Sociology*, 91: 481–510.

Greve, H., J. Baum, H. Mitsuhashi, and T. Rowley (2010) Built to last but falling apart: Cohesion, friction and withdrawal from inter firm alliances. *Academy of Management Journal*, 53(2): 302–322.

Gulati, R. (1995) Social structure and alliance formation patterns. *Administrative Science Quarterly*, 40: 619–652.

Gulati, R. (2007) *Managing Network Resources: Alliances, Affiliations and Other Relational Assets*. Oxford: Oxford University Press.

Gulati, R. and M. Gargiulo (1998) Where do inter organizational networks come from? *American Journal of Sociology*, 104(5): 1439–1493.

Hanaki, H., R. Nakajima, and Y. Ogura (2010) The dynamics of R&D network in the IT industry. *Research Policy*, 39(3): 386–399.

Hansen, M.T., M.L. Mors, and B. Lovas (2005) Knowledge sharing in organizations: Multiple networks, multiple phases. *Academy of Management Journal*, 48: 776–793.

Hargadon, A. and R. Sutton (1997) Technology brokering and innovation in a product development firm. *Administrative Science Quarterly*, 42(4): 716–749.

Heath, B., H. Raymond, and F. Ciarallo (2009) A survey of agent-based modeling practices (January 1998 to July 2008) *Journal of Artificial Societies and Social Simulation*, 12(4): 9.

Heider, F. (1958) *The Psychology of Interpersonal Relations*. New York: Wiley.

Hislop, D. (2013) *Knowledge Management in Organizations: A Critical Introduction*. New York: Oxford University Press.

Hummon, N.P. and P. Doreian (1989) Connectivity in a citation network: The development of DNA theory. *Social Networks*, 11: 39–63.

Jha, Y. and E.W. Welch (2010) Relational mechanisms governing collaborative behaviour of academic scientists in six fields of science and engineering. *Research Policy*, 39(9): 1174–1184.

Kadushin, C. (2012) *Understanding Social Networks*. Oxford: Oxford University Press.

Kastelle, T. and J. Steen (2010) Are small world networks always best for innovation? *Innovation: Management, Policy and Practice*, 12(1): 75–87.

Kilduff, M. and D. Krackhardt (2008) *Interpersonal Networks in Organizations*. New York: Cambridge University Press.

Kilduff, M. and W. Tsai (2003) *Social Networks and Organizations*. Thousand Oaks, CA: Sage Publications.

Kilduff, M, W. Tsai, and R. Hanke (2006) A paradigm too far? A dynamic stability research consideration of the network research program. *Academy of Management Review*, 31: 1031–1048.

Kim, T., H. Oh, and A. Swaminathan (2006) Framing interorganizational network change. *Academy of Management Review*, 31, 3: 704–720.

Kirkels, Y. and G. Duysters (2010) Brokerage in SME networks. *Research Policy*, 39(3): 375–385.

Knoke, D. and S. Yang (2008) *Social Network Analysis* (2nd edition). London: Sage Publications.

Koka, B.R. and J.E. Prescott (2008) Designing alliance networks: The influence of network position, environmental change, and strategy. *Strategic Management Journal*, 29: 638.

Lakatos, I. (1970) Falsification and the methodology of scientific research programs. In I. Lakatos and A. Musgrave (eds), *Criticism and the Growth of Knowledge* (pp. 91–132). New York: Cambridge University Press.

Laumann, E.O., P.V. Marsden, and D. Prensky (1983) The boundary specification problem in network analysis. In R.S. Burt and M.J. Minor (eds), *Applied Network Analysis*. Beverly Hills, CA: Sage Publications.

Lee, J. (2010) Heterogeneity, brokerage, and innovative performance: Endogenous formation of collaborative inventor networks. *Organization Science*, 21(4): 804–822.

Letterie, W., J. Hagedoorn, H. van Kranenburg, and F. Palm (2008) Information gathering through alliances. *Journal of Economic Behavior & Organization*, 66, 2: 176–194.

Li, D., L. Eden, M. Hitt, and R. D. Ireland (2008) Friends, acquaintances or strangers? Partner selection in R&D alliances. *Academy of Management Journal*, 51(2): 315–334.

Lissoni, F. (2010) Academic inventors as brokers. *Research Policy*, 39(7): 843–857.

Lissoni, F., P. Llerena and P. Sanditov (2013) Small worlds in networks of inventors and the role of academics: An analysis of France. *Industry & Innovation*, 20(3): 195–220.

Llerena, P. and M. Özman (2013) Networks, irreversibility and knowledge creation. *Journal of Evolutionary Economics*, 23: 431–453.

Luo, X.R., K. Koput, and W.W. Powell (2009) Intellectual capital or signal? The effects of scientists on alliance formation in knowledge-intensive industries. *Research Policy*, 38(8): 1313–1325.

McEvily, B. and A. Marcus (2005) Embedded ties and the acquisition of competitive capabilities. *Strategic Management Journal*, 26(11): 1033–1055.

Maggioni, M. and T. Uberti (2011) Networks and geography in the economics of knowledge flows. *Quality and Quantity*, 45(4): 1031–1051.

Maggioni, M., S. Breschi, and P. Panzarasa (2013) Multiplexity, growth mechanisms and structural variety in scientific collaboration networks. *Industry and Innovation*, 20, 3: 185–194.

Martinelli, A. (2012) An emerging paradigm or just another trajectory? Understanding the nature of technological changes using engineering heuristics in the telecommunications switching industry. *Research Policy*, 41(2): 414–429.

Meyer, P.B. (2013) The airplane as an open-source invention. *Revue Economique*, 64: 115–132.

Min, J. and H. Mitsuhishi (2012) Dynamics of unclosed triangles in alliance networks: Disappearance of brokerage positions and performance consequences. *Journal of Management Studies*, 49(6): 1078–1108.

Mina, A., R. Ramlogan, G. Tampubolon, and J.S. Metcalfe (2007) Mapping evolutionary trajectories: Applications to the growth and transformation of medical knowledge. *Research Policy* 36(5): 789–806.

Mintzberg, H. and Waters, J. (1985) Of strategies, deliberate and emergent. *Strategic Management Journal*, 6: 257–272.

Mitsuhashi, H. and H. Greve (2009) A matching theory of alliance formation and organizational success: Complementarity and compatibility. *Academy of Management Journal*, 52, 5: 975–995.

Molina-Morales, F.X. and M.T. Martinez-Fernandez (2009) Too much love in the neighborhood can hurt: How an excess of intensity and trust in relationships may produce negative effects on firms. *Strategic Management Journal*, 30(9): 1013–1023.

Moran, P. (2005) Structural vs. relational embeddedness: Social capital and managerial performance. *Strategic Management Journal*, 26: 1129–1151.

Moreno, Jacob L. (1934) *Who Shall Survive?* Washington, D.C.: Nervous and Mental Diseases Publishing.

Nelson, A. (2009) Measuring knowledge spillovers: What patents, licenses and publications reveal about innovation diffusion. *Research Policy*, 38(6): 994–1005.

Nerkar, A. and S. Paruchuri (2005) Evolution of R&D capabilities: The role of knowledge networks within a firm. *Management Science*, 51(5): 771–785.

Obstfeld, D. (2005) Social networks, the tertius iungens orientation, and involvement in innovation. *Administrative Science Quarterly*, 50(1): 100–130.

Özman, M. (2008) Network formation and strategic firm behaviour to explore and exploit. *Journal of Artificial Societies and Social Simulation*, 11(17).

Özman, M. (2010) The knowledge base of products: Implications for organizational structure. *Organization Studies*, 31(8): 1129–1154.

Paruchuri, S. (2010) Intraorganizational networks, interorganizational networks, and the impact of central inventors: A longitudinal study of pharmaceutical firms. *Organization Science*, 21: 63–80.

Perry-Smith, J.E. (2006) Social yet creative: The role of social relationships in facilitating individual creativity. *Academy of Management Journal*, 49: 85–101.

Podolny, J.M. (1994) Market uncertainty and the social character of economic exchange. *Administrative Science Quarterly*, 39: 458–483.

Polidoro, F., G. Ahuja, and W. Mitchell (2011) When the social structure overshadows competitive incentives: The effects of network embeddedness on joint venture dissolution. *Academy of Management Journal*, 54(1): 203–223.

Rosenkopf, L. and G. Padula (2008) Investigating the microstructure of network evolution: Alliance formation in the mobile communications industry. *Organization Science*, 19: 669–687.

Rosenkopf, L. and M. Schilling (2007) Comparing alliance network structure across industries: Observations and explanations. *Strategic Entrepreneurship Journal*, 1: 191–209.

Rothaermel, F. and W. Boeker (2008) Old technology meets new technology: Complementarities, similarities and alliance formation. *Strategic Management Journal*, 29: 47–77.

Rowley, T. J., D. Behrens, and D. Krackhardt (2000) Redundant governance structures: An analysis of structural and relational embeddedness in the steel and semiconductor industries. *Strategic Management Journal*, 21: 369–386.

Rowley, T.J., H.R. Greve, H. Rao, J.A.C. Baum, and A.V. Shipilov (2005) Time to break up: Social and instrumental antecedents of firm exits from exchange cliques. *Academy of Management Journal*, 48(3): 499–520.

Sasovova, Z., A. Mehra, S.P. Borgatti, and M.C. Schippers (2010) Network churn: The effects of self-monitoring personality on brokerage dynamics. *Administrative Science Quarterly*, 55(4): 639–670.

Schilling, M.A. (2008) Understanding the alliance data. *Strategic Management Journal*, 30(3), pp. 233–260.

Schoenmakers, W. and G. Duysters (2006) Learning in strategic technology alliances. *Technology Analysis and Strategic Management*, 18(2), 245–264.

Scott, J. and P. Carrington (eds) (2011) *The Sage Handbook of Social Network Analysis.* London: Sage Publications.

Scott, R. and G. Davis (2007) *Organizations and Organizing.* London: Pearson International Press.

Shipilov, A. (2009) Firm scope experience, historic multimarket contact with partners, centrality, and the relationship between structural holes and performance. *Organization Science*, 20 (1): 85–106.

Shipilov, A. and S. Li (2008) To have a cake and eat it too? Structural holes' influence on market and network performance in collaborative networks. *Administrative Science Quarterly*, 51(1): 73–108.

Simmel, G. (1950) *The Sociology of George Simmel.* Glencoe, IL: Free Press.

Singh, J. (2005) Collaboration networks as determinants of knowledge diffusion patterns. *Management Science*, 51(5): 756–770.

Singh, J., M.T. Hansen, and J.M. Podolny (2010) The world is not small for everyone: Inequity in searching for knowledge in organizations. *Management Science*, 56(9): 1415–1948.

Smith, K.G., C.J. Collins, and K.D. Clark (2005) Existing knowledge, knowledge creation capability and the rate of new product introduction in high technology firms. *Academy of Management Journal*, 48: 346–357.

Smith-Doerr, L. and W.W. Powell (2005) Networks and economic life. *The Handbook of Economic Sociology.* Princeton, NJ: Princeton University Press, pp. 379–402.

Soda, G., A. Usai, and A. Zaheer (2004) Network memory: The influence of past and current networks on performance. *Academy of Management Journal*, 47: 893–906.

Sorenson, O., J.W. Rivkin, and L. Fleming (2006) Complexity, networks and knowledge flow. *Research Policy*, 35: 994–1017.

Stam, W. (2010) Industry event participation and network brokerage among entrepreneurial ventures. *Journal of Management Studies*, 47: 625–653.

Steglich, C.E., T.A.B. Snijders, and M. Pearson (2010) Dynamic networks and behavior: Separating selection from influence. *Sociological Methodology*, 40: 329–392.

Ter Wal, A.L.J. (2013) Cluster emergence and network evolution: A longitudinal analysis of the inventor network in Sophia-Antipolis. *Regional Studies*, 47: 651–668.

Ter Wal, A. and R. Boschma (2009) Applying social network analysis in economic geography: Framing some key analytic issues. *The Annals of Regional Science*, 43: 739–756.

Tiwana, A. (2008) Do bridging ties complement strong ties? An empirical examination of alliance ambidexterity. *Strategic Management Journal*, 29: 251–272.

Tortoriello, M. and D. Krackhardt (2010) Activating cross-boundary knowledge: The role of Simmelian ties in the generation of innovations. *The Academy of Management Journal*, 531(1): 167–181.

Tsai, W., K.-H. Su, and M.-J. Chen (2011) Seeing through the eyes of a rival: Competitor acumen based on rival centric perceptions. *Academy of Management Journal*, 54: 761–778.

Uzzi, B. (1997) Social structure and competition in interfirm networks: The paradox of embeddedness. *Administrative Science Quarterly*, 42(1): 35–67.

Vanhaverbeke, W., V. Gilsing, B. Beerkens, and G. Duysters (2009) The role of alliance network redundancy in the creation of core and non-core technologies. *Journal of Management Studies*, 46: 215–244.

Verspagen, B. (2007) Mapping technological trajectories as patent citation networks: a study on the history of fuel cell research. *Advances in Complex Systems*, 10(1): 93–115.

Wagner, C.S. and L. Leydesdorff (2005) Network structure, self-organization, and the growth of international collaboration in science. *Research Policy*, 34(10): 1608–1618.

Whittington, K., J. Owen-Smith, and W.W. Powell (2009) Networks, propinquity, and innovation in knowledge intensive industries. *Administrative Science Quarterly*, 54(1): 90–122.

Windrum, P., G. Fagiolo, and M. Moneta (2007) Empirical validation of agent-based models: Alternatives and prospects. *Journal of Artificial Societies and Social Simulation*, 10, 2.

Yang, H., Z. Lin, and M. Peng (2011) Behind acquisitions of alliance partners: Exploratory learning and network embeddedness. *Academy of Management Journal*, 54(5): 1069–1080.

Zaheer, A. and G. Soda. (2009) Network evolution: The origins of structural holes. *Administrative Science Quarterly*, 54: 1–31.

6

Academic networks and the diffusion of knowledge

Rajeev K. Goel, Devrim Göktepe-Hultén, and Rati Ram

1. Introduction

How universities can contribute to economic growth has become a topical question for academics as well as policymakers. Academic networks are a key channel for dissemination and diffusion of university knowledge and thus for technological progress. They are formal and informal channels/linkages among academic researchers for collaboration and knowledge acquisition/dissemination (Arora *et al.* (2001); Bozeman *et al.* (2013); Coupé (2004); Dasgupta (1988); Goel (1999); Goel and Rich (2005); Goyal *et al.* (2006); Laband and Tollison (2000); Lam (2011); Nelson (1959); Rothaermel *et al.* (2007); Salter and Martin (2001); Skyrme (1999); Stephan (1996)). Academic networks result from interactions among various actors and organizations such as university researchers, research groups, private or public firms, technology transfer offices (TTOs), university administrators, venture capitalists, other financiers, and diverse public sector participants. Universities and academic faculty have been and remain crucial generators of new knowledge, although other kinds of organizations such as firms and research institutes are also increasingly engaged in knowledge production and dissemination.

Besides being useful to individual researchers (see D'Este and Perkmann (2011)), academic networking can be socially beneficial as it enables efficient transmission of scientific knowledge and can be instrumental in accelerating the rate of long term technological progress (Mansfield (1995)).

Networking between universities and firms is therefore in most cases encouraged by governments, direct or indirect financial assistance, or legislations. Following the Bayh-Dole Act[1] and other university–industry relations in the US (Mowery *et al.* (2001)), policymakers elsewhere have focused on patenting and licensing to overcome weaknesses of technology transfer by reforming the intellectual property regimes (Geuna and Rossi (2011)).

According to the recent OECD (2013, p. 126) report (also see OECD (2003)):

> Collaboration is a key vector of innovation-related knowledge flows both for firms that use R&D (either internally developed or externally acquired) and for those that are not R&D active … Patterns of collaboration differ in terms of partners' characteristics. Collaboration with higher education or public research institutions is mainly an important source of knowledge transfer for large firms.

Recent advances in transportation and telecommunications have facilitated networking, although greater networking might at some point have negative effects (discussed below). There is some concern that, in spite of the technological and networking progress, the publishing pace might be slowing down (Ellison (2002) and Merton (1973) for a broader discussion). Academic networks traditionally involved academic researchers, but in recent years industry–academic networking has increased, due in large part to initiatives of policymakers and university administrators (see Blumenthal *et al.* (1996); Schmoch (1999); and Varga (2009)).

Some types of networks are formal (e.g., attending academic conferences and workshops), while others are informal or involuntary (e.g., graduates of well-known large academic programs *de facto* belong to large networks) as noted by Faria and Goel (2010) and Goel and Grimpe (2013). Figure 6.1 provides an overview of the main types of academic networking. The two main forms of academic networks are university to university and university to industry. The former includes mainly transfer of basic knowledge, while knowledge transfers in the latter are mainly of an applied nature. Along another related dimension, both types of networking might be active or formal (consciously undertaken by researchers – e.g., conference participation) or passive or informal (involuntary – e.g., being alumnus of an educational institution ties one to a set of graduates with little or no conscious effort). Thus, passive networking is largely exogenous from a researcher's perspective, while active networking is endogenous. These classifications provide a simple but useful way to organize the discussion surrounding academic networking and have somewhat different implications for the diffusion of academic knowledge. However, finding the right balance of knowledge transfer through different routes remains a challenge (Mowery *et al.* (2001); Nelson (2001)).

Before going into detail, the first question that one must address is how academic networks differ from other non-academic networks (see Bozeman *et al.* (2013)). Figure 6.2 shows different channels of knowledge flows through academic networking, with the two main branches being inter-university and university to industry. Both types of interactions can be formal or might take place informally. Non-academic networks include trade associations, industry clubs, and religious and sports organizations, etc.[2]

Several differences may be mentioned between the two types of networks. First, academic research is by its very nature cumulative in the sense that discoveries/inventions/theories are developed based on incremental advances by different researchers ("standing on the shoulders of giants"). Thus, examining others' work and building upon their ideas is a part of the process, which networking facilitates. On the other hand, non-academic networks, for example industry

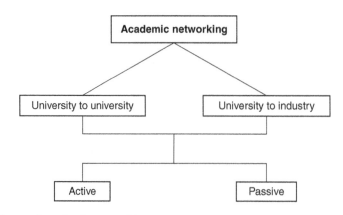

Figure 6.1 Types of academic networking

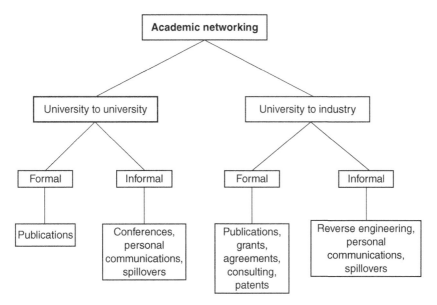

Figure 6.2 Knowledge flows through academic networking

associations, aim to increase the profits or market power of members and thus are more secretive. Second, participation in academic networks by researchers is generally voluntary, whereas non-academic networks are frequently based on institutional affiliations. Individual researchers, depending upon their disciplines/sub-disciplines and geographic location, choose to participate in a particular network (Goel and Rich (2005)). On the other hand, professional accreditations often mandate members to join certain non-academic networks or certain institutions to lobby governments for favors collectively. Third, unlike non-academic endeavors, academic research, especially basic research, is a non-zero sum game. In other words, greater use of one's research by others increases both internal (researcher's reputation, citations) and external rewards (society benefits from dissemination of new knowledge). Thus, researchers have intrinsic incentives to join networks that facilitate their research/reputation and these incentives might be absent or less-pronounced in non-academic settings where profit-maximization is viewed as a zero sum game. To summarize, academic networks are intrinsically different from non-academic networks and deserve special attention.

Given that networking can take many forms, one must try to find some classifications to effectively organize the discussion and to conduct meaningful analysis and draw conclusions. In this regard, Bozeman *et al.*'s (2013) distinction between "knowledge-focused collaborations" and "property-focused collaborations" seems useful. The knowledge-focused collaborations are mainly undertaken to foster research collaborations (i.e., to produce greater research output) and to exploit research complementarities among researchers. These are more likely to take place among university researchers and could be both formal and informal (see Figures 6.1 and 6.2). Property-based collaborations seek to produce economic value (e.g., via exploitation of commercialization) and are more likely to take place between universities or research institutions and industry. Traditionally, university researchers have been interested in knowledge-focused collaborations, but recently universities have actively tried to encourage property-focused collaborations. However, the success of such a transition has varied across universities, jurisdictions, gender, and academic disciplines (see Bozeman *et al.* (2013) for an excellent review).

Having established a case for separate treatment of academic networks, one must then dwell upon their causes and effects. Admittedly, analyzing the numerous causes and effects of networking is a tall order and beyond the scope of the present undertaking. In this chapter, we provide an overview of the literature on academic networking focusing particularly on causes and effects of individual-level collaborations among university researchers and with industry, with particular emphasis on its effect on the diffusion of academic knowledge. Knowledge diffusion is a key to long-run technological progress and consequent economic growth. We describe academic networks as scientists' interactions in order to generate and increase the amount of academic knowledge as well as to disseminate and utilize knowledge for solving industrial problems and to generate economic value, new ventures, jobs, and wealth. We also discuss some empirical evidence on the causes and effects of academic networking, making some distinction between active and passive networking.

2. Emergence of academic networks

In the related literature, broader approaches to innovation, e.g., the systems-of-innovation framework, which emerged out of interactive and evolutionary theories of innovation, emphasize the interconnectivity and interdependence between various organizations and institutions at different levels of analysis (Freeman (1987); Lundvall (1992); Nelson (1993)). Innovation systems ensure that innovation does not take place in isolation but in continuous interactions between organizations (firms, universities, government agencies as players) and within an institutional structure (in the sense of the rules of the game). The institutional structure is generated by private organizations (e.g., professional societies) and by public institutions (e.g., universities, laboratories, patent offices).

Closely related to the systems-of-innovation framework, the triple-helix mode of Etzkowitz and Leydesdorff (1997) states that increasing linkages and interactions among universities, industry, and the government facilitate technology transfer from universities to industry. In addition to increasing linkages and interactions, this model argues that each actor shares the roles of the others (Etzkowitz and Leydesdorff (1997)). Thus universities increasingly perform entrepreneurial tasks such as commercializing research results, patenting, licensing, or forming spin-offs. Firms take on academic roles such as sharing knowledge with one another and with universities (Etzkowitz et al. (2000)). As various players act complementarily, the diffusion of knowledge over time is likely to increase and its pace would likely quicken.

In addition to this scholarly debate, there has been an increasing policy interest in academic networking and the diffusion of academic knowledge, accompanied by concern with increasing this kind of activity – especially in the forms of patenting, licensing, and launching academic spin-off firms. In the European Union (EU), it has been argued that the level of commercial activity at universities is relatively low compared to the high levels of scientific performance and investment in research. This perception is exacerbated somewhat by the impression that universities in the US have done much better in commercializing their research results due to the Bayh-Dole Act. Although many other factors also came into play in the upsurge of patenting and licensing in the post-1980 period (Mowery et al. (2004); Mowery and Sampat (2004)), Etzkowitz noted that the Bayh-Dole Act improved the ability to move ideas from R&D to the marketplace and into business in the US (Etzkowitz et al. (2000); Etzkowitz (2001, 2002)).

Despite skepticism that Bayh-Dole is the only factor behind the rise of university patenting in the US (see below), this Act has received attention as one of the important factors in the commercialization of university research and thereby facilitating another channel for the diffusion of knowledge. It is also considered to be important for the institutionalization of technology transfer (i.e., streamlining the procedures for patenting and licensing of patents developed as a result of federally funded research) in US universities (see Bozeman (2000); Etzkowitz *et al.* (2000); Jensen and Thursby (2001); Mowery *et al.* (2001, 2004); Mowery and Ziedonis (2002); OECD (2003); Siegel *et al.* (2003a, b); Thursby *et al.* (2001); Thursby and Kemp (2002); Thursby and Thursby (2001, 2002, 2003, 2005, 2007)). However, there is considerable variation in the commercialization rates at individual universities.

Both in academic discussions and policy initiatives, universities are not only acknowledged as important organizations for teaching and research, they are also expected to contribute to the development of industrially relevant technologies in modern knowledge-based economies. While they have long served as sources or generators of knowledge, it has been noted that universities' relations with industry have intensified in recent years. Such arguments have been supported by references to a number of important developments, some of which can be summarized as follows:

- Closer links between scientific developments (university research) and their external utilization, e.g., important technological breakthroughs in computing (microprocessors), biotechnology (genetic engineering), molecular biology, and nanotechnology (Mowery *et al.* (2004)) made for faster utilization of university research in industry.
- A general increase in the scientific and technical content of all types of industrial production (Mowery *et al.* (2001, 2004)).
- A need for new sources of funding for academic research, due to budgetary stringency or general declines in research funds at universities (Bercovitz and Feldman (2006); Geuna (2001)).
- The US Congress's passage in 1980 of the Bayh-Dole Act, providing incentives for universities to patent scientific breakthroughs accomplished with federal funding (Etzkowitz *et al.* (2000); Henderson *et al.* (1998)).
- Increasing emphasis on government policies aimed at increasing the economic returns of publicly funded research by stimulating university–industry relations (Geuna (2001); Mowery and Sampat (2004)).
- The increase in the number and mobility of scientists and engineers, with larger numbers of scientists and engineers facilitating their movement between industrial and academic employment (Almeida and Kogut (1999); Bercovitz and Feldman (2006); Crespi *et al.* (2007)).
- The rise of venture capital, providing financing for academic start-up firms dedicated to commercializing the results of university-based research (Rothaermel *et al.* (2007)).
- Huge reduction in the cost of knowledge flows due to the explosive growth of the internet technology and its usage. However, formal analyses of the influence of the internet are in their infancy, given the relatively recent nature of the underlying innovation (see Goel and Hsieh (2002)).

These developments, among others, have attracted the attention of researchers and policymakers around the world, particularly in the US and Europe. This is especially relevant for their ability to pave the way for the "third task" activities – the inclusion of an economic development mandate for universities in addition to their traditional missions of education and research (Etzkowitz (1997); Rasmussen *et al.* (2006); Rothaermel *et al.* (2007)). It is in this spirit that university researchers and universities have been encouraged to embark upon collaborations with private companies in the UK (Geuna (2001)). Universities have also been urged to become involved in technology transfer as a way of controlling their own destiny, i.e., in order to continue their other missions and to retain their autonomy (Clark (1998)).

Several important themes have been studied within the broader area of research on university–industry relations. The literature is quite fragmented but a substantial amount of the work has been done in the last two decades. The reviews by Phan and Siegel (2006) and Siegel and Phan (2005) have focused chiefly on synthesizing the current literature on university technology transfer. They examined the objectives and cultures of the three key stakeholders in university technology transfer: (a) scientists; (b) university administrators and TTOs; and (c) firms and entrepreneurs. They found differences among the objectives, motives, and cultures of these main actors. They also showed the potential importance of organizational factors and institutional policies in effective university management of intellectual property. The authors concluded that most of the studies of the relative performance of technology transfer have explored the importance of institutional and managerial practices.

To sum up, the key actors (stakeholders) in the formation of academic networks and realization of university–industry technology transfer (UITT) are:

- Universities and university scientists (inventors, faculty, staff, researchers, graduates) who do research, discover new technologies, or lead to knowledge accumulation;
- Industrial companies and entrepreneurs who commercialize, use, and utilize university-based technology and knowledge; and
- Technology transfer organizations and technology transfer agents who manage universities' or researchers' IPR and contacts with industry (Siegel *et al.* (2003a, 2003b)).

In the university–industry knowledge transfer process, these various actors play ever-changing roles (Bercovitz and Feldman (2006); Markman *et al.* (2005a)). These roles have evolved over time and vary across nations. For instance, the process of university patenting includes initiation of research projects, achievement of research results (inventions), invention disclosures to TTOs for the evaluation of patentability, patent applications, and attempts to utilize a patent through licensing or spin-offs. However, innovations differ in their patentability and such differences are more pronounced in certain academic disciplines.

University researchers carry out the tasks of education, research, and commercial activities (third task) at universities. Despite their importance, the roles and motivations of university inventors have been relatively neglected topics of study. Most studies on university–industry relations are focusing on selected elite universities, TTOs, patent legislation, or technology transfer activities in specific sectors. There are only a few studies focusing on university inventors. For instance, a group of studies underlined the importance of institutions (*patent legislation, rules and regulations, policy mechanisms*) and organizations (*TTOs, university administration*) in the patenting activities of scientists. Another group of studies revealed the importance of individual factors such as *entrepreneurial traits, age, experience, scientific background* for scientists to commercialize their research results (see Bozeman *et al.* (2013) for a recent survey).

Most of these studies are based on data (number of patents, spin-offs, licensing revenues, etc.) available from TTOs or the Association of University Technology Managers (AUTM). However, the registers at the university-TTOs may fail to reflect the actual number of scientists who are involved in commercialization and the actual amount of commercial activities, since some scientists may avoid disclosing their inventions to TTOs officially (Audretsch *et al.* (2002); Markman *et al.* (2005b); Thursby *et al.* (2009)). As a result, the available data from AUTM or university-TTOs include mainly university-owned patents and may therefore underestimate the actual patenting activity of scientists. Thursby *et al.* (2009) have also shown that there are patents that are not registered to university-TTOs even in the post Bayh-Dole US, although at a relatively lower frequency than in the European cases as shown by Göktepe (2008) and Meyer *et al.* (2005).

Another stream of studies on academic networks has raised the question of *whether the recent increase in formal networking with commercial actors has challenged the open nature of university research and shifted academic research toward more commercialization*. A number of scholars have investigated the relationship between patenting and open dissemination of research results by scientists in the form of publications (see Agrawal and Henderson (2002); Breschi el al. (2005, 2007); Fabrizio and Di Minin (2008); Meyer (2006); Van Looy *et al.* (2006)). These studies have found that publication and patenting are complementary and *not* competing activities of university researchers. Most of these studies have found a positive relationship between scientific publication and patenting activities. These studies and the relationship between industrial interactions and publishing (scientific) activities of researchers merit more attention (see Goel and Göktepe-Hultén (2013)).

There have also been different views on how networking with industry and knowledge diffusion channels to industry may affect university scientists and the nature of university research (see Feller (1990)). Studies with a rather pessimistic view (Geuna (2001); Geuna and Nesta (2006); Nelson (2001); Slaughter and Rhoades (1996)) are concerned that, over time, this networking might be detrimental to the academic commons (Hellström (2003)) or the academic heartland (Clark (1998)). Even when major contributions to industrial growth and restructuring are desired, it is claimed that university researchers should concentrate on teaching and basic research (Rosenberg and Nelson (1994)).

On the other hand, studies with an optimistic take on such academic networks (Benner and Sandström (2000); Kleinman and Vallas (2001)) have argued that the increasing collaboration between academic and corporate research can lead to increased flexibility and autonomy for researchers. Alternately, universities may strengthen their traditional norms and their research and teaching activities as the second academic revolution leads them into becoming entrepreneurial entities with closer and more productive relationships with industry and the public sector (Etzkowitz (2001, 2002); Clark (1998); Goel and Rich (2005); Shane (2004)). Instead of being a question of either-or, successful universities and university researchers manage to combine academic excellence with industrial contacts and/or entrepreneurial contributions, according to Godin and Gingras (2000) and Van Looy *et al.* (2006).

The lack of studies on the role of university inventors is significant given the fact that possible negative consequences of patenting on the publications of scientists and other traditional scholarly pursuits have received a great deal of attention (Gray (2000)). A focus on individuals in no way involves underestimating the importance of external factors such as TTOs or patent legislation as well as research environment and groups for the patenting activities of individual scientists. A synergy between both internal and external factors is essential for optimal diffusion of knowledge. However, striking the right balance, given somewhat differing objectives of the various stakeholders and with resource constraints, is a formidable and evolving challenge.

3. Types of academic networks/knowledge diffusion channels

As mentioned at the outset, academic networks are a key channel for knowledge diffusion and technological progress. Although the transmission of university research results to industry is widely accepted as a crucial factor for industrial growth and competitiveness, there is no one single best way to promote such academic networks. Formal networks include deliberate attempts by academics to get in touch with other scholars for the exchange of ideas and attempts to collaborate, while informal networks are formed from indirect efforts, conscious or otherwise (see Grimpe and Fier (2010); Link *et al.* (2007)). Examples of informal networks include professional associations and trade groups. While many of these networks are discipline-specific, others are cross-disciplinary (see Table 6.1).

Table 6.1 Knowledge transfer mechanisms

Transferring of IPR
- Licensing of university patents
- Formation of university spin-offs

Technology transfer and co-development via formal research contracts
- R&D agreements
- R&D consortia
- Co-funding of research/co-supervision of PhD and masters theses
- Collaboration in national competence centers

Technology transfer via mobility/exchange of people
- Employment of graduates
- Faculty consultancy/university sabbaticals
- Industry scientists working at universities
- Individual collaboration

Technology transfer via casual, occasional, or collaborative means
- Conferences, seminars, workshops
- Scientific publications
- Popular lectures/university fairs
- Open university days
- Joint-labs
- Continuing education for industry

Note: This is not an exhaustive list. We are using the terms informal and casual networks interchangeably.

Table 6.1 shows the classification of technology transfer mechanisms into two main sets: patenting (licensing, spin-off company formation) and other more general types of technology transfer mechanisms. However, a few points are noteworthy. First, this list is not exhaustive and there may be other kinds of mechanisms. Second, it is difficult to separate these mechanisms from each other. Some of the mechanisms are *expanding their initial boundaries* and hence some mechanisms have started to overlap with each other. For instance, while some university spin-offs can be seen as mechanisms for the transfer of IPR, university spin-offs can also be formed by the university employees' or graduates' active involvement. Thus it is an appropriate mechanism for technology transfer via mobility of labor. Indisputably, it has become difficult to analyze one single mechanism.

Much of the literature on knowledge transfer between academe and industry has nevertheless focused on the role of patents and licensing (Autio and Laamanen (1995); Bercovitz and Feldman (2006); Bozeman *et al.* (2013); Feldman *et al.* (2002a, 2002b); Henderson *et al.* (1998); Jensen and Thursby (2001); Mowery *et al.* (2001); Siegel *et al.* (2003a, 2003b, 2004)). The formation of university spin-offs has also received a substantial amount of attention from researchers (Birley (2002); Di Gregorio and Shane (2003); Mustar (1997); Ndonzuau *et al.* (2001); O'Shea *et al.* (2005)); Perez and Sanchez (2003); Radosevich (1995); Shane (2004); Smilor *et al.* (1990)). This focus is partly data-driven and partly driven by the biases of the granting agencies (see Bozeman and Gaughan (2007)).

A substantial amount of technology/knowledge transfer may also take place through less formal mechanisms. Some of the research has focused on consulting, sponsored research, and collaboration (Cohen *et al.* (1998); Mansfield (1995, 1998); Mansfield and Lee (1996); Vohora *et al.* (2004)). These types of academic networks may be based on daily or routine transactions, resulting mostly from informal networks and informal relations between scientists and industry. Some studies have focused on mobility from academia to industry (Almeida and Kogut (1999); Crespi *et al.* (2007); Murray (2004); Zucker *et al.* (2002); Zucker and Darby (1995)). These studies have analyzed specific areas of interaction and knowledge transfer and have focused on specific types of academic networking.

The above review of the literature shows that (i) the issue of academic networking has really caught researchers' attention in recent years with a substantial growth in the literature at various levels of detail, differing in their scope and focus; and (ii) the quest for an optimal diffusion of knowledge via networking is far from over and, given the variation in the networks and the factors involved, might continue for some time. However, to shed light on the available evidence, we provide overviews from some related empirical studies.

4. A simple model of academic networking

As mentioned in the introduction, academic networking can have numerous causes and effects (see Grimpe and Fier (2010); also Figures 6.1 and 6.2). Thus, incorporation of various linkages in a single theoretical model does not seem feasible. Nevertheless, to provide some formal structure to the discussion and to anchor key ideas, we sketch a rudimentary model, borrowing from Faria and Goel (2010); also see Goel and Grimpe (2013) and Goel and Rich (2005).

The model involves a dynamic game between academic authors and journal editors, who have somewhat different objectives. One could think of the author being a faculty member at a university and the journal editor might be a university professor or an academic at a research institution. The representative academic author or researcher maximizes his/her utility (U) that is a function of the number of publications (q) and citations (c). Publications and reputation (via citations) are frequently used measures of research output and are positively related to job promotions and remunerations (Hamermesh *et al.* (1982)). Of course, there are differences across academic disciplines. For instance, researchers' output in fine arts disciplines is often measured in forms other than academic publications. The number of publications could have differing effects on the researchers' utility – increasing utility when they lead to promotions and greater compensation, while decreasing utility when pursuit of publications takes time away from other activities (Goel and Faria (2007)). The authors might be affiliated, consciously (e.g., internet blog groups) or otherwise (graduates of certain academic disciplines), to some networks (see below).

Citations for professional publications are an indicator of the quality of research output. Citations are, *ceteris paribus*, greater for networked authors (via greater exposure or word of mouth), for those with a larger stock of publications (via reputation), for more reputed journals, and for higher quality publications.

There are network externalities generated by an author's academic network membership, $z > 0$, which increase the positive impact of an author's research quality and the number of publications. If the author is not a member of a network, $z = 0$. This networking might be actively sought by going to professional conferences or might be passively acquired – for example, by the size of the peer group (e.g., academic department size). As noted above, other things being the same, there are more citations over time for networked authors ($z > 0$). The internet has decreased transactions costs for active networking in many instances.

The journal editor, on the other hand, tries to maximize the journal's reputation, taking account of the quality of papers and the author's behavior (via the number of citations and the number of articles). A more reputed journal also enhances the editor's reputation and increases his/her clout within the profession. This could in turn lead to better job offers or invitations to edit more prestigious journals. The editor can show preference toward publishing papers from networked authors if the editor thinks that these papers would receive more citations and thus contribute to the journal's reputation. There is, however, a potential cost to the bias in terms of the biased editor's journal being viewed as "parochial". Faria and Goel (2010) model cases both where the editor shows a networking bias and where the editor is impartial (also see Medoff (2003)).

Given this basic framework, Faria and Goel's (2010) analysis of the steady state of the dynamic game shows that academic networks do not have a significant bearing on the steady state number of publications of the author, or on the quality of the papers published (measured via citations). However, academic networks are found to affect citations in that citations increase with networking (i.e., $(\partial c/\partial z) > 0$). As mentioned above, citations to academic work are an indicator of research quality. Thus, in the simple stylized framework, there are returns to networking in terms of greater visibility or dissemination of one's work or showing a positive link between networking and knowledge diffusion. However, active networking efforts (e.g., attending conferences) are not costless. This positive link between networking and knowledge diffusion is shown in an empirical model based on German data in Section 5.

5. Empirical reflections

Empirical research on academic networking is hampered by limited availability of appropriate data as many networking tendencies of researchers are difficult to observe externally and researchers themselves are often reluctant to divulge such information. Relatively speaking, the data issues are more acute in the case of networks that involve industry collaborators or that are property-focused because disclosures are less forthcoming. Yet, sometimes survey level data on individual researchers' behavior are available and we provide insights from a few relevant studies.

5.1 Causes of academic networking: active and passive networking

In a recent study, Goel and Grimpe (GG) (2013) use a sample of German researchers to focus on the linkage between active and passive networking – specifically whether the two are substitutes or complements (see Table 6.1). The two may be complementary when passive networking makes active networking more likely. The authors use the number of professional conference visits as their measure of active networking, while researchers' professional discipline, employment status, etc., are used to denote passive associations. Researchers make conscious efforts and spend resources to attend academic conferences, while researchers' discipline and professional experience send indirect signals that might affect their ability to actively network. Any insights into the linkage between active and passive networking can provide useful inputs into resource allocation at academic institutions.

GG also consider the influences of various bottlenecks or obstacles to research production. When the three publication bottlenecks are considered (no access to others' research, (lack of) international cooperation, and (small) size of peer group), peer group size and lack of access to others' research do not significantly impact conference participation or active networking. International cooperation, on the other hand, seems to spur conference participation across the board. Internationally connected authors might better perceive the benefits of active networking. To summarize, some types of passive academic networking are complementary to active networking, while others are substitutes. In other words, some passive attributes of researchers do induce them to actively network.

Besides providing unique insights into researchers' propensity to network, Goel and Grimpe's (2013) findings have implications for technology policy in terms of resource allocation. For instance, not all disciplines need to be treated alike and some disciplines might need to provide greater incentives for conference participation abroad than others. Also, identification of significant research bottlenecks is a useful input in policies trying to get rid of these bottlenecks.

5.2 Effects of academic networking: industrial interactions and patenting

In this section, we present some survey evidence on the effects of networking, based on another sample of German researchers, focusing on the effects of academic networking in terms of the diffusion of knowledge. Specifically, drawing on Goel and Göktepe-Hultén (2013), hereafter GGH, we study the effects of industry–academic networking on the diffusion of knowledge as denoted by academics' attempts at patenting. Two specific interactions of university–industry networking – i.e., industrial cooperation and industrial consulting – are considered.

GGH differentiate between industrial collaboration (cooperation) and academic consulting (see Stephan *et al.* (2007); Thursby *et al.* (2009); Trajtenberg *et al.* (1997)). While consulting engagements are typically short term and seek academic expertise on a specific issue, cooperative arrangements are longer term and encompass a broad range of a research programs (see Hicks and Hamilton (1999)). Other things being the same, scientists engaging in cooperative endeavors with industry are likely to be exposed to a wider and fuller spectrum of research undertakings. They might also have a greater incentive to excel as they view themselves as part and parcel of the overall research project (which might eventually lead to part ownership of a resulting patent). Therefore, it is likely that industrial cooperation and consulting have different effects on academic patenting.[3]

The results of academic research can obviously be transferred from universities to industry via numerous channels, including: publications of basic research; patenting and licensing; spin-offs; joint research with firms; consultancy; student internships and training; and other types of informal knowledge networks (Audretsch *et al.* (2002); Bozeman *et al.* (2013); Goel and Rich (2005); Laband and Tollison (2000); and Stephan (1996)).

Based on this background, GGH hypothesize that industrial cooperation would result in patenting (see Meyer (2003); Owen-Smith and Powell (2001); Perkmann and Walsh (2007)), while it could undermine research behavior when it crowds out basic research. To test these hypotheses, they use data from Max Planck Society (MPS) survey (2009). The MPS is Germany's largest non-university public non-profit research organization, comprising 80 institutes located throughout the country. A telephone survey of over 2,500 MPS scientists was conducted from October 2007 to December 2007, and the dataset includes 2,604 interviews. In this sense, GGH's sample surveys a narrower population of German researchers than considered by GG, where all German public science researchers were surveyed. However, GGH's sample size is nearly three times that of Goel and Grimpe's sample (GG's sample survey was internet-based).

From this data, two binary variables (*Cooperate* and *Consult*, respectively) indicate whether or not a scientist has experience in research cooperation with firms and whether or not scientists had been hired for paid consultancy for firms or public institutions. Again, these forms of academia-industry networking are qualitatively different.

In their empirical setup, GGH account for several individual and external (institution specific) factors that may influence patenting behavior. The dependent variable is measured by whether scientists have been involved in a patent application. Specifically, the dependent variable captures academic patenting by a scientist (*Patent*) and can be seen as proxying for knowledge diffusion (Geuna and Nesta (2006)), while networking or industry interactions are alternately captured by consulting (*Consult*) and cooperation (*Cooperate*).

In terms of other controls for patenting behavior, professional characteristics considered include whether a scientist has a doctoral degree, or is a research group leader, and their professional/scientific discipline (*Life sciences*, *Natural sciences*). These professional characteristics capture abilities of researchers and the institutional differences across academic fields. Personal characteristics of researchers might influence patenting behavior, and age in years – to account for experience (see Levin and Stephan (1991)) – and gender were included.[4] These factors are commonly used in studies of innovation, entrepreneurship, and technology transfer (see Corley and Gaughan (2005); Goel and Grimpe (2013); Rosa and Dawson (2006); Thursby and Thursby (2005)).

Given the dichotomous nature of the dependent variable (*Patent*), GGH use Probit as the estimation technique, with alternate models including *Cooperate* and *Consult*. In the baseline, both main determinants of interest, *Consult* and *Cooperate*, have positive and statistically significant impacts on *Patent*. Thus, both types of industrial interactions lead to knowledge diffusion in the form of patents.

Turning to other controls, greater age, doctoral degree, and research group leadership make patenting more likely, and female scientists are less likely to patent. Gender is partly capturing the associated hurdles of underrepresentation (see Goel and Grimpe (2013); Goel and Göktepe-Hultén (2013); Thursby and Thursby (2005)). Further, researchers in hard sciences (*Life sciences*, *Natural sciences*) were more likely to patent – not surprising given the nature of research in these fields. These findings consistently held whether *Consult* was employed as a control or *Cooperate* was employed as a control.

Further, to account for possible simultaneity between patenting and cooperation/consulting (i.e., patenting might invite opportunities for industry cooperation or consulting), GGH report results of endogenous Probit, where *Consult* and *Cooperate* were alternately taken as endogenous. In each case, a researcher's industry experience and years of work experience at the Max Planck Institute were employed as additional instruments. Both measures of experience would affect industry interactions. The instrumental-variable regression results showed that only the effects of cooperation are positive and statistically significant, while the effects of consulting were not robust (for details, see Goel and Göktepe-Hultén (2013)). Thus, robustness checks supported the hypothesis about the positive impact of industrial cooperation on patenting; however, there was little robust evidence to support whether consultancy activities are substitute or complementary to scientists' overall research.

The key policy implication of GGH's work is that while industrial cooperation and consulting are often viewed similarly under academic-industry interactions and such interactions have found favor with administrators and public policymakers in recent years, there is a difference in their effects on patenting. Industrial cooperation is shown to robustly foster knowledge transfers in the form of patents. Thus, from a patenting viewpoint, the two types of interactions or university–industry networking are not necessarily alike and there is a case for supporting cooperation over consulting. The diffusion of knowledge, at least to the extent patents are carriers of such knowledge, is better accomplished via industrial cooperation between researchers and industry than via consulting. The effects of other forms of interactions on alternative forms of knowledge transmission must await further analysis with appropriate data. Bozeman *et al.* (2013) provide overviews of some other studies.

6. Concluding remarks and directions for future research

Academic networking's role in the diffusion of knowledge has been long recognized. A thriving knowledge-based economy depends upon how its universities develop along the entrepreneurial dimensions like patenting, licensing, start-ups, consultancy as well as other types of interaction and collaboration with firms, along with the applicability of the knowledge and skills of graduates to economic prosperity. In the context of the literature on academic networking, the systems-of-innovation and the triple-helix perspectives have both emphasized the increased interaction among universities and industry plus the diversity in the sources of knowledge and types of interaction among the producers and users of knowledge. In this chapter we review the current academic thinking on knowledge transfer channels between universities and private industry. We also highlight some research gaps indicating that further studies are needed.

In the US, several factors have facilitated the inclusion of such entrepreneurial activities in addition to the traditional roles of teaching and research at universities (Mowery *et al.* (2004)). A few studies suggest that some European universities in Germany, Sweden, the UK, and Italy that are rich in science and technology lag behind in their efficiency of knowledge transfer and innovation compared to the US universities (Rothaermel *et al.* (2007)) and that the benefits of university scientific output are not spread widely to society. The European Commission and the OECD have promoted several initiatives in which universities are tasked with the economic development mandate (so-called third mission) and reformed the intellectual property regimes after the US model and initiated support organizations (e.g., TTOs) to facilitate academic networking or, in particular, patenting and licensing of university research results.

To summarize and synthesize the vast and growing literature on academic networking, we can place the discussion by highlighting the following aspects:

1) Varieties of academic networks

We see that there are significant networking differences across disciplines (Perkmann *et al.* (2011), gender (Thursby and Thursby (2005)) and age (Levin and Stephan (1991)). However, it is not yet clear how academic networks have evolved over time.

In general, formal theoretical and empirical work on networking is difficult partly because networking comes in many forms (Figures 6.1 and 6.2) and partly because hard data on networking are scarce (because some networking is informal and due to the fact that researchers are often secretive about their ongoing research efforts).

Measurement of less formalized activities is often difficult and most efforts have focused on channels for which easily quantifiable data is available (such as publications and patents) or which are easily institutionalized (such as licensing or spin-off company formation).

In this chapter we have seen how academic networks contribute to the diffusion of knowledge, using examples of stylized theoretical and empirical settings. The theoretical model presents a stylized game between journal editors (who are gatekeepers of new knowledge) and researchers (who are producers of new knowledge). The two empirical studies alternately examine the determinants of the causes and effects of academic networking. They show that active networking might be a substitute or complement relative to different types of passive networking and that industrial cooperation might foster greater knowledge diffusion (in the form of patents) than industrial consultancy. These examples provide useful insights into an area where more formal research is warranted.

We have indicated that academic networking can have numerous causes and effects (see Grimpe and Fier (2010); also Figures 6.1 and 6.2). Thus, incorporation of various linkages in a single theoretical model does not seem feasible. The issue of heterogeneity among different universities, scientists, scientific fields, industrial sectors, as well as firm types cautions that emulating any kind of standard model that may seem to work, or even approximating "best practice", in other contexts may not necessarily yield the same outcomes and be beneficial. Instead, policymakers in different jurisdictions should try to establish competent organizations and efficient institutional set-ups that are adapted to particular – national, regional, or even local – contexts and that can be further customized to accommodate both the needs of the scientists and the nature of the technology.

While networking facilitates both personal growth of researchers and social gains via knowledge diffusion, one could envision situations where networking might have a downside.

For instance, there could be excessive resources devoted to networking (see Van Rijnsoever et al. (2008)) and, in the context of the theoretical model discussed above, if journal editors were biased in favor of networked authors, one could envision situations where the overall quality of published research might suffer (see Hicks and Hamilton (1999)). However, more research on this (negative) aspect is needed.

Arguably the most significant networking development in recent years is related to the growth of the internet (see Goel and Hsieh (2002)). The internet has been nothing short of a game-changer in networking and the diffusion of knowledge. Besides facilitating faster and more efficient transmission of scientific information, the internet has deemphasized the role of physical location and greatly reduced the costs of networking and collaboration. Researchers can now form networks in cyberspace, and thus collaborate effectively without ever having to meet physically (see Goel (2003a)). The internet has also lowered output costs related to knowledge diffusion by spurring the growth of online publishing outlets (Goel (2003a); Goel and Faria (2007)). On a note of caution, this growth has the potential to adversely affect research quality, especially given the inadequate policing of the internet. Formal research on the role of the internet, however, is in its relative infancy.

2) Complementarities and research synergies

Some studies show that academic excellence and commercial success are not incompatible but can in fact be mutually reinforcing. Goel and Göktepe-Hultén (2013) provide some novel insights regarding the relative effectiveness of various industry–academic interactions. However, more research is needed with finer distinctions between sub-disciplines and industry groups.

3) Technology policy implications

Another important issue that has received relatively little attention is related to the political economy of innovation in general and, in the present context, the nexus between politics and knowledge diffusion (see Goel (2003b, 2007), Göktepe (2008) for some related work). Existing literature and policy initiatives often emphasize the outcomes (number of patents, licensing revenues, number of start-ups) or look at the codified data (co-publications), rather than unmeasurable (unquantifiable) aspects of learning, tacit knowledge, and interaction between academic scientists and corporates.

Due to the overall positive image of academic networking, policies facilitating networking are archetypically adopted. In addition to providing sound framework conditions, policymakers will need to further differentiate the types of networking used by scientists and industry. This will require taking into account evidence on the extent to which different activities and channels complement each other. Governance of innovation at universities, however, goes beyond introducing new reforms. It entails risks and uncertainties. Rent-seeking by policymakers can affect the rules of the game and thereby have a bearing on the pace of knowledge diffusion. Vested interest groups (e.g., influential universities and research organizations) might also be able to influence research policy to their advantage and create entry barriers for newcomers.

Given that networking varies across disciplines, and gender, and comes in many forms (Figures 6.1 and 6.2), perhaps more specific policies would work better. Policies and incentives for the transfer of knowledge and its commercialization should not be limited to patents and licensing but may extend to efforts toward channels that are also favored by industry, as well as emerging channels like student entrepreneurship. For that purpose adaptive and flexible institutions and organizations may enable scientists to network with external actors by providing them with the resources and skills they may need for networking in general, whereas simply applying standard solutions to different contexts may militate such positive outcomes. Some channels like industrial collaboration are also highly valued by industry, and most knowledge transfer channels are not currently institutionalized or formalized (OECD, 2013). We also empirically highlight that industrial collaboration through consultancy is likely to yield more novel research findings that may lead to more patenting (Goel and Göktepe-Hultén, 2013). As such we suggest mutuality between the goals of university and industry as well as the view that reinforcement of different channels of knowledge transfer will generally require complex policy interventions to foster.

We noted a change toward less formal academic networking channels and open science, and a move away from the pursuit of academic patenting and licensing activity. Technology licensing and transfer offices (TTOs), which have long been central to university and government efforts to commercialize research, are also evolving in the search for more effective operational models. Many universities have sought to reform TTOs or to create new models such as regional hub-and-spoke TTOs that service multiple research institutions. In addition, some universities are also exploring new approaches to IP ownership by vesting some rights with the academic inventor while maintaining university ownership (Göktepe (2008)). Overall, without taking into account the complexity of the diffusion of knowledge and variety (diversity) of knowledge transfer channels as well as the level of complementarity of different channels, public policy efforts may not achieve an optimal pattern for university–industry knowledge transfer.

4) Role of individual network participants

Academic networks can be influenced to some degree by the incentives and motivations of individual scientists. Channels like informal contacts, conferences and professional meetings, consulting, and collaborative research that industry often finds important also have high person-to-person relational intensity. From a policy perspective it is therefore relevant to better understand the role of individuals in these relations. Researchers' behaviors are likely to be influenced by their mindset (e.g., their motivation to participate in commercialization) and their competences (e.g., understanding the needs of industrial partners). They are also influenced by their peers, institutional culture, and the leadership under which they work (Göktepe (2008)). However, while considering individuals' personal traits (researchers' seniority (tenure or not), prior industry experience, competence, gender, etc.) as well as incentives and rewards, the role of institutional culture and leadership, the literature above tends to focus on academic entrepreneurship more than other types of academic networking. Further research that investigates individual factors in the emergence of all types of academic networks and diffusion of knowledge is needed.

In short, besides providing a limited taxonomy of academic networking, some descriptive narratives, and a few theoretical and empirical reflections relative to academic networks, this chapter notes ten points. First, we restate the view that research conducted in universities has a high potential for technical change and economic growth, and, therefore, its transmission and diffusion is socially important. Second, producers of this research, and of the associated knowledge, transmit it through "active" and "passive" academic networks which extend across universities and industry. Third, there is increasing pressure to strengthen the university–industry networks and to generate patents, licensing, spin-offs, and other commercial products from the university research output. Fourth, despite the paucity of research in the area, there seems some ambiguity about the impact of such pressure, and the consequent focus on patents and licensing, on the intrinsic scientific quality of academic research. Fifth, although it is difficult to provide a tight argument, considering the somewhat diffuse nature of incentives for production and diffusion of university research output, such production and its diffusion through academic networks is likely to be socially suboptimal. Sixth, however, due to the diversity of the university research products, the wide variety of networks and other mechanisms for transmission of knowledge embodied in these products, differences in the personalities and motivations of academic researchers, and variability in the institutional contexts, it is perhaps not prudent to look for a general model of efficient transmission or a universal incentive structure to enhance production and transmission of academic research output and its contribution to economic performance. Seventh, therefore, suggestions about the "success" of measures like the Bayh-Dole Act might perhaps be interpreted somewhat cautiously. Eighth, the explosive growth of the internet has greatly lowered the costs of academic networks and probably increased the payoff from these. Ninth, we note the paucity of research in several important areas related to academic networks, particularly the impact of the internet, the relation between patenting and licensing and the intrinsic scientific quality of research output, the characteristics of the individual researcher relative to the type of network chosen, and the propensity toward commercialization of the research output. Last, academic networks need to be considered along with other types of networks and interactions that generate and transmit useful knowledge. These topics are pursued in some other chapters of this *Handbook*.

Notes

1 The Bayh-Dole Act of 1980 made changes in the ownership of inventions stemming from US federal funding. Before the Bayh-Dole Act, federal research funding obligated inventors to assign the ownership of inventions generated using federal funding to the federal government. The Bayh-Dole Act permits a university, small business, or non-profit institution to have ownership of such an invention. Policymakers and university administrators in several countries believe that such ownership of intellectual property would spur innovation (Göktepe (2008)).
2 This distinction would also justify the current attention to academic networks.
3 One should bear in mind, however, that patents do not capture all research output and are not equally applicable across all academic disciplines.
4 Note that the model in GG includes professional experience, while researcher's age is included here. On the other hand, research leadership and gender are included in both models.

References

Agrawal, A. and R. Henderson (2002) "Putting Patents in Context: Exploring Knowledge Transfer from MIT", *Management Science*, 48(1), 44–60.

Almeida, P. and B. Kogut (1999) "Localization of Knowledge and the Mobility of Engineers in Regional Networks", *Management Science*, 45(7), 905–917.

Arora, A., A. Fosfuri and A. Gambardella (2001) *Markets for Technology*, Cambridge, MA: MIT Press.

Audretsch, D.B., B. Bozeman, K.L. Combs, M. Feldman, A.N. Link, D.S. Siegel, P. Stephan, G. Tassey and C. Wessner (2002) "The Economics of Science and Technology", *Journal of Technology Transfer*, 27(2), 155–203.

Autio, E. and T. Laamanen (1995) "Measurement and Evaluation of Technology Transfer: Review of Technology Transfer Mechanisms and Indicators", *International Journal of Technology Management*, 10(7/8), 643–664.

Benner, M. and U. Sandström (2000) "Institutionalizing the Triple Helix: Research Funding and Norms in the Academic System", *Research Policy*, 29(2), 291–301.

Bercovitz, J.L. and M.P. Feldman (2006) "Entrepreneurial Universities and Technology Transfer: A Conceptual Framework for Understanding Knowledge-Based Economic Development", *Journal of Technology Transfer*, 31(1), 175–188.

Birley, S. (2002) "Universities, Academics and Spin-out Companies: Lessons from Imperial College", *International Journal of Entrepreneurship Education*, 1(1), 1–21.

Blumenthal, D., E.G. Campbell, N. Causino and K.S. Louis (1996) "Relationships between Academic Institutions and Industry in the Life Sciences – An Industry Survey", *New England Journal of Medicine*, 1996, 334(6), 368–373.

Bozeman, B. (2000) "Technology Transfer and Public Policy: A Review of Research and Theory", *Research Policy*, 29(4–5), 627–655.

Bozeman, B. and M. Gaughan (2007) "Impact of Grants and Contracts on Academic Researchers' Interactions with Industry", *Research Policy*, 36(5), 694–707.

Bozeman, B., D. Fay and C.P. Slade (2013) "Research Collaboration in Universities and Academic Entrepreneurship: The-State-of-the-Art", *Journal of Technology Transfer*, 38(1), 1–67.

Breschi, S., F. Lissoni and F. Montobbio (2005) "From Publishing to Patenting: Do Productive Scientists Turn into Academic Inventors?" *Revue d'Economie Industrielle*, 110(2), 75–102.

Breschi, S., F. Lissoni and F. Montobbio (2007) "The Scientific Productivity of Academic Inventors: New Evidence from Italian Data", *Economics of Innovation and New Technology*, 16(2), 101–118.

Clark, B.R. (1998) *Creating Entrepreneurial Universities: Organizational Pathways of Transformation*, Surrey: Pergamon.

Cohen, W.M., R. Florida, L. Randazzese and J. Walsh (1998) "Industry and the Academy: Uneasy Partners in the Cause of Technological Advance", in R.G. Noll (ed.), *Challenges to Research Universities*, Washington, D.C.: Brookings Institution, 171–199.

Corley, E. and M. Gaughan (2005) "Scientists' Participation in University Research Centers: What Are the Gender Differences?" *Journal of Technology Transfer*, 30(4), 371–381.

Coupé, T. (2004) "What Do We Know About Ourselves? On the Economics of Economics", *Kyklos*, 57(2), 197–216.

Crespi, G.A., A. Geuna and L. Nesta (2007) "The Mobility of University Inventors in Europe", *Journal of Technology Transfer*, 32(3), 195–215.

Dasgupta, P. (1988) "The Welfare Economics of Knowledge Production", *Oxford Review of Economic Policy*, 4(4), 1–12.

D'Este, P. and M. Perkmann (2011) "Why Do Academics Engage with Industry? The Entrepreneurial University and Individual Motivations", *Journal of Technology Transfer*, 36(3), 316–339.

Di Gregorio, D. and S. Shane (2003) "Why Do Some Universities Generate More Start-ups than Others?" *Research Policy*, 32(2), 209–227.

Ellison, G. (2002) "The Slowdown of the Economics Publishing Process", *Journal of Political Economy*, 110(5), 947–993.

Etzkowitz, H. (1997) "The Entrepreneurial University and the Emergence of Democratic Corporatism", in H. Etzkowitz and L. Leydesdorff (eds.), *Universities and the Global Knowledge Economy: A Triple Helix of University–Industry–Government Relations*, London: Cassell, 141–152.

Etzkowitz, H. (2001) "The Second Academic Revolution and the Rise of Entrepreneurial Science", *IEEE Technology and Society*, 22(2), 18–29.

Etzkowitz, H. (2002) *MIT and the Rise of Entrepreneurial Science*, London: Routledge.

Etzkowitz, H. and L. Leydesdorff (1997) *Universities and the Global Knowledge Economy: A Triple Helix of University–Industry–Government Relations*, London: Pinter.

Etzkowitz, H., A. Webster, C. Gebhardt and B.-R. Cantisano Terra (2000) "The Future of the University and the University of the Future: Evolution of Ivory Tower to Entrepreneurial Paradigm", *Research Policy*, 29(2), 313–330.

Fabrizio, K. and A. Di Minin (2008) "Commercializing the Laboratory: Faculty Patenting and the Open Science Environment", *Research Policy*, 37(5), 914–931.

Faria, J.R. and R.K. Goel (2010) "Returns to Networking in Academia", *Netnomics*, 11(2), 103–117.

Feldman, M., M. Feller, J. Bercovitz and R. Burton (2002a) "Equity and the Technology Transfer Strategies of American Universities", *Journal of Management Science*, 48(1), 105–121.

Feldman, M.P., A.N. Link and D.S. Siegel (2002b) *The Economics of Science and Technology*, Boston: Kluwer Academic Publishers.

Feller, I. (1990) "Universities as Engines of R&D-based Economic Growth: They Think They Can", *Research Policy*, 19(4), 335–348.

Freeman, C. (1987) *Technology Policy and Economic Performance: Lessons from Japan*, London: Pinter.

Geuna, A. (2001) "The Changing Rationale for European University Research Funding: Are There Negative Unintended Consequences", *Journal of Economic Issues*, 35(3), 607–632.

Geuna, A. and L.J.J. Nesta (2006) "University Patenting and Its Effects on Academic Research: The Emerging European Evidence", *Research Policy*, 35(6), 790–807.

Geuna, A. and F. Rossi (2011) "Changes to University IPR Regulations in Europe and the Impact on Academic Patenting", *Research Policy*, 40(8), 1068–1076.

Godin, B. and Y. Gingras (2000) "The Place of Universities in the System of Knowledge Production", *Research Policy*, 29(2), 273–278.

Goel, R.K. (1999) *Economic Models of Technological Change*, Westport, CT: Quorum Books.

Goel, R.K. (2003a) "A Market Mechanism for Scientific Communication: A Comment", *Kyklos*, 56(3), 395–400.

Goel, R.K. (2003b) "Rent-Seeking in Research Markets", *Journal of Technology Transfer*, 28(2), 103–109.

Goel, R.K. (2007) "Research Spending under Regulatory Uncertainty", *Journal of Technology Transfer*, 32(6), 593–604.

Goel, R.K. and J.R. Faria (2007) "Proliferation of Academic Journals: Effects on Research Quantity and Quality", *Metroeconomica*, 58(4), 536–549.

Goel, R.K. and D. Göktepe-Hultén (2013) "Industrial Interactions and Academic Patenting: Evidence from German Scientists", *Economics of Innovation and New Technology*, 2013, 22(6), 551–565.

Goel, R.K. and C. Grimpe (2013) "Active versus Passive Academic Networking: Evidence from Micro-level Data", *Journal of Technology Transfer*, 38(2), 116–134.

Goel, R.K. and E.W.T. Hsieh (2002) "Internet Growth and Economic Theory", *Netnomics*, 4(2), 221–225.

Goel, R.K. and D.P. Rich (2005) "Organization of Markets for Science and Technology", *Journal of Institutional and Theoretical Economics*, 161(1), 1–17.

Göktepe, D. (2008) "Identification of University Inventors and University Patenting Patterns at Lund University: Conceptual-Methodological & Empirical Findings", in S. Krishna (ed.), *Academic Patents: Emerging Issues and Challenges*, India: ICFAI University Press.

Goyal, S., M.J. Van Der Leij and J.L. Moraga-Gonzalez (2006) "Economics: An Emerging Small World", *Journal of Political Economy*, 114(2), 403–412.

Gray, D.O. (2000) "Cooperative Research: Government-Sponsored Industry-University Cooperative Research: An Analysis of Cooperative Research Center Evaluation Approaches", *Research Evaluation*, 9(1), 57–67.

Grimpe, C. and H. Fier (2010) "Informal University Technology Transfer: A Comparison Between the United States and Germany", *Journal of Technology Transfer*, 35(6), 637–650.

Hamermesh, D., G.E. Johnson and B.A. Weisbrod (1982) "Scholarship, Citations, and Salaries: Economic Rewards in Economics", *Southern Economic Journal*, 49(2), 472–481.

Hellström, T. (2003) "Governing the Virtual Academic Commons", *Research Policy*, 32(3), 391–401.

Henderson, R., A. Jaffe and M. Trajtenberg (1998) "Universities as Source of Commercial Technology: A Detailed Analysis of University Patenting, 1965–1988", *Review of Economics and Statistics*, 80(1), 119–127.

Hicks, D. and K. Hamilton (1999) "Does University–Industry Collaboration Adversely Affect University Research?" *Issues in Science and Technology Online*, University of Texas at Dallas, http://www.nap.edu/issues/15.4/realnumbers.htm, accessed January 15, 2014.

Jensen, R.A. and M.C. Thursby (2001) "Proofs and Prototypes for Sale: The Licensing of University Inventions", *American Economic Review*, 91(1), 240–259.

Kleinman, D.L. and S.P. Vallas (2001) "Science, Capitalism, and the Rise of the 'Knowledge Worker': The Changing Structure of Knowledge Production in the United States", *Theory and Society*, 30(4), 451–492.

Laband, D.N. and R.D. Tollison (2000) "Intellectual Collaboration", *Journal of Political Economy*, 108(3), 632–662.

Lam, A. (2011) "What Motivates Academic Scientists to Engage in Research Commercialization: 'Gold', 'Ribbon', or 'Puzzle'?" *Research Policy*, 40(10), 1354–1368.

Levin, S.G. and P.E. Stephan (1991) "Research Productivity over the Life Cycle: Evidence for Academic Scientists", *American Economic Review*, 81(1), 114–132.

Link, A.N., D.S. Siegel and B. Bozeman (2007) "An Empirical Analysis of the Propensity of Academics to Engage in Informal University Technology Transfer", *Industrial and Corporate Change*, 16(4), 641–655.

Lundvall, B-Å. (ed.) (1992) *National Innovation Systems: Towards a Theory of Innovation and Interactive Learning*, London: Pinter.

Mansfield, E. (1995) "Academic Research Underlying Industrial Innovations: Source, Characteristics, and Financing", *Review of Economics and Statistics*, 77(1), 55–65.

Mansfield, E. (1998) "Academic Research and Industrial Innovation: An Update of Empirical Findings", *Research Policy*, 26(7–8), 773–776.

Mansfield, E. and J.Y. Lee (1996) "The Modern University: Contributor to Industrial Innovation and Recipient of Industrial R&D Support", *Research Policy*, 25(7), 1047–1058.

Markman, G.D., P.T. Gianiodis, P.H. Phan and D.B. Balkin (2005a) "Innovation Speed: Transferring University Technology to Market", *Research Policy*, 34(7), 1058–1075.

Markman, G.D., P.T. Gianiodis, P.H. Phan and D.B. Balkin (2005b) "Entrepreneurship from the Ivory Tower: Do Incentive Systems Matter?" *Journal of Technology Transfer*, 29(3–4), 353–364.

Max Planck Society (2009) "Max Planck Society: Annual Report 2008", http://pesona.jahresbericht2008/jahresbericht2008.pdf, accessed May 22, 2012.

Medoff, M.H. (2003) "Editorial Favoritism in Economics?" *Southern Economic Journal*, 70(2), 425–434.

Merton, R.K. (1973) *The Sociology of Science*, Chicago, IL: University of Chicago Press.

Meyer, M. (2003) "Academic Patents as an Indicator of Useful Research? A New Approach to Measure Academic Inventiveness", *Research Evaluation*, 12(1), 17–27.

Meyer, M. (2006) "Academic Inventiveness and Entrepreneurship: On the Importance of Start-Up Companies in Commercializing Academic Patents", *Journal of Technology Transfer*, 31(4), 501–510.

Meyer, M., M. Du Plessis, T. Tukeva and J.-T. Utecht (2005) "Inventive Output of Academic Research: A Comparison of Two Science Systems", *Scientometrics*, 63(1), 145–161.

Mowery, D.C. and B.N. Sampat (2004) "Universities in National Systems of Innovation", in J. Fagerberg, D. Mowery and R.R. Nelson (eds.), *Oxford Handbook of Innovation*, Oxford: Oxford University Press, pp. 209–239.

Mowery, D.C. and A.A. Ziedonis (2002) "Academic Patent Quality and Quantity Before and After the Bayh-Dole Act in the United States", *Research Policy*, 31(3), 399–418.

Mowery, D.C., R.R. Nelson, B.N. Sampat and A.A. Ziedonis (2001) "The Growth of Patenting and Licensing by U.S. Universities: An Assessment of the Effects of the Bayh-Dole Act of 1980", *Research Policy*, 30(1), 99–119.

Mowery, D.C., R.R. Nelson, B.N. Sampat and A.A. Ziedonis (2004) *Ivory Tower and Industrial Innovation: University–Industry Technology Transfer Before and After the Bayh-Dole Act*, Stanford, CA: Stanford Business Books.

Murray, F. (2004) "The Role of Academic Inventors in Entrepreneurial Firms: Sharing the Laboratory Life", *Research Policy*, 33(4), 643–659.

Mustar, P. (1997) "Spin-off Enterprises – How French Academics Create Hi-tech Companies: The Conditions for Success or Failure", *Journal of Science and Public Policy*, 24(1), 37–43.

Ndonzuau, F.N., F. Pirnay and B. Surlemont (2001) "A Stage Model of Academic Spin-off Creation", *Technovation*, 22(5), 281–289.

Nelson, R.R. (1959) "The Simple Economics of Basic Scientific Research", *Journal of Political Economy*, 67(3), 297–306.

Nelson, R. (ed.) (1993) *National Innovation Systems: A Comparative Analysis*, Oxford: Oxford University Press.

Nelson, R.R. (2001) "Observations on the Post-Bayh-Dole Rise of Patenting at American Universities", *Journal of Technology Transfer*, 26(1–2), 13–19.

OECD (2003) *Turning Science into Business: Patenting and Licensing at Public Research Organizations*, Paris: OECD Publications.

OECD (2013) *OECD Science, Technology and Industry Scoreboard 2013: Innovation for Growth*, Paris: OECD Publications.

O'Shea, R.P., T.J. Allen, A. Chevalier and F. Roche (2005) "Entrepreneurial Orientation, Technology Transfer and Spinoff Performance of U.S. Universities", *Research Policy*, 34(7), 994–1009.

Owen-Smith, J. and W.W. Powell (2001) "To Patent or Not: Faculty Decision and Institutional Success at Technology Transfer", *Journal of Technology Transfer*, 26(1–2), 99–114.

Perez, M.P. and A.M. Sanchez (2003) "The Development of University Spin-offs: Early Dynamics of Technology Transfer and Networking", *Technovation*, 23(10), 823–831.

Perkmann, M. and K. Walsh (2007) "University Industry Relationships and Open Innovation: Towards a Research Agenda", *International Journal of Management Reviews*, 9(4), 259–280.

Perkmann, M., Z. King and S. Pavelin (2011) "Engaging Excellence? Effects of Faculty Quality on Industry Engagement Across Disciplines", *Research Policy*, 40(4), 539–552.

Phan, P.H. and D.S. Siegel (2006) "The Effectiveness of University Technology Transfer: Lessons Learned, Managerial and Policy Implications, and the Road Forward", *Foundations and Trends in Entrepreneurship*, 2(2), 77–144.

Radosevich, R. (1995) "A Model for Entrepreneurial Spin-offs from Public Technology Sources", *International Journal of Technology Management*, 10(7–8), 879–893.

Rasmussen, E., O. Moen and M. Gulbrandsen (2006) "Initiatives to Promote Commercialization of University Knowledge", *Technovation*, 26(4), 518–533.

Rosa, P. and A. Dawson (2006) "Gender and the Commercialization of University Science: Academic Founders of Spinout Companies", *Entrepreneurship and Regional Development*, 18(4), 341–366.

Rosenberg, N. and R.R. Nelson (1994) "American Universities and Technical Advance in Industry", *Research Policy*, 23(3), 323–348.

Rothaermel, F.T., S.D. Agung and L. Jiang (2007) "University Entrepreneurship: A Taxonomy of the Literature", *Industrial and Corporate Change*, 16(4), 691–791.

Salter, A.J. and B.R. Martin (2001) "The Economic Benefits of Publicly Funded Basic Research: A Critical Review", *Research Policy*, 30(3), 509–532.

Schmoch, U. (1999) "Interaction of Universities and Industrial Enterprises in Germany and the United States – A Comparison", *Industry and Innovation*, 6(1), 51–68.

Shane, S.A. (2004) "Encouraging University Entrepreneurship? The Effect of the Bayh-Dole Act on University Patenting in the United States", *Journal of Business Venturing*, 19(1), 127–151.

Siegel, D.S. and P. Phan (2005) "Analyzing the Effectiveness of University Technology Transfer: Implications for Entrepreneurship Education", in G. Liebcap (ed.), *Advances in the Study of Entrepreneurship, Innovation, and Economic Growth*, Vol. 16, Amsterdam: Elsevier Science/JAI Press, 1–38.

Siegel, D.S., D.A. Waldman, L.E. Atwater and A.N. Link (2003a) "Commercial Knowledge Transfers from Universities to Firms: Improving the Effectiveness of University–Industry Collaboration", *Journal of High Technology Management Research*, 14(1), 111–133.

Siegel, D.S., D.A. Waldman and A.N. Link (2003b) "Assessing the Impact of Organizational Practices on the Productivity of University Technology Transfer Offices: An Exploratory Study", *Research Policy*, 32(1), 27–48.

Siegel, D.S., D.A. Waldman, L.E. Atwater and A.N. Link (2004) "Toward a Model of the Effective Transfer of Scientific Knowledge from Academicians to Practitioners: Qualitative Evidence from the Commercialization of University Technologies", *Journal of Engineering and Technology Management*, 21(1–2), 115–142.

Skyrme, D.J. (1999) *Knowledge Networking: Creating the Collaborative Enterprise*, Abingdon, UK: Routledge.

Slaughter, S. and G. Rhoades (1996) "The Emergence of a Competitiveness Research and Development Policy Coalition and the Commercialization of Academic Science and Technology", *Science, Technology and Human Value*, 21(3), 303–339.

Smilor, R.W., D.V. Gibson and G.B. Dietrich (1990) "University Spin-out Companies: Technology Start-ups from UT-Austin", *Journal of Business Venturing*, 5(1), 63–76.

Stephan, P.E. (1996) "The Economics of Science", *Journal of Economic Literature*, 34(3), 1199–1235.

Stephan, P.E., S. Gurmu, A.J. Sumell and G. Black (2007) "Who's Patenting in the University? Evidence from the Survey of Doctorate Recipients", *Economics of Innovation and New Technology*, 16(2), 71–99.

Thursby, J.G. and S. Kemp (2002) "Growth and Productive Efficiency of University Intellectual Property Licensing", *Research Policy*, 31(1), 109–124.

Thursby, J.G. and M.C. Thursby (2001) "Industry Perspectives on Licensing University Technologies: Sources and Problems", *Industry & Higher Education*, 15(4), 289–294.

Thursby, J.G. and M.C. Thursby (2002) "Who is Selling the Ivory Tower? Sources of Growth in University Licensing", *Management Science*, 48(1), 90–104.

Thursby, J.G. and M.C. Thursby (2003) "Industry/University Licensing: Characteristics, Concerns and Issues from the Perspective of the Buyer", *Journal of Technology Transfer*, 28(4), 207–213.

Thursby, J.G. and M.C. Thursby (2005) "Gender Patterns of Research and Licensing Activity of Science and Engineering Faculty", *Journal of Technology Transfer*, 30(4), 343–353.

Thursby, J.G. and M.C. Thursby (2007) "University Licensing", *Oxford Review of Economic Policy*, 23(4), 620–639.

Thursby, J.G., A. Fuller and M.C. Thursby (2009) "US Faculty Patenting: Inside and Outside the University", *Research Policy*, 38(1), 14–25.

Thursby, J.G., R. Jensen and M.C. Thursby (2001) "Objectives, Characteristics and Outcomes of University Licensing: A Survey of Major U.S. Universities", *Journal of Technology Transfer*, 26(1–2), 59–72.

Trajtenberg, M., R.M. Henderson and A.B. Jaffe (1997) "University versus Corporate Patents: A Window on the Basicness of Inventions", *Economics of Innovation and New Technology*, 5(1), 19–50.

Van Looy, B., J. Callaert and K. Debackere (2006) "Publication and Patent Behavior of Academic Researchers: Conflicting, Reinforcing or Merely Co-existing?" *Research Policy*, 35(4), 596–608.

Van Rijnsoever, F., L.K. Hessels and R.L.J. Vandeberg (2008) "A Resource-Based View on the Interactions of University Researchers", *Research Policy*, 37(8), 1255–1266.

Varga, A. (2009) *University Knowledge Transfers and Regional Development*, Cheltenham, UK: Edward Elgar Publishers.

Vohora, A., M. Wright and A. Lockett (2004) "Critical Junctures in the Development of University High-Tech Spinout Companies", *Research Policy*, 33(1), 147–175.

Zucker, L.G. and M.R. Darby (1995) "Virtuous Circles of Productivity: Star Bioscientists and the Institutional Transformation of Industry", NBER Working Paper, no 5342.

Zucker, L.G., M.R. Darby and M. Torero (2002) "Labor Mobility from Academe to Commerce", *Journal of Labor Economics*, 20(3), 629–660.

7

Transversal or linear?

Knowledge externalities and the complexity of knowledge interactions

Phil Cooke

1. Introduction

This chapter is a research-informed contribution to a new kind of regional innovation policy analysis based on evolutionary economic geography principles. It tackles key issues in the ways in which the 'knowledge economy' has been understood by both academics and policy makers. Furthermore, it suggests that this 'framing' of 'knowledge economy' rhetoric contributed directly to the socio-spatial polarisation of modern economies. At its heart, the dominant 'knowledge economy' practice model is linear, exclusive and 'specialisationist' – for example, the EU insistence that to receive regional aid, regions must show they propose S&T *innovation* by so-called 'smart specialisation'. A seminal paper by Jensen *et al.* (2007) refers to this hegemonic approach to *innovation*, which itself has also become an almost 'totalising' rhetoric for regional and business improvement, the Science, Technology, Innovation (STI) model of innovation. As we shall see, they contrast STI with a Doing, Using, Interacting (DUI) model that is both more user-friendly than STI to most firms and much truer to Schumpeter's (1939) basic and still relevant definition of innovation as rooted in 'recombinations of knowledge' where novelty may occur, we may add, even if the 'knowledge modules' themselves are not new.

To achieve this, the chapter reports original research into a number of, first, regional and, second, business innovation schemas, models and forms of intervention that give parity if not priority to DUI modes of operation. The chapter shows how a small selection of regions are responding to economic, financial and sustainability crises by searching for models of business enhancement and development that take innovation seriously but do not confine it to an STI (science, technology, innovation) mode of 'policy framing'. Accordingly, these are not 'core, science-based' regions such as Silicon Valley, Greater Boston or Cambridge within the East Anglia region, where Nobel laureates abound and path-breaking scientific discoveries are historically made. In truth, such regions are rare, but such is the allure of their research as well as commercial fecundity that their STI has bedazzled policy 'movers and shakers'. In the non-core science regions that exemplify a more widely applicable 'framing' of innovation, each is keen to recognise and enhance formerly often-unrecognised, practical DUI innovation styles pursued by firms and other actors usually in the absence of formal science. The findings are interesting because until now there has been no 'model' of a DUI regional innovation system (RIS) either theoretically or practically, in any formalised sense.

The paper proceeds to three formalisations of RIS set-ups that formally involve DUI, albeit in a variety of hybrid forms in which STI is either weakly (Algarve) or more strongly (Centro, Skåne)[1] engaged. It begins with clarification of the differences between STI and DUI framings of innovation, after Jensen *et al.* (2007). This leads in the next section to an evolutionary theoretical discussion of typical RIS system failure around knowledge issues. This is followed by a section on the rise of 'modularity' as a new mode of policy formulation (although not of industry organisation) whose origins lie in process innovations in the ICT industry dating from the 1990s, if not earlier. Following this are brief sections based on 'deliberative research' in which the author was both 'participant observer' and 'critical friend' to the process of learning how to more fully embed DUI support into regional innovation policy processes in Portugal's Algarve region. This involved analysis of an organisational process from the management of transitions to sustainable development practice, called 'Strategic Niche Management', connecting STI and DUI, while formalising and externalising the resulting innovation processes. There are then subsections introducing different regional experiences of involving DUI alongside STI in regional innovation. Finally, there is a Discussion and Conclusions section.

2. What is STI-type innovation and what is DUI?

The Science–Technology–Innovation (STI) approach might be referred to as the classic, top-down, internal, research and innovation (R&I) model first practised in large corporate laboratories like GE and AT&T *transformed* into an externalised model of university laboratory research translated into technological innovation through 'academic entrepreneurship'. It is the source of start-up and spin-out SMEs in high-tech clusters such as Silicon Valley and Cambridge, Massachusetts. As such, it has been an innovation model, pursued with much rhetoric, investment and variable results throughout the world of regional and national economic development. It is sometimes characterised in terms of a 'patenting – seed/angel/venture fund – incubator' model of new business growth. It thrives in economic boom times when venture capital is abundant but withers in economic downturns when risk capital is scarce. The approach is inclined to be *Linear* with some interactivity among science, finance and entrepreneurship (although the finance element often drives out the scientific founder element due to the perceived weak business management skills of the latter). It is *Technology-push* in inspiration. The approach is highly *Specialist*, taking often extremely advanced scientific findings (single molecule or function) to a hoped-for exit on the relevant market. Accordingly, it is *Exclusive*, being advanced, protected and proprietorial in terms of knowledge. This is even though patenting and publication nevertheless render such knowledge to a large extent *Explicit/Codified* and finally, because of codification it is knowledge that is, in principle, *Global* in its reach and accessibility, i.e. anyone with the right skill-set can, in principle, exploit it.

This contrasts markedly with the Doing–Using–Interacting (DUI) approach to innovation. This is not immediate exploitation of laboratory bench knowledge, although some such knowledge may lie behind the current state-of-the-art or even contribute to its furtherance. DUI involves knowledge recombination among diverse knowledge and practice sets. Accordingly, it is fundamentally *Interactive* among firms and/or intermediaries characterised by 'related variety' in the first instance. However, research shows that such is the potential of Schumpeterian knowledge recombination that many innovations integrate sectorally very different firm or institutional knowledge-sets. One only has to think of the Wright brothers' first flight, the plane for which embodied boat propellers, kites, bicycle wheels and chains *inter alia*. In this respect, DUI is *Practice-driven*. Accordingly, DUI is *Diversified* in that it thrives on cross-fertilisation or cross-pollination of ideas and practices from different fields, for example the intelligent textiles for stay-clean car seats that inspired the innovation of bacteria-free medical uniforms. This means DUI is *Inclusive* to firms that have the needed information about a shared innovation possibility provided demonstration effort is made (e.g. by a Regional Innovation and Development Agency – RIDA) through presentations, roadshows or living laboratory-based 'innovation theatre'. The entailed knowledge for DUI is thus *Implicit* rather than codified, and *Regional/Local* rather than globally available. Later in the paper, designs of evolving DUI regional innovation systems (RIS) are delineated to demonstrate both the specific characteristics these have but also showing how they are open to STI involvement where desirable and appropriate.[2]

A peer-reviewer of this chapter asks why the distinction is presented as sharply distinct while most innovation systems are a mixture of the two. This belies a rather naive view of scientific method, which is to make clear conjectures then test them against reality. Reality may be messier than conceptual frameworks. However, in this case the distinctions between the two modes are more than justified. They are indeed borne out as separately 'framed' types and ways of utilising knowledge by the incumbents represented in Figure 7.2. A similar answer attends peer-reviewer question two, namely why is STI specialised but DUI diversified. There is a conceptual 'system' and a real 'system'. Nevertheless, by and large science proceeds by becoming more and more specialised down to the sub-atomic or molecular level while DUI tends to add value through a kind of 'bricolage'. The reviewer goes on to muse that both specialisation and diversification might occur in both with positive effects on innovation performance. This is true but it may likely be as much sequential as simultaneous where a diversified 'breakthrough' occurs. (E.g. the Wright brothers' bicycle wheels, chains, box-kites and boat propellers in their workshop eventuating in specialisation in refining and tailoring such parts. But later, other variety gets introduced for innovation such as turbines or 'fly-by-wire' from other engineering fields.) Finally, it is suggested DUI's openness lends itself to a 'spaceless playground' of global interactivity. However, economic geography teaches us that knowledge often doesn't travel far due to tacitness or even communities of practice and embeddedness effects. So we retain a notion of 'friction-of-distance' in our dualistic – but potentially interactive – conceptual system. Studies of this include Isaksen and Nilsson (2013); Grillitsch and Trippl (2014) and Njøs *et al.* (2014).

3. System failure from weak purposive and communicative action

We begin here with an analysis of three main kinds of system failure that occur in typical regional innovation system (RIS) set-ups. The first of these occurs because the 'system' is not a system. This means three things: first, the issue of 'nodality', second, the issue of 'connectivity' and third, the issue of 'lock-in'. In the first of these, the set-up lacks 'nodality' or the key driver organisation/institutional arrangement to give *purpose* to innovative effort. This is described in complexity theory as being in the presence of the Lego problem. That is, a person may be surrounded with all the different shapes, sizes and functionalities of Lego bricks, but without a definite purpose for such infinite variety, no design idea can exist for implementation as an innovation. Accordingly, the Lego problem, or put differently, the problem of social action, is first to identify its *purpose*, or 'purposive action' for innovation. This means injunctions for persons, firms, organisations or regions to 'be innovative' are close to meaningless without a clear purpose. This problem is exacerbated when the dominant model underpinning the injunction is STI. The 'nodality' is usually expected to be provided by the regional university, which, even if its officers and staff are 'on message', usually lacks the capacity or authority to lead regional innovation in the STI-driven way. This may be because it also lacks 'innovation assets' meaning its best research knowledge lacks 'fit' with the regional economy or the knowledge is not yet exploitable for commercial purposes, or it simply lacks the distinction or purposiveness to attract innovators.

A second absence in regions with innovation system failure is the result of a failure of communication or, to maintain the action perspective, lack of a theory of communicative action. This is a failure of processes of 'discursive rationality', meaning reasoned arguments that may lead to regional policy consensus even where, as is likely, such consensus is 'second-best' and loved by no-one but tolerated by everyone. This is often referred to as the 'networking' problem and no would-be RIS can be so without the system connectivity that rests upon modern, open, transparent networking propensities and practices. In parenthesis, 'networks' may exist in a region but they can be exclusive, closed and uncommunicative – especially where 'private languages', including STI private languages, prevail. Adopting a DUI model of innovation can mean such exclusivity disappears, especially where 'resource conditionality', meaning control of innovation funding processes, requires that, for example, STI revenue is earned by meeting business norms of being an efficient and effective contractor to a firm or firms. In RIS contexts, resources should broadly support purposive innovation not basic science.

The third source of system failure in would-be RIS set-ups is also highlighted in complexity theory as the problem of too little variety. Many regions are not only dependent on an 'industrial monoculture', they find they are 'locked-in' to that monoculture by both acts of omission and commission by higher authorities. Acts of omission occur when central government decision-makers refuse, especially, STI infrastructural investments that could help diversify the regional economy using a 'probable white elephant' discourse. Accordingly, locked-in monocultures lose any possibility of implementing STI-type innovation even if a 'spinoff in the desert' occurs unless it too reinforces the monoculture. The acts of commission occur when the same central authorities divert attention and possible investment (e.g. FDI), towards the region in precisely the inherited monoculture thus reinforcing the lock-in that regional stakeholders may wish to escape.

Complexity theory sees this as the problem of 'stasis of low numbers', meaning that where a monoculture has low or no industrial diversity with which to easily interact, no innovation can occur and lock-in retains its deadening grip (Frenken 2006). By contrast, the more evolutionary insight is that where a region has a number of points of economic energy or 'clusters'[3] interaction among them will naturally occur and from the 'interaction at interfaces' novel ideas and potential innovations may also occur. It is the increasing richness rather than monocultural isolation of the economic web that gives birth to innovation and growth. Hence 'specialisation' ('smart' or otherwise) is not a good recipe for regional growth. So, the extreme opposite scenario – of stasis and decline – is summed up in characteristics of low 'nodality' or purposelessness, absent or closed networks from which only monocultural (or 'stasis of low numbers') reinforcing of lock-in will ensue and insufficient stimulation of regional variety underlies the basic condition of regional innovation system failure.

4. New modular vision of regional innovation

This is a section that problematises 'knowledge spillovers', which tend to be treated as a feature of normally functioning markets rather than occasional triumphs by firms over market failure. Much of the argument about recombinant innovation in this chapter has pointed to the importance of open discourse in preference to cognitive dissonance. There is a huge literature on the failure of firms to innovate because of dissonance within their own corporate walls. In the externalised world of the RIS, which will have inter-regional and international connectivity too, the problem is magnified. However RIS set-ups offer possibilities, explored below, for significantly minimising such 'failures to innovate'. The core issue is how to stimulate knowledge spillovers in a facilitative, non-imposing, hierarchical way. A strong candidate solution that involves recognition that innovation involves Schumpeterian recombination of knowledge was described by CEO Andy Grove for Intel, the pioneer ICT firm that systematically realised it as 'modular assembly.'[4] This model of 'purposive action' was since copied in most manufacturing and services industries but it has made effectively no entry on to the radar of any policy community in the world – with the exception of a tiny minority involved in regional innovation, some of which feature in the following section. In the policy sphere, this means thinking of sectors as embodying modules that must be integrated to accelerate regional innovation. This modular approach is increasingly perceived to be the way forward for regional innovation policy. It overcomes the development blockage of sectoral specialisation in 'silos' by rotating recombinative interactions from the vertical into the horizontal (interaction at industry interfaces) to enhance Schumpeterian 'recombinative' innovation (Blackwell *et al.* 2010).

Translating Intel practice into policy practice might be thought simplistic and it has to be said the model is not without its faults. One of these, which *appears* to be corrective of the evolutionary economic geography advocacy of *proximity* as perhaps the key locational advantage for firms, whether SMEs in clusters or MNCs to appropriately talented labour pools, is that Intel was criticised for being slow in delivering chips to customers. Both Apple and Google, located on Intel's doorstep in Cupertino and Palo Alto, respectively, experienced this. So much so that although Apple continued to source from Intel for desktop PCs, it was Taiwanese suppliers that met its exacting standards for smartphone chip delivery. Google had to wake Intel up by getting it to optimise its chip architecture to meet Android platform requirements. Interestingly, now Google has entered the smartphone market under its own name, its products are badge-engineered by Taiwanese firm Asus. Finally, the reason this cautionary tale about the possibly unrealised advantage of *spatial* proximity strengthens the evolutionary perspective is that it has a sophisticated analysis of proximity of the *relational* or non-spatially constrained kind. Thus good inter-firm, even if inter-continental, relations such as those found in successful global innovation networks (GINs) can clearly trump geographical propinquity.[5]

Accordingly, the emergent DUI vision for the region involves the following:

- Evolving a more dynamic, sustainable and innovative region – an admirably concise 'key vision statement' – by
- Increasing openness to innovation at interfaces between innovation and entrepreneurship, by
- Implementation of new innovative content activities, e.g. a diverse food, construction or tourism offer (not simply 'mass consumption', 'mass housing' or 'sun and beach'), by
- Integration of, for example, healthcare, renewable energy, 'connectivity' and new 'creativity' (innovation by interactions among culture, heritage, ICT and performance resources) with economic processes.

This approach receives some stimulation from the EU's regional economic development instrument – Regional Innovation Strategy: version 3 (RIS3) by which member regions access regional aid (FEDER/ERDF). However the EU emphasis on 'smart specialisation' is typically backgrounded to allow regional innovation strategies to evolve a more thoroughgoing methodology, based on demonstration, learning, exploring, modularising and creating innovative products, processes and methodological/organisational forms. Accordingly, the preferred approach means absorbing suitable S&T knowledge to facilitate working out and working through a new DUI system model for regional innovation. Hence DUI by no means 'substitutes for' STI, the two are, as far as possible complementary; but as we shall see, certain status concessions and modes of discourse have to occur for this compatibility between knowledges to be found.[6]

In the policy context, learning from the weaknesses as well as strengths of innovation by modularisation involves a broad stakeholder engagement that allows preferences to be boiled down and prioritised. While 'specialisationist' STI in pursuit of, for example, a single molecule is by definition somewhat exclusive knowledge, an innovation context – especially an RIS – can legitimately require that its likely relevance and applicability in DUI practice be discussed purposively. One of the unmentioned weaknesses of STI is a tendency for its knowledge approach to be privileged, if not reified, by its practitioners and audience in equal measure. However, a more hard-headed knowledge appreciation process is needed where the purpose is to achieve innovation by means of open and transparent interaction within a functioning RIS. Accordingly, deliberation upon the possible interfaces between STI and DUI is important, as is inter-industry DUI interaction, both with a view to reducing cognitive dissonance. Modules of knowledge (and artifacts) may subsequently be assembled and thereafter be in a position to be explored, validated (examined), or exploited commercially as 'new combinations' (or recombinations) of knowledge that constitute innovation. Clearly, modularisation goes hand in hand with a project focus for the facilitation of such 'innovation at interfaces'. Accordingly, the important, unifying 'vision statement' for a regional innovation strategy will likely occur at the end of the deliberative process rather than at the beginning, where it can be myopic, constraining and excluding, as much as giving focus to a strategic exercise.

5. Actually existing DUI embracing policy models

Here, we drill down into some emergent exemplars of DUI-friendly RIS-building, starting with the climatically agreeable but monoculturally locked-in Portuguese Algarve region (Guerrero *et al.* 2013). As a case in point of 'specialisation syndrome' some coastal or mountain regions suffer from too much specialisation – in tourism, particularly for coastal regions like the Algarve, the 'sun and beach' specialism – as perceived by national government. Having said that, such regions are often highly entrepreneurial where entrepreneurs are capable of swift adaptation. So, if a niche opportunity presents itself, entrepreneurs are not slow in coming forward to make money. Notice also that local licensing can facilitate this process. There are municipal licenses and licenses for economic activity, so some advantage may accrue from regions being decentralised in terms of authority. This may even be advantageous in attracting 'prestigious' FDI (foreign direct investment) projects complementary to national priorities. But national governments may steer specialised FDI to the appropriately specialised region, too. Accordingly, specialised regions may suffer from 'lock-in', meaning the region is specialised, adaptable, but not particularly 'smart' because of old perceptions of its 'role' in the national economy. What the specialised region needs, in consequence of this character, is 'Smart Diversification'. Regions' past achievements will have moved them up the learning curve and may include: experience in managing EU Structural Funds Operational Programmes; a specific record of managing MLG (multi-level governance) innovation initiatives; the achievement of (DUI) results in raising innovative behaviour of indigenous firms; assisting traditional firms to learn about ICT and adaptations; and experience with policy decentralisation to municipalities. Now the challenge is to raise the learning and monitoring practice in the region under, for example, the EU's RIS3 programme.

An example of this is found in the Algarve region's evolving effort to establish a DUI innovation system model for that over-specialised touristic region. Part of the vision is to establish a framework for undertaking DUI innovation support governance, to be translated into clear strategic goals and objectives. The region's governance and monitoring system is the subject of analytical design in the Guerrero/Pinto report.[7] This early attempt at a DUI innovation governance model for the Algarve region revealed (Figure 7.1) an actor-centred governance model with good stakeholder engagement mechanisms which was to be further augmented with a Communication Strategy. By 2013 the demands from EU DGs for European regions to evolve *Regional Innovation Strategies* to be eligible for regional development (ERDF/FEDER) funds

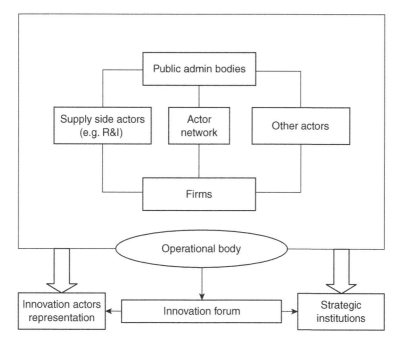

Figure 7.1   Regional innovation governance model for the Algarve, 2007

Source: Adapted from Guerrero *et al.* (2013)

would cause a *rapid* evolution in thinking, for the Algarve and elsewhere, about the appropriate governance and delivery model. In this, as can be seen (Figure 7.2), the emphasis on *innovation* as the primary mechanism for securing regional economic development meant the regional support function for, in particular, DUI innovation became of equivalence to the STI approach.

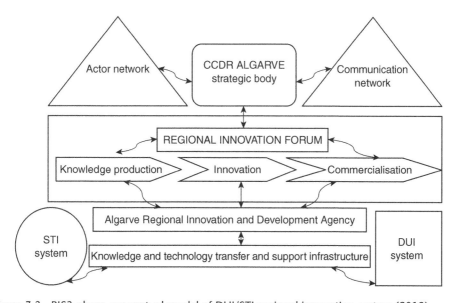

Figure 7.2   RIS3 phase conceptual model of DUI/STI regional innovation system (2013)

Source: Author's interpretation of Centro CCDR's RIS model

In parenthesis, it would be expected that highlighting DUI would produce more measurable innovation success than an exclusive reliance upon a thin infrastructure of STI institutions and assets had in the past. That is not to say that STI was to be downgraded in support or policies but rather DUI was to be introduced and stimulated as a more down-to-earth, but nevertheless valuable, mode of securing regional innovation. The newer, evolved regional innovation governance model with functional spaces for both DUI and STI approaches to innovation is shown in Figure 7.2.

This demonstrates three key 'innovation governance discoveries'. First *innovation* is now both highlighted and placed at centre stage in the governance model. It is further supported by a Regional Innovation and Development Agency (RIDA) to manage the DUI/STI project assessment and overall management function, to facilitate the 'learning from your industry' process annually, and to arrange 'innovation theatre' opportunities in living lab-type settings. Previously, as Figure 7.1 shows, all of this was outside the main ambit of the policy development arena. Second, the innovation support infrastructure is bi-directional, linking to the STI knowledge base where appropriate and available but also aligning with the more ubiquitous DUI knowledge base in the quest for more practical innovation opportunities. Third, the strategic governance body has taken on responsibility for ensuring openness and transparency towards the public by installing a Communication network function, complementing the previously included Actor network policy input function.

5.1 Centro Region's STI/DUI hybrid RIS model

The new EU regional economic development measure that embeds funding in the successful submission of a Regional Innovation Strategy (RIS3) to qualify for EU regional aid (ERDF/FEDER) has released highly DUI-dependent, over-specialised and 'locked-in' regions like the Algarve to think innovatively in policy terms. As we have seen, this has meant evolving mechanisms to enhance 'transversality' across industry boundaries and bring regional innovation from the edge to the heart of the regional economic development process by proposing a regional innovation agency (ARIDA) to lead policy governance. But what happens in regions where, while DUI has been something of a policy 'orphan', it has long been practised in a context where STI has been highlighted as the key regional economic and innovation development need? To that end, Portugal's Centro region exemplifies some of the opportunities for hybrid regional innovation system evolution by virtue of its RIS3 process.

Space does not allow for more than a sketch of how transversality among STI and DUI across the boundaries of a biotechnology, a construction and a forestry cluster are planned to facilitate such hybrid innovation strategy. In an emergent Centro field, biotechnology, BIOCANT has been a successful and fast-growing research entity (including businesses, among them FDI, a 24-firm incubator, and venture capital) that now 'translates' its findings into commercial innovations in healthcare and other biotechnology-related fields. Thus stem cells, microbial biotechnology and computational biology are BIOCANT research strengths being applied experimentally to biomaterials and agro-forestry (biofungicides; oenobiotechnology) as well as ICT diagnostics in human healthcare. One of BIOCANT's fields of expertise is in the analysis of the DNA of biofungicides, work that began in relation to biofungicidal issues in human healthcare. However, innovation opportunities arose in relation to the transfer of such biotechnological knowledge from human to agro-food and, particularly, agro-arboreal applications.

A specific development project in Centro's RIS3 programme funding bids involves the two other Centro clusters, mentioned earlier, one of which, HABITAT, is the 115-member house construction cluster within which are many timber-utilising firms. One success of this cluster has been the production of low-cost dwellings for less-developed countries, including refugee camps and slum-upgrading schemes (e.g. in Angola, Mozambique and Kurdish Iraq). In such countries high humidity causes rot to occur in native softwoods commonly used in the Centro cluster. Biotechnology knowledge from BIOCANT shows this can be controlled by the application of biofungicides to the growing tree/live timber. However, a delivery mechanism is necessary and this can be supplied from nanotechnology, or more specifically, bionanotechnology. Such a knowledge centre, capable of delivering the requisite molecule to the living tree organism, exists at Bragancia in the neighbouring Norte region. Such a partnership, crossing regional boundaries from laboratory bench biotechnology and nanotechnology (STI) to the wooden dwelling construction and furniture industries (DUI), utilising Centro regional forest products, clearly captures platform/hub integration of diverse knowledge and innovation modes at knowledge and industry interfaces.

Instead of an external regional innovation agency, Centro's RIS model builds on its past (EU and central government) match-funded investments in STI infrastructures, including new universities, Technopoles and clusters, to lead programme bids for funding its regional innovation strategy (Figure 7.3). This occurs under the regional council's (CCDR) leadership but, as with Portugal's other regions, is eventually subsumed in the national RIS3 strategy. Frequently, such asymmetric power relations would be expected to lead to conflict or stasis as local versus national developmental tensions would be worked through or become blockages to progress. However, Centro's intelligent solution to this has been consciously to engage large numbers of stakeholder interests (some 300 at least) in a process of 'socio-economic challenge' identification. Four of these – sustainable industrial solutions; endogenous resource efficiency; quality of life; and territorial (especially rural) innovation – have been adopted. Unlike the national institutional proclivity for prioritising sectors, Centro's model is deliberately issue focused and cross sectoral, as we have seen. Accordingly, tensions such as those arising from national insensitivity to local concerns seem potentially to be defused in large measure. Inspection of Figure 7.3 also shows STI and DUI to be more closely integrated in the strategising process than in the Algarve,

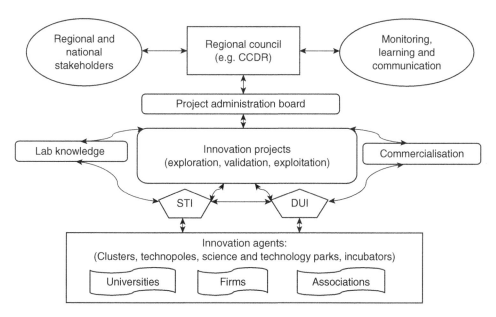

Figure 7.3   Centro's STI/DUI hybrid regional innovation system

Source: Author's interpretation of Centro CCDR's RIS model

but a project-based approach to be equally favoured and with firms, universities and business associations in the same policy-box for progressing projects to fruition.

5.2 Skåne: a further example of DUI-friendly regional innovation system architecture

The Skåne region in Sweden has DUI and STI as conscious regional innovation development mechanisms. Its system consists (Figure 7.4) of a regional innovation forum (regime) known as the 'Sounding Board', bringing together key regional and national representative stakeholders and their priorities for developing the regional economy (paradigm). The Sounding Board searches for innovation opportunities in the 'White Spaces'. Here, different sectoral or institutional interests come together to explore new innovation opportunities and means for focusing these. In Figure 7.4, this regional innovation 'regime' interacts with the regional 'paradigm' of industry, mostly SMEs, some clusters, large firms (e.g. (formerly) Astra Zeneca in life sciences or Ericsson in ICT) and public bodies (e.g. healthcare). Such interactions led to the identification of two cross-sector/cluster strategic innovation platforms that are pursuing, with project subsidy support, innovations in White Space fields of 'Sustainable Cities', on the one hand, and 'Personal Healthcare', on the other. Feedback from 'paradigm' to 'regime' then informs further refinement of policies.

Although STI-inflected innovation efforts are clearly part of this process, much of the rest is DUI such as the packaging cluster (Packbridge) working with the digital media cluster (Media Evolution) to evolve supermarket product-finding apps on smartphones. Similarly, Packbridge works on sustainability with the Food Academy cluster both to customise organic SME retail packaging and to prevent bioplastic liquid seepage in containers produced from regionally grown potato starch. Clearly each innovation quest uses knowledge derived ultimately from STI but the innovation ideas can equally be seen to be quite practical in a DUI sense.

6. DUI policy framing

We have seen how both STI *disadvantaged* and relatively STI advantaged regions now also seek to develop the productive, DUI character of their evolving innovation profiles. This involves a process not of 'picking winners' but 'learning from your own industry' what it thinks it needs for future innovation. As will be seen, some regions have already embarked on this process with 'Sounding Boards' or 'Thematic Issues' 'labs' bringing together entrepreneurs and associations in the form of 'detailed working groups' as requested, for instance, in background RIS3 documentation. In this way, a bottom-up process of Niche Identification has already been embarked upon. The question is: What is the next step? How to engage in Niche Management or even 'Strategic Niche Management'?[8]

6.1 Strategic Niche Management

This is really the new task for DUI and STI regions throughout Europe and, indeed, the world. There are a number of steps already worked out in the 'niche management' literature:

- Overcome 'critical mass' (which is mainly a nuclear engineering 'metaphor') by mixing sectoral affiliation (if any) of firms and/or their associations. As a basis for this new approach, a useful preliminary aim is to help form 'one single Regional Business Association' as occurred in the Algarve.

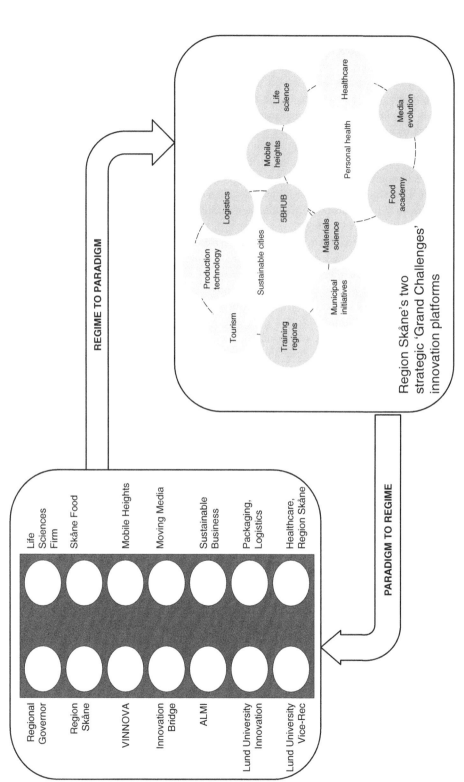

Figure 7.4 Regional innovation: DUI/STI 'Sounding Board' regime and 'transversality' paradigm

Source: Region Skåne – author's adaptation

- This can then more firmly host the 'Thematic Issues' around which panels of industry representatives and/or entrepreneurs will focus, bringing together opportunities for niche management at industry interfaces with, subsequently, entrepreneurial discovery and exploitation.[9]
- 'Learning from your industry' means the region paying serious attention to the considerations and conclusions of such panels regarding 'niche opportunities' for exploitation from knowledge recombination discussions.
- The region (through its Innovation and/or Development Agency) must then be 'catalytic' in organising 'innovation theatre' in the form of demonstrations, roadshows and exhibitions across the community of regional entrepreneurs.
- This involves: first, showing *existing* innovations from inside or outside the region, including abroad, that may be 'preadapted' (transferable) modules or whole solutions for re-use in a new problem or industry context.
- Second, showing potential innovations that may have niche value across interfaces and rests on bringing together 'knowledge modules' that are candidates for niche-based innovation.
- Third, the region must then 'orchestrate' contests in which competition for innovation subsidies and support occurs among the 'preadapted' and 'White Space' fields. Winners are rewarded with funded support projects (in which there must be substantial private as well as public investment funding).
- Fourth, these 'concept contests' will mainly be project based, (i) early stage and exploratory, (ii) mid-stage and examinatory ('validation'), and (iii) final stage and exploitative in nature and status, (three types of award per 'concept contest') with the aim always being to produce innovative outcomes.
- Finally, regions must establish a monitoring, learning and communication system to refine understanding and improvement upon successful practice. In this way, regional innovation strategy can evolve over time.

Accordingly, it is clear that both innovation-led and knowledge-based development priorities lie at the heart of DUI regional innovation (not excluding STI) ambitions and strategic process aspirations. However, crucially, this involves maintaining harmonious relations with the region's influential stakeholders. For example, municipalities may agree to more strategic thinking because 'innovation' matters are usually accepted as regional fiefdoms. This marks recognition that R&I cannot satisfactorily be done at local level. Regarding 'niche identification', especially in fields with embryonic regional innovation status, the conventional view of what constitutes 'critical mass' hardly applies. The conventional view is perceived as primarily sectoral yet lacking any definition of what the term actually means.[10] Thus, in line with its aim of de-specialisation for the regional economy by seeking 'related variety' opportunities, core SME groups in, for example ICT would be augmented by user-driven SMEs and other firms in, for instance, tourism, agro-food, bio-marine, healthcare or renewable energy to seek to broaden regional 'critical mass', innovation base, knowledge 'transversality' and application. The final stage of this analysis is to show how regions can implement DUI and DUI/STI interactive innovation strategies. These involve the two types of innovation under discussion – Preadaptive and White Spaces – and, within each, a project focus to expenditure recognising three possible types of project: knowledge exploration (leaning towards STI application); examination or 'validation' (DUI/STI hybrid); and exploitation (leaning towards DUI). In general, these are referred to here as Business Intervention Models (BIMs). These are informed by evolutionary complexity theory (ECT) notions, notably preadaptive innovation (otherwise *exaptive* as utilised in evolutionary biology).[11]

7 DUI policy recommendations

7.1 Preadaptive innovation: Business Intervention Models (BIMs)

These require innovation theatre in the form of 'fashion shows' where potential 'attractors' may be drawn together to discuss applications (i.e. both transferring and changing a pre-existing innovation). Such industry and firm 'attractors' can include both 'natural attractors' who are near to predictable, coming from neighbouring industries in the technical sense, and 'strange attractors' coming from largely unconnected industries. In 'living lab' type *innovation theatre* settings attractors can meet and absorb knowledge spillovers from sectoral 'others'. These settings should include stages (theatre style) or 'living labs' with 'red thread' narratives, 'storytelling' discourses and dramaturgies, as practised in Finland's 'Regional Platform Development Methodology' (Melkas and Uotila 2013). Fundamentally, firms in one industry or cluster are presented with accounts of useful innovations developed in a different industry. If this process sparks off some inspiration to adapt an innovation to a new field, firms begin 'conversations'. These may be brokered by a third party from the RIDA to provide 'neutral territory' and 'trusted third-party' facilitation, which also serve learning and policy co-creation purposes from an 'innovation platform' point of view.

7.2 Reverse innovation

There may also be 'reverse innovation' BIMs engaged in retro-fitting existing innovation more affordably or accessibly. A progenitor is General Electric's (GE) retro-fitting of medical scanning machines for LDC patients – targeting Prahalad's 'bottom of the pyramid' markets – in BRICs and elsewhere.[12] In the GE case this involved recognition that the world market for its Optima CT Scanners was becoming saturated as most hospitals had often purchased many of the desired models. Accordingly, the firm designed a hand-held scanner integrated with a smartphone. The imaging and data are relayed to a control centre in a host country for analysis and swiftly relayed to the clinician. The difference in price was from at least $1 million for a conventional scanner to approximately $1,000 for the smartphone-enabled hand scanner. So successful has the retro-innovation been that it is regularly deployed by police and paramedics at accident sites in GE's US homebase.

7.3 User-driven innovation

Here preadaptive innovation can occur in supply chains depending upon the shift from global production networks (GPNs) to global innovation networks (GINs). Such shifts must be understood by RIDA or equivalent intermediaries working with and learning from cluster expertise in technological and business model transitions occurring worldwide. One such shift negatively affecting former ICT leaders like Nokia, BlackBerry, Motorola and Sony Ericsson is that they pursued endogenous systems applications long after Asian competitors like Samsung, HTC and Huawei were pursuing Apple into the 'smartphone market'. The demise of Sony Ericsson and the sale of Nokia mobile telephony interests to Microsoft signify the price of not having third-party monitoring of the GIN for the kind of user-driven requirements that, for example, contemporary smartphone markets regularly display.

7.4 'White Spaces' innovation: learning from your industry

If the former three points refer mainly to 'preadaptive innovation', the next three refer mainly to 'White Spaces' adjacent possible explorations. We may refer to notion of 'Learning from your

Industry' in a context of 'From Producer Innovation to User and Open Collaborative Innovation' (Baldwin and Von Hippel 2009). Innovation development, production, distribution and consumption networks can be built up horizontally – with actors consisting only of innovation users. Some open source software projects are illustrative of such networks, and examples can be found in the case of physical products as well. It may be concluded that conditions favourable to horizontal user innovation networks are often present in the economy. In these circumstances, the BIM demands that the RIDA keeps a knowledge management system (KMS) of its large and SME 'system integrator' firms (see below). Each year all are asked what solutions they need and these become the regional system's initial innovation market for 'exploration,' 'validation' and 'exploitation' innovation projects. Thus, the 'system' learns through the RIDA of the innovation needs and functioning or projected innovation projects in demand from specific types of large firm users, and the knowledge capabilities of system integrators, regional start-ups and research laboratories. In this way, existing path dependences are exploited and renewed with the possibility that new paths may open up in consequence. The transversality in this process is managed by face-to-face meetings, presentations and adjudications before exploration or examination projects are earmarked for appropriate 'attractors'.

7.5 Regional system–integrator knowledge

This is the corollary of 'learning from your industry' what it needs, in that the region learns from its industry what innovations it can supply. Among suppliers of software and systems-based services of the kind in demand from users in increasingly automated industries such as mining, metallurgy, forest products, energy, and so on, are firms that act as 'hub' or 'pivotal' innovative systems-integrator firms. In such a knowledge distribution system, knowledge from regional research and system integrators is presented to regional client firms individually or in partnership with one or two others. Theoretically, this is a process involving 'learning about confidentiality', aiming to move gradually towards more 'open kimono' postures on the part of firms that are even today hyper-secretive. Eventually, a collective or sub-group 'showcasing' business model may be designed by the RIDA or equivalent but a major trust-building process has first to be implemented. This filters into customer minds new business practices, new technical solutions, new opportunities for exploring 'White Spaces' according to those who occupy positions as the 'internal radar' of global innovation networks (GINs). These are firms seeing, thinking about, understanding and proposing to move, if partners can be found, into new strategic niches. Here the role of innovation broker of solutions to final users in and beyond the region is also crucial – as 'orchestrator' of shared interests and relatedness 'storyteller'.

7.6 Demand-driven innovation: exploratory projects

These are especially important for 'White Spaces' and Grand Challenges (e.g. Climate Change, Ageing Demography, Personalised Healthcare). They are often, accordingly, funded across cluster interfaces evolving as a collaborative business model where 'exploratory' innovation projects may later mutate into 'exploitative' ones. New Tools for Health (NTH) is a Swedish cluster initiative in East Gotland that does this. It seeks to deliver health and social care in a distributed, domestic and personalised way, a 'White Space' issue for healthcare everywhere (e.g. sometimes linked to 'Ambient Assisted Living'). Healthcare was typically wedded to a vertical 'separation of powers' service delivery model until government statements on demographics, rising costs and declining public budgets shook its foundations. NTH commissions solutions through innovation projects between hospitals, healthcare research and existing or start-up SMEs while building relational capital with large, external firms with some relevant competence areas. However, so new is this mission that relatively few large-scale personalised healthcare providers of the kind required are to be found anywhere. Accordingly, experimentation through exploratory projects, building alliances, absorbing experience and articulating hitherto unconceived innovation demands are the drivers of this initiative.

8. Discussion and conclusions

In the preamble, this contribution spoke of certain problems of knowledge transfer and knowledge spillovers implied in the standard model of how this tends to occur in contemporary business, particularly among firms and between them and knowledge sources, notably universities. Research now shows that direct, comprehensible transfer from laboratory bench to production line across the university-to-firm interface is a rarity indeed. An exception for the majority of firms might be where the firm founder is also the discovering scientist. But even there, if venture capital is involved in fuelling the start-up it is often the case that the financier replaces the scientist with a proper business manager. In passing, this is a perfect illustration of Schumpeter's differentiation of the inventor/innovator, on the one hand, and the entrepreneur, with its separate commerce and finance business skills-set, on the other.[13] Thus knowledge spillovers may, in theory, be open because composed of codified knowledge in STI fields but they are actually very far from unproblematic.

Accordingly, this chapter opened up the debate, initiated by Jensen *et al.* (2007) regarding the importance of other kinds of knowledge for innovation than STI, namely DUI. It now seems that was a very prescient argument whereby most innovation (in any case mostly incremental, (Lundvall 1992)) is not directly STI in nature but rather DUI. However, those founders of the DUI perspective rather left it at that, having come up with the concept. The challenge, now being picked up, is to conceptualise, research and formalise the system modes by which, if true, DUI is actually operationalised in its practice. Hence the interest in this chapter in exploring extant DUI regional innovation systems. Regional, because knowledge transfer in this case being tacit rather than codified in patents or journals, the likelihood is that much knowledge transfer and even spillovers would be local rather than global. The missing link in conceptual terms is supplied by evolutionary complexity theory (ECT) with its core innovation concepts of preadaptivity and adjacency as moves firms (and, conceivably, researchers) actually make in the creative step to reaching Schumpeterian knowledge recombinations that are at the heart of innovation. Innovation, here, being understood in terms of *commercialisation* of the knowledge newly recombined.

The chapter showed how, among other things, *modularisation* captures the way in which firms innovate when they bring in elements from outside, including across industry interfaces, to piece together with pre-existing and other extant elements from elsewhere the knowledge and artifactual components of the innovation to be commercialised. Some of this involves what may not start out as but may become 'general purpose technologies' (GPT) (Jovanovic and Rousseau 2005). The chapter also showed how because of the dark side of knowledge transfer – namely, when spillover opportunities are obscured or invisible – certain regional innovation agencies exemplified in the chapter establish mechanisms to facilitate key 'let there be light' moments of revelation. It was shown that these may occur when strategies in support of regional innovation are being established by setting up 'thematic issues' groups tasked with the responsibility of identifying future 'Grand Challenges', opportunities for 'strange attractors' (as they are known in ECT) to engage across sectoral boundaries, or to seek such opportunities as ways of breaking out of the 'lock-in' associated with past regional economic path dependence.

The chapter also demonstrated how innovation policy makers may stimulate 'modularisation' among clusters, single firms or other key innovation actors or users to facilitate 'emergence' of innovation platforms based on renewed exploitation of regional assets across industry interfaces. In the few cases thus far researched there appears to be no sense of opposition between STI and DUI modes of innovation interaction. Rather, in regions disadvantaged from an endogenous STI infrastructure, DUI may be a default position from which to start, if indeed promotion of innovation is understood to be the imperative it is according to numerous innovation support incentive schemes. Some such regions are best described as operating a hybrid regional innovation system with engagement from both STI and DUI in variable quantities. The pure STI region is, however, almost certainly a rarity. This chapter has sought, using an evolutionary economic geography perspective, to open up further opportunities for research into the ways most firms (which, of course, are not large corporations) actually conduct research and innovation (R&I) as distinct from presuming they all more or less conform to some variant of an often not very appropriate STI model of innovation alone.

Notes

1 Further detail on Skåne can be found in Cooke (2012).
2 For further explication of STI/DUI characteristics, see: Jensen *et al.* (2007).
3 This term is used by Kauffman (1995) to specify 'complex adaptive systems'.
4 Grove (1996). Other writers on modularisation include Henderson and Clark (1990) and Sturgeon (2002).
5 The Google, Intel, Apple interface issues are discussed in Cooke (2013).
6 This is valuably explored in Nooteboom *et al.* (2007).
7 Where STI benchmarking stresses R&D expenditures (especially private), employment in medium- to high-tech activities (manufacturing and services), EPO patents and public–private co-publications, DUI indicators may show increasingly technical product and process improvements, regional skills enhancements, SME endogenous innovation and innovation sales new to firm and market.
8 On 'Strategic' Niche Management in the renewable energy and broader sustainable economy fields, see, for example, Geels (2004, 2010).
9 The workings of this approach are shown in Melkas and Uotila (2013) Foresight and innovation: emergence and resilience of the cleantech cluster at Lahti, Finland, in P. Cooke (ed.) *Reframing Regional Development*, London, Routledge.
10 It is a dull repeat of Zeno's Paradox where the philosopher asked, without answer: 'How many bees make a swarm?' Nowadays it is 'How many firms make a cluster?'
11 For application in economics, see Dew, Sarasvathy and Venkataranam (2004).
12 On this, see Immelt, Govindarajan and Trimble (2009); Prahalad (2005).
13 This is explored carefully by Andersen (2011).

References

Andersen, E.S. (2011) Schumpeter and regional innovation, in P. Cooke *et al.* (eds.) *The Handbook of Regional Innovation & Growth*, Cheltenham, Edward Elgar.
Baldwin, C. and Von Hippel, E. (2009) Modelling a paradigm shift: from producer innovation to user and open collaborative innovation, Cambridge, MA, Working Paper 4764-09, MIT Sloan School of Management.
Blackwell, A, Wilson, L, Boulton, C. and Knell, J. (2010) *Creating Value across Boundaries: Maximising the Return from Interdisciplinary Innovation*, London, NESTA Research Report.
Cooke, P. (2012) *Complex Adaptive Innovation Systems*, London, Routledge.
Cooke, P. (2013) Qualitative analysis and comparison of firm and system incumbents in the new ICT global innovation network, *European Planning Studies*, 21, 9, 1323–1340.
Dew, N, Sarasvathy, S. and Venkataranam, S. (2004) The economic implications of exaptation, *Journal of Evolutionary Economics*, 14, 1, 69–82.

Frenken, K. (2006) *Innovation, Evolution & Complexity Theory*, Cheltenham, Edward Elgar.

Geels, F. (2004) From sectoral systems of innovation to socio-technical systems: insights about dynamics and change from sociology and institutional theory, *Research Policy*, 33, 897–920.

Geels, F. (2010) Ontologies, socio-technical transitions (to sustainability) and the multi-level perspective, *Research Policy*, 39, 495–510.

Grillitsch, M. and Trippl, M. (2014) Combining knowledge from different sources, channels and geographical scales, *European Planning Studies*. DOI:10.1080/09654313.2013.835793.

Grove, A. (1996) *Only the Paranoid Survive*, New York, Doubleday.

Guerrero, J., Pinto, H. *et al.* (2013) *RIS3 – Algarve 2014–2020: Research & Innovation Strategy for Smart Specialisation* (Version 0.2 – 30/4/2013), Faro, Algarve CCRD.

Henderson, R. and Clark, K. (1990) Architectural innovation: the reconfiguration of existing systems and the failure of established firms, *Administrative Science Quarterly*, 35, 9–30.

Immelt, J, Govindarajan, V. and Trimble, C. (2009) How GE is disrupting itself, *Harvard Business Review*, 85, 56–65.

Isaksen, I. and Nilsson, M. (2013) Combined innovation policy: linking scientific and practical knowledge in innovation systems, *European Planning Studies*, 21, 12, 1919–1936.

Jensen, M., Johnson B., Lorenz E. and Lundvall, B. (2007) Forms of knowledge and modes of innovation, *Research Policy*, 36, 680–693.

Jovanovic, B. and Rousseau, P. (2005) General purpose technologies in P. Aghion and S. Durlauf (eds), *Handbook of Economic Growth*, Amsterdam, Elsevier.

Kauffman, S. (1995) *At Home in the Universe*, Oxford, Oxford University Press.

Lundvall, B. (ed.) (1992) *National Systems of Innovation*, London, Frances Pinter.

Melkas, H. and Uotila, T. (2013) Foresight and innovation: emergence and resilience in the cleantech cluster at Lahti, Finland, in P. Cooke (ed.) *Reframing Regional Development*, London, Routledge.

Njøs, R, Jakobsen, S., Fosse, J. and Engelsen, C. (2014) Challenges to bridging discrepant knowledge bases: a case study of the Norwegian Centre for Offshore Wind Technology, *European Planning Studies*. DOI: org/10.1080/09654313.2013.843651.

Nooteboom, B., Van Haverbeke, W., Duysters, G., Gilsing, V. and van den Oord, A. (2007) Optimal cognitive distance and absorptive capacity, *Research Policy*, 36, 1016–1034.

Prahalad, C. (2005) *The Fortune at the Bottom of the Pyramid*, London, Pearson.

Schumpeter, J. (1939) *Business Cycles: A Theoretical, Historical and Statistical Analysis of the Capitalist Process*, New York, McGraw-Hill.

Sturgeon, T. (2002) Modular production networks: a new American model of industrial production, *Industrial & Corporate Change*, 11, 3 451–496.

8

Knowledge cumulability and path dependence in innovation persistence[1]

Francesco Crespi and Giuseppe Scellato

1. Introduction

The theoretical and empirical assessment of the determinants of firm-level innovation persistence in time has important implications for our understanding of knowledge production processes, long-run industry dynamics, as well as for the evaluation of the expected impacts of specific policy tools to sustain innovative activities. The theme of innovation persistence in recent years has attracted the interest of scholars along different research perspectives, ranging from the economics of knowledge, to the economics of organization and the economics of innovation (Malerba *et al.*, 1997; Cefis and Orsenigo, 2001; Peters, 2009; Antonelli *et al.*, 2012; Clausen and Pohjola, 2013). Indeed, the theoretical reasoning about firm-level persistence of innovation activities is deeply rooted in the Schumpeterian view of industry dynamics. In the Schumpeter Mark I regime, technological change follows a process of creative destruction in which innovation creates just temporary monopoly power, with new and innovative firms replacing exiting firms. On the contrary, according to the Schumpeter Mark II regime, technological change is the outcome of a gradual process of technological accumulation. In particular, the cumulativeness of knowledge and its tacit component contribute to generate entry barriers, economies of scale and 'success breeds success' dynamics, leading to higher persistence of innovation (Malerba and Orsenigo, 1995).

As will be discussed later in this chapter, the sources of persistence have been subsequently addressed along different perspectives, going beyond explanations that refer just to sectoral or technological regimes. In so doing, the study of firm-level innovation persistence over time has proven to be a good viewpoint to observe and interpret patterns of data that have implications for diverse areas of enquiry. First, the enquiry on the sources of innovation persistence clearly contributes to our understanding of the presence of persistent heterogeneity in firms' performances, in line with the legacy of studies building on the seminal contributions by Nelson (1991) and Dosi and Malerba (1996). Second, the topic of innovation persistence is strictly related to the literature that has addressed the complex relationship between market structures and innovation (Sutton, 1998; Gilbert, 2006; Aghion *et al.*, 2005). Third, the presence of persistent innovation patterns at the firm level can be interpreted as the result of the capability of firms to exploit dynamic capabilities to sustain competitive advantage as highlighted by management studies (Teece, 2007). In this context, the role of knowledge cumulativeness and the relevance of strategic decisions to leverage internal and external knowledge emerge as crucial in shaping path dependent dynamics of innovation persistence (Antonelli *et al.*, 2013b). Once again, this finding points to the centrality of the notion of path dependence in economic theory (David, 1997; Colombelli and von Tunzelmann, 2011). Finally, the investigation of the drivers of persistent innovation can be relevant for innovation policy studies, under the hypothesis that different types of policy instruments have a diverse likelihood to induce long lasting effects on firms' innovation incentives.

Recent contributions have highlighted how the correct identification of the types of *non-ergodic* processes through which firms persistently innovate is a non-trivial task and empirical results vary significantly according to the indicators adopted to measure innovation outcomes along time. However, there have been significant advancements in the empirical tools for the study of persistency. Such methods include the use of dynamic panel data models that allow to properly account for firm-specific unobservable heterogeneity and hence allowing the identification of true state persistence, depurating the data from spurious effect (Peters, 2009; Raymond *et al.*, 2010). Moreover, transition probability matrixes have been widely adopted to provide descriptive evidence on the dynamics of innovation persistence and its path dependent character (Antonelli *et al.*, 2013a).

The recognition that innovation is a highly differentiated phenomenon that is associated with diverse strategies of firms and characterized by remarkable industry and country specificities has led researchers to try to use an array of different innovation indicators. In this respect, the availability of survey data (e.g. the European Community Innovation Surveys – CIS) has opened up a great opportunity for detailed investigations of the variety of innovation processes. These sources of data have provided researchers with new information on the innovative efforts (including but not limited to R&D investment) of firms and the diverse strategies that lead to the introduction of new products, new processes and new organizational behaviours (Archibugi and Pianta, 1996).

Available firm-level evidence suggests that the actual degree of innovation persistence varies according to the indicator adopted (Duguet and Monjon, 2004): while the works that have used patents as indicators suggest that persistence is weak, exhibiting strong values only in the case of top patentees, empirical analyses based on survey data found stronger evidence of innovation persistence, particularly for product innovation. Furthermore, the complementarities among different types of innovation activities (i.e. product or process innovation) appear to be crucial in shaping different patterns of persistence (Clausen and Pohjola, 2013; Antonelli *et al.*, 2012), including the case of organizational innovation (Le Bas *et al.*, 2011; Latham and Le Bas, 2006).

The objective of this chapter is to provide a critical overview of both the extant evidence on innovation persistence and the underlying theoretical frameworks that can provide guidance on the identification of the actual determinants of such persistence. In particular, the paper shows that the largest part of the empirical contributions reviewed provides evidence in favour of the presence of path dependent persistency patterns in innovation efforts at the firm level. Such evidence is interpreted within a theoretical framework based on the two fundamental concepts of internal and external knowledge cumulability and dynamic capabilities, which allow us to interpret the path dependent character of innovation persistence. The overall evidence on innovation persistence and the analysis on how such persistence is related to knowledge properties are discussed in terms of implications for innovation and technology policies.[2]

The reminder of the chapter is organized as follows. Section two discusses the main theoretical explanations for innovation persistence. In section three we discuss the specific link between innovation persistence, knowledge cumulativeness and path dependence. Section four is dedicated to a review of recent econometric studies on the topic. Finally, in section five we draw the main conclusions and policy implications, and highlight areas of research in this specific field that seem to deserve further investigations.

2. The standard economics of innovation persistence

The seminal contribution by Arrow (1962) addressed the incentives to innovate of a monopolist. Because of the presence of a 'replacement effect', a monopolist gains less from innovating than does a competitive firm which converts a formerly competitive market into a monopoly through innovation. This approach based on the 'replacement effect' would predict limited persistence in innovation. Gilbert and Newberry (1982) have studied a more specific case: a monopoly threatened by a potential entrant. In this case it is possible to demonstrate, under very general assumptions, that, because entry will reduce its profit, the monopolist's incentives to remain a monopolist are greater than the entrant's incentive to become a duopolist. There is clearly an asymmetric effect between the incumbent whose new innovation will destroy rents generated from prior innovations and the prospective entrant. Since these early works many scholars have contributed to our understanding of the sources of observed persistence by integrating the incentive based approach. In particular, the literature has traditionally shed attention upon two main factors that might explain the capability of firms to maintain high innovation rates along time: the role of sunk costs and barriers to entry and exit in the innovation activity; the presence of a virtuous process linking firm technological success, superior economic performance and larger amounts of financial resources to be invested in R&D activities. Below we briefly summarize the key elements of such theoretical frameworks.

2.1 The role of sunk costs and entry barriers

The generation of technological knowledge is an activity characterized by significant indivisibility and learning (Stiglitz, 1987) and the production of new knowledge deriving from R&D efforts is affected by substantial sunk costs (Máñez et al., 2009). R&D related assets are typically non-redeployable, their economic returns are defined in the long term and they require smooth investment plans. Such characteristics contribute to generate exit barriers and make technological innovation a systematic component of the firm strategy, once the firm has incurred the non-recoverable R&D start-up costs. Sutton (1991) has extensively analysed the concept of endogenous sunk costs, including R&D and advertisement, as an explanatory factor behind the evidence of many manufacturing industries becoming dominated by a few firms as they grow to a large size. The peculiar aspect of Sutton's approach (1991, 1998) refers to the distinction between exogenous sunk costs (traditional fixed costs related to the production technology) and endogenous sunk costs, which are the results of an intentional decision of incumbents to increase their price-cost margin and whose size does not depend on the level of production. In the presence of endogenous sunk costs, even in the case of an expansion in the demand, there would be a lower bound in industry concentration and the number of active firms might also get smaller. Hence, the endogenous sunk costs are likely to induce persistency in innovation.

2.2 The 'success breeds success' effect and financial constraints

According to the Schumpeterian Mark II model firms able to introduce an innovation at time t can be able to earn profits above the norm for a long period of time. Quasi-rents generated by an early innovation can be partly used to fund further R&D expenditures. High levels of R&D expenditures consequently increase the opportunity to generate further innovations and simultaneously keep high levels of profit and high rates of introduction of innovations. In this respect the 'success breeds success' hypothesis asserts that innovation feeds profitability, which later funds innovation activities (Flaig and Stadler, 1994; Latham and Le Bas, 2006). Successful innovation activities have a positive impact on the conditions for follow on innovations by providing the firm with higher permanent market power, by reducing financial constraints as well as by broadening the space of available technological opportunities. There is large and consistent evidence on financial constraints to innovation investments (Hall and Lerner, 2009) which has highlighted how the limited capability to access external financial sources significantly bound the innovation potential especially of small firms. Financing constraints are more likely to occur for innovative firms because their investment returns are uncertain, they have little collateral to secure firms' borrowing and their capital, which is mostly intangible, is also difficult to be redeployed in alternative settings (Himmelberg and Petersen, 1994; Scellato, 2007). In particular, the presence of liquidity constraints on capital investments due to capital market imperfections tends to delay the initial start of in-house research and development activities for product enhancement (Carpenter and Petersen, 2002). The fact that firms have to rely mostly on internal resources to finance R&D projects generates an additional factor inducing the emergence of innovation persistency patterns.

3. Knowledge cumulability and path dependence in the persistence of innovation

The notion of path dependence provides a comprehensive framework for the analysis of dynamic processes and indeed offers the analytical tools to understand why early innovators are likely to experience rates of introduction of innovation persistently above the average (David, 1997; Antonelli, 1997). The existence of persistence phenomena related to the introduction of innovations can be in fact hardly reconciled with the neoclassical paradigm where innovation is a 'manna from heaven', equally distributed among firms and in space. On the contrary, this evidence suggests that innovation exhibits the typical dynamic traits of a non-ergodic process in which history is important as it affects the likelihood of the different possible states in which the process may end up (David, 2007). However, a non-ergodic process may be either *past dependent*, when the features of the process are fully and exhaustively defined at its onset, or *path dependent*, when irreversibility affects its dynamics and yet small, contingent events along the process may change its key characteristics, such as path, speed and destination (David, 1997; Antonelli, 2006).

In this respect, innovation persistence would be *past dependent*, and consequently fully determined by the introduction of the first innovation, if firms built long lasting innovating capabilities after the introduction of the first innovation. This result would be consistent with the resource-based theory of the firm, which explains innovation persistence as the result of intrinsic characteristics of the firm. In this interpretative framework, innovation capabilities are time-invariant endowments that display their effects. Firms are able to learn but innovation persistence is fully driven by the initial allocation of innovation capabilities.

On the contrary, as it will be discussed in the next section, there is evidence that not only initial conditions are relevant for explaining persistence processes but contingent events significantly affect the dynamics of the process. This suggests that innovation persistence is a *path-dependent* process as opposed to a *past dependent* one, in which the probability of introducing an innovation at time *t* is influenced by previous innovative activities but the transition probability might change over time because of the effects of internal and external contingent events.

In our view the role of path dependence in innovation persistence can be framed by integrating the different theoretical ingredients stemming from the economics of knowledge and the economics of organization.

3.1 The role of knowledge cumulability

In the last decades, the economics of knowledge has made important steps forward in the analysis of the characteristics of knowledge as an economic good (Antonelli and Colombelli, 2013). In particular, on the one hand, the knowledge generation function approach allowed economists to fully appreciate the need to explicitly consider knowledge as the output of a dedicated activity and take into account the variety of inputs, complementary to R&D expenditures, that make possible the generation of new knowledge (Nelson, 1982). On the other hand, knowledge has been recognized to be at the same time an input in the generation of new knowledge and in the production of other goods (David, 1993).

In this context, building on the Arrovian analysis of knowledge as an economic good (Arrow, 1962; Nelson, 1959), the process of knowledge generation can be understood as a recombinant process where existing bits of knowledge enter as inputs in the generation of new ideas (Weitzman, 1996, 1998; Antonelli *et al.*, 2012). This approach shed new light on the role of knowledge indivisibility and, hence, non-exhaustibility, cumulability and complementarity (Antonelli and Colombelli, 2013) in the generation of new knowledge. In so doing the path dependent character of the knowledge generation process could be fully appreciated. At each point in time the generation of new technological knowledge is the result of a process of search, identification and use of bits of knowledge previously generated and stored in the stock of competence and knowledge accumulated in the past (Scotchmer, 1991). Therefore, the current levels of research efforts of each organization determine the rate and direction of innovative activities but only within a context that is shaped by knowledge accumulated in the past both inside and outside the organization (Antonelli, 2011).

The fundamental role of the stock of knowledge as an input into the generation of new knowledge allows the understanding of its non-ergodic character and, hence, to correctly interpret persistence phenomena in innovation activities. Firms that have been able to start generating new technological knowledge can rely upon their own output to generate new additional knowledge at lower costs. Moreover, since learning, together with research activities, is a major source of new knowledge, dynamic increasing returns are likely to characterize the performance of innovation activities: the larger is the cumulated size of innovation activities carried on and the larger are the positive effects on costs. In this respect, Stiglitz (1987) has added an important dynamic element with the notion of learning to learn: firms that have started to learn about the generation of new knowledge enjoy distinctive dynamic increasing returns as they are better able to learn in the subsequent attempts to generate new knowledge. By innovating, the firm explores a process of learning and discovers new ideas by recombining (re-arranging) old ones (Weitzman, 1996). Moreover, the accumulation of knowledge and the creation of routines to valorize and exploit it within the same organization eventually lead to the creation of *dynamic capabilities* that, as it will be discussed, may favour the systematic reliance upon innovation as a competitive tool (Teece *et al.*, 1997).

3.2 The role of external knowledge

A large number of empirical studies confirm the pervasive role of technological spillover in favouring the economic performances of clustered firms in terms of output, employment and innovation. The subsequent literature has interpreted these empirical findings as reliable clues to assessing the positive effects of knowledge externalities on the rate of introduction of technological changes by firms that are able to use external knowledge as an input in their own innovation processes (Acs *et al.*, 2002; Fritsch and Franke, 2004).

In this respect, the recombinant approach enables the appreciation of the central role of two important inputs into the generation of new technological knowledge such as the knowledge base of each firm as qualified by stock of knowledge that each firm possess, and the knowledge that is external but complementary to the research activities undertaken by each firm (Antonelli, 2011). The access to a high quality pool of external knowledge, in fact, may alter the current amount of knowledge that each firm is able to generate. At each point in time, no single agent in fact possesses all the necessary bits of knowledge to be used as inputs in the knowledge generation process. On the contrary, agents need to access the variety of knowledge items that are available at the system level. Hence, the search of external knowledge is necessary and its acquisition is the result of an intentional activity. The access to external knowledge is in fact possible only if dedicated resources are devoted to search, identify and eventually recombine the external elements of knowledge with the internal ones. This implies that current research efforts are a necessary investment to access, learn and absorb the stock of existing external knowledge generated by third parties.

Following this approach, external factors add to internal ones and shape the context in which the persistence of innovation occurs. The external conditions, namely the quality of local pools of knowledge and the strength of the Schumpeterian rivalry, together with the internal conditions, in particular the level of dynamic capabilities, exert a specific and localized effect on the persistent introduction of innovations. Because externalities are internal to the local system in which firms are embedded, the changing conditions exert a path dependent effect on the sequence of innovations (Antonelli *et al.*, 2013a). As with internal factors, external factors are contingent because the structure of the system in which external knowledge is generated tends to change as a result of the introduction of innovations. At each point in time, the networks of interactions and the types of transactions on factor and product markets change. Yet, at each point in time, the architecture of the system and the market exert a strong effect on the ability of firms to access and use external knowledge and to rely on it for the introduction of further innovations as a competitive tool.

3.3 The role of dynamic capabilities

As discussed so far, knowledge cumulability, related to knowledge indivisibility and knowledge non-exhaustibility, plays a central role in path dependent innovation persistence. The introduction of further innovations is easier for firms that can command a larger internal knowledge base and have access and capability to use larger knowledge bases from other agents operating in the external environment (Antonelli, 2008, 2011; Colombelli and von Tunzelmann, 2011). For this reason, the effects of internal and external knowledge cumulability are typically path dependent. Knowledge accumulated in the past exerts a strong influence in the future generation of new knowledge. Internal and external knowledge cumulability affect the dynamics of economic processes because the knowledge base that each firm can access and use internally and externally shapes the probability of the generation of new knowledge. Such effects can change over time because the rates of accumulation and the conditions of access are not fixed.

Past knowledge, however, is not a single, deterministic factor: management strategies appear to be crucial in shaping the amount of knowledge that each firm is able to generate at each point in time and in sustaining persistent innovative activities through R&D investment choices and other decisions related to the acquisition of specific pieces of external knowledge (Antonelli *et al.*, 2013a). In this respect, the economics of organization has shown that repeated interactions between the accumulation of knowledge and the creation of routines to valorize and exploit it within the same organization eventually lead to the creation of dynamic capabilities that favour the systematic reliance upon innovation as a competitive tool (Nelson and Winter, 1982; Rothaermel and Hess, 2007; Verona and Ravasi, 2003). Dynamic capabilities are defined as 'the subset of competence/capabilities which allow the firm to create new products and processes, and respond to changing market circumstances' (Teece *et al.*, 1997: 510).

> If an enterprise possesses resources/competences but lacks dynamic capabilities, it has a chance to make a competitive return (and possibly even a supra-competitive return) for a short period; but it cannot sustain supra-competitive returns for the long term except due to chance.
>
> *(Teece, 2007: 1344)*

In particular, only firms able to leveraging their dynamic capabilities can innovate persistently over a long period of time.

This framework emphasizes that the past displays a relevant impact on current and future performances. However, the dynamic capabilities approach recognizes that the business enterprise is shaped but not necessarily trapped by its past. Management can make big differences through investment choice and other decisions. The generation of new knowledge and the introduction of innovations are in fact the conditional results of a creative and localized reaction that occurs when firms face unexpected events in both factor and product markets (Antonelli, 2008, 2011). The positive loop between accumulation of knowledge, generation of dynamic capabilities and continuous innovation performance is clearly sustained by the contingent generation of extra profits that can feed the process. Hence, managers can act creatively and strategically for shaping firms' paths. It remains possible to get portions of space – within a corridor constraint by path dependent dynamics – in which creative solutions could be implemented through managers' decisions (Antonelli, 2011; Vergne and Durand, 2011; Le Bas and Scellato, 2014).

We still have limited empirical evidence but the few available contributions that have tried to link innovation persistence, dynamic capability and strategic approaches seem to suggest that indeed, in addition to industry specificities and technological regimes, firm-level innovation strategies do matter. Firm heterogeneity in the form of strategic differences across firms constitutes a key driving force behind a firm's probability to innovate over time (Clausen *et al.*, 2013). In this perspective, firms focusing their strategy on acquisition, assimilation and exploitation of externally available knowledge are able to continuously renew their knowledge stock and strengthen their dynamic capabilities. Hence, managers can deal with, and even take benefit from, path dependence if they are able to select the appropriate self-reinforcing mechanisms along the capability paths that emerge from the firm–environment interaction (Vergne and Durand, 2011). Management strategies appear to be crucial to sustain superior innovation performance over time through investment choices and other decisions related to the leveraging of dynamic capabilities and the exploitation of strategic assets. Managerial contingencies in fact affect the non-ergodic dynamics of innovation persistence (Clausen *et al.*, 2013; Antonelli *et al.*, 2013b).

The recognition of the relevance of internal and external knowledge cumulability in the generation of innovations allows us to appreciate how dynamic capabilities co-evolve with firm innovation persistence in a path dependent way (Le Bas and Scellato, 2014). There is co-evolution as a very general form of adaptation when the strategic actions taken by firms have a certain impact on their environment and subsequently on their future evolution as well. The access conditions to the local pools of knowledge that engender externalities at the firm level are clearly endogenous to the system as they are emergent properties of a system that is itself exposed to changes at both the macro and meso levels. For the same reason, it can be argued that the internal characteristics that affect innovation persistence are subject to a time variability that shapes the dynamics of the process in a step-wise manner. Hence, persistence is path dependent rather than past dependent: knowledge cumulability shapes the process together with a number of contingent and localized conditions that exert significant effects on the non-ergodic dynamics of the process and change its path, its speed and its duration (David, 1997, 2007; Antonelli, 2008; Antonelli *et al.*, 2013b). This implies that innovation persistence can no longer be regarded as the result of an intrinsic capability of the firm that behaves as an endowment, given once and lasting forever; rather, it should be regarded as the conditional result of a systemic and interactive process that keeps changing over time.

4. Empirical evidence on innovation persistence

The different frameworks that have been summarized in the previous paragraphs provide complementary and self-reinforcing rather than competing hypotheses about the source of persistency. The concept of endogenous sunk costs is clearly correlated to the generation of internal competencies through the investment in learning. The effects of knowledge accumulation and the 'success breeds success' hypothesis interplay, giving rise to a virtuous circle in which profits fund R&D and other technology activities and, a time period later, they enable the learning process to continue (Le Bas and Scellato, 2014). In this respect, the assessment of the prevailing factors is likely to depend on industry and technology contingent conditions. In this section we review a selection of available econometric evidence on innovation persistence in which we highlight the relevance of the different theoretical frameworks.

The empirical analysis of the persistence of innovation activities at the firm level is a relatively recent undertaking in the economic literature. In the special issue of the *International Journal of Industrial Organization* dedicated to the economics of path dependence, Malerba, Orsenigo and Petretto (1997) pave the way to this new area of investigation. Currently available evidence can be grouped into a subset of studies that build upon the analysis of large samples of patents and a subset of empirical studies that make use of data from innovation surveys repeated along time. In the following paragraphs we provide a review of the most relevant econometric studies, highlighting their specific contributions to our understanding of the relative importance of the different potential drivers of the analysed phenomenon. Table 8.1 shows a synopsis of the reviewed articles. The review builds on the introductory article by Le Bas and Scellato (2014) for a recent special issue on the theme of innovation persistence.

4.1 Empirical studies based on patent data

Malerba *et al.* (1997) tested the evidence provided by the OTAF-SPRU data base for five European countries (Germany, France, UK, Italy and Sweden) for the period 1969–1986 for 33 technological categories. Their econometric evidence confirms the existence of persistence patterns in innovative activities, with the contemporaneous presence of serial innovators and persistent non-innovative firms. The paper does not investigate the determinants and the features of the persistency but rather analyses its effects. It shows in fact that the persistence of the innovative activity plays an important role in explaining the concentration of technological activity, that is the share of patents granted to the firms, the stability of the ranking of innovators and their innovative intensity. Geroski, Van Reenen and Walters (1997) study the innovative history of UK firms in the period 1969–1988 using patent records and the introduction of 'major' innovations. The empirical analysis is based upon the estimate of a proportional hazard model to capture the drivers of the duration of innovation spells. Results seem to indicate that 'success only follows really major success, and then for only a limited period of time'. Indeed patent data seem to suggests that just

Table 8.1 Main recent empirical contributions on innovation persistence

Authors	Country, time period, industry	Type of econometric model	Main results
Alfranca, Rama, and von Tunzelmann (2002)	US (1977–1994) 103 global firms in the food and beverage industry	Time series analysis	Global firms exhibit a stable pattern of technological accumulation in the 'success breeds success' perspective. Potential stimuli to technological change have only transitory effects on innovation
Antonelli, Crespi, Scellato (2012)	Italy (1998–2006) Sample of 451 manufacturing firms	Transition probability matrixes and dynamic random effects probit model	Level of persistence differs according to the typology of innovation: higher persistence for R&D investments and for product innovation
Antonelli, Crespi, Scellato (2013a)	Italy (1996–2005) Sample of 7020 manufacturing firms	Transition probability matrixes and dynamic discrete panel data	Evidence of path dependent persistence due to both internal and external factors
Cefis (2003)	UK (1978–1991) Patent data on 577 firms	Transition probability matrixes	Evidence of little persistence characterized by a strong threshold effect. Only great innovators have a stronger probability to keep innovating
Cefis and Ciccarelli (2005)	UK (1988–1992) Patent data on	Bayesian approach and classical estimation methods	Positive effect of innovation on profits. Persistence of profit differentials
Cefis and Orsenigo (2001)	Germany, Italy, Japan, US, and France (1978–1993)	Transition probability matrixes	Evidence of weak persistence; both low innovators and great innovators generally remain in their classes
Clausen and Pohjola (2013)	Norway (1997–2006)	Dynamic random effects probit model	Breakthrough product innovation is persistent at the firm level and driven by dynamic learning effects
Clausen, Pohjola, Sapprasert, Verspagen (2013)	Norway (1995–2004)	Dynamic random effects probit model	Innovation strategies provide an important source of innovation persistence. Scale of persistence differs between product/process innovation and low/high tech sector
Duguet and Monjon (2004)	France (1986–1996) 621 manufacturing firms	Propensity score matching models	Strong evidence of innovation persistence
Huang (2008)	Taiwan (1998–2003)	Dynamic random effect probit model	Effect of state dependence + dynamic increasing return to innovation. Importance of initial conditions
Huang, Yang (2010)	Taiwan (1990–2003)	Dynamic random effect probit model	True state dependence especially within firms rather than between industries. Importance to take into account initial conditions and individual unobserved heterogeneity
Jang and Chen (2011)	Taiwan (1990–2001) 125 publicly listed IT firms	Survival model	Evidence of the state dependent but transient nature of the competitive advantage attributable to innovative persistence

Study	Country (period)	Model	Main results
Johansson, Loof (2010)	Sweden (1997–2006)	Dynamic panel models (Cobb-Douglas production function)	Persistent R&D firms have higher sales, value added and export value
Le Bas and Poussing (2014)	Luxembourg (2002–2008) Panel of 243 firms	Probit model (cross section)	Complex innovators (product *and* process innovators) are more persistent than single innovators (product *or* process innovators); pure product innovators have an advantage over pure process innovators
Le Bas, Mothe, and Nguyen (2014)	Luxembourg (2004–2008) Panel data on 287 firms	Multinomial probit models	Organizational innovation is shown to be a determinant factor for innovation persistence
Malerba, Orsenigo, and Petretto (1997)	Five EU countries (1969–1986)	Dynamic panel data model	The econometric evidence shows that innovative activity is persistent
Máñez, Rochina-Barrachina, Sanchis and Sanchis (2009)	Spain (1990–2000)	Dynamic binary choice model	Existence of sunk costs in firm's R&D activities. Sunk costs explain the persistence of R&D activities (barrier to both entry and exit from R&D activities) but quick depreciation of the effects of prior R&D activities over time (not many differences between the re-entry costs of a firm that previously performed R&D activities and a firm that never conducted R&D)
Martínez-Ros and Labeaga (2009)	Spain (1990–1999) Manufacturing firms	Random effect probit models	Evidence of persistence with relevant complementarities between product and process innovation
Peters (2009)	Germany (1994–2002) Panel of manufacturing and service firms	Dynamic random effects panel probit model	True state dependence: innovation is persistent over time (higher effects of innovation in manufacturing sector)
Raymond, Mohnen, Palm, van der Loeff (2010)	Netherlands (1994–2002) Panel of firms	Dynamic panel data bivariate Tobit model	Persistence in the high tech industries
Rogers (2004)	Australia (1994–1997) Sample of around 4500 firms	Probit regression model	Persistence of innovation for (non-) manufacturing firms + little role for traditional factors of innovation (market share, industry concentration, tech. opportunity…)
Roper, Hewitt-Dundas (2008)	Ireland (1991–2002) Panel of 2277 firms	Quantitative approach and qualitative case-studies analysis	Persistence for product and process innovations and persistence of high level of innovative product sales declines monotonically from its initial level
Suarez (2014)	Argentina (1998–2006)	Random effects dynamic probit	Innovation persistence is strongly conditioned by firm's ability to respond to changes in the external environment
Triguero and Corcoles (2013)	Spain (1990–2006) Sample of manufacturing firms	Random effects dynamic probit	Differences between input and output dynamics

Source: Adapted from Le Bas and Scellato (2014)

a minority of firms is persistently innovative. The somehow weak persistence of patenting activity is confirmed by Cefis and Orsenigo (2001) who apply a transition probability matrix approach to analyse the persistence of innovative activity in the years 1978–1993 for a samples of about 1400 manufacturing firms in each country, respectively in Germany, Italy, Japan, US and France. The results show that on average innovative activities are characterized by a weak persistency. More specifically, both low innovators and top innovators tend to remain in their classes. Much of the persistence in innovation activities however seems to be determined by the 'economic' persistency of the firms themselves. This study provides original evidence about inter-sectoral differences that confirm the importance of technology-specific factors. A subsequent study by Cefis (2003) focuses on 577 UK patenting firms in the period 1978–1991. Also in this case the transition probability matrix shows little persistence in general and it is characterized by a strong threshold effect. Only great innovators, in other words, have a stronger probability to keep innovating. Cefis and Ciccarelli (2005) contribute to the literature on the persistence of innovation by exploring the persistence of the effects of innovation rather than the persistence of innovation *per se* and its causes. Their paper investigates the effects of innovative activity on profitability using a panel of 267 UK firms in the period 1988–1992. The innovativeness of firms is measured by means of patent statistics. The econometric model tests with both a Bayesian approach and classical estimation methodology the hypothesis that past innovations exert a short and long term positive effect upon the profits of firms. The results of the Bayesian approach confirm that the impact of innovation on profits is cumulative and long lasting. This work provides a tangential contribution to the identification of persistence of innovation, as it confirms that because past innovations have a long lasting effect on profitability, innovation at time *t* can be positively influenced by past innovation via the greater availability of financial resources. The approach by Alfranca, Rama and von Tunzelmann (2002) is quite original in this context. They study the persistence of innovation in a specific sector with a focus on a well-identified group of firms. They analyse 16,698 patents granted in the United States from 1977 to 1994 to 103 global firms in the food and beverage industry. They test whether patent time series are trend stationary or difference stationary to detect how large the autoregressive parameter is and how enduring is the impact of past innovation on current ones in these companies. Their results show that the 18 years' patent series are not consistent with the random walk model. The evidence confirms that global firms, both of very large and smaller size, in this industry, exhibit a stable pattern of technological accumulation in which 'success breeds success'. Latham and Le Bas (2006) make an important contribution to the field with a systematic investigation of the persistence of innovation based upon the analysis of French and US patents. Their results confirm that the persistence of innovation takes place, but only and mainly in a limited time span. They test the hypothesis that size and profitability exert a major positive effect on the spell of innovation activities: the larger are the firms and the larger their profitability and the longer the time spell over which firms are able to sustain a sequence of innovations. The work coordinated by Latham and Le Bas expands further the investigation with the analysis of the persistence of innovation among individual inventors, as distinct from firms. The persistence of innovation is stronger among individuals than among firms. This result provides strong evidence about the important role of 'serial inventors': creative individuals that are characterized by high levels of productivity and are able to generate a persistent flow of inventions through time.

4.2. *Empirical studies based on survey data*

The use of survey data allows differentiating the analysis of persistence as captured by different input and output indicators of innovation activities, including R&D activities, product and process innovations, organizational innovations. The joint use of such indicators makes it possible to account for the effects of complementarities between different types of innovation and for the interrelations between innovation inputs and outputs. Indeed, the rich information on firm-level characteristics, deriving from survey data, can improve our understanding of the actual determinants of persistence and identify the relevance of true state persistence in innovation activities and eventually qualify it as past or path dependent.

Peters (2009) provides strong evidence in favour of persistence of innovation activities both in terms of innovation inputs, in terms of R&D activities, and innovation outputs as measured by the number of innovations introduced by German manufacturing and service firms in the years 1994–2002. The research exploits the Manheim Innovation Panel. A firm is defined as an innovator when it exhibits positive innovation expenditures and has introduced a new product or a new production process. The results of the empirical investigation confirm that firms experience high levels of persistence in undertaking innovation activities: almost half of the difference across firms in the propensity to innovate between previous innovators and non-innovators in the German manufacturing industry can be explained by the state dependence, i.e. whether the firm was already involved in innovation activities at time t-1. The persistence of innovative activities is explained by the levels of human skills, support of public funding, financial liquidity and size. Notably, the author pointed out the importance of unobserved heterogeneity, which explains a considerable amount of variation of the dependent variables. Raymond *et al.* (2010) find contrasting evidence. They study the persistence of innovation in Dutch manufacturing firms using firm data from three Community Innovation Surveys (CIS), in the years 1994–2002. The innovations that each firm claims to have introduced in each period of observation is the unit of analysis. They test the hypothesis of persistence with a maximum likelihood dynamic panel data Tobit model accounting for individual effects and handling the initial conditions problem. Their findings suggest that there is no evidence of true persistence in achieving technological product or process innovations. At each point in time, however, the shares of sales stemming from innovative products, introduced in the past, have a (small) effect on the current shares of sales of innovative products. Roper and Hewitt-Dundas (2008) use innovation survey data and show that in the case of 3604 plants covered by the Irish Innovative Panel in the period 1991–2002 both product and process innovations are strongly persistent. In this case the size and ownership of plants matters: large plants that are part of multinational companies are more able to sustain the innovation process through time than smaller ones locally owned. The persistence in the introduction of product innovations is associated to strategic variables, while the persistence in the introduction of process innovations is associated to market pressure. Antonelli *et al.* (2012) show an empirical analysis based on a sample of 451 Italian manufacturing companies observed during the years 1998–2006. Results highlight the relevance of innovation persistence. The highest level of persistence is found for R&D-based innovation activities, witnessing the actual presence of significant entry and exit barriers to innovation activities. Moreover, they obtain more robust evidence of persistence for product innovation than for process innovation, once complementarity effects between the two types of innovation are accounted for. This research outcome can be explained by the closer link between product innovation, R&D activities and knowledge cumulability with respect to process innovation (Crespi and Pianta, 2008). The levels of R&D intensity, as measured by the two indicators R&D expenditures per employee and the share of internal R&D over total, as well as the level of fixed capital investment enhance the probability of subsequent innovation outcomes. Such result confirms the idea that R&D investment activity is associated with the presence of sunk costs that might motivate the continuous undertaking of innovation activities

Triguero *et al.* (2014) examine the relationship between firm-specific characteristics, technological regimes and persistence measured by innovative spells. The results are based on a sample of Spanish manufacturing firms over a period of 19 years (1990 to 2008) and show that high technological opportunities, patents, cumulativeness of learning based on previous experience and accumulated R&D, as well as the use of knowledge provided by universities, enhance persistence in innovative activity. The analyses are based on discrete-time duration models controlling for some of the existing problems in the continuous-time duration models used in previous studies. Using the same data source, Triguero and Corcoles (2013) apply a dynamic random effect panel model and find that R&D (input) and innovation (output) are highly persistent at the firm level. Among external/environmental factors, market dynamism affects R&D and innovation. Regarding firm specific characteristics, size and outsourcing also have a positive impact on both processes. Past innovative behaviour is shown to be more decisive in explaining the current state of R&D and innovation activities than external factors or firm-level heterogeneity. The crucial role of external factors in innovation persistence, as measured by total factor productivity (TFP), is further analysed by Antonelli *et al.* (2013a) who showed that the external conditions, namely the quality of local knowledge pools and the strength of the Schumpeterian rivalry, along with the internal conditions exert a specific and localized effect upon the persistent introduction of innovations.

Hecker and Ganter (2013) examine the persistence of technological and organizational innovation for a sample of German firms over the time span from 2002 to 2008, using a balanced panel data from the fourth, fifth and sixth wave of the German Community Innovation Survey. Results confirm also for this dataset a significant persistency effect for technological innovation (product and process) while results are mixed in the case of organizational innovation. Clausen and Pohjola (2013) focus the innovation persistence analysis on comparing breakthrough product innovation (product innovations that are new and previously unknown to the market) and incremental innovation (innovations that are new to the firm but not new to the market). They use a panel database created by merging four waves of Community Innovation Survey (CIS) and R&D survey data collected by Statistics Norway between 1997 and 2006. They find that previous innovation output persistency effects tend to override the effect of R&D in generating new innovation output. The authors interpret this as evidence of knowledge accumulation effect through innovation output over that of R&D investments. The positive and significant effect on persistence of the share of internal R&D expenditures supports this interpretation: knowledge accumulated internally within the firm has an effect over time. Interestingly, such pattern is present only in the case of radical innovations, suggesting that breakthrough product innovation is driven not just by past investment but also by 'dynamic learning effects'. Clausen *et al.* (2013) address the role of innovation strategies as a source of persistent innovation. Their results support the idea that the differences in innovation strategies across firms are an important determinant of the firms' probability to repeatedly innovate. In particular, they identify five innovation strategies that capture the main differences of the innovation activities. The authors employ two dependent variables: product innovation and process innovation. Their database contains information about all enterprises which have participated in at least one of the R&D surveys conducted by Statistics Norway since 1993. The results confirm the general finding in the literature that innovation is persistent at the firm level. Moreover, they find that firm heterogeneity – in the form of initial strategic differences – constitutes a relevant driver of firms' probability to keep innovating over time. The econometric results seem to suggest that the effects of innovation strategies are, in many cases, larger than the 'pure' effect of lagged innovation.

Martínez-Ros and Labeaga (2009) use the Spanish database ESEE and find evidence in favour of persistence in product and process innovation. The authors highlight the importance of complementarity between product and process innovation as a determinants of subsequent innovation activities. Le Bas and Poussing (2014) use two waves of the Community Innovation Survey (2002–2004, 2006–2008) conducted in Luxembourg and show that complex innovators (i.e. those performing jointly product and process innovation) are more inclined to remain persistent innovators than single innovators. Within the group of single innovators pure product innovators have an advantage over pure process innovators.

Haned *et al.* (2014) analyse the impact of organizational innovation on the patterns of technological innovation persistence, using firm-level data from three waves of French Community Innovation Surveys. Their results indicate a positive effect of organizational innovation on the dynamics of technological innovation, according to various measures of organizational change that capture their degree of continuity and diversity. Such effect is more substantial for complex innovators, that is, those companies that innovate in both products and processes. In particular, the evidence suggests that the more organizational practices are implemented by the firm, the higher the probability that it will remain an innovator (although this pattern does not apply to pure process innovators). Lhuillery (2014) provides an analysis of the influence of marketing activities on innovation success and in particular on persistent innovation success, using three waves of the French CIS innovation survey covering the period 2002–2008. Results seem to indicate that innovation in marketing does not positively influence persistent innovation success in low-tech industries. The impact of innovation in marketing is found to be more complex in high tech industries: innovation marketing positively influences persistent innovation success for incremental innovation but negatively influences it for radical innovation. Such evidence is in line with existing literature which, for the most part, associates incremental innovation success with marketing and radical innovation success with R&D resources. Frenz and Prevezer (2012) analyse the link between technological regimes and persistence in innovation at the firm level using a balanced panel of around 4000 firms that responded to the latest three waves of the UK version of the CIS. Key explanatory variables include measures of appropriability, cumulativeness, technological opportunity and closeness to the science base. They find strong persistence in innovation in the short run; less so, and only with respect to new-to-market product innovation, in the longer run. The extent to which firms exchange knowledge with other companies, the intensity of R&D investments, as well as their size matters in explaining innovation persistence. The authors claim that their results suggest the presence of a pattern of technological accumulation at the level of the firm rather than at the industry level (measured by the average share of new-to-market sales within the industry). High levels of technological opportunity increase the chance of persistent product innovation among the services firms. Deschryvere (2014) analyses the role of persistence of innovation output on the relationship between R&D investment and growth in SMEs. The analysis is based on an unbalanced firm-level panel of 516 firms containing 1998–2008 data from the R&D surveys and the Business Register of Statistics Finland and the Community Innovation Survey (CIS). The empirical analysis of the relationship between innovation and firm performance is performed through vector autoregression models. Results indicate that only continuous innovators have positive associations, albeit small, between R&D growth and sales growth. The correlation between sales growth and subsequent R&D growth is not always stronger for continuous innovators than for occasional innovators, particularly in the case of process innovators. Suarez (2014) discusses the concept of innovation persistence in the context of unstable economic environments. The author studies the innovative behaviour of Argentinean firms using data from national innovation surveys in three distinct macroeconomic environments: the 1998–2001 economic crisis, the 2002–2004 recovery period and the 2005–2006 growth phase. Results suggest that persistence is conditioned by firms' ability to respond to changes in the environment. The instability of the environment induced sporadic short-term innovations, with limited impact on the firms' capabilities and resources. Actual innovation persistence is observed only among firms that changed together with the environment.

The largest part of the empirical contributions reviewed seems to provide evidence in favour of the presence of persistency patterns in innovation efforts at the firm level, due to true state dependence and not driven just by firm-specific time variant unobservable factors. Still, the results also show relevant nuances that can provide further hints about the economic determinants and implication of persistence.

The early papers that have used patent-based indicators to account for persistency have found indeed a rather limited evidence of persistence. In this regard, however, it has to be remarked that patent application intensity, especially for smaller firms, might reflect to some extent the appropriation strategies adopted to secure the outcomes of innovation investments rather than the intensity of underlying innovation effort. At the same time, survey-based studies are forced to adopt a dichotomic approach given the structure of available data (whether a firm has performed or not a certain type of innovation in a certain time period) and this in turn represents a clear limitation of this second class of analyses.

However, this class of studies has provided important insights to qualify the patterns of innovation persistence, with relevant implications for the theory of the economics of knowledge. Independently of the sectors and country analysed, product innovation appears to be more persistent in time than process innovation. Different studies have explicitly investigated the complementarities between the two macro typologies of innovation highlighting that, also for the firms performing both of them, it is product innovation that drives the persistency dynamic. Moreover, radical product innovation (related to the introduction of products new to the market and not only new to the company) shows a more persistent impact on subsequent innovation persistence. Results tend to be more mixed in the case of organizational innovation and marketing-related innovation. Such type of innovation activities are indeed more sporadic, although some studies have revealed that organizational change can have an impact on the persistency of product innovation under specific circumstances. As predicted by the sunk-cost approach, expenditures in research and development, and particularly the share of internal R&D costs, show substantial persistence even after accounting for firm-specific characteristics. Finally, interesting evidence pertains to the presence of an export premium: companies exporting a relevant share of their turnover tend to show higher innovation persistence.

5. Conclusions

The reviewed empirical evidence provides key lessons on the nature of innovation activities with relevant implications regarding the theory of the firm and the relevance of the notion of path dependence in economic thinking.

The largest part of the empirical contributions reviewed in this chapter seems to provide evidence in favour of the presence of persistency patterns in innovation effort at the firm level. Such evidence confirmed the presence of true state dependence in innovative activities as the detected persistence effects showed to be robust when controlling for firm-specific time variant unobservable factors. Moreover, the contemporaneous significant influence on current innovation performance exerted by past innovative efforts and different, internal and external, contingent factors confirms the path dependent character of the identified persistence. In particular, the introduction of radically new products, which requires the development and exploitation of specific skills, seems to be more likely to induce and support subsequent persistent innovation patterns. This can be attributed to the presence of technological learning processes that eventually generate new knowledge for the innovating company. Organizational change results in increased subsequent innovation capabilities only when knowledge accumulation has already reached a significant threshold. The exporting companies have higher learning opportunities that in turn have a positive impact on firms' capabilities and innovation persistence.

The results originating from the analysis of the drivers of innovation persistence appear to be fully coherent with a theoretical framework based on the two fundamental concepts of knowledge cumulability and dynamic capabilities which allow us to fully interpret the path dependent character of innovation persistence. In this context, dynamic capabilities follow a sort of co-evolution with the intensity of firms' innovation persistence in a systemic and interactive process that keeps changing over time.

The overall evidence on innovation persistence and its links with knowledge properties has also relevant implications for innovation and technology policies.

First, the recognition that innovation persistence is a path dependent rather than past dependent process implies that there is room for public intervention as firms' initial conditions can be modified along the process through properly designed policy instruments. Second, the identification of persistence in innovative activities suggests that public policies can produce long lasting effects on firms' innovation performances if they are able to induce firms to shifting towards more innovative patterns. In this context a cumulative process of learning of both benefiting companies and public authorities can lead to virtuous processes able to increase the overall effectiveness of policy interventions (Antonelli and Crespi, 2012, 2013). Third, the reviewed empirical evidence provides clear indications on the different potential of alternative policy instruments in inducing persistent effect on innovation performances. In particular, public efforts to sustain the introduction of product rather than process innovations or radical innovations rather than incremental ones appear to be more effective in producing long lasting effects on firms' innovation activities. In addition, as knowledge cumulability has been found to be central in explaining innovation persistence, it is possible to conclude that when the target of public policies is centred on economic sectors characterized by high knowledge cumulability the potential long term impact of policy instruments can be maximized (Antonelli and Crespi, 2012). Moreover, the interpretation of the evidence on financial constraints to innovation investments and on the role of sunk R&D costs in innovation persistence seems to suggest the importance of policy tools addressing the financial support of the start-up phases of firm's R&D infrastructures. Finally, some empirical analyses of innovation persistence patterns have also showed the positive impact of external factors. The learning opportunities stemming from the access to localized and qualified pools of knowledge are likely to exert a positive impact on the generation of dynamic capabilities within firms. In this perspective, policies aiming at enhancing R&D networking and knowledge exchange can have a long lasting effect.

Despite the large number of contributions produced on the analysis of innovation persistence, extant empirical results leave unanswered some relevant questions. First, while we have convincing evidence of a link between firm-level knowledge cumulativeness and innovation performance, the relationship between specific properties of firms' knowledge bases, such as the degree, coherence and variety, and their capability to continuously innovate through the exploitation of dynamic capabilities has not yet been deeply investigated. Second, the study of innovation persistence under different technological regimes would deserve further analyses. Third, in terms of managerial implications the literature has clearly stated how individuals are decisive to the formation of dynamic capabilities (Rothaermel and Hess, 2007). This calls for further specific analyses of the role of highly talented individuals, such as serial inventors, within organizations. Fourth, external relationships have received limited attention. Indeed, the access conditions to the local pools of knowledge that engender externalities at the firm level represent a relevant factor driving firm-level innovation persistence. With respect to these issues, the increasing availability of long panel databases for conducting empirical analyses and the possibility to make international comparisons in persistence drivers and behaviours accounting for the influence of local and national systems of innovation will provide new opportunities to further investigate this phenomenon.

Notes

1 This paper is part of the research project 'Policy Incentives for the Creation of Knowledge: Methods and Evidence' (PICK-ME), funded by the European Union D.G. Research with the Grant number 266959 within the context Cooperation Program/Theme 8/Socio-economic Sciences and Humanities (SSH).
2 The analysis of the implications in terms of firms' economic performances is left out from the discussion as it is beyond the scope of the chapter.

References

Acs, Z.J., L. Anselin, and A. Varga. (2002). Patents and innovation counts as measures of regional production of new knowledge, *Research Policy* 31: 1069–1085.

Aghion, P., N. Bloom, R. Blundell, R. Griffith, and P. Howitt. (2005). Competition and innovation: an inverted U relationship, *Quarterly Journal of Economics* 120: 701–728.

Alfranca, O., R. Rama, and N. von Tunzelmann. (2002). A patent analysis of global food and beverage firms: the persistence of innovation, *Agribusiness* 18: 349–68.

Antonelli, C. (1997). The economics of path-dependence in industrial organization, *International Journal of Industrial Organization* 15(6): 643–675.

Antonelli, C. (2006) Path dependence, localised technological change and the quest for dynamic efficiency. In *New Frontiers in the Economics of Innovation and New Technology. Essays in Honour of Paul A. David*, eds C. Antonelli, D. Foray, B.H. Hall, and E. Steinmueller. Cheltenham: Edward Elgar Publishing, pp. 51–69.

Antonelli, C. (2008). *Localized Technological Change: Towards the Economics of Complexity*, London: Routledge.

Antonelli, C. (ed.) (2011). *Handbook on the Economic Complexity of Technological Change*, Cheltenham: Edward Elgar.

Antonelli, C. and A. Colombelli. (2013). Knowledge cumulability and complementarity in the knowledge generation function, Department of Economics and Statistics Cognetti de Martiis. Working Papers 201305, University of Turin.

Antonelli, C. and F. Crespi. (2012). Matthew effects and R&D subsidies: knowledge cumulability in high-tech and low-tech industries, *Giornale degli Economisti e Annali di Economia* 71 – N. 1: 5–31.

Antonelli, C. and F. Crespi. (2013). The Matthew effect in R&D public subsidies: the case of Italy, *Technological Forecasting and Social Change* 80: 1523–1534.

Antonelli, C., F. Crespi, and G. Scellato. (2012). Inside innovation persistence: new evidence from Italian micro-data, *Structural Change and Economic Dynamics* 23, 4: 341–353.

Antonelli, C., F. Crespi, and G. Scellato. (2013a). Internal and external factors in innovation persistence, *Economics of Innovation and New Technology* 22, 3: 256–280.

Antonelli, C., F. Crespi, and G. Scellato. (2013b). *Path Dependent Patterns of Persistence in Productivity Growth*, Department of Economics and Statistics Cognetti de Martiis LEI & BRICK.

Archibugi, D. and M. Pianta. (1996). Measuring technological through patents and innovation surveys, *Technovation* 169, 451–468.

Arrow, K.J. (1962). Economic welfare and the allocation of resources for invention. In *The Rate and Direction of Inventive Activity: Economic and Social Factors*, ed. R.R. Nelson. Princeton, NJ: National Bureau of Economic Research and Princeton University Press, pp. 609–626.

Carpenter, R. and Petersen B., (2002). Capital market imperfections, high-tech investment and new equity financing, *Economic Journal* 112: 54–72.

Cefis, E. (2003). Is there any persistence in innovative activities? *International Journal of Industrial Organization* 21: 489–515.

Cefis, E. and M. Ciccarelli. (2005). Profit differentials and innovation, *Economics of Innovation and New Technology* 14: 43–61.

Cefis, E. and L. Orsenigo. (2001). The persistence of innovative activities. A cross-countries and cross-sectors comparative analysis, *Research Policy* 30: 1139–1158.

Clausen, T.H. and M. Pohjola. (2013). Persistence of product innovation: comparing breakthrough and incremental product innovation, *Technology Analysis & Strategic Management*, 25, 4, 369–385.

Clausen, T.H., M. Pohjola, K. Sapprasert, and B. Verspagen. (2013). Innovation strategies as a source of persistent innovation, *Industrial and Corporate Change* 21: 553–585.

Colombelli, A. and N.G. von Tunzelmann. (2011). The persistence of innovation and path dependence. In *The Handbook of the System Dynamics of Technological Change*, ed. C. Antonelli. Cheltenham: Edward Elgar, pp. 105–119.

Crespi, F. and M. Pianta. (2008). New processes and new products in Europe and Italy, *Rivista di Politica Economica* II: 119–146.

David, P. A. (1993). Knowledge property and the system dynamics of technological change. In *Proceedings of the World Bank Annual Conference on Development Economics*, eds L. Summers and S. Shah. Washington: The World Bank, pp. 215–248.

David, P.A. (1997). *Path Dependence and the Quest for Historical Economics: One More Chorus of Ballad of QWERTY*, Oxford University Economic and Social History Series 020, Economics Group. Oxford: Nuffield College, University of Oxford.

David, P.A. (2007). Path dependence: a foundational concept for historical social science, *Cliometrica: Journal of Historical Economics and Econometric History* 1: 91–114.

Deschryvere, M. (2014). R&D, firm growth and the role of innovation persistence: an analysis of Finnish SMEs and large firms, *Small Business Economics,* forthcoming. DOI: 10.1007/s11187-014-9559-3.

Dosi, G. and F. Malerba. (1996). *Organization and Strategy in the Evolution of the Enterprise*, London: MacMillan Press.

Duguet, E. and S. Monjon. (2004). Is innovation persistent at the firm level? An econometric examination comparing the propensity score and regression methods. *Cahiers de la Maison des Sciences Economiques*, Université Panthéon-Sorbonne.

Flaig, G. and M. Stadler. (1994). Success breeds success. The dynamics of the innovation process, *Empirical Economics* 19: 55–68.

Frenz, M. and M. Prevezer. (2012). What can CIS data tell us about technological regimes and persistence of innovation? *Industry and Innovation* 19, 4: 285–306.

Fritsch, M. and G. Franke. (2004). Innovation, regional knowledge spillovers and R&D cooperation, *Research Policy* 33: 245–255.

Geroski, P., J. Van Reenen, and C.F. Walters. (1997). How persistently do firms innovate? *Research Policy* 26: 33–48.

Gilbert, R.J. (2006). Looking for Mr. Schumpeter: Where are we in the innovation competition debate? In *Innovation Policy and the Economy*, vol. 6, eds A.B. Jaffe, J. Lerner, and S. Stern. Cambridge: The MIT Press, pp. 159–215.

Gilbert, R., and D. Newberry. (1982). Pre-emptive patenting and the persistence of monopoly, *American Economic Review* 72: 514–526.

Hall, B. and J. Lerner. (2009). The financing of R&D and innovation. NBER Working paper 15325.

Haned, N., C. Mothe, and U. Nguyen. (2013). Firm persistence in technological innovation: The relevance of organizational innovation, *Economics of Innovation and New Technology* 23, 5–6: 490–516.

Hecker, A. and A. Ganter. (2013). Persistence of innovation: discriminating between types of innovation and sources of state dependence, *Research Policy* 42: 1431–1445.

Himmelberg, C. and B. Petersen. (1994). R&D and internal finance: a panel study of small firms in high-tech industries, *Review of Economics and Statistics* 76: 38–51.

Huang, C.H. (2008). A note on the persistence of firms' innovation behavior: a dynamic random effect probit model approach, *Economics Bulletin* 15, 5: 1–9.

Huang, C.-H. and C.H. Yang. (2010). Persistence of innovation in Taiwan's manufacturing firms, *Taiwan Economic Review* 38, 2: 199–231.

Jang, S.-L. and J.H. Chen. (2011). What determines how long an innovative spell will last? *Scientometrics* 86, 1: 65–76.

Johansson, B. and H. Loof. (2010). Innovation strategy and firm performance. What is the long-run impact of persistent R&D? *Cesis Electronic Working Paper Series* no. 240.

Latham, W. and C. Le Bas. (2006). *The Economics of Persistent Innovation: An Evolutionary View*, Berlin: Springer.

Le Bas, C. and N. Poussing. (2014). Is complex innovation more persistent than single? An empirical analysis of innovation persistence drivers, *International Journal of Innovation Management* 18, 1, February.

Le Bas, C. and G. Scellato. (2014). Firm innovation persistence: a fresh look at the frameworks of analysis, *Economics of Innovation and New Technology* 23, 5–6: 432–446.

Le Bas, C., C. Mothe, and T.U. Nguyen. (2011). *Technological Innovation Persistence: Literature Survey and Exploration of the Role of Organizational Innovation.* SSRN e-library. DOI: 10.2139/ssrn.1969293.

Le Bas, C., C. Mothe, and T.U. Nguyen. (2014). The differentiated impacts of organizational innovation practices on technological innovation persistence, *European Journal of Innovation Management*, forthcoming.

Lhuillery, S. (2014). Marketing and persistent innovation success, *Economics of Innovation and New Technology* 23, 5–6: 447–468.

Malerba, F. and F. Orsenigo. (1995). Schumpeterian patterns of innovation, *Cambridge Journal of Economics* 19(1): 47–65.

Malerba, F., L. Orsenigo, and P. Petretto. (1997). Persistence of innovative activities, sectoral patterns of innovation and international technological specialization, *International Journal of Industrial Organization* 15: 801–826.

Máñez, J.A., M.E. Rochina-Barrachina, A. Sanchis, and J.A. Sanchis. (2009). The role of sunk costs in the decision to invest in R&D, *The Journal of Industrial Economics* 57, 4: 712–735.

Martínez-Ros, E. and J.M. Labeaga. (2009). Product and process innovation: persistence and complementarities, *European Management Review* 6: 64–75.

Nelson, R.R. (1959). The simple economics of basic scientific research, *The Journal of Political Economy* 67, 5: 297–306.

Nelson, R.R. (1982). The role of knowledge in R&D efficiency, *Quarterly Journal of Economics* 97: 453–470.

Nelson, R.R. (1991). Why do firms differ and how does it matter? *Strategic Management Journal* 12: 61–74.

Nelson, R. and S. Winter. (1982). *An Evolutionary Theory of Economic Change*. Cambridge, MA: The Belknap Press of Harvard University Press.

Peters, B. (2009). Persistence of innovation: stylized facts and panel data evidence, *Journal of Technology Transfer* 34: 226–243.

Raymond, W., P. Mohnen, F.C. Palm, and S. Schim van der Loeff. (2010). Persistence of innovation in Dutch manufacturing: is it spurious? *Review of Economics and Statistics* 92, 3: 495–504.

Rogers, M. (2004). Networks, firm size and innovation, *Small Business Economics* 22, 2: 141–153.

Roper, S. and N. Hewitt-Dundas. (2008). Innovation persistence: survey and case-study evidence, *Research Policy* 37: 149–162.

Rothaermel, F.T. and A.M. Hess. (2007). Building dynamic capabilities, *Organization Science* 18, 6: 898–921.

Scellato, G. (2007). Patents, firm size and financial constraints: an empirical analysis for a sample of Italian manufacturing firms, *Cambridge Journal of Economics* 1: 55–76.

Scotchmer, S. (1991). Standing on the shoulders of science: cumulative research and the patent law, *Journal of Economic Perspectives* 5(1): 29–41.

Stiglitz, J. (1987). Learning to learn, localized learning and technological progress. In *Economic Policy and Technological Performance*, eds P. Dasgupta and P. Stoneman. Cambridge: Cambridge University Press, pp. 125–153.

Suarez, D. (2014). Persistence of innovation in unstable environments: continuity and change in the firm's innovative behavior, *Research Policy* 43: 726–773.

Sutton, J. (1991). *Sunk Costs and Market Structure*, Cambridge, MA: MIT Press.

Sutton, J. (1998). *Technology and Market Structure*, Cambridge, MA: The MIT Press.

Teece, D. (2007). Explicating dynamic capabilities: the nature and micro-foundations of sustainable enterprise performance, *Strategic Management Journal* 28: 1319–1350.

Teece, D.J., G. Pisano, and A. Schuen. (1997). Dynamic capabilities and strategic management, *Strategic Management Journal* 18: 509–533.

Triguero, A. and D. Corcoles. (2013). Understanding the innovation: an analysis of persistence for Spanish manufacturing firms, *Research Policy* 42: 340–352.

Triguero, A., D. Corcoles, and M. Cuerva. (2014). Measuring the persistence in innovation in Spanish manufacturing firms: empirical evidence using discrete-time duration models, *Economics of Innovation and New Technology*, forthcoming.

Vergne, J.-P. and R. Durand. (2011). The path of most persistence: an evolutionary perspective on path dependence and dynamic capabilities, *Organization Studies* 32: 365–382.

Verona, G. and D. Ravasi. (2003). Unbundling dynamic capabilities: an exploratory study on continuous product development, *Industrial and Corporate Change* 12 (3): 577–606.

Weitzman, M.L. (1996). Hybridizing growth theory, *American Economic Review* 86: 207–212.

Weitzman, M. L. (1998). Recombinant growth, *Quarterly Journal of Economics*, 113: 331–360.

9

Social responsibility and the knowledge production function of higher education

A review of the literature

Christopher S. Hayter

1. Introduction

Policymakers around the world recognize that universities have a responsibility to serve the needs of the societies in which they are embedded. Clark Kerr, former Chancellor of the University of California System, framed this responsibility in terms of the creation and dissemination of new knowledge:

> We are just now perceiving that the university's invisible product, knowledge, may be the most powerful single element in our culture, affecting the rise and fall of professions, even social classes, of regions and even of nations. Because of this fundamental reality, the university is being called upon to produce knowledge as never before … and it is also being called upon to transmit knowledge to an unprecedented proportion of the population.

> *(2001)*

From an economics perspective, new knowledge is a critical ingredient for economic growth and technological progress (Romer 1986; Solow 1956). The economic contributions of universities are therefore tied to their role in the knowledge production function, the creation and spillover of new knowledge (Griliches 1979). Neoclassical traditions assume that knowledge, once created, automatically spills over into society justifying ever-increasing public expenditures for university R&D.

Recent research posits, however, that new knowledge does not fall "like manna from heaven" but is instead subject to institutional, geographic, and cost constraints illustrated in the substantial differences among regional economies, despite the presence of preeminent, well-funded research universities (Almeida and Kogut 1999; Braunerhjelm *et al.* 2010; Jaffe 1989; Jaffe *et al.* 1993; Nelson 2005). Seeking to explain differences in regional economic growth, Acs *et al.* (2009) consequently recommend that scholars not only examine barriers to the spillover of knowledge, but also investigate *how* and *why* it spills over.

Of course, the primary purpose of new knowledge created in colleges and universities is not economic but rather to support the social goals of the regions and nations where higher education institutions are located. And while high-profile discussions relating to the role of higher education in society are frequent, a conspicuous gap exists in the literature relating to the social responsibilities of higher education, how these responsibilities are specifically carried out, and their impact. In contrast, a voluminous and ever-growing body of research examines corporate social responsibility (CSR), the conceptualization and practice of how for-profit firms can address society's needs.

This chapter is motivated by a desire to explore this gap in the literature and address the question: what is the *social responsibility* of higher education related to the creation and dissemination of new knowledge? We assume that the knowledge production function of colleges and universities is congruent with the traditional teaching and research missions of universities (Braunerhjelm *et al.* 2010; Kerr 2001), allowing comparison among disparate literatures.

This chapter is among the first to review the extant research on the social responsibility of higher education as compared to a robust CSR literature. Exploring the social responsibility literature will not only allow for the establishment of a research agenda focused on colleges and universities, it might also provide insight to policymakers and academic leaders interested in understanding and maximizing the social and, potentially, economic impact of higher education.

The remainder of the paper is outlined as follows. In Section 2 we discuss the emerging CSR literature from the Management disciplines. In Section 3, we review the related higher education literature. The paper concludes in Section 4 with an interpretation of our findings for articulating a social responsibility strategy for policymakers and university leaders interested in knowledge dissemination and commercialization.

2. Corporate social responsibility

While the objective function of the firm is typically viewed as profit generation, CSR examines a broader question: what are the overall contributions that firms make to society (Crane *et al.* 2008; Handy 2002)? A robust and growing literature seeks to address this question; Carroll (1999), for example, reviews more than 25 different definitions of CSR in the academic literature and De Bakker *et al.* (2005) finds over 500 articles relating to both CSR theory and empirical research.

The CSR literature is increasingly empirical and, as Marens (2004) points out, often accompanied by normative inquiries to determine what corporations *should* be responsible for in society. Views of the appropriate role of firms range from Milton Friedman's (1970) contention that "the social responsibility of the firm is to increase its profits" to Davis (1973) who argues that CSR requires "consideration of issues beyond the narrow economic, technical, and legal requirements of the firm."

Table 9.1 presents several conceptual models of CSR based on the extant literature. While time and space do not permit a thorough critique of each model, CSR has developed over time through six separate, yet interrelated phases (Carroll 2008). These development phases include:

I.   **Awareness.** Prior to the 1950s, discussions on the role of a firm in society focused primarily on its profit-making objective function. However, some research emerged relating to the treatment of employees (child labor, workers' rights, role of unions) and philanthropy. In the 1950s, leaders such as Bowen (1953) and others helped create awareness of CSR by

Table 9.1 Models of corporate social responsibility derived from the literature

Model	Explanation	Mechanisms	Motivation	Target	Measured by	Authors
Shareholder Value Theory	The only social responsibility of business is upholding the desires of shareholders by maximizing profits	Corporate governance and managerial systems that defend shareholders' interests	Business is a private and autonomous activity only restricted by the regulations of the government, with no responsibilities other than profits and creating wealth; public and private spheres should be completely separated	Owners	Profit	Friedman, M. (1970) Ross, S. A. (1973) Jensen, M. C. and W. Meckling (1976) Jensen, M. C. (2002)
Cost Reduction	The firm chooses to engage or not engage in CSR-related activities in order to reduce costs and risks to the firm	The demands of outside stakeholders should be recognized; corporate economic interests are served by adopting a threshold level of social or environmental performance	Cost avoidance, including negative publicity that often results in reduced sales	Stakeholders with the firm as primary	Tradeoff between costs of social performance and financial performance	Friedman, M. (1962, 1970) Lerner, L. D. and G. E. Fryxell (1988)
Corporate Social Performance	Business has power which has social impact; business is responsible for social problems created by business	Firms can create and incorporate policies and programs that strengthen its relationships with society Comply with DSI index—criteria include diversity, employee relations, human rights. Excludes all firms involved with alcohol, tobacco, firearms, gambling, nuclear power, and military weapons	Socio-economic responsibility for general economic welfare Socio-human responsibility for preserving and developing human values	Society	Response to social requirements Domini 400 Social Index (DSI) that classifies firms as "socially responsible" — conducted by the indexing firm KLD Research and Analytics	Davis, K. (1967) Carroll, A. B. (1979) Preston, L. E. and J. E. Post (1981) Wartick, S. L. and P. L. Cochran (1985) Wood, D. J. (1991a, 1991b) Van Oosterhout, J. H. (2005)

(Continued)

Table 9.1 (Continued)

Model	Explanation	Mechanisms	Motivation	Target	Measured by	Authors
Supply and Demand Theory	Firms only need to supply the level of environmental and social performance that is demanded of them	Firms should incorporate environmentally and socially responsible actions into business operations, but only the minimum which satisfies demand by consumers	Profit maximization, efficiency	Stakeholders/consumers	Profit	Anderson, J. C. and A. W. Frankle (1980) Freedman, M. and B. Jaggi (1982) Aupperle K. E. et al. (1985) McWilliams, A. and D. Siegel (2001)
Stakeholder Theory	The firm is a system of stakeholders operating within the larger system of the host society	Firms are managed for the benefit of its stakeholders to ensure their rights and ability to participate in critical decisions and for the long-term survival of the firm	Society provides the necessary legal and market infrastructure for the firm's activities, so firms have a responsibility to take stakeholders' rights and interests into account	Stakeholders directly involved in the operation of the firm, including investors and management	Profit and other types of value created for stakeholders	Jones, T. M. (1980) Evan, W. M. and R. E. Freeman (1988) Clarkson, M. B. E. (1995)
Reputation and Legitimacy	Exploiting CSR activities creates value through gains in firm reputation and legitimacy	Corporations should engage in philanthropy, marketing, and efforts to demonstrate socially and environmentally responsible behavior	A firm's corporate social performance generates positive reputational effects; failure to meet stakeholder needs has a negative impact on firm reputation; the costs of CSR activities are less than potential benefits	Stakeholders	Firm's reputation	Murray, K. B. and J. R. Montanari (1986) Cornell, B. and A. C. Shapiro (1987) Drumwright, M. (1996) Pava, M. L. and J. Krausz (1996) Preston, L. E. and D. P. O'Bannon (1997) Varadarajan, P. R. and A. Menon (1998)

Theory	Description	Mechanism	Outcome	Level of analysis	Key focus	References
Critical Theory Model of Stakeholder Participation	Meeting economic and social goals requires inclusive communication and decision-making processes that incorporate both business and the community	Firms manage conflict among labor unions, supplier cartels, consumer groups, and others to create "win-win" responses; communication constitutes participation	Enhanced creativity, productivity, economic performance, greater fulfillment of social good	Stakeholders	Opportunities for stakeholder involvement/decision-making	Gray, B. (1989) Bowie, N. E. (1991) Donaldson, T. and L. Preston (1995) Scherer, A. G. and E. T. Palazzo (2007)
Corporate Citizenship	Business should play an active (positive) role in society	Corporations can provide social rights (education, healthcare, etc.), enable civil rights, and act as a channel for political rights	Companies have an obligation to play a positive role in civil and ethical dimensions of society, respect and defend human rights, and contribute to social welfare and human development	Society	How active firms are engaged in acts or programs to promote human welfare or goodwill	Carroll, A. B. (1991, 2004) Logsdon, J. M. and D. J. Wood (2002) Matten, D. and A. Crane (2005)
Competitive Advantage	Value creation occurs when firms adapt to their external context in order to optimize competitive advantage within their industry	Responsiveness to stakeholders; firms strategically orient and direct their resources in order to meet the needs of stakeholders	Stakeholder demands, such as expectations of social investments and philanthropy, are opportunities that can be leveraged for the benefit of the firm	Firm/stakeholders	Competitiveness within industry	Smith, N. C. (1994) Porter, M. E. and M. R. Kramer (1999, 2002) Bruch F. and F. Walter (2005)
Synergistic Value Creation	Firms maximize impact by creating pluralistic definitions of value, connecting stakeholder interests	Firms combine slack resources and good management in order to invest in human, social, financial, and ecological capital	Creating connections among stakeholders will open up heretofore unseen opportunities for collective value creation	Stakeholder/ community/ society/ environment	New opportunities for mutual gain	Pava, M. L. and J. Krausz (1996) Preston, L. E. and D. P. O'Bannon (1997) Waddock, S. and S. B. Graves (1997) Stanwick, P. A. and S. D. Stanwick (1998) Wheeler et al. (2005)

asking the question "What responsibility to society may businessmen reasonably be expected to assume?" As Carroll (2008) points out, this is a question that we continue to ask today.

II. **Conceptual development.** In the 1960s and 70s, scholars focused on the definitional aspects of CSR. At least two contrasting models emerged, including the view that a manager's decisions and actions must be motivated at least partially beyond a firm's direct economic or technical interests (Frederick 1960; Davis 1967) and shareholder value theory (SVT), which posits that firms are private and bear little responsibility to society other than creating profits and wealth (Freidman 1970). These two models have helped frame a basic dichotomy of CSR: to what extent should (and can) the actions of a firm produce private benefits for its shareholders compared to public benefits for society?

III. **Issues and practice.** During the late 1960s and early 1970s, discussions of CSR broadened to include specific issues, policies, and practices for advancing the concept (Heald 1970; Murphy 1978). Given the social activism of the time, the Cost Reduction model (Friedman 1962, 1970) posits that a firm's economic interest can be served by adopting a minimum level of social or environmental performance defined by specific programs that emphasize, for example, minority hiring, the environment, civil rights, and education (Eilbert and Parket 1973). Programs were considered ancillary functions of firms and rarely related to core functions.

IV. **Engagement.** As derivations of CSR, such as corporate social performance (Carroll 1979), continued to emerge in the late 1970s and 1980s, Jones (1980) viewed CSR as a *process* for firms to understand the needs and demands of society. The Stakeholder Theory model and its derivative, the Critical Theory of Stakeholder Participation, hold that while firms are made up of internal and external stakeholders, they nonetheless operate in a broader public context and must therefore keep society's interest in mind in day-to-day operations through continuous communications and engagement. This view is also especially important in the Reputation and Legitimacy model, which finds that CSR performance leads to positive (or negative) reputational effects in society that can, in turn, result in positive (or negative) economic outcomes for a firm.

V. **Integration.** Criticisms of CSR models, such as Corporate Social Performance, focus on the lack of integration between normative aspects (of CSR) and business activity (Melé 2008). The 1990s saw the emergence of the Competitive Advantage model, which posits that firms create value by adapting to external contexts; specific to CSR, stakeholder demands for social investments and philanthropy can be seen as an important market opportunity for firms (Porter *et al.* 1999, 2002). Therefore, social responsibility may be integrated into the strategy and operations of firms and, in the case of the Synergistic Value Creation model, may help create unforeseen value.

VI. **Empirical research, best practices, and internationalization.** The twenty-first century has seen a shift in emphasis from the definitional and conceptual aspects of CSR to the empirical research employing Corporate Social Performance, Stakeholder Theory, and Corporate Citizenship models, often complemented with other emerging frames such as business ethics and sustainability (Carroll 2008). Practice-related empirical research has grown rapidly during the 2000s largely driven by calls from industry for researchers to justify the "business case" for CSR; previous empirical research did not typically frame CSR practices in terms of competitive advantage (Kotler and Lee 2005). The emergence of CSR best practices and legal vehicles, such as the benefit corporation—the so-called B-corp—further encourage the integration of social goals into business operations. Finally, while CSR concepts were rapidly adopted and developed in Europe at least during the past 20 years, the 2000s saw increasing interest in CSR and its application in other parts of world (Carroll 2008).

3. Social responsibility of higher education

As noted in the previous section, CSR has evolved from a rudimentary philanthropic philosophy to an increasingly integrated practice among firms around the world reflected in emerging strategies, management, products, and services. Nonetheless, the creation of wealth—and resulting employment and economic development outcomes—remains the most important and appropriate objective function of industry. Conversely, we assume that colleges and universities are *de facto* social organizations and that their objective function is the creation and dissemination of new knowledge in service to society.

Social responsibility has long been integral to the development of higher education institutions world-wide. In the United States, for example, the social responsibility of colleges was reflected in early colonial charters and was the principal logic behind the Morrill Acts of 1862 and 1890 that led to the establishment of the nation's land-grant universities and agriculture experiment stations and cooperative extension service. In the twentieth century the social mission of emerging public institutions, including flagship universities and normal schools, was reflected in their (typical) non-profit status and receipt of substantial public funding, especially regular appropriations from state governments. Social responsibility was also a critical dimension of the Truman Commission report in 1947 that recommended the establishment of a nation-wide network of community colleges and financial aid for students of limited means, the latter of which led indirectly to the Higher Education Act of 1965 and its subsequent reauthorizations (Thelin 2004).

From contemporary political speeches to scholarly publications, the traditional responsibilities of higher education are specifically defined as teaching, research, and service (Bok 2003). Other responsibilities mentioned in the literature include developing the arts and humanities, advancing democratic principles, adopting environmentally friendly operational practices, critiquing public policy, preserving knowledge and making it available to communities, supporting curriculum development in primary and secondary schools, spurring economic development, and supporting local and regional communities, among others (Bok 1982; Gumport 2000; Kezar 2004; Kezar *et al.* 2005). The sections below explore how social responsibility is defined in the extant literature relating to the knowledge production function of colleges and universities.

3.1 Education

Education is a long-accepted responsibility of colleges and universities—and perhaps the oldest form of knowledge dissemination. In 1858, Cardinal John Henry Newman's *The Idea of a University Defined and Illustrated* posited that universities benefited society by educating *gentlemen* with "a cultivated intellect, a delicate taste, a candid, equitable mind, noble and courteous bearing in the conduct of life" (1919, Discourse 5, pt. 9).

In the twentieth century, higher education rapidly evolved from a luxury largely reserved for the wealthy, to a large and increasingly accessible public enterprise designed to meet the educational needs of a growing nation (Thelin 2004). This "massification" of higher education was viewed as a way to produce leaders who, in the post–World-War Two era, could serve society by improving international relations, the ethics of the free enterprise system, and the rights of citizens (Mead 1949).

Higher education's responsibility for educating civic-minded individuals, especially undergraduates, remains a common theme in contemporary research (Checkoway 2001; Iverson and James 2010; Thornton and Jaeger 2007). UNESCO (2009) deems an educated populace critical to a vibrant, democratic society. Intellectual inquiry creates awareness of the principles and practice of social obligation manifest in civic missions and community service (Kantanen 2005; Sawer 1987). Civic education, service learning courses, applied research within local communities, and other forms of community service equip students with the relevant knowledge and skills to address society's problems (Astin and Sax 1998; Bryant *et al.* 2012; Checkoway 2001; Schneider 2005; Thornton and Jaeger 2008).

In addition to providing a general education to students, higher education helps meet critical local and national workforce needs, such as the nation-wide demand for highly qualified math and science teachers (Bok 2003; National Governors Association [NGA] 2007; Ramaley 2005). This "human capital" responsibility has historical roots within the United States and was the rationale behind the creation of United States Military Academy at West Point and, later, the establishment of American land-grant universities and community colleges (Thelin 2004). Benefits of higher education meeting its workforce responsibilities include social mobility, poverty alleviation, regional development, and national competitiveness (Bok 2003; Kerr 2001; NGA 2007, 2011; National Research Council 2006; Zemsky 2010).

Finally, a growing number of policy reports articulate the importance of education attainment and the resulting need to provide higher education access to all individuals in society, especially older workers and the disadvantaged (Lumina Foundation 2013; NGA 2007, 2011). Kempner and Connett (1990) similarly posit that society must care for the higher education needs of all youths and see community colleges as the most important mechanism for remediation and skill development among high school dropouts. Zumeta (2011) finds that society should provide higher education to all population groups, exclusive of socio-economic status, and should therefore educate *more* students overall.

3.2 Academic research

As mentioned, the knowledge creation mission of higher education is a well-accepted responsibility. More than sixty years ago, Vannevar Bush—science advisor to President Franklin D. Roosevelt—advocated for federal support for academic research due to its importance in addressing issues of national security, human health, and commerce (Bush 1945). More recent policy discussions also emphasized the critical role of academic research in employment, technological advance, industry creation, and national competitiveness (NGA 2007; National Research Council 2006; Roberts and Easley 2009).

Despite the importance of the research mission, its function and impact are not well integrated into other discussions of other higher education responsibilities (NGA 2007). For example, discussing his role in the Spellings Commission on Higher Education for Postsecondary Reform convened in the mid-2000s, Zemsky (2010) is surprised by how "unimportant the research and discovery mission had become among higher education's would-be reformers." The literature that does exist ties the increasing preeminence of the research mission in higher education to a diminished focus on undergraduate education (Slaughter and Rhoades 2004). Related concerns include the emergence of elitist definitions of scholarship, narrow tenure and promotion guidelines, individualistic behavior among faculty, and mission creep among traditionally education-focused institutions (Boyer 1991; NGA 2007; Slaughter and Rhoades 2004). In other words, knowledge creation in colleges and universities is often not well linked to various forms of knowledge dissemination.

To help address some of these challenges, Boyer (1991) recommends that the definition of scholarship be broadened to include not only discovery, but also the scholarship of teaching, integration, and application. Similarly, Stokes (1997) and, more recently, Ramaley (2005) recommend that colleges and universities simultaneously connect discovery and theory to problem solving and the development of new, useful products. Several scholars recommend that the research mission of higher education focus on solving real-world, local community problems (Benson *et al.* 2005).

3.3 *Public engagement and service*

Thelin (2004) finds that, in addition to providing education, public colleges and universities were established to serve the needs of states and the nation. Scholars maintain that public service should remain an important social responsibility and, specifically, that colleges and universities should mobilize faculty in order to help solve problems in society, especially local communities (Checkoway 2001; Jacoby 2003; Slaughter and Rhoades 2004; van Ginkel 2002; Zumeta 2011). Similarly, Thornton and Jaeger (2007, 2008) posit that higher education should only receive financial resources from the government if it fulfills well-defined service obligations.

While public engagement and service has long been a part of the higher education policy lexicon, critical views have long existed relating to the commitment, substance, and effectiveness of higher education service missions (Checkoway 1997). Lee (1970), for example, finds that campus culture in the early twentieth century promoted hedonism far more than it inspired the fulfillment of civic duties. Thelin (2011) describes the recent efforts of colleges and universities to create new administrative posts, such as vice provosts for engagement, which rarely lead to substantial change. Bok (1982) observes that the (diminished) service mission of higher education can be linked to faculty incentives and culture and a narrow definition of service responsibilities in terms of what Ward (2003) calls "internal service," including administrative committees, hiring panels, and reviewing publications.

In addition to student education, scholarly publication and conference presentations are well-accepted forms of knowledge dissemination within higher education (Slaughter and Rhoades 2004; van Ginkel 2002). However, Nowotny *et al.* (2001) find that publication, a codified form of knowledge dissemination, does not account for other, more tacit forms of knowledge exchange. Weerts (2007) agrees, recommending that higher education institutions move away from the so-called expert model of knowledge dissemination and adopt a perspective that emphasizes knowledge sharing and co-creation with community stakeholders. Both Nowotny *et al.* (2001) and Weerts (2007) base their assumptions on constructivism whereby the knowledge creation process is localized, complex, and dynamic with learning and impact taking place during its application and utilization.

In addition to the aforementioned service learning programs, other types of outreach programs, such as agriculture extension, aid in the transmission of tacit knowledge while providing a vehicle to understand and address society's needs (McDowell 2001; Nowotny *et al.* 2001; Walshok 1995). Unfortunately, extension programs do not often exist outside of schools of agriculture at large public land grant universities (McDowell 2001), are structured as an ancillary support function with a particular school or university (Thornton and Jaeger 2007; Weerts and Sandmann 2008), or are viewed as unimportant or irrelevant by core faculty (Checkoway 2001).

Scholars recommend broadening extension programs beyond agriculture to include other research disciplines and renewing programmatic focus on research problems relevant to society (Boyer 1991; Kantanen 2005; McDowell 2001; Nowotny *et al.* 2001; Strand *et al.* 2003). One example in the literature is the creation of the Center for Research and Extension Services for Schools established at the University of California at Davis to support elementary and secondary school faculty in the Sacramento metropolitan area (Wagner 1993). Evidence shows that broadening scholarship in this way strengthens public financial support to colleges (Weerts and Ronca 2006; Weerts and Sandmann 2008).

3.4 Economic development and commercialization

Economic development has emerged in policy lexicon as the so-called fourth mission of higher education. The term can describe the direct impact of colleges and universities on their local economies through student spending, university procurement, and local employment. Efforts to measure the direct economic impact of colleges and universities are evident in the emergence of economic impact studies in higher education (Beck *et al.* 1995; NGA 2007).

The term economic development has also been used to describe the technology transfer role of research universities and resulting benefits, including the establishment of university spinoff companies, development of new technologies, employment, and attraction of talented individuals to work in the surrounding region (Phan and Siegel 2006; Rothaermel *et al.* 2007; Shane 2004). Colleges and universities encourage and support technology commercialization and entrepreneurship through a variety of mechanisms, including incubators, science parks, proof-of-concept centers, and venture funds (Bradley *et al.* 2013; Link and Scott 2003).

Critics fear that more entrepreneurial colleges and universities may compromise traditional values, including academic freedom, "disinterested" inquiry, and the ideals of liberal education. These concerns are framed in terms of commercialization (Bok 2003), academic capitalism (Slaughter and Rhoades 2004), or privatization (Altbach 1999). At one extreme, some fear that "public policy that subjects higher education to the market is a bad policy" (de la Fuente 2002). Other scholars approach market-driven changes more rhetorically, asking questions such as: to what extent should higher education adapt to market forces and what values should be upheld and reinforced as higher education interacts with other groups with different value systems (Kezar 2004; Kirp 2003; Slaughter and Rhoades 2004)?

Others take a more positive view of university entrepreneurship, finding little impact on traditional faculty responsibilities and, in some cases, a positive impact on publishing and research skills (Azoulay *et al.* 2009; Mansfield 1995). Mars and Rhoades (2012) suggest that social and economic goals may be complementary; they find that social entrepreneurs benefit from the infrastructure put in place to support market-oriented entrepreneurship.

To address concerns associated with commercialization, Bok (2003) recommends that universities adopt a "management approach" whereby social responsibilities are emphasized and promoted through a range of activities, including commercially oriented ventures. For example, both Zemsky (2010) and Slaughter and Rhoades (2004) recommend that universities use the proceeds from their market activities to fund areas that may not be self-sustaining like the arts and humanities, service to disadvantaged communities, and scholarships for the disadvantaged.

3.5 Adaptation, strategy, and efficiency

Organizational adaptation and efficiency are increasingly viewed as a responsibility of higher education (Tierney 1999; Zemsky 2010). Adaptation ranges from expanding higher education to the underserved (Kempner and Connett 1990) to transforming the nature of academic research (Nowotny *et al.* 2001), to improving educational quality (Zemsky 2010). Schneider (2005) cites "engaged learning" as an adaptive higher education response to growing research on cognition and intellectual development, the rise of new disciplinary and technological fields, growing interest in integrative learning, the emergence of diversity as an educational value, and the importance of teaming skills to employers.

While often viewed negatively by traditional academic communities, strategy and efficiency—co-opting market forces and management practices into higher education—are viewed as ways to control costs (Zemsky 2010), more effectively meet the responsibilities of higher education (Ward 2005), and increase the contributions of higher education to the public good (Longanecker 2005). Van Ginkel (2002) and Zemsky (2010) recognize that, given its decentralized nature, colleges and universities have difficulty implementing cross-campus strategies, as do state systems (NGA 2007). Related to civic engagement, Schneider (2005) recommends that higher education institutions adopt a comprehensive approach to civic engagement that spans schools and departments rather than relying on the uncoordinated actions of individual faculty and students. The Kellogg Commission (2000) found that evaluation practices and data systems should complement strategy in order to "make an open accounting of our progress toward achieving our commitment to the public good."

3.6 Accountability

Seeking to avoid the perceived excesses of academic life at Oxford, American colonialists created higher education governance structures to promote accountability among students and faculty (Thelin 2004). Rajaoson (2002) posits that the tradeoff for traditional "full academic authority and freedom" among higher education faculty is "clear and transparent accountability." As mentioned, Zemsky (2010) describes more modern versions of accountability, which focus almost exclusively on the education mission of universities and emphasize access, affordability, and quality. Specifically, rising costs, static (if not declining) graduation rates, and persistently low levels of higher education participation among disadvantaged populations have led to increasing pressure for colleges and universities to communicate and provide evidence of their broad usefulness (Breneman 1995; Fairweather 1996; Hearn and Holdsworth 2002; Tierney 1998).

3.7 Determination of social responsibilities

Few articles in the literature discuss *how*, specifically, social responsibilities for higher education should be determined; only a handful of articles examine how social responsibilities *are* determined. Some contend that responsibility should rest solely with individual colleges and universities. Rajaoson (2002) and de la Fuente (2002), for example, posit that academic freedom provides complete autonomy for faculty to define and carry out higher education's social responsibilities as best they see fit.

As mentioned above, Rajaoson (2002) acknowledges that with this autonomy comes accountability but does not articulate how this accountability is "enforced." De la Fuente (2002) disagrees that public financing allows governments to determine the social responsibilities of higher education; he articulates that "the autonomy of universities is somehow limited" and "the principle 'he who pays commands' does not apply." Thornton and Jaeger (2007, 2008) differ, finding that it is exactly the government's provision of financial resources that should motivate higher education to address the needs of the communities in which they are located.

Kezar *et al.* (2005) frame the determination of social responsibilities in terms of a public process: "A dialogue is needed to understand what the public expects of higher education and for leaders in higher education to talk about opportunities for serving the public good."

During this process, responsibilities would be negotiated among government, community, and higher education leaders through a social contract—or compact—mechanism (Kallison and Cohen 2010; Kezar *et al.* 2005; Neave 1997; NGA 2007). Further, society's expectations change regularly and, given that society provides authority and financial support to higher education, the social compact must be redefined and revitalized within the context of the capabilities of higher education (Kezar 2004; Neave 1997; Zemsky 2010).

Kezar *et al.* (2005) emphasize the reciprocal nature of a social contract, positing that society must provide political and financial support in return for higher education effectively meeting its responsibilities. Kallison and Cohen (2010) posit that a compact would place more responsibility on public colleges and universities for reform and accountability but, in turn, should guarantee stable levels of funding. Examples of social compacts in the literature include the California Master Plan and, more recently, the Virginia Restructuring Act (Douglass 2010; Pusser 2008).

3.8 Capability to fulfill social responsibilities

A relatively modest literature explores contextual factors that impact the capability of higher education to meet its social responsibilities, including political, organizational, and professional factors (Hearn and Holdsworth 2002; NGA 2007). Part of capability relates to the demands of society: as Bowen (1977) notes, colleges and universities have been asked to provide wide, equitable access; quality instruction; and world-class research—all at a low cost to students and taxpayers. Hearn and Holdsworth (2002), among others, point out that "painful tradeoffs" must be made among these goals because "do(ing) good work for everyone at low costs" is not possible. Further, as Zemsky (2010) notes, higher education's traditional emphasis on egalitarianism, free thought, and open inquiry is typically at odds with the increasing need for strategic management.

Given the centrality of faculty to university missions, Hearn and Holdsworth (2002) point out that divided faculty loyalty may also limit the ability of colleges and universities to meet social responsibilities. They identify at least six (potentially) conflicting loyalties of university faculty, including (1) institutional—loyalty to their college or university as an employee; (2) departmental—loyalty to their home units as players to competition for resources on campus; (3) disciplinary—loyalty to the lexicon, training, and advancement of their home discipline; (4) extramural—loyalty to those outside the institution who fund their research; (5) professional—loyalty to their individual career advancement; and (6) personal—loyalty to their own career and personal happiness. While these loyalties are not mutually exclusive, they certainly create tension relating to the ability of faculty—and therefore institutions—to serve broader goals within society.

Organizational incentives also play a mediating role in fulfilling the social responsibilities of higher education. Sanctions and incentives can be focused individually (through salary, promotions, and tenure), in groups (through allocation of resources and research programs), and institution-wide (through the nature of the work environment, the quality of benefits, the condition of the physical plant) (Hearn and Holdsworth 2002). A growing body of literature examines these incentives and explores how campus leadership, structure, faculty rewards, and institutional culture might be managed to facilitate closer alignment with the needs of society and promote engagement (Bringle and Hatcher 2000; Holland 1997; Maurrasse 2001; NGA 2007; Votruba 1996; Walshok 1999; Ward 1996; Zlotkowski 1998). Further, several state and system-wide efforts have been undertaken to restructure higher education governance systems and introduce performance funding systems, though their efficacy is unknown (NGA 2007; Zemsky 2010).

4. Discussion

This chapter reviews the extant literature relating to the social responsibility of higher education, relative to CSR, framed in terms of the creation and dissemination of new knowledge. The review uncovers a modest literature conceptualizing social responsibility within higher education, understanding that the majority of publications reviewed are what Marens (2004) calls normative exercises. In other words few, if any, publications explore empirically how faculty, students, or administrators define social responsibility in higher education, not to mention policymakers, community leaders, or the general public. Furthermore, there are few systematic analyses of how, beyond the ubiquitous three-pronged mission of teaching, research, and service, social responsibilities are *specifically* defined. For example, illustrated by Ward (2003), to what extent do higher education faculty define service in terms of internal administrative duties compared to external community-based activities?

Compared to the conceptualization of social responsibilities—and certainly the CSR literature—recent research relating to the practice of identifying and fulfilling the social responsibilities of higher education is lacking. This is not surprising given what Thornton and Jaeger (2007) observe in higher education as few common references or practices to social responsibility can be "cited by biology professors, groundskeepers, and athletic directors alike." In other words, if common visions of social responsibility are not clearly articulated, then it is difficult at best to understand how social responsibilities are implemented and, therefore, how knowledge is disseminated beyond academic publication. Even within the context of long-standing practices, such as extension and civic education, there is a dearth of (recent) analyses of how these programs have evolved, and their efficacy.

From reviews of the technology transfer and university entrepreneurship literature we find, however, a robust and growing body of work relating to the creation and dissemination of new, "economically-useful" knowledge. On one hand, this may motivate additional discussion and research related to the question: is commercialization of technologies derived from academic research a *social* responsibility of higher education? On the other hand, given our original premise that colleges and universities are inherently social organizations, to what extent do other (social) responsibilities relate to and take preference over these commercial endeavors?

While many scholars and critics have posed these questions, we do not yet have the conceptual frameworks, much less the empirical research, to address them fully though Hearn and Holdsworth (2002) and Weerts (2007) certainly offer a promising start. Our review of the CSR literature is instructive: compared to the CSR phases of development mentioned above, notions of the social responsibility for higher education may be at a point similar to its conceptual development phase.

The findings unearthed in this review present an extraordinary opportunity for scholars to explore and craft a related research agenda to understand better how social responsibility is conceptualized in higher education. A research greenfield also exists to examine how social responsibilities are determined, along with individual, institution, and system-level practices for their execution. This examination might include new higher education organizational structures, best practices for defining and implementing the social good, public–private partnerships, and emerging models of higher education outreach. These research avenues could be further framed in terms of the relationship between social responsibility in higher education and the creation and dissemination of new knowledge, allowing coordination between Economics and other relevant social sciences.

Thankfully, we can also draw upon CSR for conceptual guidance; Stakeholder Theory and Corporate Social Performance, for example, may offer useful frameworks for application to higher education. Further, CSR is part of a much larger Management literature that examines nearly every operational and strategic aspect of for-profit and, increasingly, non-profit organizations. Perhaps it's time for scholars to develop strategic management concepts for higher education, with social responsibility as the foundation.

Acknowledgements

Thanks to Samantha Bradley at the Research Triangle Institute for her able research assistance. Thanks also to Jim Hearn at the University of Georgia and John Thelin at the University of Kentucky for their helpful comments and suggestions.

References

Acs, Z., Braunerhjelm, J. P., Audretsch, D. B., and Carlsson, B. (2009). The knowledge spillover theory of entrepreneurship. *Small Business Economics*, 32(1), 15–30.

Almeida, P., and Kogut, B. (1999). Localization of knowledge and the mobility of engineers in regional networks. *Management Science*, 45(7), 905–917.

Altbach, P. G. (1999). *Private Prometheus: Private higher education and development in the 21st century*. Westport, CT: Greenwood.

Anderson, J. C., and Frankle, A. W. (1980). Voluntary social reporting: An iso-beta portfolio analysis. *The Accounting Review*, 55, 467–479.

Astin, A. W., and Sax, L. J. (1998). How undergraduates are affected by service participation. *Journal of College Student Development*, 39, 251–263.

Aupperle, K. E., Carrol, A. B., and Hatfield, J. D. (1985). An empirical examination of the relationship between corporate social responsibility and profitability. *Academy of Management Journal*, 28(2), 446–463.

Azoulay, P., Ding, P., and Stuart, T. (2009). The impact of academic patenting on the rate, quality, and direction of (public) research output. *Journal of Industrial Economics*, 57, 637–676.

Beck, R., Elliott, D., Meisel, J., and Wagner, M. (1995). Economic impact studies of regional public colleges and universities. *Growth and Change*, 26(2), 245–260.

Benson, L., Harkavy, I., and Hartley, M. (2005). Integrating a commitment to the public good into the institutional fabric. In K. Adrianna (Ed.), *Higher education for the public good*. San Francisco: Jossey-Bass, 185–216.

Bok, D. (1982). *Beyond the ivory tower: Social responsibilities of the modern university*. Cambridge, MA: Harvard University Press.

Bok, D. (2003). *Universities in the marketplace: The commercialization of higher education*. Princeton, NJ: Princeton University Press.

Bowen, H. R. (1953). *Social responsibilities of the businessman*. New York: Harper & Row.

Bowen, H. R. (1977). *Investment in learning*. San Francisco: Jossey-Bass.

Bowie, N. E. (1991). The firm as a moral community. In R. M. Coughlin (Ed.), *Morality, rationality, and efficiency: New perspectives on socio-economics*. Armonk, NY: M. E. Sharp, 169–183.

Boyer, E. L. (1991). The scholarship of teaching. In: Scholarship reconsidered: Priorities of the professoriate. *College Teaching*, 39(1), 11–13.

Bradley, S. R., Hayter, C. S., and Link, A. N. (2013). Proof of concept centers in the United States: An exploratory look. *Journal of Technology Transfer*, 38, 349–381.

Braunerhjelm, P., Acs, Z. J., Audretsch, D. B., and Carlsson, B. (2010). The missing link: Knowledge diffusion and entrepreneurship in endogenous growth. *Small Business Economics*, 34(2), 105–125.

Breneman, D. W. (1995, September 8). Sweeping, painful changes. *Chronicle of Higher Education*, B1–B2.

Bringle, R. G., and Hatcher, J. A. (2000). Institutionalization of service learning in higher education. *Journal of Higher Education*, 71(3), 273–290.

Bruch, F., and Walter, F. (2005). The keys to rethinking corporate philanthropy. *MIT Sloan Management Review*, 47(1), 49–55.

Bryant, A. N., Gayles, J. G., and Davis, H. A. (2012). The relationship between civic behavior and civic values: A conceptual model. *Research in Higher Education*, 53(1), 76–93.

Bush, V. (1945). *Science – The endless frontier*. A Report to the President on a Program for Postwar Scientific Research (July) and Reprinted by the National Science Foundation: Washington, DC.

Carroll, A. B. (1979). A three-dimensional conceptual model of corporate performance. *Academy of Management Review*, 4(4), 497–505.

Carroll, A. B. (1991). The pyramid of corporate social responsibility: Towards the moral management of organizational stakeholders. *Business Horizons*, 34(4), 39–48.

Carroll, A. B. (1999). Corporate social responsibility: Evolution of a definitional construct. *Business & Society*, 38(3), 268–295.

Carroll, A. B. (2004). Managing ethically with global stakeholders: A present and future challenge. *Academy of Management Executive*, 18(2), 114–120.

Carroll, A. B. (2008). A history of corporate social responsibility: Concepts and practices. *The Oxford Handbook of Corporate Social Responsibility*, Oxford: Oxford University Press, 19–46.

Checkoway, B. (1997). Reinventing the research university for public service. *Journal of Planning Literature*, 11(3), 307–319.

Checkoway, B. (2001). Renewing the civic mission of the American research university. *Journal of Higher Education*, 125–147.

Clarkson, M. B. E. (1995). A stakeholder framework for analyzing and evaluating corporate social performance. *Academy of Management Review*, 20(1), 92–117.

Cornell, B., and Shapiro, A. C. (1987). Corporate stakeholders and corporate finance. *Financial Management*, 16, 5–14.

Crane, A., McWilliams, A., Matten, D., Moon, J., and Siegel, D. (2008). The corporate social responsibility agenda. *The Oxford Handbook of Corporate Social Responsibility*, Oxford: Oxford University Press, 3–18.

Davis, K. (1967). Understanding the social responsibility puzzle: What does the businessman owe to society?. *Business Horizons*, 10 (Winter), 45–50.

Davis, K. (1973). The case for and against business assumption of social responsibilities. *Academy of Management Journal*, 16(2), 312–322.

De Bakker, F. G., Groenewegen, P., and Den Hond, F. (2005). A bibliometric analysis of 30 years of research and theory on corporate social responsibility and corporate social performance. *Business & Society*, 44(3), 283–317.

De la Fuente, J. R. (2002). Academic freedom and social responsibility. *Higher Education Policy*, 15(4), 337–339.

Donaldson, T., and Preston, L. (1995). The stakeholder theory of the corporation: Concepts, evidence, implications. *Academy of Management Review*, 20, 65–91.

Douglass, J. A. (2010). *From chaos to order and back? A revisionist reflection on the California master plan.* For Higher Education @ 50 and Thoughts about its Future. Available at: http://www.cshe.berkeley.edu/chaos-order-and-back-revisionist-reflection-california-master-plan-higher-education50-and-thoughts. Accessed July 11, 2014.

Drumwright, M. (1996). Company advertising with social dimension: The role of non-economic criteria. *Journal of Marketing*, 60, 71–87.

Eilbert, H., and Parket, I. R. (1973). The current status of corporate social responsibility. *Business Horizons*, 16, 5–14.

Evan, W. M., and Freeman, R. E. (1988). A stakeholder theory of the modern corporation: Kantian capitalism. In T. Beauchamp and N. Bowie (Eds.), *Ethical theory and business*. Englewood Cliffs, NJ: Prentice Hall, 75–93.

Fairweather, J. S. (1996). *Faculty work and public trust: Restoring the value of teaching and public service in American academic life.* Needham Heights, MA: Allyn and Bacon.

Frederick, W. C. (1960). The growing concern over business responsibility. *California Management Review*, 2, 54–61.

Freedman, M., and Jaggi, B. (1982). Pollution disclosures, pollution performance and economic performance. *Omega*, 10(2), 167–176.

Friedman, M. (1962). *Capitalism and freedom.* Chicago: University of Chicago Press.

Friedman, M. (1970). The social responsibility of business is to increase its profits. *New York Times Magazine*, 13 September.

Gray, B. (1989). *Collaborating: Finding common ground for multi-party problems.* San Francisco: Jossey-Bass.

Griliches, Z. (1979). Issues in assessing the contribution of research and development to productivity growth. *The Bell Journal of Economics*, 10(1), 92–116.

Gumport, P. J. (2000). Academic restructuring: Organizational change and institutional imperatives. *Higher Education*, 39(1), 67–91.

Handy, C. (2002). What is a business for? *Harvard Business Review*, December.

Heald, M. (1970). *The social responsibilities of business: Company, community, 1900–1960.* Cleveland, OH: Case Western Reserve University Press.

Hearn, J. C., and Holdsworth, J. M. (2002). The societally responsive university: Public ideals, organisational realites, and the possibility of engagement. *Tertiary Education & Management*, 8(2), 127–144.

Holland, B. A. (1997). Analyzing institutional commitment to service: A model of key organizational factors. *Michigan Journal of Community Service Learning*, 4, 30–41.

Iverson, S. V., and James, J. H. (2010). Becoming "effective" citizens? Change-oriented service in a teacher education program. *Innovative Higher Education*, 35(1), 19–35.

Jacoby, B. (ed.) (2003). *Building partnerships for service-learning.* San Francisco: Jossey-Bass.

Jaffe, A. (1989). Real effects of academic research. *American Economic Review*, 79(5), 957–970.

Jaffe, A., Trajtenberg, M., and Henderson, R. (1993). Geographic localization of knowledge spillovers as evidenced by patent citations. *Quarterly Journal of Economics*, 108(3), 577–598.

Jensen, M. C. (2002). Value maximization, stakeholder theory, and the corporate objective function. *Business Ethics Quarterly*, 12(2), 235–256.

Jensen, M. C., and Meckling, W. (1976). Theory of the firm: Managerial behavior, agency cost, and capital structure. *Journal of Financial Economics*, 3(4), 305–360.

Jones, T. M. (1980). Corporate social responsibility revisited, redefined. *California Management Review*, 22(2), 59–67.

Kallison Jr., J. M., and Cohen, P. (2010). A new compact for higher education: Funding and autonomy for reform and accountability. *Innovative Higher Education*, 35(1), 37–49.

Kantanen, H. (2005). Civic mission and social responsibility: New challenges for the practice of public relations in higher education. *Higher Education Management and Policy*, 17(1), 1–16.

Kellogg Commission. (2000). Renewing the covenant: Learning, discovery, and engagement in a new age and different world. *Kellogg Commission on the Future of State and Land-Grant Universities.*

Kempner, K., and Connett, D. (1990). Social responsibility in community colleges: Rethinking the commitment to alternative education. *Innovative Higher Education*, 14(2), 83–92.

Kerr, C. (2001). *The uses of the university.* 5th edn. Cambridge, MA: Harvard University Press.

Kezar, A. J. (2004). Obtaining integrity? Reviewing and examining the charter between higher education and society. *The Review of Higher Education*, 27(4), 429–459.

Kezar, A. J., Chambers, T. C., and Burkhardt, J. C. (2005). *Higher education for the public good: Emerging voices from a national movement.* San Francisco: Jossey-Bass.

Kirp, D. L. (2003). *Shakespeare, Einstein, and the bottom line: The marketing of higher education.* Cambridge, MA: Harvard University Press.

Kotler, P., and Lee, N. (2005). *Corporate social responsibility: Best practices for doing the most good.* Hoboken, New Jersey: John Wiley & Sons.

Lee, C. B. T. (1970). *The campus scene, 1900–1970.* New York: David McKay.

Lerner, L. D., and Fryxell, G. E. (1988). An empirical study of the predictors of corporate social performance: A multi-dimensional analysis. *Journal of Business Ethics*, 7(12), 951–959.

Link, A. N., and Scott, J. T. (2003). US science parks: The diffusion of an innovation and its effects on the academic missions of universities. *International Journal of Industrial Organization*, 21(9), 1323–1356.

Logsdon, J. M., and Wood, D. J. (2002). Global corporate citizenship: From domestic to global level of analysis. *Business Ethics Quarterly*, 12(2) 155–187.

Longanecker, D. (2005). State governance and the public good. In A. Kezar (Ed.), *Higher education for the public good*, 166–181. San Francisco: Jossey-Bass.

Lumina Foundation. (2013). *A stronger nation through higher education.* Indianapolis, IN: Lumina Foundation.

McDowell, G. (2001). *Land-grant universities and extension into the 21st Century: Renegotiating or abandoning a social contract.* Ames, IA: Iowa State University Press.

McWilliams, A., and Siegel, D. (2001). Corporate social responsibility: A theory of the firm perspective. *Academy of Management Review*, 26(1), 117–127.

Mansfield, E. (1995). Academic research underlying industrial innovations: Sources, characteristics, and financing. *The Review of Economics and Statistics*, 77, 55–65.

Marens, R. (2004). Wobbling on a one-legged stool: The decline of American pluralism and the academic treatment of corporate social responsibility. *Journal of Academic Ethics*, 2(1), 63–87.

Mars, M. M., and Rhoades, G. (2012). Socially oriented student entrepreneurship: A study of student change agency in the academic capitalism context. *The Journal of Higher Education*, 83(3), 435–459.

Matten, D., and Crane, A. (2005). Corporate citizenship: Towards an extended theoretical conceptualization. *Academy of Management Review*, 30(1), 166–179.

Maurrasse, D. J. (2001). *Beyond the campus: How colleges and universities form partnerships with their communities.* New York: Routledge.

Mead, A. R. (1949). The moral responsibility of the university. *Peabody Journal of Education,* 26(6), 354–358.

Melé, D. (2008). Corporate social responsibility theories. *The Oxford Handbook of Corporate Social Responsibility,* Oxford: Oxford University Press, 48–82.

Murphy, P. E. (1978). An evolution: Corporate social responsiveness. *University of Michigan Business Review,* 6(30), 19–25.

Murray, K. B., and Montanari, J. R. (1986). Strategic management of the socially responsible firm: Integrating management and marketing theory. *Academy of Management Review,* 22(4), 853–856.

National Governors Association. (2007). *A compact for postsecondary education.* Washington, D.C.: NGA.

National Governors Association. (2011). *Complete to compete: Improving postsecondary attainment among adults.* Washington, D.C.: NGA.

National Research Council. (2006). *Rising above the gathering storm: Energizing and employing America for a brighter economic future.* Washington, D.C.: National Academies Press.

Neave, G. (1997). Markets, higher education and social responsibility. *Higher Education Policy,* 10(3/4), 161–162.

Nelson, R. R. (2005). *Technology, institutions and economic growth.* Cambridge, MA: Harvard University Press.

Newman, J. H. (1919). *The idea of a university defined and illustrated: I. in nine discourses delivered to the Catholics of Dublin: II in occasional lectures and essays addressed to the members of the Catholic university.* New York: Longmans, Green, and Company.

Nowotny, H., Scott, P., and Gibbons, M. (2001). *Re-thinking science: Knowledge and the public in an age of uncertainty.* Malden, MA: Polity.

Pava, M. L., and Krausz, J. (1996). The association between corporate social responsibility and financial performance: The paradox of social cost. *Journal of Business Ethics,* 15, 321–357.

Phan, P. H. C., and Siegel, D. S. (2006). *The effectiveness of university technology transfer.* Hanover, MA: Now Publishers Inc.

Porter, M. E., and Kramer, M. R. (1999). Philanthropy's new agenda: Creating value. *Harvard Business Review,* 77(6), 121–130.

Porter, M. E., and Kramer, M. R. (2002). The competitive advantage of corporate philanthropy. *Harvard Business Review,* 80(12), 56–68.

Preston, L. E., and O'Bannon, D. P. (1997). The corporate social-financial performance relationship: A typology and analysis. *Business and Society,* 35(4), 419–429.

Preston, L. E., and Post, J. E. (1981). Private management and public policy. *California Management Review,* 23(3), 56–63.

Pusser, B. (2008). The state, the market and the institutional estate: Revisiting contemporary authority relations in higher education. In *Higher Education,* 105–139. Netherlands: Springer.

Rajaoson, F. (2002). Academic freedom and social responsibility: Reflections from the African experience. *Higher Education Policy,* 15(4), 375–379.

Ramaley, J. A. (2005). Scholarship for the public good: Living in Pasteur's dream. In A. Kezar (Ed.), *Higher education for the public good,* 166–181. San Francisco: Jossey-Bass.

Roberts, E. B., and Easley, C. (2009). *Entrepreneurial impact: The role of MIT.* Kansas City, MO: Kauffman Foundation for Entrepreneurship.

Romer, P. M. (1986). Increasing returns and long-run growth. *The Journal of Political Economy,* 1002–1037.

Ross, S. A. (1973). The economic theory of agency: The principal's problem. *American Economic Review,* 63(2), 134–139.

Rothaermel, F., Agung, S., and Jiang, L. (2007). University entrepreneurship: A taxonomy of the literature. *Industrial and Corporate Change,* 16, 691–791.

Sawer, M. (1987). Academic freedom and social responsibility. *Politics,* 22(1), 1–7.

Scherer, A. G., and Palazzo, E. T. (2007). Towards a political conception of corporate responsibility: Business and society seen from a Habermasian perspective. *Academy of Management Review,* 32, 1096–1120.

Schneider, C. G. (2005). Liberal education and the civic engagement gap. In A. Kezar (Ed.), *Higher education for the public good,* 166–181. San Francisco: Jossey-Bass.

Shane, S. (2004). *Academic entrepreneurship: University spinoffs and wealth creation.* Northampton, MA: Edward Elgar.

Slaughter, S., and Rhoades, G. (2004). *Academic capitalism and the new economy: Markets, state, and higher education.* Baltimore, MD: Johns Hopkins University Press.

Smith, N. C. (1994). The new corporate philanthropy. *Harvard Business Review,* 72(3), 105–116.

Solow, R. M. (1956). A contribution to the theory of economic growth. *The Quarterly Journal of Economics,* 70(1), 65–94.

Stanwick, P. A., and Stanwick, S. D. (1998). The relationship between corporate social performance and organizational size, financial performance, and environmental performance: An empirical examination. *Journal of Business Ethics*, 17, 195–204.

Stokes, D. E. (1997). *Pasteur's quadrant: Basic science and technological innovation*. Washington, DC: Brookings Institution Press.

Strand, K., Marullo, S., Cutforth, N., Stoecker, R., and Donohue, P. (2003). *Community-based research and higher education*. San Francisco: Jossey-Bass.

Thelin, J. R. (2004). *A history of American higher education*. Baltimore, MD: The Johns Hopkins University Press.

Thelin, J. R. (2011). Talk is cheap: The university and the national project—a history. In Feith, D. (Ed.), *Teaching America: The case for civic education*. Lantham, MD: Rowman and Littlefield.

Thornton, C. H., and Jaeger, A. J. (2007). A new context for understanding civic responsibility: Relating culture to action at a research university. *Research in Higher Education*, 48(8), 993–1020.

Thornton, C. H., and Jaeger, A. J. (2008). The role of culture in institutional and individual approaches to civic responsibility at research universities. *The Journal of Higher Education*, 79(2), 160–182.

Tierney, W. G. (1998). *The responsive university: Restructuring for high performance*. Baltimore, MD: The Johns Hopkins University Press.

Tierney, W. G. (1999). *Building the responsive campus: Creating high performance colleges and universities*. Thousand Oaks, CA: Sage Publications.

UNESCO. (2009). *World conference on higher education: The new dynamics of higher education and research for societal change and development*. Final communiqué. Paris: United Nations Educational, Scientific, and Cultural Organization.

Van Ginkel, H. (2002). Academic freedom and social responsibility: The role of university organisations. *Higher Education Policy*, 15(4), 347–351.

Van Oosterhout, J. H. (2005). Corporate citizenship: An idea whose time has not yet come. *Academy of Management Review*, 30(4), 677–681.

Varadarajan, P. R., and Menon, A. (1998). Cause-related marketing. A coalignment of marketing strategy and corporate philanthropy. *Journal of Marketing*, 52(3), 58–74.

Votruba, J. C. (1996). Strengthening the university's alignment with society: Challenges and strategies. *Journal of Public Service and Outreach*, 1(1), 29–36.

Waddock, S., and Graves, S. B. (1997). Quality of management and quality of stakeholder relationships: Are they synonymous? *Business and Society*, 36(3), 250–279.

Wagner, J. (1993). Social contracts and university public service: The case of agriculture and schooling. *The Journal of Higher Education*, 64(6), 696–729.

Walshok, M. L. (1995). *Knowledge without boundaries: What America's research universities can do for the economy, the workplace, and the community*. San Francisco: Jossey-Bass.

Walshok, M. L. (1999). Strategies for building the infrastructure that supports the engaged campus. In R. G. Bingle, R. Games, and E. A. Malloy (Eds.), *Colleges and universities as citizens*. Boston, MA: Allyn and Bacon.

Ward, K. (1996). Service learning and student volunteerism: Reflections on institutional commitment. *Michigan Journal of Community Service Learning*, 3, 55–65.

Ward, K. (2003). *Faculty service roles and the scholarship of engagement*. ASHE Higher Education Report, 29(5), San Francisco: Jossey-Bass.

Ward, K. (2005). Rethinking faculty roles and rewards for the public good. In A. Kezar (Ed.), *Higher education for the public good*, 166–181. San Francisco: Jossey-Bass.

Wartick, S. L., and Cochran, P. L. (1985). The evolution of the corporate social performance model. *Academy of Management Review*, 10(4), 758–769.

Weerts, D. J. (2007). Toward an engagement model of institutional advancement at public colleges and universities. *International Journal of Educational Advancement*, 7(2), 79–103.

Weerts, D. J., and Ronca, J. M. (2006). Examining differences in state support for higher education: A comparative study of state appropriations for research I universities. *The Journal of Higher Education*, 77(6), 935–967.

Weerts, D. J., and Sandmann, L. R. (2008). Building a two-way street: Challenges and opportunities for community engagement at research universities. *The Review of Higher Education*, 32(1), 73–106.

Wheeler, D., McKague, K., Thomson, J., Davies, R., Medalye, J., and Prada, M. (2005). Creating sustainable local enterprise network. *MIT Sloan Management Review*, 47(1), 33–40.

Wood, D. J. (1991a). Toward improving corporate social performance. *Business Horizons*, 34(4), 66–73.

Wood, D. J. (1991b). Corporate social performance revisited. *Academy of Management Review*, 16(4), 691–718.

Zemsky, R. (2010). *Making reform work: The case for transforming American higher education*. New Brunswick, NJ: Rutgers University Press.

Zlotkowski, E. (1998). *Successful service-learning programs: New models of excellence in higher education*. Bolton, MA: Anker Publishing Company, Inc.

Zumeta, W. M. (2011). What does it mean to be accountable? Dimensions and implications of higher education's public accountability. *The Review of Higher Education*, 35(1), 131–148.

10

An alternative to the economic value of knowledge

Heather Rimes, Jennie Welch, and Barry Bozeman

1. Introduction

Neoclassical economic theory asserts that value can be derived from the interaction of the market supply and demand for a particular good or service. In societies with market economies, assuming that a good's value is synonymous with the good's market price is often appropriate. The great advantage of equating price with value is that price provides a common metric by which to compare value across a wide range of goods and services. In most cases, assigning a market price changes neither the production of the good nor how the good is used. However, some social scientists and policy makers argue that the marketization of particular goods and services, for example the topic of this chapter—knowledge—can affect the product itself, crowding out particular behaviors of producers and consumers based on the value assigned and altering the nature of the good or service produced.

In this chapter we concern ourselves with the limitations of market-based tools for evaluating knowledge production. We suggest that we can begin to address these limitations by taking a non-economic approach to knowledge valuation. We argue that the true value of scientific knowledge lies in how often and how widely it is applied—information that is not captured in its market price. In other words, the value of knowledge derives from *the intensity and range of its use*. It is important to note that we do not advocate that the economic value of knowledge should be ignored. Knowledge is often treated as a commodity, and because it can generate tangible outputs, there is utility to using market-based evaluation methods. For instance, cost-benefit analysis is useful for justifying science and technology expenditures or as a method for choosing between R&D alternatives. However, this chapter posits that market-based notions of value and value evaluation are limiting because they ignore the capacity of knowledge to produce new uses.

The chapter introduces churn theory as an alternative way of measuring the value of knowledge that cannot be captured using market-based strategies alone. Its core purpose is to provide a rich description of churn theory. We begin with a brief overview of economic approaches to knowledge valuation and describe ways in which churn theory addresses the limitations of these approaches. We then provide a thorough discussion of the theory's core assumptions, illustrate how it has been applied in the literature, and highlight the findings these applications have produced. Next, we compare the similarities and differences between churn theory and other methods of valuing knowledge, both economic and non-economic. Finally, we conclude with a discussion of the future promise of churn theory, summarizing developments and applications of the theory and discussing implications for future research.

2. Economic approaches to knowledge valuation

As discussed above, churn theory offers an alternative to the economic value of knowledge. To underscore why an alternative is warranted, we briefly describe economic approaches and their shortcomings (see Audretsch *et al.*, 2002; Ballandonne, 2012; and Stephan, 1996 for more in-depth treatments of the development of the economics of science as a field of study). First, the traditional economic approach treats knowledge as a durable public good, non-rivalrous and non-excludable, and thus apt to produce market failures (Mowery, 1983). Specifically, knowledge creation generates positive externalities known as knowledge spillovers, informal exchanges of ideas and information among market participants (Carlino, 2001; Forni and Paba, 2002; Griliches, 1979). Because the net social benefit of knowledge creation exceeds the net private benefit, an undersupply of knowledge occurs when knowledge generation activities are guided solely by the market's invisible hand (Arrow, 1962; Nelson, 1959). From this perspective, knowledge value is reflected by market value and pricing mechanisms, which can be analyzed by utilizing appropriate econometric models. Examples of studies that use a traditional economic approach for knowledge valuation include research on production functions for assessing national economic growth related to science and technology (Griliches, 1979; Solow, 1957), investigations into the appropriability of research and development (R&D) returns (Levin *et al.*, 1987), and attempts to estimate the market value of a firm's knowledge assets (Czarnitzki *et al.*, 2006).

There have long been critiques of the adequacy of the traditional economic paradigm to fully address the complexities of scientific and technical knowledge production (Bozeman and Rogers, 2002). In response to some of these criticisms, Partha Dasgupta and Paul David (1994) call for a "new economics of science". They argue that the traditional approach largely ignores the norms, reward systems, and institutional structures of knowledge generating institutions. They point out that these features have important implications for resource allocation and knowledge production. For instance, they discuss credit as a particularly important incentive mechanism for academic scientists, drawing the focus of economic analysis to individual scientists rather than firms. Others have suggested the individual scientist as a critical unit of analysis as well (Acs *et al.*, 2009). Additionally, Dasgupta and David (1994) outline ways that tools of economic analysis such as game theory can be used to analyze knowledge production processes and influence public policy decisions. Research drawing upon the new economics of science approach is varied and fruitful. To illustrate, a sampling of studies that adopt the perspective includes the following: an analysis of the relationship between industrial scientists' wages and autonomy to pursue their own research agendas (Stern, 2004), an examination of the relationship between university scientists' royalty shares and university licensing income (Lach and Schankerman, 2008), and an economic explanation for why publication practices in biomedicine may be distorting research (Young *et al.*, 2008).

Despite their differences, several criticisms apply to both traditional and new economics of science approaches to knowledge valuation. For instance, some scholars cite the marketization effect, suggesting that assigning price and measuring performance using market tools alone may change the behavior of producers, consumers, or both (Sandel, 2012). Others critique the approaches for their strict focus on discrete outputs, such as scientific publications or products of R&D projects, which ignores the long-term positive (or negative) effects of knowledge production endeavors (Bozeman *et al.*, 2001). Of particular importance for churn theorists is the objection that "the rents one captures for scientific and technical knowledge often seem quite unrelated to anyone's conception of the actual social and intellectual value of the knowledge" (Bozeman and Rogers, 2002, p. 771). Because of this, churn theory offers an alternative, non-economic approach to knowledge valuation.

3. Theoretical building blocks of churn theory

As the title of the theory suggests, churning describes the process through which knowledge is created, used, and transformed. The image of churning relays the idea that knowledge and production process is not directional, and it does not assume linear scientific progress (Bozeman and Rogers, 2002). The process is represented by a cycle of unpredictable periodicity consisting of information use and transformation which creates new knowledge and information, followed by information use and transformation once again. In order to explain this cycle, churn theory weaves together specific definitions of knowledge and information, two core assumptions, and two key conceptual elements. In doing so, the theory offers an alternative to economic approaches to knowledge valuation. Each of these elements is discussed in turn below.

3.1 Defining knowledge and information

Knowledge is a broad concept that scholars define and apply in a variety of ways (see Alavi and Leidner, 2001 or Godin, 2010 for an overview). Of particular importance to the development of churn theory, contributors to the knowledge and information literatures have posited hierarchical models that distinguish between knowledge and other related concepts (Ackoff, 1989; Zeleny, 1987). Rowley (2007) examines the evolution of these models, paying particular attention to the data, information, knowledge, wisdom (DIKW) hierarchy. Hierarchical models such as these include links that facilitate transformation of lower levels of the hierarchy to higher. For example, mechanisms for processing data create the links that transform data into information (Ackoff, 1989). Bozeman and Rogers (2002) draw on ideas embedded in hierarchical models, coupled with the scientific and technical context, to generate distinct definitions of knowledge and information.

> Information: descriptors (e.g. coded observations) and statements (e.g. language-based synthetic propositions) concerning empirically-derived observations about conditions and states of affairs in the physical world and the realm of human behavior.
>
> Knowledge: information *put to use* [emphasis added] in furtherance of scientific understanding (i.e. empirically-based, generalizable explanation of states of affairs and behavior) or in the creation, construction, or reshaping of technological devices and processes.
>
> *(Bozeman and Rogers, 2002, p. 773)*

These definitions adopt the above-mentioned perspective that knowledge and information are distinguishable and hierarchically related. Moreover, they specify that the link transforming information into knowledge is a person or persons' use of the information. Defining knowledge in this way creates the foundation for the two key assumptions of churn theory.

3.2 Key assumptions

First, a central underlying assumption of churn theory is that the value of knowledge is not transitive among users. Non-transitivity of knowledge value signifies that it is not possible to weight or rank varying knowledge uses. For instance, one cannot say that using knowledge to increase understanding of the physical world is any more or less valuable than using the same knowledge to develop a new product that will increase a firm's profits. The theorists frame this as the "equality of use" principle.

> The equality of use principle is a direct consequence of the observation that scientific and technical knowledge does not contain its consequences and potential within itself ... Clients' use *defines* success. Therefore, the array of uses that reflect attribution of value of research output must be established empirically rather than being imposed a priori.
>
> *(Bozeman and Rogers, 2002, p. 773)*

Thus, it is possible to evaluate knowledge use in terms of various aspects of its use (suggestions include repetition, intensity, and range of uses), but the uses themselves are non-transitive (Bozeman and Rogers, 2002). Bozeman and Rogers (2002) provide an overview of the criticisms that the equality of use principle might provoke. Importantly, they discuss that the theory is not a theory of the good, meaning that it does not imply anything about the morality of knowledge uses.

In addition to the equality of use principle, the second core assumption of the churn model is the "use-transformation-value" assumption. The label describes the process by which knowledge value is created. Specifically, *use* of information *transforms* information into knowledge, and knowledge *value* in turn derives from its use. The implication is that use and valuation of knowledge are identical. Moreover, information alone has no inherent value, but rather it gains value as it is transformed through use. Thus, as knowledge is used more broadly or intensely, it becomes more valuable. This process of use-transformation-value drives the churn process of innovation. Information in use is knowledge; knowledge use produces new information. In turn, the new information may be used, thereby creating new knowledge, or it may remain unused and valueless. The churning of the use and transformation cycle can (although it is not inevitable that it does) produce new uses of knowledge.

3.3 Scientific and technical human capital and the KVC

The use-transformation-value churning process is driven by the individuals who are participating in the cycle of knowledge creation and use. These individuals and their social configurations are the focus of churn theory's two major conceptual elements: S&T human capital and the knowledge value collective. S&T human capital "encompasses not only the individual human capital endowments...but also the sum total of researchers' tacit knowledge, craft knowledge, and know-how...[It] further includes the social capital that scientists continually draw upon in creating knowledge" (Bozeman et al., 2001, p. 5). In other words, S&T human capital refers to the bundles of knowledge, skills, abilities, and social capital, both formally and informally attained, that are possessed by researchers in a specified domain. As individuals participate in the knowledge creation process, they simultaneously increase their S&T human capital which enhances their capacity to generate and use new knowledge. Because capacity precedes the ability to generate new uses of information, individuals, research groups, or networks with higher levels of capacity are capable of creating more value (through broader or more intense uses of knowledge) than those with lower levels of capacity. In this way, capacity is value, and it can be operationalized and used as a tool for evaluation (Bozeman and Rogers, 2002).

Additionally, individual scientists and their varying levels of capacity are rooted in social configurations called knowledge value collectives. The KVC is the second core conceptual element of churn theory, and it refers to the "set of individuals who interact in the demand, production, technical evaluation, and application of scientific and technical knowledge" (Bozeman and Rogers, 2002, p. 769). These are loosely connected collectives of actors who share a knowledge goal but do not necessarily share the same purposes for pursuing that goal (Bozeman et al., 1998). Loose connections indicate that it is not necessary for members of a KVC to interact or even have knowledge of the other members of the collective. Furthermore, there are no expectations that KVCs must be a certain size. A KVC includes only actors who are involved in the process of using and reshaping information and creating knowledge; it excludes actors who are pure consumers of knowledge (Rogers and Bozeman, 2001). As the churning process generates new knowledge within a particular KVC, "the KVC validates the knowledge produced by individual members (though not through conventional social controls) and relies on the constituent members' S&T human capital for its functioning and growth" (Bozeman and Rogers, 2002, p. 780). The KVC concept allows for a more comprehensive assessment of knowledge value beyond the boundaries of a specific research project, program, or even scientific discipline.

4. Applications of churn theory

Churn theory has been applied and adapted in a variety of ways since its inception. Much of this work is a product of the Research Value Mapping Project[1] for which a focal objective was advancing the state of the art of research evaluation, with emphasis on evaluation of government-sponsored research projects.[2] The fundamental question for the project was "how can we best understand the value of scientific knowledge and its applications including, especially, the ways in which we enhance capacity to create new knowledge, innovation and new uses for knowledge?" (Bozeman, 2003, p. 20). Churn theory provides a framework for answering this question.

A major way the theory has been utilized is to trace the churn process of knowledge generation and highlight instances in which economic reasoning does not offer satisfying explanations for knowledge development. These studies tend to use case study methodology. For example, in their original explication of churn theory, Bozeman and Rogers (2002) apply the lens of churn theory to the development of the Internet. They sketch the constituents of the complex Internet KVC and demonstrate that the development of Internet technology resulted from the knowledge churning process throughout the KVC rather than the strategic aim of any one scientific community or discipline. Consequently, they argue that understanding both the KVC and the dynamics of knowledge churn within it offers a more complete picture of the value of the knowledge used to create Internet technology. Furthermore, they contend that it is impossible to assess the current value of the Internet by merely aggregating the market value of its components. As evidence, they point out that some of the most popular Internet applications such as email would not have been developed if their development rested solely on the market signals available at the time. Bozeman and Rogers conclude that churn theory has valuable applications for understanding the social structures driving knowledge creation, transformation, and use and that it also offers a qualitative approach to valuing knowledge and evaluating scientific research.

Studies conducted by Rogers (2008) and Rogers, Martin and NCDDR Knowledge Translation Task Force (2009) apply churn theory in a manner similar to the Bozeman and Rogers (2002) study mentioned above. Both of the more recent studies examine knowledge production activities related to accessible currency (currency design and assistive technologies that are designed to aid the visually impaired). The researchers present case studies that detail the churn process of knowledge creation in the accessible currency KVC. Importantly, they add the idea of Knowledge Value Mapping (KVM): "a strategy to identify all user-producers of knowledge and trace all paths of circulation of knowledge and information together with the incentives and disincentives that may have an effect on the process" (Rogers, 2008, p. 240). The output of the KVM process is a map of the knowledge system that illustrates the knowledge transformation and selection processes based on the values of the actors within the system (Rogers, 2008). In this way, the researchers use the core concepts of churn theory, but rather than estimating the non-economic value of accessible currency knowledge, they examine the *values* of members in the KVC that drive the knowledge flows within the collective. This allows them to draw conclusions about where gaps exist and knowledge flows are not reaching relevant members of the KVC. This has implications for increasing the value of knowledge by identifying potential users.

A second application of churn theory involves its use as a practical tool for research evaluation. This is a rarer application of the theory, likely due to the fact that it requires significant resources. Corley (2007) presents the most concrete use of churn theory in this manner. She utilizes the theory's use and transformation model for evaluating the impacts of publicly funded R&D. Notably, her approach provides a pathway for evaluating individual research programs or groups by comparing them to the larger KVC within which they operate. She develops a six stage evaluation process to assess research units by measuring their capacity to generate new uses of information. She employs the KVC associated with polycystic ovarian syndrome (PCOS) research as an exemplar, and outlines the evaluation process.

The initial stage includes broadly mapping the boundaries of the specified KVC along with smaller units within the KVC, such as a research group funded by a particular grant. Step two involves bibliometric and patent analyses to identify uses of KVC and sub-unit knowledge. This step stems from an extension of the equality of use principle. Corley asserts that if all uses of knowledge are equally valued, then in order to operationalize uses one must also accept an equality of medium assumption. Specifically, she states that "all media used to carry information outputs within a KVC are of equal value" (Corley, 2007, p. 27). Therefore, evaluators must identify and document as many of the information outlets as possible within a KVC. Following these analyses, Corley recommends employing an expert panel to review and refine the information gathered in the preliminary stages. Next, evaluators should conduct a survey of the KVC population to develop indicators for success based on the extent of knowledge use. These include but are not limited to indicators of KVC growth, knowledge development, social capital, and resilience. In the final step of the evaluation, the evaluator compares the sub-unit of interest with the KVC as a whole using the success indicators. In this way, evaluators are able to offer an alternative to economic valuations of research by assessing growth of capacity within the KVC.

While the above uses of churn theory focus on non-economic valuation of scientific and technical knowledge in terms of capacity, a third application relies on the same theoretical framework but shifts the focus to the social impacts and outcomes of scientific research. This approach is labeled Public Value Mapping (PVM), and it offers a toolkit to assess and evaluate public value failures and successes in publically funded research. Churn theory provides one of its theoretical underpinnings by prescribing the KVC as the unit of analysis. The PVM approach has been fairly popular for evaluating research programs and scientific policies (Bozeman and Sarewitz, 2011; Fisher *et al.*, 2010; Gaughan, 2003; Gupta, 2003; Logar, 2011; Maricle, 2011; Meyer, 2011; Slade, 2011).

Moreover, Bozeman (2002, 2007) also expands PVM beyond the research evaluation context by connecting the analytical approach to public value failure theory which offers public value failure analogues for the familiar market failure concepts. Researchers in other fields, particularly public administration and management (Chen, 2009; Feeney and Bozeman, 2007; Moulton, 2009), utilize public value failure theory. However, the linkages between churn theory and processes of social innovation have not been fully explored and remain indistinct, thereby limiting the theory's current usefulness in this realm (Welch *et al.*, in press).

In addition to the previous direct applications of churn theory, a fourth group of studies focuses on further development of the KVC elements of the theory. For example, Corley, Boardman, and Bozeman (2006) propose a stage model of the development of epistemic norms within a scientific discipline. The model includes five stages of maturation ranging from burgeoning research topic to established scientific field of study; they argue that the knowledge value collective represents the third stage of institutionalization. It is at this stage that boundaries of the network lose their fuzziness and the first elements of formal interactions among network actors begin to emerge. In a related study, Youtie, Libaers, and Bozeman (2006) apply this maturation model. They explore the role of the multidiscipline, multipurpose university research center (MMURC) as an institutional mechanism for supporting and increasing the pace and progress of scientific research through the stages of maturation.

A final group of studies does not directly apply churn theory or its constituent elements but rather tacitly accepts the utility of the theory. For example, researchers cite churn theory in order to provide support for arguments that economic valuation of scientific and technical knowledge is often insufficient (Capece *et al.*, 2008; Dietz and Bozeman, 2005), to illustrate the importance of scientific and technical human capital considerations (Ireland and Hine, 2007; Klenk *et al.*, 2010), and to corroborate the importance of analyzing networks of scientific collaboration (Rigby and Edler, 2005; Shapira and Youtie, 2008). Additionally, Arnold (2004) indicates that future research should explore the effect that government interventions have on particular KVCs as well as how current levels of research support fit their needs.

5. Churn theory in comparison

As discussed previously, churn theory offers a non-economic approach to knowledge valuation. Bozeman and Rogers (2002) contrast the theory with economic approaches to knowledge valuation, and Corley (2007) extends this comparison to include a comparison with state-of-the-art valuation. The following discussion draws on both of these sources to offer an overview of the similarities and differences between churn theory and both economic and state-of-the-art approaches to knowledge valuation.

First, economic approaches to knowledge valuation focus on the exchange value (quantified worth) of knowledge products. Value is indicated by market and pricing mechanisms. Because of the nature of prices, economic valuation approaches lend themselves to quantitative analyses. Econometric models are standard tools for analysis, as are cost-benefit analyses. Moreover, these evaluations focus on the knowledge outputs of individuals or specified research projects and programs. However, scientists and others argue that economic valuation does not present the full picture of the true value of knowledge produced by scientific research. In this vein, state-of-the-art valuation techniques move in the opposite direction of economic valuation. Rather than focusing on external mechanisms like pricing, state-of-the-art evaluations emphasize

Table 10.1 Churn theory of knowledge valuation in comparison

	Churn theory	Traditional economics	New economics of knowledge	State of the art
Valued object	Capacity to produce new uses: S&T human capital	Discrete products: papers, patents, jobs created	Discrete products: papers, patents, jobs created	Impact or potential impact on knowledge growth: improvements in state of the art
Standard index of value	Range and repetition of uses	Pricing mechanisms	Dependent on institution: pricing mechanisms and scientific credit	Research outputs
Methodological tools	Case studies and other in-depth qualitative methods, network/KVC analysis	Econometric models, cost-benefit analysis, input-output models	Econometric models, game theory, bibliometric techniques	Bibliometric techniques, peer review
Knowledge value generator	Collective/KVC	Individual/firm	Individual/scientist or project	Both collective and individual

the internal impacts that scientific knowledge has within the research community. Its value lies in its ability to improve the state of the art. Evaluations utilizing this perspective focus on research outputs such as publications, citations, or patents, and analytic methods include bibliometric techniques and peer review processes. The use and transformation model suggested by churn theory offers an alternative to both economic and state-of-the-art approaches. It equates knowledge value with use and is concerned with estimating the capacity (S&T human capital) within KVCs to transform information into knowledge. Methods for this type of evaluation tend to be qualitative and concerned with research collectivities rather than single projects or programs. As illustrated above, each of these approaches differ in terms of the object that is valued, the standard index of value, methodological tools, and the knowledge value generator. Table 10.1 summarizes this discussion by adapting and extending the comparison table found in Bozeman and Rogers (2002).

6. Theoretical extensions and conclusion

During the past decade, the churn theory of knowledge valuation has seen only modest direct improvements and extensions. Likewise, the theory, while having some applications, has not provided remarkable changes in theory of innovation or value of knowledge. However, this is not to say that churn theory has proved static or that it has been consigned to a blind alley in the history of ideas about knowledge and innovation. Churn theory has taken its place alongside a growing number of alternatives to economic valuation of knowledge and innovation. Thus, such cognate activities as public value mapping and studies of scientific and technical human capital have found churn theory useful even when no direct lineage can be claimed. More important, churn theory is emblematic of a certain Zeitgeist that encourages a fundamental rethinking of approaches to knowledge value and evaluation and innovation.

Current interest in such topics as social equity in innovation impacts, public value innovation, and public participation in science and technology evaluation demonstrates the notion that economic impacts of innovation tell only part of the story.

If we take together the variety of non-market approaches to understanding knowledge and innovation we can consider the "what next?" question more broadly and perhaps more usefully than if we simply focus on research and theory needed for fleshing out a churn theory of knowledge. As is the case for nascent social or political movements, intellectual and scientific movements are characterized by fragmentation and miscommunication. There is a great need presently for an overarching theory of non-market knowledge valuation that will draw up the strands of the many good but poorly developed relevant ideas and then tie those strands together. In doing so, it is certainly the case that some strands will prove weak and will break off, but others will sustain the collectivity of ideas. Presently, there is little evidence that such an integrative effort is even underway much less that it is likely to succeed. But the strands are there and the theoretical work now needed is studies that will put these strands to good explanatory use.

Regarding the churn theory itself, the most important step to be taken is to move from broader conceptualization and case examples to more systematic and empirical proof of concept. The work previously done on the Internet (Bozeman and Rogers, 2002) clearly shows how the premises of churn theory play out and provides sufficient context and propositions to permit researchers to determine for themselves whether this particular alternative has promise. Taking churn theory to the next step, providing more specific and better integrated propositions, developing hypotheses, and identifying a set of data adequate to their test remains daunting. But that must be the next step. Absent some improved empirical proof of concept the churn theory too much resembles a set of metaphysical assumptions and too little resembles an explanatory theory.

Perhaps the key to making churn theory more viable is to latch together its implications for innovation and knowledge valuation. A suitable test for current theory, albeit one that would require prodigious resources, would be to use it as a framework for developing a series of interrelated case studies of innovations, with a mix of innovations that has a diverse set of uses, benefits, and costs. By examining multiple cases with very different motives, diverse stakeholder impacts of innovation and knowledge, and even a wide array of types of knowledge used in innovation, it might be possible to provide an entirely satisfactory side-by-side test of the explanatory value of the churn theory against a more conventional neoclassical interpretation of innovation and the value of knowledge.

Notes

1 This project originated at the Georgia Institute of Technology in 1996. The Department of Energy Office of Science provided the original funding for the project; additional funding came from a variety of sources. The project later moved to Arizona State University's Consortium for Science Policy and Outcomes.
2 See http://archive.cspo.org/rvm/index.htm

References

Ackoff, Russell L. (1989). From data to wisdom. *Journal of Applied Systems Analysis*, 16, 3–9.
Acs, Zoltan, Braunerhjelm, Pontus, Audretsch, David, and Carlsson, Bo. (2009). The knowledge spillover theory of entrepreneurship. *Small Business Economics*, 32(1), 15–30.
Alavi, Maryam, and Leidner, Dorothy E. (2001). Review: knowledge management and knowledge management systems: conceptual foundations and research issues. *MIS Quarterly*, 25(1), 107–136.

Arnold, Erik. (2004). Evaluating research and innovation policy: a systems world needs systems evaluations. *Research Evaluation, 13*(1), 3–17.

Arrow, K. (1962). Economic welfare and the allocation of resources for invention. In R.R. Nelson (Ed.), *The Rate and Direction of Inventive Activity: Economic and Socal Factors.* Princeton, NJ: Princeton University Press.

Audretsch, David B., Bozeman, Barry, Combs, Kathryn L., Feldman, Maryann, Link, Albert N., Siegel, Donald S., … Wessner, Charles. (2002). The economics of science and technology. *The Journal of Technology Transfer, 27*(2), 155–203.

Ballandonne, Matthieu. (2012). New economics of science, economics of scientific knowledge and sociology of science: the case of Paul David. *Journal of Economic Methodology, 19*(4), 391–406.

Bozeman, Barry. (2002). Public value failure: when efficient markets may not do. *Public Administration Review, 62*(2), 145–161.

Bozeman, Barry. (2003). *Public Value Mapping of Science Outcomes: Theory and Method.* Washington D.C.: Center for Science, Policy and Outcomes.

Bozeman, Barry. (2007). *Public Values and Public Interest: Counterbalancing Economic Individualism.* Washington D.C.: Georgetown University Press.

Bozeman, Barry, and Rogers, Juan D. (2002). A churn model of scientific knowledge value: internet researchers as a knowledge value collective. *Research Policy, 31*(5), 769–794.

Bozeman, Barry, and Sarewitz, Daniel. (2011). Public value mapping and science policy evaluation. *Minerva, 49*(1), 1–23.

Bozeman, Barry, Rogers, Juan, Roessner, David, Klein, H., and Park, J. (1998). *The R&D Value Mapping Project: Final Report. Report to the Department of Energy, Office of Basic Energy Sciences.* Atlanta, GA: Georgia Institute of Technology.

Bozeman, Barry, Dietz, James S, and Gaughan, Monica. (2001). Scientific and technical human capital: an alternative model for research evaluation. *International Journal of Technology Management, 22*(7), 716–740.

Capece, Guendalina, Gitto, Simone, and Campisi, Domenico. (2008). Beyond the learning frontier and the human capital development: new and old technological opportunities for the competence-based enterprises. *Knowledge & Process Management, 15*(4), 270–279.

Carlino, Gerald A. (2001). Knowledge spillovers: cities' role in the new economy. *Business Review* (Q4), 17–26.

Chen, Chung-An. (2009). Antecedents of contracting-back-in: a view beyond the economic paradigm. *Administration & Society, 41*(1), 101–126.

Corley, Elizabeth A. (2007). A use-and-transformation model for evaluating public R&D: illustrations from polycystic ovarian syndrome (PCOS) research. *Evaluation and Program Planning, 30*(1), 21–35.

Corley, Elizabeth A., Boardman, P. Craig, and Bozeman, Barry. (2006). Design and the management of multi-institutional research collaborations: theoretical implications from two case studies. *Research Policy, 35*(7), 975–993.

Czarnitzki, Dirk, Hall, Bronwyn H., and Oriani, Raffaele. (2006). The market valuation of knowledge assets in US and European firms. In D. Bosworth and E. Webster (Eds), *The Management of Intellectual Property.* Cheltenham Glos, UK: Edward Elgar, 111–131.

Dasgupta, Partha, and David, Paul A. (1994). Toward a new economics of science. *Research Policy, 23*(5), 487–521.

Dietz, James S., and Bozeman, Barry. (2005). Academic careers, patents, and productivity: industry experience as scientific and technical human capital. *Research Policy, 34*(3), 349–367.

Feeney, Mary Kathleen, and Bozeman, Barry. (2007). Public values and public failure: implications of the 2004–2005 flu vaccine case. *Public Integrity, 9*(2), 175–190.

Fisher, Erik, Slade, Catherine, Anderson, Derrick, and Bozeman, Barry. (2010). The public value of nano-technology? *Scientometrics, 85*(1), 29–39.

Forni, Mario, and Paba, Sergio. (2002). Spillovers and the growth of local industries. *Journal of Industrial Economics, 50*(2), 151.

Gaughan, Monica. (2003). *Public Value Mapping Breast Cancer Case Studies.* Washington, D.C.: Center for Science Policy and Outcomes.

Godin, Benoît. (2010). The knowledge economy: Fritz Malchup's construction of a synthetic concept. In R. Viale and H. Etzkowitz (Eds), *The Capitalization of Knowledge: A Triple Helix of University–Industry–Government.* Northampton, MA: Edward Elgar Publishing.

Griliches, Zvi. (1979). Issues in assessing the contribution of research and development to productivity growth. *The Bell Journal of Economics, 10*(1), 92–116.

Gupta, Aarti. (2003). *Public Value Mapping in a Developing Country Context: A Methodology to Promote Socially Beneficial Public Biotechnology Research and Uptake in India.* Washington, D.C.: Center for Science Policy and Outcomes.

Ireland, David C., and Hine, Damian. (2007). Harmonizing science and business agendas for growth in new biotechnology firms: case comparisons from five countries. *Technovation*, *27*(11), 676–692.

Klenk, Nicole L., Hickey, Gordon M., and MacLellan, James Ian. (2010). Evaluating the social capital accrued in large research networks: the case of the sustainable forest management network (1995–2009). *Social Studies of Science*, *40*(6), 931–960.

Lach, Saul, and Schankerman, Mark. (2008). Incentives and invention in universities. *The RAND Journal of Economics*, *39*(2), 403–433.

Levin, Richard C., Klevorick, Alvin K., Nelson, Richard R., Winter, Sidney G., Gilbert, Richard, and Griliches, Zvi. (1987). Appropriating the returns from industrial research and development. *Brookings Papers on Economic Activity*, 783–831.

Logar, Nathaniel. (2011). Chemistry, green chemistry, and the instrumental valuation of sustainability. *Minerva: A Review of Science, Learning & Policy*, *49*(1), 113–136.

Maricle, Genevieve. (2011). Prediction as an impediment to preparedness: lessons from the US hurricane and earthquake research enterprises. *Minerva: A Review of Science, Learning & Policy*, *49*(1), 87–111.

Meyer, Ryan. (2011). The public values failures of climate science in the US. *Minerva: A Review of Science, Learning & Policy*, *49*(1), 47–70.

Moulton, Stephanie. (2009). Putting together the publicness puzzle: a framework for realized publicness. *Public Administration Review*, *69*(5), 889–900.

Mowery, David C. (1983). Economic theory and government technology policy. *Policy Sciences*, *16*(1), 27–43.

Nelson, Richard R. (1959). The simple economics of basic scientific research. *Journal of Political Economy*, *67*(3), 297–306.

Rigby, J., and Edler, J. (2005). Peering inside research networks: some observations on the effect of the intensity of collaboration on the variability of research quality. *Research Policy*, *34*(6), 784–794.

Rogers, Juan D. (2008). Evaluation in R&D management and knowledge use: a knowledge value mapping approach to currency accessible to the visually impaired. *Research Evaluation*, *17*(4), 237–249.

Rogers, Juan D., and Bozeman, Barry. (2001). "Knowledge value alliances": an alternative to the R&D project focus in evaluation. *Science, Technology, & Human Values*, *26*(1), 23–55.

Rogers, Juan D., Martin, Frank H., and NCDDR Knowledge Translation Task Force. (2009). Knowledge translation in disability and rehabilitation research: lessons from the application of knowledge value mapping to the case of accessible currency. *Journal of Disability Policy Studies*, *20*(2), 110–126.

Rowley, Jennifer. (2007). The wisdom hierarchy: representations of the DIKW hierarchy. *Journal of Information Science*, *33*(2), 163–180.

Sandel, Michael J. (2012). *What Money Can't Buy: The Moral Limits of Markets*. New York: Farrar, Straus and Giroux.

Shapira, Philip, and Youtie, Jan. (2008). Emergence of nanodistricts in the United States: path dependency or new opportunities? *Economic Development Quarterly*, *22*(3), 187–199.

Slade, Catherine. (2011). Public value mapping of equity in emerging nanomedicine. *Minerva: A Review of Science, Learning & Policy*, *49*(1), 71–86.

Solow, Robert M. (1957). Technical change and the aggregate production function. *The Review of Economics and Statistics*, *39*(3), 312–320.

Stephan, Paula E. (1996). The economics of science. *Journal of Economic Literature*, *34*(3), 1199.

Stern, Scott. (2004). Do scientists pay to be scientists? *Management Science*, *50*(6), 835–853.

Welch, Jennie, Rimes, Heather, and Bozeman, Barry. (in press). Public Value Mapping. In J. Bryson, B. Crosby, and L. Blomberg (Eds.), *Valuing Public Value*. Washington, D.C.: Georgetown University Press.

Young, Neal S., Ioannidis, John P.A., and Al-Ubaydli, Omar. (2008). Why current publication practices may distort science. *PLoS medicine*, *5*(10), e201.

Youtie, Jan, Libaers, Dirk, and Bozeman, Barry. (2006). Institutionalization of university research centers: the case of the national cooperative program in infertility research. *Technovation*, *26*(9), 1055–1063.

Zeleny, Milan. (1987). Management support systems: towards integrated knowledge management. *Human Systems Management*, *7*(1), 59–70.

11

The international dissemination of technological knowledge

Fabio Montobbio and Rodrigo Kataishi

in order to analyze the problem, to imagine possible solutions to it, to estimate their relative cost and difficulty, and to reduce one or more to practice, the inventor must use the science and technology bequeathed in the past…

(Schmookler, 1966, p.12)

1. Introduction

Exactly because the creation of new technologies is more geographically concentrated relative to production and value added, international knowledge diffusion is considered a powerful driver of economic growth and catching up. As emphasized by Keller (2004), in many countries 90 percent of productivity growth can be related to foreign technology. Comin and Hobijn (2010) and Comin *et al.* (2008) show that the cross-country variation in the adoption of technologies accounts for at least 25 percent of per-capita income differences and that technology usage lags are large and correlated with lags in per-capita income.

The analysis of the determinants and channels of international knowledge dissemination is therefore very important to understand our economies, their growth and productivity, in particular in a phase of increased economic integration. One key feature that attracts the interest of economists is that knowledge diffuses for intentional and non-intentional reasons. Economists have studied especially the non-intentional component because it reveals the mirage of a productive factor potentially unlimited and reproducible at very low cost. In fact if knowledge were a pure public good, this would create two consequences: it would disseminate very quickly but, at the same time, there would be no incentive to produce it. Actually the economic literature shows that neither of these two consequences is systematically observed. Knowledge is produced even without strong legal protection showing that many different forms of appropriability can take place and, second, many barriers exist to international knowledge diffusions. The economic literature shows that the diffusion of knowledge is neither inevitable nor automatic.

This paper surveys the vast number of theoretical and empirical papers on this issue keeping in mind that other extremely interesting and complete surveys exist on the topic (e.g. Branstetter, 2000; Keller, 2004; Belderbos and Mohnen, 2013). Here, far from being exhaustive, we focus mainly on technological knowledge and take the following perspective: in Section 2 we first discuss the issue of knowledge dissemination within the broad literature on pure and pecuniary knowledge spillovers. Second, we discuss the impact of international knowledge flows on growth with some examples from a set of seminal endogenous growth models. We show how knowledge can generate increasing returns if it is considered a public good, how the geographical scope of knowledge spillovers can affect growth patterns across countries, and how different dissemination channels (like trade) affect the growth path. In addition, we raise the issues of technological obsolescence; new knowledge makes previous knowledge less useful. Finally, we argue that knowledge does not diffuse automatically and therefore absorptive capacity and incentives to transfer and adopt have to be considered. In addition it is important to assess which are the specific vehicles of international knowledge dissemination.

Section 3 considers the empirical literature that studies these different channels and asks whether trade, foreign direct investment, licencing, R&D ventures and other forms of collaborations generate knowledge externalities at the international level. It is important to underline that this survey focuses on the knowledge dissemination that takes place at the *international* level. The comparison between national and international knowledge diffusion might be misleading because, on the one side, contemporary economies are increasingly integrated at supranational level (e.g. the European Union and the NAFTA) and, on the other side, there is a large consensus that knowledge tends to remain localized in geographical units that are typically smaller than nations (e.g. cities and districts). This issue is empirically discussed in two ways. The first approach recognizes that knowledge may flow *at a distance*, so it studies how geographical distance affects knowledge dissemination. Geographical distance can represent a proxy for some types of costs necessary to disseminate and absorb knowledge like communication, codification and transport costs. The second and complementary approach explores whether *national borders* provide a barrier to knowledge dissemination. This second perspective underlines how cultural (like language) and legal aspects can constitute barriers to knowledge dissemination. So Sections 4 and 5 explore different types of potential barriers to these channels of international dissemination of knowledge. In particular, Section 4 discusses the empirical evidence on the role of geography and physical distance together with other potential cultural and institutional barriers (like legal rules or languages) that make national borders significant obstacles to knowledge dissemination. Section 5 explores the issue of the impact of the reinforcement of intellectual property rights on international spillovers. Finally Section 6 attempts to make a methodological assessment on the empirical literature on knowledge dissemination, emphasizing the main limits and possible prospects.

It is important to underline immediately a set of issues that are implicit throughout the entire chapter. First of all, international knowledge dissemination is clearly more important for small countries that typically are more open and where the contribution to growth from foreign R&D can be very strong. In particular countries that are poor and have a relatively low level of domestic R&D can benefit substantially from access to foreign technology. At the same time, since learning is not automatic, absorptive capacity at different levels is very important together with the effort to engage in international economic activities. Finally, most of the literature addressed in this survey analyzes knowledge dissemination as an input to a production process that might lead eventually to economic and productivity growth thanks to some forms of externalities. Of course international knowledge dissemination is very important for many other aspects affecting countries' welfare (and only indirectly economic growth) like knowledge related to the protection of the environment, education practices and human health (e.g. Green et al., 2009).

2. Knowledge diffusion and knowledge externalities

Knowledge dissemination attracts a lot of attention in the economic literature because knowledge cannot be considered a normal good. The potential non-rival and non-excludable nature of substantial portions of knowledge implies – using the famous Jefferson's words – that "who lights his taper at mine, receives light without darkening me" (Jefferson, 1886). These characteristics of knowledge generate the possibility of a quick and large worldwide diffusion of ideas with potential substantial improvement in human conditions. We know however that in many cases technological knowledge does not disseminate very quickly even in the presence of increased communication possibilities created by advanced information and communication technologies and the worldwide web.

Economists have therefore tried to understand the role of knowledge in economics having in mind that its potential non-rivalry and non-excludability raise a very interesting set of economic issues: under which conditions is knowledge really produced in the form of a public good? And which is the right balance between appropriability and diffusion? Our point of departure, as emphasized by the Schmookler quote at the start, is that firms and individuals use knowledge produced by other firms and individuals. Economic agents can buy such knowledge or can learn without paying a monetary price, possibly via multiple forms of interactions. It is no surprise that most of the economic literature has provided a substantial effort in trying to understand which is the fraction of knowledge that spills over and, actually, generates externalities (resulting from various types of activities). This is exactly because its potential public nature makes knowledge production and diffusion a key topic to understand and support economic growth and improve well-being.

2.1 Knowledge dissemination, pure spillovers and pecuniary externalities

The economic literature has defined separately two types of knowledge spillovers: pure knowledge spillovers and rent (or pecuniary) spillovers (Griliches, 1979 and 1992; Antonelli and Ferraris, 2012; Antonelli, 2014). *Pure knowledge spillovers* are externalities. Ideas generated in research or production by some agents increase the (research) productivity undertaken by others. Existing knowledge may generate new ideas which, in turn, lead to innovations (idea-creating spillovers) or may be simply absorbed and used to imitate (imitation-enhancing spillovers). Imitation-enhancing spillovers are more likely to occur within the same industry while the former category is likely to take place within and across industries (Breschi and Lissoni, 2001). It is important to note that imitation-enhancing spillovers are considered a key source of market failure in R&D.[1]

A *pecuniary or rent spillover* is mainly generated through the purchase of an R&D-intensive input or capital equipment. If the input is not sold at the full "quality" price, part of the improvement of the input is appropriated by downstream firms. This type of rent depends directly on how much inputs and capital goods are important for the production of a specific firm. In addition, upstream industry structure is very important and we can expect that pecuniary spillovers are larger when there is a lot of competition among suppliers. Empirically hedonic prices are used to analyze the impact on downstream firms.

The international dissemination of knowledge can take place within the same industry and across industries. Many papers show that rent spillovers through imported machinery have a significant effect on productivity in technology-intensive industries (e.g. Keller, 2002; Parameswaran, 2009), supporting the argument that trade openness promotes technological progress and economic growth in both developed and developing countries.

For example, Daveri and Olmo (2004) suggest that the increase in productivity growth in the IT related services industries in Finland in the 1990s has been generated by declining costs of production in higher quality machinery and equipment due to worldwide technical change in the supply side (e.g. semiconductor improvements due to Moore's law, which states that, simultaneously, there is an exponential growth of the number of components inside a chip and a trend of lower cost per unit over time).

It is evident that the precise empirical identification of actual knowledge spillovers (vs. rent spillovers) is a daunting challenge because the distinction between borrowing ideas generated elsewhere and input purchase flows is often impossible. It is very difficult in particular to figure out whether two industries, which do not buy from each other, exploit research on similar topics and, as a consequence, can benefit from each other's R&D efforts. Confounding the two types of spillovers may lead to overestimating true spillovers. This is because prices underestimate the value of the inputs and, as a result, the benefits on Total Factor Productivity (TFP) are overestimated. More clearly TFP of industry i appears to be increased through quality improvement in upstream sectors even if there are no real productivity improvements in industry i.

Once it is recognized that knowledge spillovers are a key element to understanding different productivity performances and innovation trends, it is important to point out that firm-level performance is also affected by internal knowledge, i.e. the capacity of firms to understand and modify their products and technologies and to absorb external knowledge (e.g. Cohen and Levinthal, 1989; Keller, 2004). R&D expenditures therefore not only generate discoveries and innovation but also help firms to learn from external sources. Firms do not absorb technological abilities in an automatic cost-free fashion: they invest resources and time to absorb knowledge (Antonelli, 2008 and 2013).

An additional aspect to consider regards the difference between knowledge transfer and innovation diffusion. Diffusion can be understood as a process that takes place when an innovation appears. The study of diffusion terminates when the rate of adoption of the innovation is zero. The innovation diffusion literature is interested in explaining a set of stylized facts in usage patterns, typically the specific form of the S-shaped curve. A substantial number of surveys define this field and different models have been much discussed elsewhere.[2]

Section 2.2 addresses the issue of knowledge diffusion in the context of growth models while we focus more on the mechanism of knowledge transfer in Section 3. Knowledge transfer processes are mainly focused on specific economic interactions and take place when one economic agent intentionally passes on knowledge to another one mainly via face-to-face interactions, through a multiplicity of channels. This process entails a bidirectional nature, modifying the amount, quality and capacity to process new knowledge of the parts involved. Hence, while technological transfer is not a necessary requirement for the existence of knowledge diffusion, it may reinforce the dissemination dynamics. Of course, several conditions can be linked to the transfer process, such as the proximity (technological, spatial) of the institutions involved (firms, countries), the level of cumulated knowledge they have (and the existence of a threshold to access some knowledge), the nature of the interaction process and its social and institutional context, and other factors that will be discussed in the next pages.

2.2. From a macro to a micro analysis of international knowledge dissemination

Macroeconomic models analyze the key role played by knowledge diffusion and externalities for growth. The theoretical representations of knowledge diffusion in macro and growth models are becoming more complex over time; our effort here is to give an overview of the main macroeconomic relationships between knowledge diffusion and growth. In particular we provide four examples based on Romer (1986), Grossman and Helpman (1991), Caballero and Jaffe (1993) and, finally, Keller (2004) that builds on Eaton and Kortum (1999).

Following Romer (1986), knowledge externalities are described in the following production function

$$Y_i = F\left(z_i, Z, x_i\right) \tag{1}$$

where x_i stands for capital (K) and labor (L) inputs, and $Z = \sum_{i=1}^{x} z_i$ is the aggregate stock of knowledge generated by the investment of firm i in knowledge production z_i. Romer generates increasing returns assuming concavity and homogeneity of degree one in z_i and x_i. If firms maximize their profits taking Z for given, externalities from the aggregate level of knowledge generate endogenous growth with the well-known consequence that income per capita does not need to converge across countries.

One challenge is to measure, in this context, the size of the external effect relative to the internal effect (e.g. Barro and Sala-i-Martin, 2004; Li et al., 2011). In fact, an empirically tractable possible spillover measurement compares the amount of knowledge produced at the internal and external levels of the economy. Formally, the index can be constructed as the absolute difference between externally and internally generated knowledge:

$$Spillover = \frac{\left(Social\ Marginal\ Product\ of\ Knowledge - Private\ Marginal\ Product\ of\ Knowledge\right)}{Social\ Marginal\ Product\ of\ Knowledge} \tag{2}$$

Romer (1986, p. 1027) shows that assuming a simple production function in which $f\left(z, Z\right) = z^\delta Z^\varepsilon$ equation (2) can be expressed as the ratio of the private and social marginal products: $\varphi = \varepsilon / \left(\delta + \varepsilon\right)$. The ratio ($\varphi$) is constant and depends upon two types of output-elasticities, the aggregated one (δ) and the one that is derived at the firm level (ε).

The first generation of endogenous growth models raises two interesting issues related to the so-called inter-temporal *scale effects*. The first one is that the per-capita growth of an economy is a function of the level of knowledge that is produced. So the key question is which is the correct spatial dimension to capture the external effect. If international spillovers are very important even small countries can expect to access global knowledge. The second issue is related to the process of creative destruction and knowledge decay. Is a company producing *more* knowledge today compared to a company active 50 years ago with the same level of human capital? In principle the company can use the knowledge accumulated in the last 50 years. However without knowledge depreciation and/or decreasing returns in knowledge production this would imply a process of exponential growth (see Jones and Williams, 1998, for a discussion).

While in Romer's framework spillovers are automatic and no difference exists between local and international knowledge spillovers, Grossman and Helpman (1991) show the conditions under which learning from *international trade* related knowledge spillovers generates endogenous growth. Trade and innovation (expressed in term of product varieties) generate a learning dynamic that drives the knowledge based economic growth. In their framework the labor productivity of new varieties depends upon the level of scientific and engineering know-how in a country. They call this know-how *knowledge capital (K)* and assume that it is a function of the cumulative amount of domestic research and foreign stock of knowledge. The former is the standard spillover benefit for the stock of knowledge capital from each domestic research project, i.e. number of product varieties that an economy is able to produce over time. The latter is the cumulated volume of export and import. In this way Grossman and Helpman are able to describe how (trade related) international knowledge spillovers affect the growth path and the relative welfare and policy implications. This is one of the first attempts to formalize how exactly international spillovers take place. At the same time Grossman and Helpman recognize that not all traded commodities serve as a channel of knowledge spillover in the same way and suggest that there can be many other channels of international knowledge dissemination.

In general, the Grossman and Helpman model provides inspiration for a substantial amount of empirical work on the size of the international spillovers and their model is compatible with the standard representation of weighted spillovers (starting from Arrow, 1962; Griliches, 1979; Coe and Helpman, 1995), in which the TFP is calculated from standard labor and capital factors and is estimated as a function of R&D expenditures. Knowledge spillovers are represented as proportions of external knowledge that are incorporated in the knowledge production function according to a weighting function ω_k in the following way: $TFP = g\ (R_k,\ \Sigma_k\ \omega_k R_k)$. In the next section we show how this approach has been empirically extended in many different directions (trade related spillovers, FDI spillovers, etc.).

Our third example is the model provided by Caballero and Jaffe (1993). They describe a process of Schumpeterian growth through creative destruction and knowledge spillovers exploiting quality ladders and, differently from previous endogenous growth models, the idea that knowledge diffusion takes time and is subject to obsolescence. The creative destruction part of the paper contains two types of research spillovers. The first one depends on the fact that it takes the same amount of resources to produce new *superior* qualities; this is a sort of learning process on what firms have done before. The second one is a *negative* pecuniary externality since new qualities substitute the old ones. In addition the model specifies how the aggregate knowledge stock affects the way research is translated into innovation. In particular they define a specific functional form for research productivity that contains parameters of knowledge diffusion and obsolescence. Note that what creates obsolescence is not time *as such* but the continuous emergence of new ideas (i.e. the usefulness of old ideas depends on how many *qualities* – goods indexed by their qualities – have been produced between the old idea and the new one). Diffusion depends upon time under the assumption that inventors need time to learn from others' inventions. Notably the model allows Caballero and Jaffe to build the first empirical work on research spillovers and creative destruction based on micro-data, patents and patent citations.

To conclude this section, it is interesting to dedicate attention to Keller's contribution (2004) based on Eaton and Kortum (1999).[3] The Keller–Eaton and Kortman approach considers N countries that at time t produce an output Y_{nt} using J intermediate inputs. Their specification of productivity includes a term related to the quality of the inputs, understood as knowledge accumulation as follows.

$$\ln\left(Y_{nt}\ /\ J\right) = J^{-1} \int_0^J \ln\left[Z_{nt}\left(j\right) X_{nt}\left(j\right)\right] dj \tag{3}$$

where $X_{nt}(j)$ stands for the amount of intermediate inputs j at time t for country n (J is the total number of inputs). $X_{nt}(j)$ is produced by capital and labor following a CRS Cobb-Douglas. $Z_{nt}(j)$ is the quality of that input that grows over time through new technologies that are the result of research efforts of high-skilled workers. In each country n, if α_{nt} is research productivity, s_{nt} is the share of R&D employment, new technologies are created at a rate $\alpha_{nt}(s_{nt})^{\beta} L_{nt}$, with β equal to the talent or experience of R&D workers. Also in this model α_{nt} depends upon the stock of knowledge in country n and the total stock of knowledge in all countries. Keller–Eaton and Kortman assume that the quality of a technology is random, common to all countries and become productive only when it has diffused.

In their model knowledge is therefore embodied in intermediate goods. In addition domestic output can be produced using knowledge produced by foreign R&D without additional costs because new quality inputs produced in one country may become available in other countries according to a diffusion rate. The key issue is how international knowledge dissemination enters into the picture. So diffusion is a stochastic process and ε_{in} is the bilateral diffusion speed between country i and country n. Technologies diffuse (if $\varepsilon_{in} > 0$) but their use depends upon a quality threshold of a country's technological stock and the aggregate knowledge growth rate (which in the model is the mean of quality across sectors). If the diffusion rate is lower than the threshold, a new worldwide available technology is used.

This model relaxes multiple assumptions with respect to other endogenous growth models. The interaction between national and aggregate level plays a key role in the definition of the use of a technology (and transitively its diffusion). Additionally, it has a clear specification of the technology growth determinants, incorporating specialized labor and a threshold between the conveniences of adopting a particular technology regarding its diffusion rate in comparison with the stock of knowledge available. From the model, several implications can be underlined. First, that both internal and foreign knowledge growth affect positively TFP; second, the faster the diffusion speed, the faster the technological growth rate (and, hence, the TFP); third, a country has a greater influence in the world's knowledge stock, the higher its idea production rate (particularly $\alpha_{nt}\,(s_{nt})^\beta\,L_{nt}$) and the greater its diffusion rate ε_{in}.

In this process what matters is not just pecuniary externalities, but also spillovers "to the extent that the intermediate good costs less than its opportunity costs—which include the R&D costs of product development" (Keller, 2004, p. 755). More generally, firms may have productivity gains from two channels: the first is the inputs and the second is the diffusion of new technologies that increase the productivity of skilled workers. On the one side third-party improved inputs induce adaptation or innovation processes within the firm, triggering learning processes. On the other side the acquisition of intermediate goods also requires repeated forms of interactions (even collaborations) that can generate knowledge absorption and learning.

In sum the four examples considered here (among many others) raise a set of important issues regarding the role of the international dissemination of knowledge on growth. Romer (1986) emphasizes how knowledge stock generates increasing returns, Grossman and Helpman extend it to an international dimension assuming trade as a channel of knowledge diffusion. Caballero and Jaffe introduce the notion that diffusion takes time and that the impact of specific knowledge inputs decays over time. Finally with Keller–Eaton and Kortman it is extremely clear that the key question is to understand how knowledge disseminates and which are exactly the most important channels of knowledge diffusion.

These models are aimed at understanding the endogenous growth path and the role that international spillovers have on it. The mathematical complexity of this task generally requires simplifying assumptions in order to perform empirical exercises. The use of specific functional forms may be one of the most important issues to consider, especially regarding the level of aggregation and the available data in order to test the model. At a theoretical level, in the former example the learning processes are assumed as *automatically* carried out during the production processes, which may lead to an underestimation of the role of endogenous absorptive capacities (Cohen and Levinthal, 1989) and omit the discussions on knowledge transfer and diffusion disaggregation. In such general models, knowledge homogeneity is generally assumed in order to make calculations simpler, but at a cost of considering all types of knowledge as "the same". This may disregard differences among countries and firms related to path dependence heterogeneity, accessibility issues and skills required to learn and use different technologies.

In addition, it is worth mentioning that knowledge externalities may affect different patterns of economic performance, raising the challenge of specialization over time of an economy. Specialization strategies are non-ergodic, non-reversible processes that have a history-based dynamic. The evolution over time of firms and countries is important since path dependence impacts not only on the present but also on the future behavior of the economic institutions.

The consideration of specialization patterns and path dependence leads to key discussions that address knowledge externalities trends and adoption. The debates around technological congruence (e.g. Antonelli, 2014) emphasize the relation between available resources and expected specialization patterns according to the direction of technological change. If an economic institution (firm, region, country) diverges from the fields in which there are substantial technological opportunities, then at the local level it can have difficulties in the adoption of new technologies and the related benefits in terms of externalities. This is a key issue in the study of catching-up processes that opens a fruitful field of research on the role of externalities and on the dynamic of technological congruence.

3. The empirical analysis of international knowledge spillovers and the different channels of knowledge dissemination

In the previous section we have shown that economic growth is importantly affected by knowledge creation and dissemination. A relevant part of the productivity growth can be related to these external sources of knowledge, making the technological diffusion processes of crucial importance in the understanding of the worldwide technical change. The channels of knowledge dissemination refer to those mechanisms through which codified and tacit knowledge passes, in voluntarily or involuntary ways, from one agent to another (or others). This implies that one side of the relation holds some specific knowledge, while the other, the receptor, processes and tries to incorporate the circulating information. This interaction is not limited to firm-to-firm interactions but may also occur through firm-to-institution interactions, such as independent inventors or universities that transfer their ideas to enterprises and vice versa (Breschi and Lissoni, 2009).

The literature has underlined the importance of different channels of knowledge diffusion. In particular, this work will discuss those related to trade, foreign investment, licensing and R&D cooperation.[4] In order to explore the effect of international knowledge spillovers on productivity, different research methodologies have been applied. There are three broad strategies to estimate this phenomenon (Branstetter, 1998; Lee 2006): first, the country-level panel data in which the estimations are based on the identification of a relationship between foreign R&D and TFP indicators (e.g. Coe and Helpman, 1995). The second approach is based on firm-level data (e.g. Branstetter, 2001): in this case technological proximity indicators are widely used to explore the similarity of the knowledge portfolios of firms. This approach uses knowledge production functions that depend upon the weighted sum of external knowledge. Of course, the availability of international and *comparable* firm-level micro-data is the main limitation of this approach, although its level of detail allows rich and revealing analysis. The third method considers the use of patents (Caballero and Jaffe, 1993). While a technological proximity approach *infers* spillover relations according to firms' behavior, the currently available information on patents and patent citation[5] makes technology transfer dynamics relatively more explicit.

It is important to note that these econometric approaches, assuming that parameters of foreign R&D are different from parameters related to domestic R&D, claim that national borders have a significant impact on knowledge dissemination. The impact of national borders depends upon cultural (like language) and legal aspects that are indeed important but often only implicitly considered. A second possibility is to recognize that knowledge may flow at a distance, so international knowledge diffusion is analyzed asking how geographical distance affects knowledge dissemination. This approach can be integrated adding other types of distances (e.g. cultural, technological, institutional, legal distances). In what follows we describe the literature that, using these different approaches, has analyzed the different channels of international knowledge dissemination. In Sections 4 and 5 we discuss in more depth the horizontal theme of the different types of distances and discuss the impact of different possible institutional settings in terms of intellectual property rights.

3.1. Trade as a knowledge diffusion channel

The relation between trade and technological knowledge dissemination is based upon two complementary visions: the traditional approach (Grossman and Helpman, 1990 and 1991; Coe and Helpman, 1995; Xu and Wang, 1999) is based on the idea that knowledge is embedded in traded goods. Trade triggers a learning dynamic in the productive agents, especially the importers, modifying their production process and, eventually, their productivity levels. A complementary approach focuses on the interactions between agents. Specifically, it refers to the way reciprocal communication and personal contact lead to knowledge diffusion, by the transmission of non-formalized or codified experiences and/or problem solving strategies. According to this view, interaction itself implies an involuntary process of knowledge transfer.

One of the main concerns of trade related knowledge dissemination literature is the problem of "what to measure". Trade includes imports and exports, but in many economies, imports are more relevant to absorb external knowledge. The literature uses different types of indicators focused around a specific sector's inputs, goods or technological classes to evaluate the dissemination of external knowledge (Xu and Wang, 1999).

The seminal work of Coe and Helpman (1995, CH) uses, for the construction of foreign R&D capital stocks, import weighted sums of trade partners' cumulative R&D spending (as proxy of knowledge stock). This approach proposes that all goods carry *per se* the ability to transfer (at least partially) the foreign knowledge incorporated into the local economy. Another important approach (Keller, 1998) is based on the idea that *capital goods* are carriers of embedded technology, hence they are relatively more important than other goods.

Two issues can be underlined: the first one is methodological and the second one is conceptual. The first regards the weights used by CH to build their spillover indicator. The early critics claim the existence of an indexation bias and an aggregation bias (Lichtenberg and Pottelsberghe de la Potterie, 1998, LPP). The indexation problem consists in the fact that CH didn't consider a link between the import rate (which according to them is the source of external knowledge) and the local R&D intensity, leading them to interpret in the same way the effect of imports on countries with different amounts of R&D activities. The aggregation problem, on the other hand, has to do with the construction of the foreign R&D stocks. Despite these potential biases related to the indexation and aggregation issues, the overall results of LPP support the original results of the CH paper, confirming the original hypothesis that spillovers are trade related.

The second issue concerns the conceptual aspect, particularly the differentiation between measurements of general imports versus capital goods. This may be relevant under the assumption that capital goods are used by firms directly on productive activities, while non-capital goods are generic and potentially spurious in the carrying of new productive knowledge (or at least not as important as capital goods). Xu and Wang (1999) show that using the two types of indexes and aggregation weightings developed by CH and LPP, non-capital goods are statistically irrelevant in the productivity performance, and capital goods showed to be more significant on the explanation of TFP variability.

Keller (1998) provides the main critique to the idea of knowledge transfer derived from total imports. Departing from the CH idea of weighted R&D stocks, he weights R&D intensity and imports using a randomized Monte Carlo simulation, obtaining more significant results than CH. Keller argues that total knowledge stocks at global level (the sum of worldwide R&D over time) are more relevant than the weighted time-dependent measure of CH, since Keller's model achieves better fitting on the explanation of the variability of TFP over time than the CH model. The conclusion is that knowledge diffusion should be considered global and trade independent, supporting the hypothesis of a global pool of knowledge worldwide available for producers, in contrast with CH's hypothesis of knowledge diffusion based on the import's structure (Fracasso and Marzetti, 2011).[6]

Regarding the exports, following the classic ideas of Vernon (1966), the technological advantages of an economy can be associated to its export level, giving innovators a favorable competitive position. The relationship between innovation and exports has been increasingly studied during the last decades (Wakelin, 2001; Keller, 2009; Damijan *et al.*, 2008; Helpman *et al.*, 2004). A number of works are focused on the issue of learning-by-exporting at the firm level. The idea is that exports improve the productive system capabilities with some time lags (Salomon and Shaver, 2005). It is worth mentioning that the exports and productivity relation involves a self-selection problem (Clerides *et al.*, 1998; López, 2004) because exporters are more productive, larger and more likely to survive than other types of firms (Bernard *et al.*, 2006). Empirical evidence shows that such differences remain, even if exporting activities do not enhance productivity levels (Aw *et al.*, 2000).

The relation between exports and innovation performance can be better understood by exploring with higher detail the characteristics of firms, as Lööf and Nabavi (2013) suggest. That is, there are differences between the impact that exports have on innovation performance if one discriminates between innovative and non-innovative firms before their access to international markets. Firms that weren't innovative before export show less probability to become innovative than those who were active in doing innovations before their internationalization. So, already innovative exporters are more likely to have a positive innovative impact from exports than the others.

León-Ledesma (2005) argues that international knowledge spillovers may have a positive impact on the export rate. His argument considers foreign knowledge as an incremental stock that permeates into local knowledge structures, boosting them and hence affecting the export amount and quality. The results of this work underline that less developed countries' exports are positively affected by the international knowledge flow, especially because of a relative backwardness effect that leads to relative advantages to catch-up.

Exporting activities *per se* don't trigger an increment in innovation activities, but the interaction with other actors does. Particularly for the case of Swedish manufacturing firms, Lööf and Nabavi (2013) relate the frequency and openness of different user–producer interactions, underlining the iterative learning process that takes place on the exchange. This process shows that not only more innovative exporters but also export-intensive firms are able to benefit from knowledge-intensive contexts.

3.2 Foreign Direct Investment (FDI)

An additional channel of international knowledge spillover is related to Foreign Direct Investments (FDIs). As in trade, FDIs can be separated into inflows – an economy receiving investments – and outflows – local firms performing investments in other countries. The main idea behind this knowledge diffusion channel is that firms who are able to perform FDIs have relatively higher capabilities. Hence FDIs bring a set of specific knowledge into the hosting economy leading to learning-by-interaction knowledge transfers and catching up dynamics.[7]

There are three main processes possibly related to knowledge dissemination generated by new FDIs. The first refers to the benefits that local firms may achieve by imitating practices of multinational firms, especially through reverse engineering of products and emulation of practices and strategies (Saggi, 2002). This process may be also referred to as the demonstration effect of FDIs (Hale and Long, 2006). The second aspect is related to the dissemination of external knowledge into the local economy (Kugler, 2006) due to specific forms of interaction. This perspective is centered in the analysis of vertical linkages among firms (Markusen, 1986; Markusen and Trofimenko, 2007). If multinational companies making FDIs interact with the local structure in order to produce, they could transfer knowledge and capabilities during their interaction with local suppliers and the implementation of novel, formerly non-diffused, quality standards. Finally, the third dimension is related to workers' mobility (Smeets, 2008; Smeets and Vaal, 2005). Spin offs and relocation of human resources from subsidiaries to the local companies could generate a process of knowledge dissemination (know-how and a set of other tacit abilities) (Fosfuri and Motta, 1998; Poole, 2007). There is a considerable debate regarding the actual impact of FDI on knowledge diffusion, which involves inconclusive and heterogeneous empirical evidence (Smeets, 2008). The ideas of *catch-up advantages* and *technological backwardness* (Findlay, 1978) are important in this vision, because underdeveloped economies are considered technological followers, so there is a relatively large potential for improvement. Thus, the presence of FDIs should impact positively in hosting economies that are technological followers.

At the same time, empirical evidence doesn't support unanimously the hypothesis of benefits derived from FDIs in terms of knowledge spillovers. At a general level, the existence of heterogeneous firms (Griffith *et al.*, 2004) may limit the knowledge transfer from one to another, especially if that transfer is based on sell-buy interactions. FDIs can also be heterogeneous because of the division between the activities of the headquarters and its subsidiaries. Since the subsidiaries' objectives are generally attached to a multinational strategy, resource allocation may lead to different types of subsidiaries according to the hosting economy characteristics. This phenomenon has to be combined with the local heterogeneity present in enterprises within countries (Zhang *et al.*, 2009). Hence, the existence of a variety of firms and subsidiaries in diverse contexts may impact on the localized ability of learning from the presence of foreign multinational firms in a given territory (Moran, 1992), affecting the idea of the existence of straight-forward knowledge spillovers derived from FDI.

Moreover, local firms can be heterogeneous along a variety of dimensions: not only structural dimensions such as the number of employees or the sectors of activity, but also, and more importantly, firms differ in terms of absorptive capacities. The idea of the existence of a threshold that limits the local capacity to benefit from the presence of foreign firms is largely discussed elsewhere (e.g. Strube, 2011; Girma and Wakelin, 2001). Therefore, economies with lower technological absorption capacities will be less susceptible to take advantages from the FDI presence (Abramovitz, 1986; Cohen and Levinthal, 1989). The discussion around FDI spillover's determinants and its diverse international impact is vast and complex. Additional factors that the literature takes into account are related to geographical proximity and regulatory conditions (Smeets, 2008). Regarding the first one, FDI's knowledge diffusion may depend upon geographical distance, especially for some of the mechanisms that conduct spillovers, such as workers' mobility (Girma and Wakelin, 2001). The evidence in this sense shows that local proximity of FDI affects positively a firm's performance and productivity (Resmini and Nicolini, 2007). Regarding the regulations, intellectual property rights play a significant role in FDI analysis. A complete discussion on the role of geographical proximity and intellectual property rights is developed in the following sections 4 and 5.

3.3. Licensing

Licensing constitutes also an important and interesting channel of international knowledge dissemination. It is important to note that licensing is a voluntary and marked-based mechanism of dissemination. A license consists in a transfer of specific knowledge from an innovator to a third party. In Nelson's (2009) words "technology licenses are contractual agreements that grant organizations permission to use a particular piece of patent-protected knowledge held by another organization". The most common mechanisms to implement these agreements are through a monetary transaction, where the price can be based on a percentage of the revenues on related products. In some cases licensing agreements are at the core of a strategic alliance (Anand and Khanna, 2000). As result, the buyers of licenses gain access to new technologies and innovators increase their revenues in the process of selling new knowledge.

The importance of revenues originated from licenses at the international level has been significant in the past decades, especially in some sectors like chemicals, biotechnology, software, computers and electrical machinery, and is a key determinant of multinationals' strategies (Anand and Khanna, 2000). These strategic alliances aim at enhancing a specific market demand, through an indirect selection of competitors,[8] or at deterring competitors' entry into some market. From an economic system perspective, these strategies become extremely relevant for knowledge dissemination (Arora and Gambardella, 1990).

A traditional vision (Markusen, 1986) claims that licenses and FDIs are substitute strategies, so firms choose *ex ante* their expansion strategy. FDIs imply a closed, secret based production strategy, while licensing is more open because the technology is sold to another firm in exchange for a fee. The second approach is linked to a complementary set of strategies that firms may apply in order to minimize the risk of non-appropiability (Teece, 1986). Thus, licenses are seen as a complementary asset to patents and FDIs, not necessarily implying a trade-off among different appropriation possibilities (Nelson, 2009), even though there is a delegation in terms of commercialization (Fosfuri, 2006; Arora and Fosfuri, 2003).

Markusen (1986) studies the multinationals' decision of licensing vs. FDIs. Departing from the idea that the knowledge market is risky and imperfect, this decision strongly depends upon key elements like the strength of intellectual property rights in the hosting country, their actual enforcement especially with respect to the licensing process, and the characteristics of the host economy. Horstmann and Markusen (1987) consider the degree of imperfect information, the "reputation" of the economy and its system of relative prices. While firms are interested in appropriating the rent of their innovation, these models evaluate the decision of choosing FDI over licensing. To do so they consider not only the costs of moving the production process (FDI and licenses versus exports), but also incorporate the knowledge dissipation costs associated to licenses within a particular Intellectual Property Rights (IPR) system. In sum, the common denominator of this work is that stronger IPR systems should be positively correlated with a stronger knowledge diffusion via FDIs.

Despite the discussion around different IPR systems and its impact on innovation, the former works do not provide an explanation of the fact that licensed technological knowledge increased significantly during the last 30 years. At the same time evidence suggests also a more than exponential growth of FDI levels and, especially, a rise in the number of strategic alliances with local partners centered on the delegation of technological capabilities, especially in the most technologically intensive sectors (Arora and Fosfuri, 2003). As it is, in spite of the strength of particular IPR systems, the tension between FDI and licensing could be spurious. Although licensing activities could be indeed affected by different regulatory frameworks (and their effective enforcements), in order to understand the growth of FDIs and licensing it is important to analyze multinational global strategies and local market-level incentives. Implications of different IPR systems on innovation activities are also discussed in Section 5.

There is a complex relation between FDI and licensing. These two channels can be complementary or substitute activities and are especially affected by IPR legislation. On the one hand, FDI investments could lead to the implementation of license agreements after the investment of the foreign firm in the hosting country. On the other hand, the two mechanisms may be substitutes: if IPRs are strong, then FDI will be the dominating strategy (because of the traditional arguments that stronger IPRs attract new FDIs). Substitution takes place in a weaker IPR context, where licensing agreements will give to the knowledge owner more control of what to share, of the conditions, and especially of possible counterparts. At the extreme, this can result in a secrecy strategy (Arora, 1997).

From a methodological perspective, licenses can be used to disambiguate the measurement problems derived from indicators based on patents (Nelson, 2009; Arora, 1996; Arora and Fosfuri, 2003). Since organizations that buy licenses are making use of other organizations' patents, a clear nexus between knowledge user and supplier can be established. License based indicators are also useful to single out patents with a relatively low importance for the productive system (patents with a low impact on the firm's activities), or strategies based on limiting (blocking) the use and diffusion of specific innovations in some technological fields (Murray and Stern, 2008; Calderini and Scellato, 2004).

Indicators based on licensing also show some limitations: evidence shows that when the knowledge producers have an interest in the market in which the license takes place, only minor innovations are licensed (Gallini, 1984). Additionally, licensing processes are based on the transfer of tacit know-how (as patents, they relay on a codification process). This tacit factor makes it difficult to evaluate if the transfer of such know-how (and especially other kinds of tacit knowledge like know-who and know-when) really takes place.

3.4 International R&D collaborations

One additional channel of voluntary international knowledge dissemination is related to collaboration activities. Particularly, international R&D collaborations are characterized by the interaction between economic agents to carry out the development of new products and processes or to exchange specific knowledge (Larsson et al., 1998). The nature of these interactions may be divided into two groups, private–private (inter-firm linkages) and private–public, that involves relations with universities,[9] research institutes, governments and other non-private organizations[10] (OECD, 2011).

The main objective behind a collaboration activity is to share, directly or indirectly, R&D costs and the related risk with the partner (e.g. Tether, 2002). This is generally characterized by the joint development of a piece of knowledge (i.e. product, process or service) in which both parties share an interest. In this sense, heterogeneous types of partnership can take place (Gallié and Roux, 2008), from informal exchanges based on meetings and conferences, to formal coalitions such as joint research activities (ad hoc or coordinated in time) or academic article publications (Link and Vonortas, 2000). The relevance of face-to-face interactions stands as an important characteristic of this process (Arai, 2002) since the tacit component of knowledge plays a key role in cooperation activities (Hall and Ritchie, 1975).

Empirical evidence shows that during the last decades international R&D collaborations have increased significantly (OECD, 2013; Hagedoorn, 2002; Montobbio and Sterzi, 2013; Cappelli and Montobbio, 2014). The carriers of this activity, though, were mainly big enterprises that used to invest in R&D before collaborations took place, leaving a marginal role for SMEs in these interactions, especially in firm-to-firm interactions (Edwards-Schachter *et al.*, 2012; OECD, 2013).

The traditional literature points out that inter-firm collaborations (Hagedoorn, 2002) take place because of three main reasons: transaction costs, technological motivations and market strategies. Recent, more complex approaches characterize motives of R&D collaborations in five groups, the first one, driven by knowledge access: a firm can benefit from another firm's specialization; the second, driven by market access, centered on how to monitor or enter a specific market; the third is risk sharing, which is based on the traditional complementary assets and transaction costs vision; the fourth, R&D complementarities, focused on joint alliances to develop a particular knowledge exploiting technological proximity; the fifth is based on learning reasons, especially relevant for uneven relations like developing-developed economies' firms or small and big enterprises, in which one party intends to catch up (Edwards-Schachter *et al.*, 2012). Complementary visions also explain firm-to-firm R&D cooperation as relations motivated by market power or driven by resource ownership (Combs and Ketchen, 1999).

Geographical proximity plays a key role in R&D collaborations because physically closer organizations interact more frequently and their interaction is more successful. An important portion of the literature argues that, since these relations are mainly oriented to tacit knowledge transfers, face-to-face interactions are very important. This gives a crucial role to both geographical and socio-cultural proximity (Keller, 2004; Hagedoorn, 2002; Edwards-Schachter *et al.*, 2012). This vision, however, has been challenged recently by the decreased costs of telecommunication brought about by the Internet and other ICT technologies. In principle this would decrease the role of geography in knowledge dissemination (Arai, 2002; Arai and Handayani, 2012).

From a methodological perspective, the uses of cooperation based indicators are affected by a potential selection bias. In this case, there is a strong effect of incomplete measurement because non-successful collaborations are not declared (and hence not computed) in the surveys and statistics. This may lead to observing only successful cases of cooperation.

To conclude, R&D collaborations, as with the other knowledge diffusion channels discussed, are affected by the regulatory dimension. According to Wu *et al.* (2013) IPR regimes have an influence on the number of R&D cooperation projects that are carried out. Moreover, R&D collaboration activities may be constrained by barriers to trade and other non-tariff limitations that may increase the costs of these activities, often implemented with protectionist intentions (Edwards and Poyago-Theotoky, 2013).

4. Geographical, technological and cultural barriers

The analysis of the different channels of knowledge dissemination clearly suggests that international technological diffusion can be shaped by different types of barriers. The channels described in the previous section generate some communication and transport costs that in turn depend upon a vast array of geographical, technological, cultural and institutional variables. In this section we discuss primarily the role of geographical and technological distances but it is important to underline that cultural and institutional factors can play a key role (note that as a consequence also national borders can provide significant barriers to knowledge dissemination). Technological and scientific knowledge can disseminate more rapidly when the language is similar and when there are specific political and economic relationships deriving from colonial and/or common legal origins.

Communication and transport costs can be relevant as learning is not automatic even when knowledge is codified and available in the public domain (e.g. in patents, publications and blueprints). This is because a substantial portion of knowledge can be tacit and linked to specific individuals and, as a consequence, learning requires in many cases active participation in a specific network of knowledge exchange (e.g. Keller and Yeaple, 2013; Montobbio and Sterzi, 2011 and 2013). Many authors have underlined that, in particular for technological knowledge, face-to-face interactions are a superior form of knowledge communication relative to, for example, telephone calls or e-mails. Face-to-face interactions provide some advantages because it is possible to have instantaneous feedback and direct correction of wrong interpretations. Clearly how strong these advantages are depends upon the complexity and specificity of knowledge. The level of international dissemination of knowledge could vary considerably across industries. In particular, as a consequence of the discussion in the previous sections, it is possible to claim that in industries where international trade, FDI and labor mobility are important and demand is global, the cost of knowledge communication may be low, particularly so when the source and the destination of the flows share the same knowledge base.

There is a wide consensus among scholars that geography constrains knowledge flows and that knowledge spillovers tend to be localized. In addition these communication and transport costs not only depend on geography but are also affected by technological distance. As emphasized in Section 2 knowledge spillovers are also generated across industries and technological distance could be a barrier to these externalities because it is more costly to learn from different technologies with a different knowledge base (Dosi, 1988; Antonelli, 2013 and 2015a). However the production of new ideas, products and processes use (knowledge) inputs that come from other fields; industries benefit from inter-sectoral spillovers depending upon how much their knowledge base uses knowledge from other fields.

Geographical and technological barriers are generated by different types of communication and learning costs (Malerba *et al.*, 2013). If it is less costly for inventors and companies to recognize and absorb knowledge that is similar to their knowledge base, intra-sectoral knowledge flows are less affected by distance than the inter-sectoral ones. At the same time when innovating firms need knowledge and technological inputs from (possibly complementary) other industries, international spillovers may be more costly to extract. In principle we should expect that intra-sectoral spillovers are more global than the inter-sectoral ones. This is because in the presence of communication and transport costs it is easier for innovators to identify, communicate and absorb knowledge coming from geographically closer economic agents and institutions.

There are not many papers that compare in a unified framework (international) intra-sectoral and inter-sectoral spillovers. Keller (2002) estimates international and inter-sectoral R&D spillovers on TFP and finds that the difference between intra-sectoral and inter-sectoral international spillovers changes according to the way inter-sectoral spillovers are calculated. Wieser's (2005) survey suggests that inter-sectoral spillovers are more significant than the intra-sectoral ones even if it is impossible to directly compare intra-sectoral with inter-sectoral spillovers because different studies measure spillovers in different ways and use different econometric strategies. Finally Malerba *et al.* (2013) estimate a patent function at the level of narrowly defined technological classes for a small set of advanced countries and show that the estimated intra-sectoral international spillover effects are more than twice the national ones. In addition they show that inter-sectoral knowledge flows are much more affected by geographical distance (and in particular national borders) than intra-sectoral ones.

5. International knowledge dissemination and intellectual property rights

The issue of knowledge spillovers is tightly linked with the issue of intellectual property rights (Antonelli, 2015b). In Section 2 we discussed how knowledge spillovers are key drivers of economic growth. The basic rationale is that the returns from knowledge investment are partly public and partly private. Both the amount of investment in knowledge creation and the portion of it that remains private depend in a complex way on how the legislation on intellectual property is designed. In addition the effectiveness of the different channels of international knowledge transfers described in the previous sections are affected by the international IPRs agreements. It would be out of the scope of this chapter to survey all the literature on IPRs and knowledge transfer. We limit ourselves to mentioning here what we think are the main issues and some results, keeping in mind that there is not strong evidence that IPRs reinforcement has a strong impact on the international dissemination of knowledge in particular to low-income countries. For further details and a more detailed discussion we can refer to many complete surveys on the issue of international IPRs legislation and international knowledge dissemination (e.g. Park and Lippoldt, 2008; Hall, 2014; Qian, 2007).

In recent years, the adoption of the Agreement on Trade Related Aspects of Intellectual Property Rights (TRIPs) and the consequent increase in IP protection in many countries has affected trade, FDIs and cooperation patterns across emerging and advanced countries. New harmonized legislation and stricter enforcement could provide greater incentives to disclose technological knowledge, especially when technological spillovers are linked to international trade. In addition, the strength of IPRs in an emerging country should reassure multinational companies willing to invest and develop technologies in these countries.

In addition, strong IPRs could generate a monopoly power, limiting competition and raising prices. As a consequence, stronger IPRs and stricter enforcement may generate fewer international knowledge flows through imitation and adoption and may cause the closing down of infringing activities. Finally, worries have also been expressed that stronger IPRs generate higher costs of access to imported technologies and difficulties in accessing basic scientific knowledge (Mazzoleni and Nelson, 1998; McCalman, 2001; Grossman and Lai, 2004; Lissoni *et al.*, 2011).

There are no general empirical results on the relationship between IPRs and international knowledge diffusion. A consensus tends to emerge showing that the positive effects of national patent law implementation increase with the development level, educational attainment and economic freedom of countries (e.g. Qian, 2008). Recent evidence about the impact of the TRIPs in the pharmaceutical sectors (Laforgia *et al.*, 2007) on investments and trade can be also found in Kyle and McGahan (2011) and Delgado *et al.* (2008).

Several works study knowledge transfer via international collaborations between patent inventors (Breschi *et al.*, 2007; Montobbio and Sterzi, 2013). These collaborations are an important vehicle of dissemination because both codified and tacit knowledge can be communicated via face-to-face interactions. Their evidence suggests that the impact of IPR reinforcement varies according to the type of collaboration considered and country of origin (emerging vs. advanced) of the companies involved. For collaborations deriving from laboratories of multinational subsidiaries we have a positive effect of IPR reinforcement. On the contrary, for collaborations that involve only a company from the emerging market the effect of the reinforcement of IPRs is negative. Finally, they show that a positive result may be confined to pairs of countries that are close trade partners.

These results tend to suggest that it is the interaction between the strength of IPRs and a certain level of absorptive capacity that could generate learning from imported technology.

However, it has to be noted that a multinational company takes decision on R&D investment in a foreign country based on factors like the size of the recipient economy, its expected growth and the presence of skilled personnel rather than IP protection.

6. Methodological issues

This last section is dedicated to the discussion of a set of methodological issues that concern the econometric methods used to identify international knowledge spillovers. These issues cut across all the econometric literature that estimates international spillovers via the different channels discussed in Section 3 (e.g. Mairesse and Sassenou, 1991) and point to the conceptualization, the measurement and the econometric estimations of knowledge externalities. First of all many econometric studies suffer an important omitted variable bias. Second, measurement error is also a recurrent issue, applying to any case in which the available indicator used in the empirical exercise doesn't reflect exactly the variable of the researchers' interest. This is an important aspect in particular for the knowledge variables in which *what to measure* and *how to measure* are still open questions.

In fact knowledge spillovers, despite being recognized as a key element to understanding economic growth, are still a black box in terms of their measurement in the empirical work. A classic contribution that triggered most of the current literature regarding measurement errors and misleading estimations of R&D is attributed to Schankerman (1981) and his work on biased R&D measures due to duplicated accounting. His approach consists in the identification of two types of distortions: the "excess returns bias" and the "expensing bias". The first takes place when R&D is represented as an expansion of production factors (e.g. in the form $L(1+d)$ where d is the proportion of labor – equivalent for the capital case – that is engaged in research) which leads to a double counting of the factor shares, having a downwards bias effect. The "expensing bias" deals with the nature of R&D as an intermediate cost: if that's the case then R&D growth rate has to be subtracted from gross product growth rate and weighted for the proportion of R&D in value added. The expensing bias doesn't have a clear behavior, since it can be positive or negative, depending on the rate of growth of both the economy and the share of R&D. According to Schankerman the "expensing" bias is expected to be less relevant than the "excess returns bias".

Shankerman's seminal observation remains valid for all the R&D based estimations of international knowledge spillovers. In addition to that we provide two examples of recent papers that point at further econometric challenges. Eberhardt *et al.* (2013) underline the limitations of the traditional spillover measurement, particularly pointing that the measurement of $TFP = g (R_k, \Sigma_k \omega_k R_k)$ not only assumes linear spillovers but also a linear relation between the effects of local R&D and foreign knowledge. Econometrically, the term $\Sigma_k \omega_k R_k$ enters as a regressor that affects TFP linearly – in a traditional fixed effects model form. Since all the regressors have to be orthogonal to the error term, the traditional specification assumes that the R&D spillover effect can be separated from the R&D investment effect on TFP. They conclude that measurement of spillovers using the classic Griliches' representation may mislead the estimations because of the presence of serially correlated non-stationary residuals specially related to the violation of the orthogonality condition. The linear expressions may be considered to be replaced for complex mixes of own R&D efforts and spillover derived knowledge.

The second example is Luintel and Khan (2004). They address the issue of international knowledge spillovers with the usual panel at country level and underline that heterogeneity of knowledge diffusion across countries is very important. Their result shows that the elasticity of total factor productivity with respect to domestic and foreign R&D stocks is extremely heterogeneous across countries. The important consequence is that they reject the typical restriction that TFP elasticity to R&D is common across countries. Luintel and Khan (2004) point at two characteristics of knowledge diffusion: first, knowledge externalities are related to some skill level of the adopting economy, supporting the idea of a minimum level of absorptive capacity that allows the exploitation of available knowledge (if a minimum level of capacity is not present, then there is no spillover). Second, in knowledge spillover dynamics the partner matters, so it is not trivial to exchange knowledge with one partner or another. In this sense, factors such as geographical proximity and technological congruence of firms and specific two-sided relations are extremely relevant in the analysis of knowledge transfer relationships.

Finally, a group of factors related to the nature of knowledge may be stressed. Knowledge transfers are often tacit, subjective and unobservable phenomena. This implies a difficulty to measure knowledge spillovers, since typically spillover estimates use proxies of unobserved variables that are known to be inaccurate. In addition to that, different knowledge types exist, meaning that knowledge heterogeneity is a relevant factor to consider in the building of empirical measurements. Knowledge poolability is an implicit assumption that actually can be considered as a particular case. Contrasting with the traditional approaches based on the knowledge homogeneity assumption, heterogeneity of knowledge has been considered as a critical matter during recent years (Patuelli et al., 2010; Sun, 2009).

Knowledge transfers are difficult to measure, regardless the intention of the receiver or the transmitter. The transformation that codified information suffers in order to become knowledge is an introspective, internal process that takes place at individual or organizational level (Nonaka and Takeuchi, 1995), and even if the researcher is able to measure the amount of information flow within an interaction, the intrinsic procedure of assimilation remains as an omitted variable (that might be proxied with recurrent qualitative in-depth interview methods). Therefore the tacit nature of knowledge acquisition in many circumstances persists as an empirical enigma. The aggregated consequence in econometric terms of these issues leads to a mix between an omitted variable bias and a measurement error bias, depending on the research subject.

A final remark can be made relative to the Griliches distinction between pure and pecuniary spillovers discussed at the beginning of the chapter. We have shown that a lot of progress has been made trying to understand the impact of international knowledge spillovers and the different channels through which knowledge disseminates. However the distinction between pecuniary and pure spillover still remains difficult to disentangle empirically, in particular when international knowledge dissemination is considered. Pooling, double counting and omitted variables considerations keep having a relevant role in this matter.

7. Conclusions

This chapter is an attempt to provide a map to the recent literature on international knowledge dissemination. We have explained why the international dissemination of technological knowledge is important. We surveyed a few endogenous growth models to show how the growth literature has incorporated the idea of knowledge dissemination. The key aspect is that knowledge creates increasing returns if a portion of it is not appropriable and creates positive externalities. In this vein various growth models have described the conditions under which knowledge accumulation may generate an equilibrium growth path. In particular we have emphasized the issue of the speed of knowledge diffusion and decay and, relatedly, the importance of identifying channels of knowledge diffusion like international trade. Theorists have demonstrated that international knowledge spillovers are key for understanding growth, and trade and policy prescriptions should pay attention to the scope and types of knowledge dissemination. However, the impact of these theories is (and will be) defined by the empirical evidence.

The empirical literature has studied different forms of international knowledge transmission: international trade, foreign direct investments, markets for technologies and international collaborations. We have surveyed here the empirical literature that explains the determinants of these channels and to what extent these channels really have an economic impact via knowledge dissemination. International knowledge dissemination implies that knowledge can flow to distant locations. So we have dedicated a section to discuss the role of geographical distance. In addition to that we have discussed geographical distance together with other forms of distances that the literature suggests are very important, in particular technological and cultural distances. Second, intellectual property rights are a key issue that regulates the trade-off between knowledge creation and diffusion and drives the degree to which knowledge actually spills over. So we have discussed how all the international channels of knowledge dissemination are affected by specific intellectual property design.

Despite the enormous number of empirical papers on the issue, the empirical estimation of international knowledge dissemination faces some problems. In the last section we emphasized some measurement and methodological problems, in particular in relation to standard econometric panel data analysis that estimates R&D international spillovers on TFP.

Notes

1 In Section 5 we address the issue of intellectual property rights and the trade-off between innovation and knowledge diffusion.
2 Among many valuable contributions see Stoneman and Battisti (2010), Comin and Hobijn (2004) and Comin *et al.* (2008).
3 Keller (2004) is a key survey on the topic of international knowledge dissemination.
4 There is a vast literature that covers these aspects. Among them, Keller (2004) makes explicit reference to the mentioned processes.
5 See also Bacchiocchi and Montobbio (2009 and 2010).
6 Keller has modified his vision in his subsequent work. Fracasso and Marzetti (2011) write "Keller starts from an hypothesis of 'global pool' of technology (Keller, 1998) and ends up with the idea that spillovers are geographically concentrated because they mainly depend on factors that are not directly related to international trade (Keller, 2004) ...".
7 There is a vast literature that is focused on multinational corporations' commercial, productive and innovative strategies. This literature, mainly represented by the Global Value Chains perspective (Feenstra, 1998; Gereffi *et al.*, 2005), will not be treated in this chapter, although it represents an important milestone in the research on international knowledge flows and FDI characteristics.
8 The intentional selection of a partner in an R&D alliance may reduce the number of competitors and, in this sense, an alliance may modify the nature of competition. If the market is concentrated, then alliances could be a collusive strategy against those firms that are outside the alliance.
9 Even though universities may be privately owned, the type of interaction can be broadly characterized as firm-university.
10 In this section we focus on inter-firm relations. The main idea behind this choice is that usually universities and governments' firm oriented interactions consist of within-country collaborations, while our interest remains on the international knowledge flows. This, however, was revisited in recent last years when a number of European Union projects pushed inter-country collaboration programs (e.g. Hottenrott and Lopes-Bento 2012). Also inventors and universities' actors carry different types of knowledge, which may impact in different productive systems through international mobility. Shapiro (2007) and Binder (2007) provide further discussion on public–private collaborations.

Bibliography

Abramovitz, M. (1986). Catching up, forging ahead, and falling behind, *The Journal of Economic History*, 46(2): 385–406.

Anand, B. N. and Khanna, T. (2000). The structure of licensing contracts, *Journal of Industrial Economics*, 48(1): 103–135.

Antonelli, C. (2008). *Localized Technological Change. Towards the Economics of Complexity*, Routledge, London.

Antonelli, C. (2013). Knowledge governance, pecuniary knowledge externalities and total factor productivity growth, *Economic Development Quarterly*, 27, 62–70.

Antonelli, C. (2014). Globalization and technological congruence: An interpretative framework of the slow growth of the knowledge economy, in Patrucco, P. (ed.), *The Economics of Knowledge Generation and Distribution: The Role of Interactions in the System Dynamics of Innovation and Growth*, Routledge, London, forthcoming.

Antonelli, C. (2015a). The dynamics of knowledge governance, forthcoming, in Antonelli, C. and Link, A. (eds.) *Handbook on the Economics of Knowledge*, Routledge, London.

Antonelli, C. (2015b). Towards non-exclusive intellectual property rights, forthcoming, in Antonelli, C. and Link, A. (eds.) *Handbook on the Economics of Knowledge*, Routledge, London.

Antonelli, C. and Ferraris, G. (2012). *Endogenous Knowledge Externalities: An Agent Based Simulation Model where Schumpeter Meets Marshall*. Dipartimento Di Economia "S. Cognetti De Martiis" – Working Paper No. 02/2012.

Arai, K. and Handayani, A. N. (2012). Question answering system for an effective collaborative learning. *International Journal of Advanced Computer Science and Applications*, 3(1): 60–64.

Arai, Y. (2002). Face-to-face and internet communications in R&D activities in Japan: An empirical study in Kyushu, *Networks and Communication Studies Netcom*, 16: 1–2, 5–16.

Arora, A. (1996). Contracting for tacit knowledge: The provision of technical services in technology licensing contracts, *Journal of Development Economics* 50: 233–256.

Arora, A. (1997). Patents, licensing and market structure in the chemical industry, *Research Policy* 26: 391–403.

Arora, A. and Fosfuri, A. (2003). Licensing the market for technology, *Journal of Economic Behavior and Organization*, 52: 277–295.

Arora, A. and Gambardella, A. (1990). Complementarity and external linkages: The strategies of the large firms in biotechnology, *Journal of Industrial Economics*, 38, 4: 361–379.

Arora, A., Fosfuri, A., and Roende, T. (2012). *Managing Licensing in a Market for Technology*, NBER Working Papers 18203.

Arrow, K. (1962). Economic welfare and the allocation of resources for invention, in Nelson, R.R. (ed.) *The Rate and Direction of Inventive Activity: Economic and Social Factors*, National Bureau of Economic Research, Inc. Princeton, NJ: Princeton University Press, pp. 609–626.

Aw, B.Y., Chung, S., and Roberts, M.J. (2000), Productivity and turnover in the export market: Micro-level evidence from Taiwan (China) and the Republic of Korea, *World Bank Economic Review*, 14, 1: 65–90.

Bacchiocchi, E. and Montobbio, F. (2009). Knowledge diffusion from university and public research. A comparison between US, Japan and Europe using patent citations, *Journal of Technology Transfer*, Springer, 34(2): 169–181.

Bacchiocchi, E. and Montobbio, F. (2010). International knowledge diffusion and home-bias effect. Do USPTO & EPO patent citations tell the same story? *Scandinavian Journal of Economics*, 112 (3): 441–470.

Barro, R. and Sala-i-Martin, X. (2004). *Economic Growth*, Second Edition, The MIT Press, Cambridge.

Belderbos, R. and Mohnen, P. (2013). *Intersectoral and International R&D Spillovers*, Unu-Merit Wp 7.

Bernard, A., Jensen, B., and Schott, P. (2006). Trade costs, firms and productivity, *Journal of Monetary Economics*, 53: 917–937.

Binder, M. (2007). *Collaborative Enterprise Governance: Sustainable Management of Inter-Firm R&D Relationships in the German Car Industry*, Aston University – Phd Thesis.

Branstetter, L.G. (1998). Looking for international knowledge spillovers: A review of the literature with suggestions for new approaches, *Annales d'Economie et de Statistique*, No. 49/50, Économie et Économétrie de l'innovation/The Economics and Econometrics of Innovation (Jan–Jun): 517–540.

Branstetter, L. (2000). *Is Foreign Direct Investment a Channel of Knowledge Spillovers? Evidence from Japan's FDI in the United States*, NBER – Working Paper No. 8015.

Branstetter, L. (2001). Are knowledge spillovers international or intranational in scope? Microeconometric evidence from Japan and the United States, *Journal of International Economics*, 53: 53–79.

Breschi, S. and Lissoni, F. (2001). Knowledge spillovers and local innovation systems: A critical survey, *Industrial and Corporate Change*, 10, 4: 975–1005.

Breschi, S. and Lissoni, F. (2009). *Mobility of Inventors and the Geography of Knowledge Spillovers. New Evidence on US Data*, Cespri Working Paper No. 142 (October).

Breschi, S., Lissoni, F., and Montobbio, F. (2007). The scientific productivity of academic inventors: New evidence from Italian data, *Economics of Innovation and New Technology* 16(2): 101–118.

Caballero, R.J. and Jaffe, A.B. (1993). How high are the giants' shoulders: An empirical assessment of knowledge spillovers and creative destruction in a model of economic growth, *NBER Macroeconomics Annual* 8 (January): 15–86.

Calderini, M. and Scellato, G. (2004). *Intellectual Property Rights as Strategic Assets: The Case of European Patent Opposition in the Telecommunication Industry*, Cespri Working Paper No. 158.

Cappelli, R. and Montobbio, F. (2014). European integration and knowledge flows across European regions, *Regional Studies*, DOI: 10.1080/00343404.2014.931572.

Clerides, S., Lach, S., and Tybout, J. (1998). Is learning by exporting important? Micro-dynamic evidence from Colombia, Mexico, and Morocco, *Quarterly Journal of Economics*, 113(3): 903–947.

Coe, D.T. and Helpman, E. (1995). International R&D spillovers, *European Economic Review*, 39: 859–887.

Cohen, W.M. and Levinthal, D.A. (1989). Innovation and learning: The two faces of R&D, *Economic Journal*, 99: 569–596.

Combs, J. and Ketchen, D. (1999). Explaining interfirm cooperation and performance: Toward a reconciliation of predictions from the resource based view and organizational economics, *Strategic Management Journal*, 20: 867–888.

Comin, D.A. and Hobijn, B. (2004). Cross-country technological adoption: Making the theories face the facts, *Journal of Monetary Economics*, 51: 39–83.

Comin, D.A. and Hobijn, B. (2010). An exploration of technology diffusion, *American Economic Review* 100 (5): 2031–2059.

Comin, D.A., Hobijn, B., and Rovito, E. (2008). A new approach to measuring technology with an application to the shape of diffusion curves, *Journal of Technology Transfer*, 33(2): 187–207.

Damijan, J., Kostevc, C., and Polanec, S. (2008). *From Innovation to Exporting or Vice Versa? Causal Link Between Innovation Activity and Exporting in Slovenian Microdata*, Vienna University of Economics and Bussiness, 1–31.

Daveri, F. and Olmo, S. (2004). Not only Nokia: What Finland tells us about "new economy" growth, *Economic Policy* 91(38): 117–163.

Delgado, M., Kyle, M., and McGahan, A.M. (2008). *The Influence of TRIPS on Global Trade in Pharmaceuticals, 1994–2005*, University of Toronto Working Paper.

Dosi, G. (1988). Sources, procedures, and microeconomic effects of innovation, *Journal of Economic Literature*, 26(3): 1120–1171.

Eaton, J. and Kortum, S. (1999). International technology diffusion: Theory and measurement, *International Economic Review*, 40(3): 537–570.

Eberhardt, M., Helmers, C., and Strauss, H. (2013). Do spillovers matter when estimating private returns to R&D? *Review of Economics and Statistics*, 95(2): 436–448.

Edwards, H. and Poyago-Theotoky, J. (2013). Regulatory protection when firms decide first on technical collaboration and R&D, *Review of International Economics*, 21(4): 750–764.

Edwards-Schachter, M., Anlló, G., Castro-Martínez, E., and Sánchez-Barrioluengo, M. (2012). *Motives for Inter-Firm Cooperation on R&D and Innovation: Empirical Evidence from Argentine and Spain*, Ingenio Working Paper Series No. 2012/04.

Feenstra, R.C. (1998). Integration of trade and disintegration of production in the global economy, *Journal of Economic Perspectives*, 12 (4): 31–50.

Feldman, M.P. and Kelley, M.R. (2006). The ex ante assessment of knowledge spillovers: Government R&D policy, economic incentives and private firm behavior, *Research Policy*, 35(10): 1509–1521.

Findlay, R. (1978). Relative backwardness, direct foreign investment, and the transfer of technology: A simple dynamic model, *Quarterly Journal of Economics*, 92(1): 1–16.

Fosfuri, A. (2006). The licensing dilemma: Understanding the determinants of the rate of technology licensing, *Strategic Management Journal*, 27: 1141–1158.

Fosfuri, A. and Motta, M. (1998). *Foreign Direct Investments and Spillovers through Workers' Mobility*, Department of Economics, Universitat Pompeu Fabra, 0663.

Fracasso, A. and Marzetti, G.V. (2011). *Taking Keller Seriously: Trade and Distance in International R&D Spillovers*, Trento University, Department of Economics Working Paper No. 6/2011.

Gallié, E-P. and Roux, P. (2008). *Forms and Determinants of R&D Collaborations: New Evidence on French Data*, Druid Working Paper No. 08-15.

Gallini, N. (1984). Deterrence by market sharing: A strategic incentive for licensing, *American Economic Review*, 74(5): 931–941.

Gereffi, G., Humphrey J., and Sturgeon T. (2005). The governance of global value chains, *Review of International Political Economy*, 12(1): 78–104.

Girma, S. and Wakelin, K. (2001). *Regional Underdevelopment: Is FDI the Solution? A Semiparametric Analysis*, CEPR Discussion Papers 2995.

Green, L.W., Ottoson J.M., García C., and Hiatt R.A. (2009). Diffusion theory and knowledge dissemination, utilization, and integration in public health, *Annual Review of Public Health*, 30: 151–174.

Griffith, R., Redding, S., and Van Reenen, J. (2004). Mapping the two faces of R&D: Productivity growth in a panel of OECD industries, *Review of Economics and Statistics*, 86(4): 883–895.

Griliches, Z. (1979). Issues in assessing the contribution of Research and Development to productivity growth, *Bell Journal of Economics*, 10(1): 92–116.

Griliches, Z. (1992). The search for R&D spillovers, *Scandinavian Journal of Economics*, 94: S29–47, Supplement.

Grossman, G.M. and Helpman, E. (1990). Trade, innovation and growth, *American Economic Review*, 80(2): 86–91.

Grossman, G. M. and Helpman, E. (1991). Trade, knowledge spillovers and growth, *European Economic Review*, 35 (2–3): 517–526.

Grossman, G. M. and Lai, E.L.C., (2004). *Parallel Imports and Price Controls*, CEPR Discussion Papers 5779.

Hagedoorn, J. (2002). Inter-Firm R&D partnerships: An overview of major trends and patterns since 1960, *Research Policy*, 31: 477–492.

Hale, G. and Long, C. (2006). *What Determines Technological Spillovers of Foreign Direct Investment: Evidence from China.* Center Discussion Paper No. 934.

Hall, B. H. (2014). Does patent protection help or hinder technology transfer?, in S. Ahn, B. H. Hall, and K. Lee (eds) *Intellectual Property for Economic Development: Issues and Policy Implications*, Edward Elgar, Cheltenham, UK, 11–32.

Hall, K.R. and Ritchie, E. (1975), A study of communication behaviour in an R&D laboratory, *R&D Management*, 5: 243–245.

Helpman, E., Melitz, M. J., and Yeaple, S. R. (2004). *Export versus FDI with Heterogeneous Firms*, Department of Economics, Harvard University.

Horstmann, I. and Markusen J. (1987). Licensing versus direct investment: A model of internalization by the multinational enterprise, *Canadian Journal of Economics*, 20(3): 464–481.

Hottenrott, H. and Lopes-Bento, C. (2012). *International R&D Collaboration and SMES: The Effectiveness of Targeted Public R&D Support Schemes*, Leuven University – Working Paper No. 2012–36.

Jefferson, T. (1886). *The Writings of Thomas Jefferson.* Edited by Andrew A. Lipscomb and Albert Ellery Bergh. 20 vols. Washington: Thomas Jefferson Memorial Association, 1905.

Jones, C. I. and Williams, J.C. (1998). Measuring the social return to R&D, *Quarterly Journal of Economics*, 113: 1119–1135.

Keller, W. (1998). Are international R&D spillovers trade-related? Analyzing spillovers among randomly matched trade partners, *European Economic Review*, 42: 1469–1481.

Keller, W. (2002). Geographic localization of international technology diffusion, *American Economic Review*, 92(1): 120–142.

Keller, W. (2004). International technology diffusion, *Journal of Economic Literature*, XLII: 752–782.

Keller, W. (2009). *International Trade, Foreign Direct Investment and Technology Spillovers*, NBER Working Paper 15442.

Keller, W. and Yeaple, S.R. (2013). The gravity of knowledge, *American Economic Review*, 103(4): 1414–1444.

Kugler, M. (2006). *Spillovers from Foreign Direct Investment: Within or Between Industries?* Department of Economics, University of Southampton (September): 1–43.

Kyle, M. and McGahan, A. (2011). *Investments in Pharmaceuticals before and after TRIPS*, CEPR Discussion Papers 8371.

Laforgia, F., Montobbio, F., and Orsenigo, L. (2007). *IPRs, Technological and Industrial Development and Growth: The Case of the Pharmaceutical Industry*, Cespri Working Paper No. 206.

Larsson, R., Bengtsson R., Henriksson K., and Sparks J. (1998). The inter-organizational learning dilemma: Collective knowledge development in strategic alliances, *Organization Science* 9: 285–305.

Lee, G. (2006). The effectiveness of international knowledge spillover channels, *European Economic Review*, 50: 2075–2088.

León-Ledesma, M. (2005). Exports, product differentiation and knowledge spillovers, *Open Economies Review*, 16: 363–379.

Li, J., Shen, K., and Zhang, R. (2011). Measuring knowledge spillovers: A non-appropriable returns perspective, *Annals of Economics and Finance*, 12–2: 265–293.

Lichtenberg, F.R. and Potterie, B.Van P. de la. (1998). International R&D spillovers: A comment, *European Economic Review*, 42: 1483–1491.

Link, A.N. and Vonortas, N.S. (2000). *Participation of European Union Companies in US Research Joint Ventures*, The IPTS Report, Contents Report 43.

Lissoni, F., Mairesse, J., Montobbio, F., and Pezzoni, M. (2011). Scientific productivity and academic promotion: A study on French and Italian physicists, *Industrial and Corporate Change*, 20(1): 253–294.

Lööf, H. and Nabavi, P. (2013). *Learning and Productivity of Swedish Exporting Firms: The Importance of Innovation Efforts and the Geography of Innovation*, Working Paper Series in Economics and Institutions of Innovation 296, Royal Institute of Technology, CESIS – Centre of Excellence for Science and Innovation Studies.

López, R.A. (2004). *Self-Selection into the Export Markets: A Conscious Decision?* Department of Economics, Indiana University, 1–23.

Luintel, K.B. and Khan, M. (2004). Are international R&D spillovers costly for the United States? *Review of Economics and Statistics*, 86(4): 896–910.

McCalman, P. (2001). Reaping what you sow: An empirical analysis of international patent harmonization, *Journal of International Economics*, 55(1): 161–186.

Mairesse, J. and Sassenou, M. (1991). *R&D and Productivity: A Survey of Econometric Studies at the Firm Level*, Working Paper No. 3666 (8).

Malerba, F., Mancusi, M.L., and Montobbio, F. (2013). Innovation, international R&D spillovers and the sectoral heterogeneity of knowledge flows, *Review of World Economics*, 149: 697–722.

Markusen, J.R. (1986). Explaining the volume of trade: An eclectic approach, *American Economic Review*, 76(5): 1002–1011.

Markusen, J. R. and Trofimenko, N. (2007). *Teaching Locals New Tricks: Foreign Experts as a Channel of Knowledge Transfers*, NBER Working Paper 12872.

Mazzoleni, R. and Nelson, R. (1998). The benefits and costs of strong patent protection: A contribution to the current debate, *Research Policy*, 27(3): 273–284.

Montobbio, F. and Sterzi, V. (2011). Inventing together: Exploring the nature of international knowledge spillovers in Latin America, *Journal of Evolutionary Economics*, 21: 53–89.

Montobbio, F. and Sterzi, V. (2013). The globalization of technology in emerging markets: A gravity model on the determinants of international technological collaborations, *World Development*, 44: 281–299.

Moran, T.H. (1992). *Harnessing Foreign Direct Investment for Development: Policies for Developed and Developing Countries*, Center for Global Development, Center for Global Development Washington, D.C. 1–1.

Murray, F. and Stern, S. (2008). *Learning to Live with Patents: A Dynamic Model of a Knowledge Community's Response to Legal Institutional Change*, MIT Sloan School of Management and Kellogg School of Management Northwestern University, (November).

Nelson, A.J. (2009). Measuring knowledge spillovers: What patents, licenses and publications reveal about innovation diffusion, *Research Policy*, 38: 994–1005.

Nonaka, I. and Takeuchi, H. (1995). *The Knowledge Creating Company: How Japanese Companies Create the Dynamics of Innovation*, Oxford University Press, New York.

OECD (2006). *Government R&D Funding and Company Behaviour*. OECD, Paris.

OECD (2011). *Hand-Out from Lessons to Principles for the Use of Public–Private Partnerships*. 32nd Annual Meeting of Working Party of Senior Budget Officials, 1–17.

OECD (2013). Collaboration on innovation, in *OECD Science, Technology and Industry Scoreboard 2013: Innovation for Growth*. OECD, Paris.

Parameswaran, M. (2009). International trade, R&D spillovers and productivity: Evidence from Indian manufacturing industry, *Journal of Development Studies*, 45(8): 1249–1266.

Park, W.G. and Lippoldt, D.C., (2008). *Technology Transfer and the Economic Implications of the Strengthening of Intellectual Property Rights in Developing Countries*, OECD Trade Policy Working Papers, No. 62.

Patuelli, R., Vaona, A., and Grimpe, C. (2010). The German East West divide in knowledge production: An application to nanomaterial patenting, *Tijdschrift voor Economische en Sociale Geografie*, 101(5): 568–582.

Poole, J.P. (2007). *Multinational Spillovers Through Worker Turnover*. Department of Economics, University of California (September).

Qian, Y. (2007). Do national patent laws stimulate domestic innovation in a global patenting environment? A cross country analysis of pharmaceutical patent protection, 1978–2002, *Review of Economics and Statistics* 89(3): 436–453.

Qian, Y. (2008). Impacts of entry by counterfeiters, *Quarterly Journal of Economics*, 123(4): 1577–1609.

Resmini, L. and Nicolini, M. (2007). *Productivity Spillovers and Multinational Enterprises: In Search of a Spatial Dimension*, Papers DYNREG10, Economic and Social Research Institute (ESRI).

Romer, P. (1986). Increasing returns and long-run growth, *Journal of Political Economy*, 94(5): 1002–1037.

Saggi, K. (2002). Trade, foreign direct investment, and international technology transfer: A survey, *The World Bank Research Observer*, 17(2): 191–235.

Salomon, R. and Shaver, J.M. (2005). Learning by exporting: New insights from examining firm innovation, *Journal of Economics & Management Strategy*, 14(2): 431–460.

Schankerman, M. (1981). The effects of double-counting and expensing on the measured returns to R&D, *Review of Economics and Statistics*, 63(3): 454–458.

Schmookler, J. (1966). *Invention and Economic Growth*, Harvard University Press, Cambridge.

Shapiro, M. (2007). Public–private R&D collaboration in Korea: A cross-sector survey of incentive structures, in Mahlich, G. and Peschea, W. (Eds) *Innovation and Technology in Korea*, Physica-Verlag HD (Pub), 93–113.

Smeets, R. (2008). Collecting the pieces of the FDI knowledge spillovers puzzle, *The World Bank*, 23: 107–138.

Smeets, R. and Vaal, A. De. (2005). *Knowledge Spillovers from FDI: Towards a General Framework*, Druid Tenth Anniversary Summer Conference 2005, 1–29.

Stoneman, P. and Battisti, G. (2010), The diffusion of new technology, in Hall, B.H. and Rosenberg, N. (eds.), *Handbook of the Economics of Innovation*, Elsevier, Amsterdam.

Strube, D. (2011). *Threshold Effects from Absorptive Capacity and the Effectiveness of Innovation Policy*, Department of Economics, Johannes Guttenberg University Mainz, 1–29.

Sun, S. (2009). *Impact of Aggregation on Measuring FDI Spillovers: A Monte Carlo Appraisal*, Munich Personal Repec Archive Impact Mpra Paper No. 15340.

Teece, D. (1986). Profiting from technological innovation: Implications for integration, collaboration, licensing and public policy, *Research Policy*, 15(6): 285–305.

Tether, Bruce S. (2002). Who co-operates for innovation, and why: An empirical analysis, *Research Policy*, 31(6): 947–967.

Vernon, R. (1966). International investment and international trade in the product cycle, *The Quarterly Journal of Economics*, 80(2): 190–207.

Wakelin, K. (2001). Productivity growth and R&D expenditure in UK manufacturing firms, *Research Policy*, 30: 1079–1090.

Wieser, R. (2005). Research and development productivity and spillovers: Empirical evidence at the firm level, *Journal of Economic Surveys*, 19(4): 587–621.

Wu, C., Lam, L. X., and Hsing, Y. M. (2013). Intellectual property in inter-firm R&D collaboration, an examination on the role of IP management core components, *International Journal of Science and Engineering*, 3(1): 1–12.

Xu, B. and Wang, J. (1999). Capital goods trade and R&D spillovers in the OECD, *Canadian Journal of Economics*, 32(5): 1258–1274.

Zhang, Y., Li, H., and Li, Y. (2009). FDI spillovers in an emerging market: The role of foreign firms' country origin diversity and domestic firms' absorptive capacity, *Strategic Management Journal*, 31: 969–989.

12

The economic nature of knowledge embodied in standards for technology-based industries

Gregory Tassey

1. Technological complexity and the policy relevance of standards

In today's technology driven economy, multiple standards are required to specify attributes of products, processes, and services.[1] In so doing, they affect both technological innovation and diffusion. Examples are

- specifying the architecture of a microprocessor;
- specifying performance (quality) levels for solid state lighting (LED) products;
- defining the calibration process for photolithography equipment;
- characterizing nanomaterials in research databases;
- providing performance data for attributes of optical fiber to facilitate market transactions.

In essence, standards are a form of technical infrastructure and therefore have considerable public-good content. In a simplified economic view, their content is both non-excludable (leaks/ spill overs) and non-rival (multiple users without congestion costs).

More accurately, however, the "infratechnologies" that provide the technical basis for standards can be partially excludable, at least for periods of time. This fact leads to complex public–private models for standards development and management. The reason is the underlying intellectual property rights (IPR) can be owned/controlled by individual firms or groups of firms, which allows them to influence the structure of standards and/or their use. This situation is often manifested in the formation of competing market segments that adopt their own version of a standard (so-called "local" standards).

As for the degree of rivalry or access to a standard, the adoption of a local standard by a system integrator can favor market access for some component suppliers over others. The vested interest acquired in each local standard can retard the movement toward a single or "global" standard that provides maximum economic benefits.[2]

Therefore, technology-based growth policies, including those elements affecting standardization, must be based on both static and dynamic contexts. Doing so, however, is complicated by the fact that the complexity of modern technologies, especially their system character, has led to a steady increase in the number and variety of standards that affect a single industry or market. Standards impact the efficiency of R&D, the variety and quality of production, the rate of market penetration, and the scope of potential markets through specification of product interfaces. In the longer term, standards influence industry structure and in particular broaden opportunities for small and medium firms to enter and prosper in high-tech industries.

While economic growth policy is increasingly concerned with standards due to their proliferation and pervasiveness in many new high-tech industries, their economic roles are unfortunately poorly understood. The result is confusion for policy makers. Standards are alternatively characterized as a proprietary corporate strategy or as a public good. In fact, both characterizations have merit. The problem is that standards have a number of distinctly different economic roles and these roles change over a typical technology life cycle. Both characteristics affect private investment incentives and hence the optimal public–private asset mix.

The greater complexity of technologies, the trend in corporate strategy toward specialization (core competences), and the resulting networks of firms and supporting infrastructure that develop, disseminate, and integrate these technologies mean that supply chains are becoming the most important level of policy analysis.[3] Greater distribution of R&D among materials, components and equipment suppliers, manufacturers of products, and providers of services now characterize high-tech supply chains. The consequent increase in market transactions involving technology demands a large infrastructure of standards to reduce the greatly increased transaction costs.[4]

An additional issue raised by this framework is whether the functionality of system-level standards is simply the result of the aggregation of specific component standards, or do they have a structure and role based on the intrinsic nature of the system technology. As a general proposition, a technology system is determined to a significant extent by the structure of its components, but system design also drives both component structure and the interfaces among components. In other words, the relationship is recursive.

2. The roles of standards in the knowledge economy

In a modern economy, standards constitute a pervasive infrastructure affecting technology-based economic activity in a number of important and relatively complex ways. Some of these impacts even appear contradictory. For example, whereas the traditional economic function of standards in production is to restrict product choice in exchange for the cost advantage of economies of scale, other types of standards common to advanced production and service systems can actually facilitate product variety and hence choice for the customer. It is therefore necessary to define four basic functions of standards, as summarized in Table 12.1, and then describe the economic targets and mechanics of each generic function along with their recursive interactions with an industry's technology and its industry structure and markets (Tassey, 2000).

The four basic functions are integral parts of technology-based economic activity and have substantial impacts on the efficiency of R&D, the cost and quality of production, and even commercialization.[5] Without such standards, R&D would be less efficient and stretched out in time, production yields and overall quality of new products would be lower, and commercialization of new technologies would be slower because transaction costs (incurred to assure performance, including interoperability) add to the price of a product and thereby slow its market penetration.[6]

With respect to market dynamics, standardization can and does occur without formal promulgation as a "standard". This distinction between *de facto* and promulgated (*de jure*) standards is important because their content is affected by the elements of an industry structure that are

Table 12.1 Functions of standards in knowledge-intensive industries

Function	Examples	Economic impacts
Specify quality and reliability	• Performance metrics, such as minimum quality levels • Procedures, such as equipment calibrations	• Expand market share through performance assurance and reduction in transaction costs
Provide information	• Measurement and test methods • Science and engineering data bases, standard reference materials • Terminology	• Increased research efficiency through more accurate research inputs and verifiable research results • Higher productivity and quality through better process control • Reduced transaction costs and hence lower prices for new products
Assure interoperability	• Interconnection among system components • Portability of software across implementations of a computer system[1]	• Achieve network externalities and thereby expand value/cost ratios • Facilitate open systems and thereby enable more competition at component and subsystem levels
Enable variety reduction	• Microprocessor architecture, size of silicon wafers	• Achieve economies of scale and compatibility across components

Note: [1] As used here a computer system means a particular processor and operating system (Isaak, 1995).

involved in the standardization process. *De facto* standards are driven by market dynamics so that first movers and companies with market clout are typically the drivers. In contrast, *de jure* standards result from a more orderly and inclusive process. The latter may seem more "democratic" in that an entire industry or even several industries are involved in the standardization process. However, the latter process is much slower and may result in an inferior standard due to the need to reach a consensus. As the following discussion shows, which process might be preferable depends in part on the nature of the standard, that is, its underlying "infratechnologies" and economic role.

3. Types of standards and their economic roles

The economic functions of standards should be assessed in two basic categories—product and non-product. Distinctions between the two categories are important because their strategic and marketplace roles are distinctly different and hence so are the rationales for and the processes by which each category of standards is set. The differences in public-good content have important implications for policy because the rationales for government intervention are very different in the two cases.

3.1 Product standards

Product-element standards typically focus on one of the key attributes or "elements" of a product, as opposed to the entire product. That is, the product as an entity is not standardized. When a product is new, i.e., an innovation has recently occurred, most or even all product attributes are fluid. As time goes on, competitors enter the market with competing designs. With subsequent growth in the aggregate market for the product, users begin to resist excessive diversity because substitution (switching) costs will be high. Eventually, therefore, at least one major attribute of the generic product technology achieves dominant market status and becomes a *de facto* standard. An example is the architecture of a microprocessor.[7]

As implied above, market dynamics usually determine the timing of product-element standards and scale and scope economies determine the product element to be standardized. The evolutionary process by which a product element becomes standardized is important because standardization of the design of the entire product is increasingly unlikely in an era of complex system technologies where complexity facilitates competition among suppliers and better serves the increasingly heterogeneous demand of users. In fact, complete standardization would most likely mean "lock-in" to a dominant supplier, which would be a suboptimal result (David and Greenstein, 1990).[8]

Alternative technologies intensely compete until one version gains sufficient market share to become the single *de facto* standard. If the innovator is a large firm, its market control can subvert the competitive process by which a product-element standard is achieved. Such control can accelerate increasing returns by forcing acceptance of the monopolist's proprietary technology element as the standard. However, the globalization of high-tech markets with more competitors is making single-firm dominance increasingly difficult. In response, various combinations of vertical and horizontal consortia are promulgating product-element standards by consensus, at least within single large economies or regional trading blocs.

3.2 Non-product standards

In contrast to product standards, non-product standards tend to be competitively neutral, at least within an industry or trading block. Hence, they tend to get less attention. Yet, this latter category can be critical to the entire industry's efficiency and its overall market penetration rate. The semiconductor industry is estimated to have over 1000 standards, most of which are non-product. Take away these standards and this industry could not function.

As observed by Matutes and Regibeau (1989), specifying the required performance attributes and the interface between the component and the rest of the product system leaves the choice of design at the product/component level to individual companies. Farther down the supply chain, system integration companies benefit from competition at the component level and thus economic welfare is increased.

Non-product standards, as the name implies, derive from a different technical base than that upon which the attributes of the product itself depend. In the United States, industry organizations often set these standards using a consensus process. The technical bases for such standards ("infratechnologies") have large, although not total, public-good content, so that their provision frequently depends upon a combination of industry and government investment. Examples of infratechnologies frequently embodied in non-product standards include measurement and test methods, interface standards, scientific and engineering databases, and artifacts such as standard reference materials (Tassey, 2007).

The number of non-product standards is proliferating due to the complexity of component technologies and the system technologies they form. Thus, both early research and subsequent market development require large cooperative efforts to put the many needed standards in place. The information technology (IT) arena is a prime example of this emerging form of standards setting.[9]

3.3 The origin and hierarchy of non-product standards

Many infratechnologies and therefore the resulting industry standards are derived from basic standards (fundamental constants of nature). Basic standards represent the most accurate statements of the fundamental laws of physics and have such diverse applications that they qualify as pure public goods and hence are provided entirely by government. Basic or fundamental standards are relatively few in number and are not easily transported to or efficiently used by industry. Thus, they have to be embodied in a "primary" standard.

Such primary standards are typically artifacts that are expensive to produce, as they require extensive development and maintenance processes using a specialized measurement science infrastructure that firms and even industries need to draw upon but individually do not make sufficient use of to justify the needed investment. In fact, many generic measurement and test methods that are derived from basic standards have wide applications in industry, so economies of scope make sufficient private investment unlikely.[10]

Because primary standards become the basis for measurement and test methods that can have wide utility across multiple firms and even several industries, their public-good content leads to government supply roles. As a result, most large industrialized economies have a national measurement function. In the United States, this function is performed by NIST. NIST maintains the basic standards and develops a set of standard reference materials (SRMs) based on them. These artifacts are then sold to industry, which produces larger numbers of secondary (and even tertiary level) standards for use in its laboratories and production lines. Such a hierarchy of standards is the most cost-effective approach to industry standards management where the standards have strong infratechnology underpinnings.

In addition, NIST develops conformance testing standards to help industry demonstrate to its customers that it is in compliance with agreed upon test methods. Doing so greatly reduces the potentially high transaction costs associated with marketing technologically complex products. Such costs add to the price of products and thereby retard market penetration.

3.4 The economic context of standards

The roles of product and non-product standards described above can only be fully understood in the context of the elements of the typical industrial technology—their investment patterns and how they interact to achieve commercially viable technologies.

Specifically, modern industrial technologies are not "black boxes". Rather, they consist of a number of discrete elements that tend to evolve in different market and institutional settings. These elements have unique characteristics and require different types and combinations of standards to achieve efficient development and utilization. Broadly defined, they fall into the three major categories shown in Figure 12.1: "generic" or "platform" technologies (the fundamental technical concepts derived from basic science from which market applications are derived), "infratechnologies" (technical methods, techniques, data, and interfaces, which enable efficient conduct of R&D, production, and market transactions), and "proprietary" technologies (actual market applications developed by companies derived from platform technologies using infratechnologies).

These technology elements, along with subsequent production, commercialization, and market development, are all affected by standardization, as shown in Figure 12.1. The thicker arrows indicate the direction of knowledge flows in a technology-based industry, with solid and compound stems indicating private-sector and public-sector produced knowledge, respectively. The thinner arrows indicate the points of impact on technology-based economic activity of each type of standard. This conceptual framework emphasizes the fact that "standards" are not a homogeneous or random collection of normative decisions. Instead, they constitute a ubiquitous technical infrastructure affecting all stages of technology-based economic activity. And, as described below, they interact in a number of important ways with industry structure and behavior.

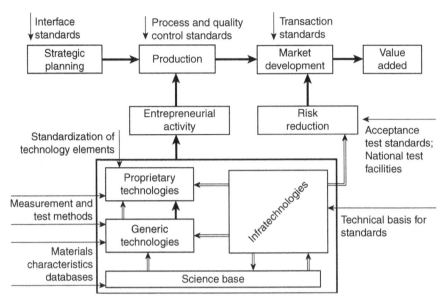

Figure 12.1 Roles of standards in technology-based industries

4. The interaction of market structure and standardization

4.1 Local vs. global product standards for single markets

Changes in the nature and the stability of the technology over its life cycle result in iterative changes in both standards and market structure. For example, early in a technology's evolution, global product standards are hard to achieve because technological content is changing and several versions of the product technology frequently coexist. As a result, submarkets often evolve around several versions of a product standard ("local" standards) and can exist for some time.

On the one hand, the competition among these submarkets helps sort out the most productive technology alternatives, which eventually maximizes economic welfare. On the other hand, during this process scale economies are not realized and customers are faced with the risk of choosing the wrong local standard (the risk that it doesn't become the eventual global standard). The latter situation is caused by high switching costs relative to perceived benefit gains by users. These switching costs can be increased when suppliers with monopolistic control of portions of the market for the generic product (such as a computer) fail to agree on a single standard for a complementary product (such as the operating system). The UNIX operating system is an example.

Companies often participate in organizations that set industry standards, while at the same time they are developing or marketing products based on proprietary or local standards. These firms have installed bases of customers and are attempting to gain or maintain market leadership and force industry acceptance of their standards. In the short run, one or even several of these competing groups of companies may maximize profits, subject to scale constraints. However, long-run profits will be diminished as aggregate market growth is constrained by customer dissatisfaction and hence reduced demand resulting from (1) lack of price competition and scale efficiencies, and (2) lower productivity from an inability to optimize system design by integrating components from a larger number of vendors made possible by standardized interfaces.

In contrast, a local standard can sometimes rapidly become the global standard due to aggressive marketing by the innovator or initial buy-in by a large user. While economies of scale are realized quickly, the probability is high that this version of the technology is not the optimal one. Moreover, increasing returns can result in a monopoly position for the innovator. If the product happens to be an especially critical component, that monopoly can be extended into related component markets; that is, the component innovator can evolve into a turnkey system supplier.

4.2 Non-product standards and system productivity

Further evolution of the industry can result in several turnkey suppliers. This phenomenon results in large part from the absence of interface standards, which significantly raises the cost of integrating an externally supplied component into a technology system. Under such conditions, market participation is difficult for small innovative firms who have a superior version of a component technology but have to incur substantial costs engineering the interface to meet the unique integration requirements of customers, each of whom has a proprietary interface specification. That is, a strategy of selling into markets characterized by proprietary turnkey systems requires a high degree of product segmentation in order to service multiple turnkey system integrators.

In such situations, small innovative suppliers experience difficulty achieving scale economies. Whatever the estimated level of risk for a single R&D project, a smaller firm with limited diversification will typically attach greater risk premiums (i.e., require a higher expected RoR) than larger firms with more diversified R&D portfolios. For emerging technologies characterized by high levels of technical risk, but which are not particularly capital intensive (e.g., software), small firms can be created and successfully introduce innovative products and services. But even in these cases, success can be predicted only if the supporting infrastructures (including interface standards) are available.

The general industry supply chain framework for these interactions is depicted in Figure 12.2. Platform technologies provide the conceptual basis for specific product innovations, which include product attributes that eventually become standardized (examples: microprocessor architecture

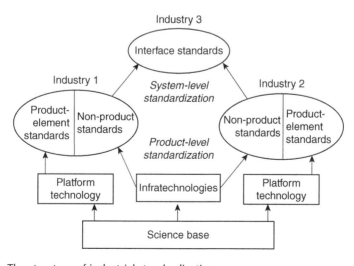

Figure 12.2 The structure of industrial standardization

and HDTV broadcast system specifications such as frame size, scanning system, and frame rate). Infratechnologies provide the technical basis for a range of measurement and testing methods, equipment calibration procedures, evaluated science and engineering data, etc., at the component industry level (Industries 1 & 2) and for interface standards at the system integration industry level (Industry 3).

One issue raised by this framework is whether system-level standards are simply the result of the aggregation of specific product-element and non-product standards, or if they have a structure based on the intrinsic nature of the system technology. A technology system is determined to a significant extent by the structure of its components, but system design also drives both component structure and the interfaces among components (Jervis, 1997; Meadows, 2008).

The lack of conformity to interface standards by the supply side of a market can be a conscious strategy or a reflection of the poor quality of the standard. Large firms with market strategies focusing on turnkey systems have an incentive to resist open systems to protect the market shares resulting from their horizontally integrated strategy. In cases of increasing returns, such strategies may result in a monopoly position being attained by one supplier or prolonged market segmentation by several competing suppliers. Either situation has the potential to constrain economic efficiency (David and Greenstein (1990).

More generally, the industry structure impacts from standardization have important effects on the achievement of economic growth objectives. "Open systems" allow small and medium companies to participate in markets for system technologies by supplying components in which they have a competitive advantage. This diversification on the supply side of the market allows system optimization by users (increases productivity) and greater price competition (lowers costs).[11]

In rare cases, open and closed systems coexist. The most prominent example is the smart phone. Apple is the innovator and based on its early monopoly position adopted a closed system. It is the sole provider of phones based on its operating system (OS X) and controls all applications that run on it. In contrast, Google's Android is a "quasi-open" operating system in that smart phone developers, such as Samsung and LG, can cheaply license Android and produce their own line of phones. However, Android companies' phones are not interoperable; that is, applications from one company's phones will not run on another company's phones. Still, this quasi-open system strategy has resulted in a collective global market share that is much larger than Apple's.

In non-vertically integrated high-tech supply chains, large users (e.g., smart phone designers and manufacturers) are likely to want to have access to several different classes or brands of critical components, or at a minimum have a second source of supply. Such component users have substantial need for effective interfaces. The ability to integrate equipment and software from different vendors has several economic benefits. First, system performance can be optimized thereby increasing productivity. Second, competition among vendors for each element of the system lowers prices. Third, responding to technological or functional obsolescence is facilitated by replacing individual components at relatively low cost (same interface specifications).

Finally, because many standards exist within modern technology systems, standards development cannot take place totally from the bottom up. For example, two machines can be made to communicate through interface standards. However, as more machines are added to, say, automate a factory (the "system"), chaos ensues without some overall "system architecture". The architecture provides an integrating force for all product-level standards in the system, driving the structure of the interfaces among the several layers constituting the control hierarchy of the automated factory.

In summary, the interactions over a technology's life cycle between technology elements and types of standards (Figure 12.1) are complex. While the potential benefits of standardization are significant, it can also result in negative economic effects such as restricting domestic competition by promulgating standards that favor certain proprietary technologies and restricting foreign competition by using standards to create exclusionary trade barriers. Equally important, poorly timed standards can retard achieving economies of scale and scope (too late) or the ability to innovate (too early), thereby significantly reducing economic welfare gains over the technology's life cycle. Further, standards in high-tech industries frequently are based on intellectual property rights (IPR) of one or several companies. These companies can withhold the IPR in an attempt to maintain monopoly positions or they can extract monopoly rents for its use in the standard. Finally, as technologies are increasingly complex systems (Figure 12.2), system design will drive standardization simultaneously with standardization at the product/component level.

5. Market failure in high-tech industries and the rationales for standards

The public-good character of standards requires an understanding of the types of underinvestment that occur in technology-based markets. To this end, innovation economists have identified, at least at a general level, a range of systemic underinvestment phenomena (Tassey, 2005). The following is a list that is probably close to inclusive with respect to the various types of market failure affecting high-tech markets:

- excessive risk (increase costs)
- long development time (reduce benefits)
- knowledge spillovers (reduce benefits)
- economies of scope (reduce benefits)
- price (rent) spillovers (reduce benefits)
- information asymmetries (increase costs)
- coordination failures (increase costs).

The first three types listed above are fairly widely recognized. R&D is generally regarded as a "high-risk" investment with "long gestation" periods. Both characteristics reduce private-sector estimates of the rates of return from investments. Once developed, technical knowledge tends to leak or "spillover" from the originating source, thereby further reducing the expected rate of return. The tendency for technical knowledge to spillover varies with the phase of the R&D cycle, being greater in the earlier phases when knowledge is more tacit (less codified) and less targeted to specific market applications. By making the R&D process more efficient, standards can partially mitigate these negative effects on investment.

The last four types of market failure are not as widely recognized and are therefore not typically used as rationales for government policy responses. First, "economies of scope" refers to the fact that many modern technology platforms have a wide range of market applications.[12] Pursuing multiple markets increases the return on the early-phase R&D investment in the technology platform, but in today's highly competitive global markets acquiring the unique set of economic assets for each market sufficient to rationalize the required investment is a daunting prospect even for the largest high-tech companies. The existence of interface, R&D-related, and product-element standards can reduce the costs of targeting a particular market to some degree, but the required investment is still substantial.

Second, "price spillovers" are a manifestation of the existence of unbalanced market structures in which the benefits from a commercialized technology are unevenly distributed between buyer and seller. Specifically, the distribution of benefits is determined by how the technology is priced, which, in turn, is affected by the relative market clout of the buyer versus the seller. Neither side of the market captures all the benefits; otherwise, one side would have no incentive to participate in that market. In reality, distributions vary widely across markets.

Particularly skewed distributions of benefits would, for example, have negative consequences for the overall supply chain by limiting investment incentives for the low-profitability industry, for which in turn imposes a constraint on the supply chain's overall growth. In contrast, if the supplier has a strong market position relative to buyers, a high price can be charged so that most of the benefits from the innovation are captured by the supplier (increasing the innovator's rate of return), which reduces the buyer's incentive to purchase the innovation. A similar negative impact on the overall supply chain's rate of growth will likely be the result.

However, the dynamics of competition can in some cases mitigate such problems with the help of product standards, which allow imitators to enter the market. Doing so results in the monopoly price being bid down so that the user industry benefits (i.e., they get the same product with the same productivity benefit for a lower price). The profit stream for the innovator may be reduced, but presumably the better balance between the supplier and consumer industries is a net gain for the growth of the supply chain as a whole.

In other cases, the buyer side of the market may have the clout and suppliers of the new technology will not realize the monopoly rents considered by economic theory to be necessary for continued investment in the more risky next generation technology. Standards can partially mitigate the negative effects of a monopsonistic (single buyer) market through open systems, which encourages other buyers in the next tier in the supply chain to enter this industry.

Third, "information asymmetries" can occur when the size distribution of firms in two adjacent tiers in a supply chain have marked differences in average firm size. They can therefore manifest themselves as price spillovers. Smaller firms incur larger relative search and transaction costs, which places them at a disadvantage. Interface standards allow small firms to compete for business with more than one large customer without having to acquire unique interface specification information from each customer. Also, product acceptance testing standards reduce transaction costs, which can have an especially positive impact on small firms who often compete in lower volume versions of a generic product technology and cannot afford to develop/acquire in order to reach agreement with customers on the required product acceptance protocols.

Finally, "coordination failures" occur in single high-tech industries and also between industries in high-tech supply chains when a technology element has significant public-good content (advanced technology platforms and infratechnologies). Failure to find a mechanism to produce and diffuse public technical knowledge in such cases results in suboptimal amounts and composition of these two technology elements. Increasingly, this problem is being addressed by research consortia, frequently embedded in "innovation clusters". These new organizational infrastructures often involve more than one industry in a high-tech supply chain. The consortium and, more broadly, the cluster mechanism adopt standardized formats for product data and other information exchanges.

6. Increasing returns, standardization, and the evolution of markets

A frequent phenomenon in the early phases of a new technology's market penetration is a highly skewed distribution of benefits among the suppliers of a technology. The benefiting firms are either the innovator or a "fast second" imitator who is large enough to rapidly acquire and effectively manage all categories of assets required to take market share.

This pattern is pronounced because the life cycles of many emerging technologies are characterized by increasing returns (Arthur, 1996). This phenomenon results from the capacity in modern economies to both rapidly achieve minimum efficient scale of production and make improvements in the initial version of the technology and thereby acquire market share in multiple related markets.

During the Industrial Revolution, technological change was relatively slow compared to today and was primarily embodied within discrete pieces of equipment. Thus, the dominant corporate strategy was simply to use more and more of the existing technology in larger and larger production configurations, until diminishing returns set in from the use of progressively less productive units of one or more factors (land, labor, or equipment). The main requirement for market entry in these traditional industries was capital. The inevitability of diminishing returns established equilibrium prices, which usually preserved at least minimally acceptable levels of competition (more than one company could acquire the technology and then invest in a large amount of plant and equipment to produce moderately differentiated products). These companies did not face the need to rapidly improve the original version of the technology or to conform to interface requirements demanded by a larger technology system of which the product was a component.

During this long period of industrial growth dominated by large manufacturing entities, a few examples of increasing returns appeared. The most frequently cited case is the telephone. Because telephone communications is a system, more specifically a network of users, the more consumers with telephones the more valuable a telephone is to any one user. This phenomenon of increasing value per user from growth in the number of users is a network externality and can have significant economic impact. On the supplier side, such growth meant realizing further efficiencies from economies of scale. Many such networks were capital intensive, and a single network implied a single provider. The policy solution therefore was to label such technologies as natural monopolies and regulate the price charged.

Today, however, the phenomenon of increasing returns is widespread but results from economies of scale realized through network externalities, which in turn results from R&D-based market strategies that can "lock in" consumers not just to individual products but to product systems. This pattern is the result of the fact that modern "products" are increasingly knowledge intensive rather than resource intensive and frequently act as a centerpiece or hub of a larger system of products. Within such systems, a particular technology product often becomes the "technology driver" of the broader system technology. As this technology evolves towards a particular version (standard), the supplier of this element benefits disproportionately from increasing returns to scale.

The manifestations of this phenomenon are significant. On the demand side of the market, lock-in of consumers can take place because of technological complexity, which results in significant learning costs being incurred. For example, a microprocessor's architecture drives the other components of a computer and all software that runs on it. This situation means consumers will incur significant "switching" (re-learning) costs, if the decision is made to adopt an alternative version of this critical technology. The growing number of existing users attracts new users who can interact with (learn from) existing users and a growing infrastructure.

The technology driver also determines the structure and functionality of complementary technology elements and products. Suppliers of these other products have to conform to the driver. They incur considerable sunk costs to do so and thus also become "locked in." Such sunk costs must be traded off against any prospective increase in productivity benefits, which can make market penetration by competitors difficult. Thus, if one firm gains sufficient control of the market for a product, it can set a *de facto* standard and capture much of the increasing returns to scale.

The large "installed base" of users also provides a strong incentive for suppliers of complementary products to focus on the existing *de facto* standard. As the market for the lead version of the technology expands, product costs fall for all suppliers due to economies of scale.

Management by the owner of the technology driver can also affect its long-term ability to dominate markets. In the early 1980s, three operating systems (CP/M, DOS, and Apple's Macintosh system) were competing for the PC market. The IBM PC–DOS platform was a kludge. However, partly because of the IBM name and partly because IBM made a tactical decision to open the PC's architecture, its version gained a large market share. The open-system tactic enabled the entry of a large number of IBM-compatible hardware suppliers, which lowered prices and increased market penetration. In addition, the increasingly large installed base led to a substantial supply of third-party software, which further enhanced the value of the overall "computing system".

As this example shows, network externalities accelerate and extend increasing returns. The critical enabling technologies driving advanced economies around the world, particularly the automation of manufacturing and the increasingly dominant services based on information technology, display network externalities. In such situations, companies fight vigorously to establish their version of the technology as the "standard" in order to acquire the substantial potential economic benefits.

7. Timing and degree of standardization

From both the corporate strategy and public policy points of view, standardization is not an all-or-nothing proposition. In complicated system technologies, such as distributed data processing, telecommunications, or factory automation, standardization typically proceeds in an evolutionary manner in lock step with the evolution of both embodied and disembodied technologies. The pattern of evolution is determined by several factors: the pace of technological change embodied in each component category; disembodied technology development, which determines the overall system architecture and organization; and changes in market structure, which affect the incentives and ability to force the standardization process.

7.1 Timing of standardization

The evolution of numerically controlled machine tools would have suffered from early total standardization of data formats in that doing so would have severely compromised the range of performance attributes potentially available to different users in future generations of machine tools. This is because standardized data formats are used to compare and assess different vendors' products, so the baseline for comparison is developed based on current technology platforms. Investment in new platforms that might not be able to be evaluated by existing data formats would therefore be inhibited.[13] Thus, only a degree of standardization was initially optimal in the technology's evolution. In other words, complete standardization too early in the technology life cycle can constrain innovation.

In contrast, delaying the decision of standardization of a critical product technology element can retard private investment and thereby impede realization of consumer and producer surplus. This situation creates an incentive to choose a standard early in the technology's life cycle.

The bottom line is that as technology-based systems become increasingly important and "windows of opportunity" for making successful investments in the associated markets continue to shrink, the relevant standards will have to be efficiently managed. If a standard is fixed, even if it is competitively neutral, it will eventually act to stifle the introduction of new technology into the system. However, if the standard is updated frequently, then version consistency (forward mobility of current system components) can become a problem.

For example, efficient data processing and communications networks are possible only if standard interfaces are provided on all the communication paths in the network. Such interfaces need to be defined between application programs, data formats, network protocols, printer control codes, human/machine interfaces, and so on. But, these system elements are all evolving at different rates and thus need updated interfaces at different points in time. Thus, with new technologies continuously being introduced into ever expanding networks, the pressure on the standards infrastructure to adapt is substantial.

7.2 Degree of standardization

The systems nature of the technology-based economy, which has been emphasized here and elsewhere (Tassey, 2007, 2010), increases the importance of the need for all components of a system—both public and private—to be assessed within the context of not only their intrinsic performance but also how such performance affects the performance of the system—for it is the system that delivers the ultimate economic benefit.

Just as modern systems technologies have a hierarchical structure, so must the associated set of standards (Figure 12.2). The evolution of component technologies drives the need for standardization at each level in the product system. Standardization at one level then creates demand for standards at adjacent levels in the system. For example, a numerically controlled machine tool is a system of components such as the controller and numerous sensors. The multiple interface standards involved in a machine tool allow modularization of the product, which permits custom design and prevents overall tool obsolescence. However, these standards must be linked by a common data format (and this updated accordingly), if all components are to function together as an efficient system (Link and Tassey, 1987).

Within a technology system, the establishment of a new standard, no matter how well conceived, can be costly to comply with. For example, a new interface standard for electronic product data exchange can require conversion of existing databases, which can be time consuming and expensive. Also, introducing such a data format standard may solve one problem (data exchange) but create another (security). Within a technology life cycle, initial standards can be hard to modify/update due to time and cost requirements coupled with installed-base effects. This can be particularly true for standards such as those providing interoperability as markets grow and the number of participants increases. And, participants can include stakeholders other than producers and consumers (e.g., system consultants) who want to have a say in evolving standards. In summary, standards can facilitate innovation and subsequent market penetration. However, the content, timing, and flexibility of standards have to be right or new technologies will have difficulty penetrating markets or even reaching the marketplace (Branscomb and Kahin, 1995).

Once a product-element standard is set, network externalities are typically realized. However, the marketplace dynamics that result in one firm's version of the technology becoming the standard do not guarantee that this version is the optimal one. The lock-in effect ensues, whereby many developers of related products conform to the standard and purchasers of the standardized technology invest substantial resources in learning to absorb and use it as well as complementary technologies and infrastructures. These sunk costs create a reluctance to switch to a new standard and related cluster of technologies. Considerable resources are then allocated to an inferior technology, which can extend over long periods of time.[14]

As described above, the firm that controls the product–element standard captures increasing returns to scale as initial market penetration begets dominance. This may be an acceptable price for rapid market growth from an economic welfare perspective, as long as the standardized version of the technology element is at least a good one and sufficient opportunity exists for market forces to periodically replace the standard.[15]

Unfortunately, the tendency for modern technologies to have systems structures increases the economic consequences of the lock-in phenomenon. In particular, most technologies today have clusters of standards embedded in them. One, however, is frequently the dominant or driver standard. Thus, the controller of that standard can have even greater impact on the evolutionary development of the overall technology and related markets.

While lock-in affects the demand side, the installed-base effect impacts the supply side. Dominant suppliers of a technology, who either control or adhere to the standard, have invested substantial resources in developing and servicing the markets based on this standard (Tassey, 2007). Their established market positions promote evolutionary as opposed to revolutionary migration of customers, who demand backward mobility to existing technology. Mobility is more difficult and expensive, the more radical the new technology. If Microsoft, Apple, and IBM were freed from maintaining compatibility with existing hardware and software, new generations of systems software would likely evolve at a faster pace.

8. The complexity and impact of standardization: the Internet Protocol

One of the most important characteristics of the knowledge revolution is the way services are structured and delivered. The conventional "service" for decades has been delivered by a person at the site of consumption. Information technology (IT) in general and the Internet in particular have radically changed this paradigm.

However, increasingly dominant IT-based services are complex, geographically distributed systems. As previously discussed, the systems nature adds complexity because often incompatible elements must be connected through standardized interfaces that are themselves technically complex. In addition, the information flows also must have standardized formats to allow efficient movement over networks while assuring the integrity of the information and providing for its security.

One of the most dramatic examples of both the complexity and the global competitiveness impacts of standardization of information technology is the Internet Protocol (IP). This standard, which is really many standards integrated into a single system of standards, controls information flows over the Internet and enables applications (software-based services provided to users of the Internet) to be implemented efficiently. It does this by providing a standardized "envelope" or "header" that carries addressing, routing, and message-handling information. The information in this header enables a message to be transmitted from its source to its final destination over the various interconnected networks that comprise the Internet.

The IP is an excellent case study in the many factors necessary for modern technical infrastructure to complement private investment over all phases of the technology life cycle. The Internet is thought of by most as a network of autonomous communications/data networks electronically connecting independent host computers for a variety of public and private entities around the world. In fact, it is a highly structured system of hardware and software, linked by a controlled and tightly specified set of standards that have considerable technical content. The complexity of this infrastructure becomes apparent when the standards infrastructure needs to be replaced by a new generation.

8.1 Motivations for the transition to a new Internet Protocol

The emergence of wireless sensor networks and machine-to-machine communications will enable a proliferation of devices that connect to the Internet in an "always on" mode (the so-called "Internet of Things"). Specifically, automobile components or subsystems, refrigerators, cameras, and home systems such as computers and security systems are being assigned IP addresses, linked together on networks, and connected to the Internet. Such potential "remote access" applications can yield substantial benefits such as increased life expectancies of consumer durables and an associated decrease in service/repair costs, thereby minimizing life-cycle costs.

However, such innovation will require a combination of virtually an infinite number of direct addresses and levels of network efficiency that the current Protocol, IPv4, cannot support.[16] Moreover, such applications also require the flexibility to reconfigure the network automatically, as users connect and disconnect or simply move the point of connection. The much larger Internet address space will be provided by the slowly emerging version 6 of the IP. In addition, IPv6 will simplify allocation of addresses, enable efficient route aggregation, and allow implementation of special addressing features.[17]

This complex interaction between proprietary applications and the supporting infrastructure means that making general predictions of technology trajectories is an insufficient incentive to stimulate needed investment in both new applications and the underlying infrastructure. From the private sector's perspective, estimating the projected benefits (e.g., forecasting the emergence of new applications and their economic impact) is increasingly complex. A major reason is the fact that the marketplace function and performance of an application, typically defined by at least several attributes (such as stability, usability, and operational efficiency), are strongly influenced by a second set of attributes associated with the Internet's infrastructure.

Part of the private sector's rate of return calculations is the projected costs to understand, acquire, and thus comply with a set of highly complex technical standards central to the functioning of this infrastructure. The nature and magnitude of these costs mean that considerable time and expense are required by the domestic economy in accomplishing the transition to a new version of the existing standard. The result is a slow deployment and utilization pattern.

In fact, in the face of the need for national economies to plan for and begin to execute what will be a long transition to the new Protocol, several important barriers exist. These barriers are common to transitions between generations of a complex standard and, to varying degrees, affect most users. Two of the most important barriers are the "installed-base" and "chicken-or-egg" effects.[18]

8.2 Resistance to transitioning to a new standard: the installed-base effect

The transition between generations of a complex standard requires years of effort and considerable expense. As a result, a number of countervailing economic forces appear that make the pattern, efficiency, and timing of the transition highly uncertain. This situation presents policy makers with the difficult problem of determining the best way to manage this critical infrastructure.

Deploying a new standard in an approximately optimal timeframe requires overcoming the effect of existing investments in economic assets targeted at optimizing performance based on the current standard. The installed base of hardware, software, trained labor, organizational models, and knowledge of markets for applications that conform to the current standard result in resistance to migration to the new one.

The greatest resistance often comes from the innovators of the product/service technologies that the current standard supports. In the case of IPv4, the United States cornered a large share of available address space and consequently has shown less concern over address capacity—the primary motivation in other economies for transitioning to the new Protocol, IPv6. Moreover, over a substantial period of time, the incumbent standard (IPv4) established an installed base of hardware and software, an IT labor pool trained in maintaining it, and many applications that were designed for the current version of the standard.

In response to growth of the Internet over its lifetime, inadequacies in IPv4 have been patched repeatedly. For example, separate devices, including so-called "middle boxes" (known as Network Address Translation devices or NATs), have been developed to deal with the increasing inadequacy of available addresses (nodes on the Internet). The net result is a complex installed standards architecture and large application base that have managed to run reasonably efficiently and thereby reduce incentives to migrate to the next generation of the standard. Equally important, the cost of restructuring the installed base is substantial. Many of the myriad of current Internet software applications will have to be scrapped or significantly modified at considerable cost.

In addition, some users have come to view NATs as providing some measure of security through anonymity, which they do not want to give up. Such preferences pose a barrier to the transition to IPv6, which offers ample globally addressable nodes and therefore obviates the need for NATs.

8.3 The chicken-or-egg effect

In addition to the installed-base effect, a recursive (chicken-or-egg) relationship exists between private investment in market applications and some combination of private and public investment in the standards infrastructure. On the one hand, improvements in technical infrastructure facilitate innovation and potential innovators take its availability into account when estimating rates of return from investment in new technologies. On the other hand, investment in complex and expensive infrastructure may not happen without the pulling effect of demand from emerging innovations that require it.

A transition strategy for IPv6 was developed over a number of years by an international standards body, the Internet Engineering Task Force (IETF). The dominant view expressed by U.S. industry was that this transition strategy (a dual-standard approach) would mitigate an investment-blocking, all-or-nothing situation (that is, the entire new standard must be deployed and the old one simultaneously turned off). However, while the proposed transition mechanisms largely avoid such a "throw-the-switch" decision for both Internet service providers (ISPs) and Internet users, the technical and economic deficiencies of early implementations of IPv6 coupled with the cost of the transition itself have slowed the perceived natural market penetration rate.

Thus, American ISPs have resisted investment in IPv6 infrastructure until major customers request IPv6 services, but the emergence of this customer demand requires that IPv6 infrastructure be available. One potential attribute of IT standards that might reduce this chicken-or-egg problem is the fact that IPv6 *capability* can diffuse into the market at relatively low cost to users and vendors. This is because the marginal cost to vendors of including additional functionality in hardware and software is relatively low. Similarly, the acquisition cost of such capability by users is also low, as long as it is acquired within normal hardware and software expenditure cycles. Hence, IPv6 capabilities have been slowly penetrating many segments of the network infrastructure for a number of years. For example, most routers and operating systems currently sold already include IPv6 functionality, so as industry and government purchase new routers for various reasons, they will acquire IPv6 capabilities at little additional cost.

However, considerable transition costs still must be incurred to *enable* or turn on these capabilities, and the incentives to do so are not strong in the early phases of the transition, hence stretching out the transition in time. Specifically, a few modest IPv6 applications are not sufficient incentive to stimulate incurring these additional deployment costs (in particular, labor training and conversion of IPv4 applications to run on IPv6, both of which are expensive undertakings).

On the other side of the public–private technology interface, inadequate deployment of an active and fully functional IPv6 infrastructure will mean that application developers have reduced incentive to invest in R&D for potential IPv6 markets. That is, first-mover incentives are constrained.

The fundamental economic reason for this situation is that small markets limit network externalities, thereby inhibiting increases in the performance/price ratio and thus in demand. Such investment barriers coupled with high transition costs contribute to the flatness of the initial portion of the S-shaped market penetration curve (Tassey, 2013). In a highly competitive global market, an extension of the flat initial portion of the curve can place domestic industries at a disadvantage that, in some cases, is never removed over the entire technology life cycle (Tassey, 2013). Therefore, addressing the chicken-or-egg problem in developing and implementing an effective transition strategy is a major imperative for both government and industry.

8.4 The economic impacts of slow transition to the new standard

The implication of the above analysis is that, in the early phase of market penetration, neither the available but incomplete infrastructure nor the limited applications are strong enough to induce significant numbers of users to transition to the new IP. Individual companies, caught up in managing the current life cycle of their infrastructure equipment, lack the knowledge and/or the risk tolerance with respect to investment in new networking technology to perceive the importance of the emerging life cycle and, therefore, the associated new standard. Instead, most users continue to attempt to modify new applications to run on IPv4, albeit inefficiently, while the unavailability of advanced applications requiring IPv6 slows testing and hence certification of IPv6 infrastructure.

Over time the new standards infrastructure will become more complete and applications will evolve that have sufficiently high need for constant connections and automatic network reconfiguration. At some point, IPv4 will be deemed incapable of further adaptation and its inadequacies will become apparent to a majority of Internet providers and users. Thus, the slow iterative pattern of investment in infrastructure and applications will eventually overcome the installed-base and chicken-or-egg effects and the rate of market penetration will accelerate, as represented by the steeper portion of the S-shaped growth curve. However, because the Internet is now global in scope, "eventually" can mean that first-mover advantages will accrue to industries in economies where both the infrastructure evolution and the development of market applications have been facilitated.

Equally important, most technologies only appear initially in isolated pockets within the market space of the defender technology. These "islands" of the new technology are initially compromised by the inability to realize economies of scale or scope, further reducing their early net benefit relative to the defender technology. In the case of a standard such as IPv6, early implementations will have to cross Internet space controlled by IPv4. The IETF has evolved a transition strategy to deal with this problem, which includes ways to "tunnel" through IPv4 space (basically, encapsulating the IPv6 application in an IPv4-compatible envelope) or using dual stacks of routers, switches, and so on for each standard.

The problem is that running a dual standard increases the complexity of an already complex infrastructure, thereby raising operating costs and creating other problems such as security risks that must be addressed and that further increase costs. For example, in dual-standard infrastructures, two paths are available to attack protocol or applications, multiplying the complexity of security approaches. A new (and incomplete) standard will have security problems that will only be discovered with actual use. Moreover, in the projected lengthy transition stage, encapsulating IPv6 applications is the equivalent to creating a Trojan horse (its IPv4 envelope), in which malicious computer code can hide while transversing IPv4 space, only to "open" at its destination (inside perimeter defenses such as firewalls) and unleash its mischief.

Although IPv6 offers network efficiency advantages and at some point will likely support major innovations in Internet services, the costs of transition will be substantial, especially if the transition process is accelerated. Government policy is therefore faced with the desire to have its domestic IT infrastructure capable of accepting innovative market applications in order to remain competitive versus the realization that

- Premature transition will result in sunk private costs (hardware, software, training) without immediate benefit.
- Accelerated transition imposes the time-cost tradeoff, in which the various phases of investment in and activation of the new infrastructure are compressed in time and overlapped with each other, leading to excessive costs.
- Operating a dual-standard infrastructure for an extended period of time imposes additional costs due to interoperability problems and possibly creates serious problems with important infrastructure attributes such as security management.

Gallaher and Rowe (2006) estimated that the total development and deployment costs associated with the transition to IPv6 within the U.S. economy over the period 2000–2025 would be approximately $25 billion (present value in 2003 dollars) with industry and government accounting for most of those costs. Eight years later, the percentage of users reaching Google services over IPv6 surpassed 3 percent for the first time.[19] The policy implication is given that technical infrastructure has strong public-good content, then the chicken-and-egg dilemma must be solved largely by government subsidizing early deployment through internal procurement policies and facilitating transition strategies in the private sector.

9. Conclusions

In knowledge-intensive industries, standards facilitate (1) knowledge production, (2) use of knowledge, and (3) the economic impact of knowledge in the marketplace. The overall economic value of a standard is determined by its functionality in terms of benefits from removing market failures less the costs of development, implementation, and management. Standards should be competitively neutral, which means adaptable to alternative applications of technology platforms.

Over the past two decades, the infrastructure roles of standards have increased in importance because (1) many new technologies are systems or networks so that increasing returns to scale or network externalities can generate huge economic rewards providing the entire system is supported by an efficient standards infrastructure, (2) the demand for quality and reliability in technologically complex products and systems requires a range of standards based on sophisticated infratechnologies, (3) the systems nature of critically important technologies means that competition is greatly affected by the degree and nature of standardization both within product structures and at the interfaces between components of these systems, and (4) the shortening of the average technology life cycle has on average increased the pressure on the standards setting process with respect to timing and overall efficiency.

Finally, standards in high-tech industries have strong public-good characteristics. Thus, their development and utilization depend on combined public and private investment and standards process management over the entire technology life cycle.

Notes

1 More formally, an industry standard is a set of specifications to which all elements of products, processes, formats, or procedures under its jurisdiction must conform. The process of standardization is the pursuit of this conformity, with the objective of increasing the efficiency of economic activity.

2 Swan (1987) points out through a case study of the early microprocessor industry that the interactions between large buyers and sellers can lead to a prolonged set of local standards. Apple and Microsoft/Intel are a highly visible example of long-standing local standards in the PC industry.

3 The term "supply chain" refers to the vertical structure of industries that begins with raw materials and eventually serves a final demand. An example of a first-level tier (industry) in a supply chain would be silicon and other semiconductor materials. These materials are used by the next tier to manufacture semiconductor devices, which are then combined by a third tier to form electronic components and equipment. The latter are further integrated into product/service systems (a car or electronic banking) that constitute final demand in an economic accounting framework.

4 Transaction costs are an important consequence of buying and selling technology-based products and services. The complexity of such products and services means that considerable costs can be incurred in assuring buyers that performance is as specified in the sales agreement. Such costs add to the effective price of the product or service and thus retard market penetration.

5 With respect to commercialization, transaction costs can be particularly high when quality and product acceptance standards are not available.

6 As an example of transaction cost reduction, when solid state (LED) lighting was commercialized, quality standards were not available. The result was high transaction costs for buyers because comparing price and quality across suppliers was time consuming and likely not totally successful. With government (NIST) assistance, an industry standards committee accelerated the development and implementation of quality standards, which appeared to accelerate market penetration. See Leech (2012).

7 Microprocessor architecture refers to the layout of components within a computer's central processing unit or CPU. See http://www.ask.com/question/microprocessor-architecture-diagram.

8 Occasionally, a product-element standard is imposed on an industry to ensure economies of scale. An example is the specification of the number of lines of resolution for HDTV broadcasts (see http://en.wikipedia.org/wiki/High-definition_television).

9 Most examples in IT are in the area of interoperability/compatibility/portability, although even the dominant product-element positions of Microsoft (operating system) and Intel (processor architecture) have come under challenge. Major IT standards such as the Internet Protocol are set by international committees.

10 An example is voltage measurement, as represented by the Josephson Volt Standard. NIST developed this standard and transferred it to 40 private and public institutions worldwide. A NIST economic impact study identified a number of economic impacts, but the major one was a significant shortening of the R&D cycle and hence earlier commercialization by instrument manufacturers. See TASC, Inc., *Economic Impact Assessment of the NIST's Josephson Volt Standard Program* (NIST Planning Report #01-1) (http://www.nist.gov/director/planning/upload/report01-1.pdf).

11 In the case of information infrastructures, attaining truly open systems has been extremely difficult. One of the major reasons for this difficulty is the complexity of IT systems technology. Each one of a number of layers in the hierarchical structure of a typical information system must have its own architecture and these architectures must be integrated into a larger network. Today, systems technologies not only have complex hardware and software platforms, but require "portability" rules and protocols to manage information flows.

12 For example, advanced ceramic materials can be adapted to such widely diverse applications as heat engines, medical devices, machine tools, electronic components, and sensors.

13 The more performance oriented the standard, the less will be the risk of inhibiting innovation. See http://news.thomasnet.com/IMT/2001/05/18/the_move_toward/.

14 For more than a decade, DOS—a clearly inferior operating system to alternatives such as Apple Computer's operating system (Mac OS)—dominated the personal computing market because the Microsoft/IBM combination was able to lock in the PC market.

15 Arthur (1996) provides an excellent analysis of the increasing returns-to-scale phenomenon that characterizes many technology-based industries and the consequent motivation for firms to set and control product-element standards.

16 IPv4 stands for Internet Protocol, version 4.

17 See http://en.wikipedia.org/wiki/IPv6 for more detail.

18 See Tassey, Gallaher, and Rowe (2009) for an analysis of the evolution of IPv6 and its policy implications and Gallaher and Rowe (2005, 2006) for more detail and estimates of the costs of transitioning to the new Protocol.

19 "IPv6". *Google Statistics*. Google. See Wikipedia (http://en.wikipedia.org/wiki/IPv6).

References

Arthur, Brian (1996), "Increasing Returns and the New World of Business," *Harvard Business Review* 74 (July–August): 100–109.

Branscomb, Lewis and Brian Kahin (1995), "Standard Processes and Objectives for the National Information Infrastructure," in Brian Kahin and Janet Abbate (eds), *Standards Policy for Information Infrastructure*. Cambridge, MA: MIT Press.

David, Paul A. and Shane Greenstein (1990), "The Economics of Compatibility Standards: An Introduction to Recent Research," *Economics of Innovation and New Technology* 1: 3–41.

Gallaher, Michael and Brent Rowe (2005), IPv6 Economic Impact Assessment: Final Report (Planning Report 05-2). Gaithersburg, MD: National Institute of Standards and Technology. Available at: http://www.nist.gov/director/planning/upload/report05-2.pdf, accessed January 2014.

Gallaher, Michael and Brent Rowe (2006), "The Costs and Benefits of Transferring Technology Infrastructures Underlying Complex Standards: The Case of IPv6," *Journal of Technology Transfer* 31: 519–544.

Jervis, Robert (1997), *System Effects: Complexity in Political and Social Life*. Princeton, NJ: Princeton University Press.

Leech, David P. (2012), *The Economic Impacts of NIST's Role in the Transition to Solid State Lighting Technology*. Gaithersburg, MD: National Institute of Standards and Technology (GCR 12-971).

Link, Albert N. and Gregory Tassey (1987), *Strategies for Technology-Based Competition*. Lexington, MA: Lexington Books.

Matutes, Carmen and Pierre Regibeau (1989), "Standardization across Markets and Entry," *Journal of Industrial Economics* 37(4): 359–371.

Meadows, Donell (2008), *Thinking in Systems: A Primer*. White River Junction, VT: Chelsea Green Publishing, pp. 145–165.

Swan, Peter (1987), "The Emergence of Industry Standard Microprocessors and the Strategy of Second Source Production," in H. Landis Gabel (ed.), *Product Standardization and Competitive Strategy*. Amsterdam: North Holland.

Tassey, Gregory (2000), "Standardization in Technology-Based Markets," *Research Policy* 20 (April): 587–602.

Tassey, Gregory (2005), "Underinvestment in Public Good Technologies," in F.M. Scherer and A.N. Link (eds), *Essays in Honor of Edwin Mansfield*, special issue of *Journal of Technology Transfer* 30: 89–113.

Tassey, Gregory (2007), *The Technology Imperative*. Northampton, MA: Edward Elgar.

Tassey, Gregory (2010), "Rationales and Mechanisms for Revitalizing US Manufacturing R&D Strategies," *Journal of Technology Transfer* 35 (June): 283–333.

Tassey, Gregory (2013), "Technology Life Cycles," in D. Campbell and E. Caryannis (eds), *The Encyclopedia of Creativity, Invention, Innovation, and Entrepreneurship*. New York/Heidelberg: Springer.

Tassey, G., M. Gallaher, and M. Rowe (2009), "Complex Standards and Sustained Innovation: the Internet Protocol," *International Journal of Technology Management* 48(4): 448–472.

13

Towards non-exclusive
intellectual property rights[1]

Cristiano Antonelli

1. Introduction

The recent advances in the economics of knowledge make the limitations of the current intellectual property rights (IPR) regime more and more evident. The generation of technological knowledge is a recombinant process where the stock of existing knowledge is a necessary, non-disposable input strictly complementary to other inputs such as competence and research and development expenditures. Because of the intrinsic cumulability of technological knowledge, the limits to the access and use of existing knowledge caused by the current IPR regime risk reducing the actual number of innovations that an economic system is able to generate. It is clear in fact that if on the one hand IPR increases the appropriability of the economic benefits stemming from the generation of new technological knowledge and hence the incentives to generate new technological knowledge, then on the other hand the limits to the use of existing knowledge cause major obstacles and engender major costs to the recombinant generation of new technological knowledge.

In the quest for non-exclusive intellectual property rights little attention has been paid to compulsory licensing. Compulsory licensing has been practiced for quite a long time in the copyright regime and in the patent regime but only for special cases, typically for drugs and medical knowledge. Recently its generalized use has been advocated in patent law and especially in the debates on trade related intellectual property rights. The shift of compulsory licensing from copyright to patent law can be considered an important institutional innovation that can help foster the pace of generation of technological knowledge and the rate of introduction of technological innovations (Antonelli, 2013).

Generalized compulsory licensing is an important institutional innovation that improves knowledge governance and can help foster the pace of generation of technological knowledge and the rate of introduction of technological innovations. So far the analysis of the effects of compulsory licensing has been focusing on the effects in the markets for the products that embody the new proprietary knowledge. Recent advances in the economics of knowledge solicit a shift in perspective calling attention to the characteristics of the knowledge generation process. These, recent, advances in the economics of knowledge have fully confirmed the medieval wisdom according to which to make knowledge it is necessary to stand on giants' shoulders.[2] In this new approach the access to existing knowledge, including the stock of knowledge owned by third parties as well as their current research efforts, is no longer viewed as a supplementary input that makes it possible to augment output levels. In the new approach existing technological knowledge is a complementary and indispensable input without which the generation of new technological knowledge is most difficult if not impossible (Antonelli, 2014).

In this context intellectual property right regimes based upon exclusivity may increase the incentives to generate new technological knowledge but reduce not only the efficiency, but the actual viability of the knowledge generation process. Generalized compulsory licensing for technological knowledge can increase the rate of generation of new technological knowledge only if the appropriate level of royalties is identified. This chapter contributes to the debate with a simple model that enables us to identify the correct levels of royalties for compulsory licensing, analyzing the generation of knowledge rather than the markets for the products that embody it.

The analysis of compulsory licensing has been implemented so far assuming the markets for the products that embody new knowledge as the single relevant perspective. Much progress can be made with the tools of the economics of knowledge, implementing the analysis of the role of compulsory licensing directly in the generation of new knowledge.

Generalized compulsory licensing-cum-royalties has not yet been analyzed with sufficient depth with the tools of the economics of knowledge. This chapter aims at using this framework of analysis to expand the analytical foundations of this important institutional innovation so as to facilitate its fast diffusion and widespread adoption. From an analytical viewpoint generalized compulsory licensing seems an intriguing device that, when it is coupled with mandatory royalties, may help address in an innovative way the well-known Schumpeterian trade-off between static and dynamic efficiency (Schumpeter, 1942).

The chapter contributes to the debate on the role of compulsory licensing within intellectual property right regimes in three ways. First it articulates the advantages of mandatory licensing as an institutional innovation that can provide a fertile solution to the new and old trade-offs of intellectual property right regimes. To do this, it applies the tools of the economics of knowledge to show why compulsory licensing can be considered an actual improvement in the allocation of property rights and hence a reduction in social costs. Second, the chapter stresses the limits of the attempts implemented so far to base the search for the optimum levels of royalties on the analysis of the markets for products that embody the new technological knowledge. Finally, it provides a simple approach based upon the economics of knowledge that enables the identification of the optimum level of royalties.

The rest of the chapter is structured as follows. Section 2 elaborates the implications of the new understanding of knowledge as both an input and an output to grasp the importance of compulsory licensing with an optimum level of royalties. Section 3 highlights the positive role of appropriate intellectual property rights and contrasts the suggestion that patents could be dismissed. Section 4 presents compulsory licensing as an institutional innovation that makes it possible to improve the IPR regime. Section 5 synthesizes the results of the literature on the effects of compulsory licensing and stresses the limits of the analysis implemented, so far, exclusively on the markets for the products that embody new technological knowledge. Section 6 presents a simple model that makes it possible to identify the correct levels of royalties, building upon the recent achievements of the economics of knowledge. Section 7 elaborates a tentative framework for the practical implementation of the generalized mandatory licensing with a fair level of royalties. The conclusions summarize the results of the analysis and provide a tentative framework for the practical implementation of a new regime of non-exclusive property rights.

2. Intellectual property rights when knowledge is both an output and an input

For quite a long time the economics of knowledge has focused attention on the negative consequences of the limited appropriability, non-excludability and intrinsic information asymmetries of technological knowledge as an economic good. Limited appropriability and non-excludability limit: a) the benefits stemming from generation and exchange in the market place, b) the incentives to allocate resources to generate it, and c) the opportunities for division of labor and hence specialization. These limits make the case for market failure. Because knowledge is 'worse-than-standard-economic-goods', markets are unable to allocate the correct amount of resources into the generation of technological knowledge. Public intervention is deemed necessary to help sustain the generation of adequate quantities of knowledge in the economic system (Nelson, 1959; Arrow, 1962 and 1969).

Figure 13.1 illustrates the point. The dotted line of the actual schedule of the marginal product of knowledge in value (VP'K) lies below the levels of the straight line that it would exhibit were it a normal economic good. Because of limited appropriability and non-excludability, the value of the knowledge that has been generated is lower than it would be with standard goods. For a given cost schedule of research development and learning activities (R&D), the equilibrium level is found in B rather than in A and the system is led to engage in levels of R&D activities that are lower than equilibrium levels with standard goods.

The size of the segment $R\&D_A - R\&D_B$ measures the undersupply of research, development and learning activities in the economic system engendered by the 'worse-than-standard-economic-goods' characteristics of knowledge.

Intellectual property rights are an important institutional remedy as they enable 'inventors' to (better) appropriate the results of the generation of technological knowledge and its application to the production of other goods. As a consequence intellectual property rights and specifically patents can increase the incentives to generate new technological knowledge and reduce the risks of market failure and undersupply. Repeated attempts to build up a consensus to dismantle intellectual property rights highlighting their negative consequences on the product markets have failed (Machlup and Penrose, 1950; Boldrin and Levine, 2002).

Much attention has been paid to the analysis of the consequences of the characteristics of patents in terms of breadth, length and assignment procedure in the attempt to identify their

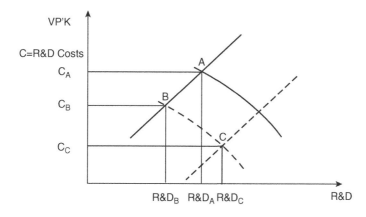

Figure 13.1   From knowledge non-appropriability to knowledge as a non-exhaustible input

best mix from the viewpoint of the trade-off between the negative effects of patents, in terms of static efficiency in product markets, and their positive effects, in terms of dynamic efficiency, on the actual levels of appropriability and hence on the incentives to introduce further innovations (Gilbert and Shapiro, 1990; Ayres and Klemperer, 1999).

The growing empirical evidence provided by the economics of knowledge has progressively made clear that the generation of new technological knowledge consists in the recombination of existing modules of knowledge. Technological knowledge is at the same time an output and an input of the recombinant generation of new technological knowledge and external knowledge is an essential – indispensable – input. Eventually knowledge enters the production function of all goods; as such it is twice an input: an input into the generation of new technological knowledge and an input into the generation of all the other goods (Weitzman, 1996 and 1998).

According to the latest advances in the economics of knowledge, new technological knowledge is generated by means of the recombination of existing technological knowledge. As Brian Arthur puts it:

> I realized that new technologies were not 'inventions' that came from nowhere. All the examples I was looking at were created – constructed, put together, assembled – from previously existing technologies. Technologies in other words consisted of other technologies, they arose as combinations of other technologies.
>
> *(Arthur, 2009:2)*

The theoretical analysis of technological knowledge has unveiled and stressed new characteristics that had received less attention, namely indivisibility and hence complementarity and cumulativity, and, most importantly, non-exhaustibility. Because of non-divisibility new technological knowledge impinges necessarily upon the stock of knowledge. Hence it can be generated only if and when existing technological knowledge can be used as an intermediary input. Its non-exhaustibility makes these repeated uses not only possible, but actually more and more effective along with the increase of the stock of knowledge (Scotchmer, 1991; Bessen and Maskin, 2009).

Figure 13.1 illustrates the point. Now the dotted cost schedule of research and learning activities lies well below the straight line that would be appropriate if knowledge were a standard good. The dotted line accounts for the positive effects of knowledge non-exhaustibility and non-divisibility. The costs of conducting research and learning activities are lower than those of any other standard good because of the positive effects of knowledge externalities stemming from its non-exhaustibility and cumulability. Because of non-exhaustibility and cumulability, technological knowledge, once generated, adds on to the stock of existing knowledge that can be used as an intermediary input into the generation of new technological knowledge again and again. When the positive effects of knowledge non-exhaustibility are accounted for and the role of knowledge non-divisibility is properly considered, the equilibrium is found in point C. The amount of R&D activities in the system is now $R\&D_C$, well above the levels of a standard good. In fact on the vertical axis the size of the segment $C_B - C_C$ measures the reduction in the costs of research and learning activities made possible by knowledge externalities. Now, because of non-exhaustibility and cumulability, the equilibrium costs of knowledge are lower than those of standard economic goods and the equilibrium quantities are far larger. Knowledge exhibits idiosyncratic characteristics that make it a good far 'better-than-standard-economic-goods' (Antonelli, 2005).

Technological knowledge appears to be 'better-than-standard-economic-goods' to the point that the increase of total factor productivity growth can be accounted by the amount of knowledge that, like a pure externality, spills from inventors to third parties (Griliches, 1979 and 1992). Building upon this thinking, the first wave of models of the new growth theory elaborated an interpretative framework according to which a system, where existing knowledge generated for a specific purpose by an agent spills freely in the atmosphere and is used as an intermediary input in the production of other goods by third parties, can experience fast rates of growth of both output and productivity (Romer, 1994).

The empirical evidence about the relevant absorption costs that are necessary to actually benefit from knowledge spillovers has enabled an appreciation of the role of both the systemic conditions and the intentional strategies of actors in qualifying the access to existing knowledge and stressed the role of pecuniary knowledge externalities – as opposed to pure externalities – in shaping the actual costs of the use of the stock of knowledge. As pecuniary knowledge externalities can measure the actual costs of external knowledge, they can actually account for the differentiated rates of productivity growth across regions, countries and firms (Mokyr, 1990 and 2002; Antonelli and Teubal, 2012).

The discovery of the dual role of technological knowledge as both an input and an output throws new light upon intellectual property right regimes. It becomes clear, in fact, that all barriers and delays to the use of existing knowledge as an input into the generation of new technological knowledge may increase the appropriability and hence the incentives to generate new technological knowledge but damage or even hinder the possibility to generate new technological knowledge as they impede the necessary use of the indispensable stock of knowledge as an intermediary input (David, 1993; Antonelli, 1999).

Intellectual property right regimes based upon full excludability force inventors to invent around and invent again bearing duplication costs that reduce the overall efficiency of the generation process. In the extreme case, an actual case for knowledge rationing takes place when existing knowledge cannot be used at all and no inventing around can overcome the non-availability of the existing knowledge. Inventors may be forced to wait until the expiry of the patent to use it as an input into the generation of new technological knowledge with major social loss in terms of reduced pace of technological advance (Jaffe and Lerner, 2004; Buzzacchi and Scellato, 2008).

The discovery of the dual role of knowledge as an output and an input unveils a second additional, inter-temporal, bundle of trade-offs. The exclusive intellectual property rights traditionally associated with patents provide patent holders at time t with the exclusive use of knowledge as an input in the production of knowledge at time t+1. Hence patent holders can generate new technological knowledge at incremental costs while all the other knowledge producers should bear the full costs of rediscovering the knowledge that is possessed by the inventor. In order to generate new technological knowledge that uses the incumbent technological knowledge as an input, patent holders bear only the additional costs while the costs of the existing knowledge are already sunk. Patent holders enjoy the benefits of substantial economies of density from which non-patent holders are excluded.[3] If prospective inventors cannot replicate the existing technological knowledge by means of inventing-around strategies, the monopolistic rights are likely to stay forever and actually increase over time as the working of knowledge cumulability displays its exclusive effects over historic time. In both cases it is clear that monopoly rights at time t are likely to become persistent and convey asymmetric cost advantages that are most likely to reduce not only static efficiency in product markets, but also dynamic efficiency in the long-term generation of knowledge (Antonelli *et al.*, 2012).

From the social viewpoint it is clear that a new bundle of dynamic knowledge trade-offs is at work. Patents have negative effects not only because they imply monopoly rights in the markets for products that apply technological knowledge, but also because they may delay and in any event create twisting asymmetries in the sequential generation of new technological knowledge.

As Heller and Eisenberg (1998) note, the strengthening of the intellectual property right regime that has characterized the last decades may actually deter innovation and make the case of an anticommons. The current intellectual property right regime together with high transaction costs in the markets for knowledge and excess expectations of patentees on the value of their knowledge assets produce a fragmented knowledge landscape where owners of small complementary bits of knowledge are unable to participate in the collective effort that is necessary to generate new knowledge as an output while using existing knowledge as input (David, 2010).

The understanding of the new trade-off has stirred the search for a new functionality of patents, trying to combine their indispensable role to enforce the necessary property rights on technological knowledge with the need to increase the dissemination and access to existing knowledge. Intellectual property rights may become an obstacle not only to static efficiency and the working of competitive product markets but also to the actual use of technological knowledge as an input into the sequential generation of new technological knowledge (Boldrin and Levine, 2002 and 2013; Corbel and Le Bas, 2011).

The positive experience of free software has attracted much attention in this context and suggested that this specific evidence might be generalized. Software provides strong evidence about the central role of knowledge complementarity and cumulability in the recombinant generation of new technological knowledge. New software produced by each developer impinges upon the source that has been generated in the past and in the myriad of applications that have been and are being, at each point in time, generated by other developers. In the software industry it seems quite clear that a bottom-up spontaneous mechanism of knowledge governance centered upon a general public license to the advances in the software source being made available by each developer to any other has become the common practice (Stallman, 1998).

The spreading of the FLOSS (Free Libre Open Source Software) practice in a fast growing industry characterized by high levels of knowledge complementarity and cumulability coupled with the clear evidence of the fast advances in software technology have suggested the viability of an intellectual property regime based upon the citation mechanism and led to the articulation of the hypothesis that gains of the free access to new technological knowledge embodied in the advances in the software source were sufficient to counterweight the lack of incentives associated with intellectual property rights (Dalle *et al.*, 2008).

At a closer analysis, however, it seems that the specificities of the software industry matter more than is recognized. In the case of free software the social recognition of the contribution made available by each 'inventor' and implemented by the general public license that provides each developer a cite, and hence the social recognition of its contribution, plays a crucial role. Specifically it seems that the free access to software made available by the software expert with the full social recognition provided by the compulsory cite is compensated by the increase in reputation and its direct valorization in the adjacent markets of professional services. The markets for professional services are not only adjacent but strictly complementary to the markets for software: the assistance of the developer in the actual implementation of a new program is in fact absolutely necessary for its effective use. The proximity of the markets for professional services to the markets for software, in other words, works as a crucial compensating mechanism as it creates complementary rewards that compensate for the lack of direct appropriation. As in academia, where publications qualified by citations secure chairs and hence long-term salaries, each quote carried by the general public license is often worth more than a penny in the working of adjacent professional markets (Trajtenberg, 1990).

The appreciation of the crucial role of the professional rewards to the citations stemming from the general public license limits the possibility of a generalized use of an intellectual property right regime based upon implicit or explicit citations. Where and if adjacent markets – where the professional reputation can be effectively valorized – are missing, the lack of appropriability has negative and direct effects on the incentives to generate new technological knowledge and hence, ultimately, the supply of new knowledge (Antonelli, 2007).

3. The need for intellectual property rights

The rising criticisms about the limits of patents and the increasing awareness that they can actually reduce the capability of an economic system to generate new technological knowledge have pushed some authors to articulate the extreme solution that patents should be suppressed (Boldrin and Levine, 2013). This position cannot be shared.

Intellectual property rights play a key role not only to secure the necessary appropriability, and hence the incentives to the generation of technological knowledge, but also to make possible the tradability of knowledge and ultimately to favor its dissemination, contrasting with the active search for secrecy, as the extreme remedy implemented by 'inventors', to reduce non-appropriability. Without effective intellectual property rights 'inventors' may try and disguise the knowledge that they have been able to generate, relying upon secrecy with great harm to the generation of new technological knowledge. Patents, even with exclusive property rights, do disseminate effective information about the existence of new technological knowledge (Cohen et al., 2000; Arundel, 2001; Bessen, 2005; Cugno and Ottoz, 2006 and 2011).

An intellectual property right regime is necessary to support the generation of new technologies for five classes of argument:

A) patents increase the appropriability of the economic benefits of the applications of knowledge to economic activities. Increased levels of appropriability in turn increase the incentives to its generation. In turn the accrued incentives make possible the specialization of individuals and organizations in the generation of knowledge, with all the well-known advantages in terms of division of labor, identification of talents and accumulation of dedicated competence.

B) Patents are a powerful tool for the dissemination of information about existing technological knowledge. Patent offices carry out the *de facto* central role of universal repositories of the relevant knowledge. In so doing patents contribute to reducing the high costs of search and screening of existing knowledge for all the other firms that are looking for external sources of knowledge that can complement the internal ones. From this viewpoint patents favor the effective and cheap identification of existing knowledge as an input both for the recombinant generation of new knowledge and for its application to the production processes of all the other goods.

C) Secrecy has always been the classical alternative to IPR and the basic remedy to non-appropriability. Inventors that could not rely upon patents have always tried to use secrecy to increase their chances of participating in the economic benefits stemming from the application of new knowledge to economic activities. Secrecy however has major negative effects upon the actual possibility to use knowledge as an input into the generation of new knowledge. Secrecy limits the dissemination of all information about the new knowledge. Potential users are not even aware that it exists already. Inventors make systematic efforts to delay the dissemination of all information about both the content and the procedures that have made possible its generation. Patents, on the contrary, help the dissemination of information about the existence of a specific knowledge item and about the specific characteristics of its content. As a matter of fact patents are the most effective vehicle for the broad dissemination of new knowledge.

D) Trade and the division of labor are key mechanisms for improving specialization and consequently competence and efficiency. IPR are strictly necessary to make knowledge transactions possible. Without a clear definition of the limits and contents of a knowledge item, trade in knowledge would not be possible. The intrinsic information asymmetries between vendors and customers would in fact impede all market exchange. Vendors would be most reluctant to reveal the actual content of their knowledge item before the transaction because of the high risk of opportunistic behavior by potential customers. Potential customers would be most reluctant to access the actual content of the new knowledge item only after the transaction.

E) Knowledge interactions are necessary for knowledge transactions to take place efficiently. Technological knowledge is characterized by high levels of tacitness that can be reduced only to a point. Even when knowledge reaches the highest levels of codification, relevant portions remain characterized by irreducible elements of tacitness. The interaction between the producers of knowledge and its users is made necessary by tacitness. Knowledge interactions accompany and qualify knowledge transactions so as to make the access to knowledge actually possible.

Summing up, it seems clear that the combined effects of these complementary and yet distinct arguments make intellectual property rights necessary not only to increase the appropriability of knowledge but also to avoid and reduce the recourse to secrecy and to favor knowledge transactions and the associated knowledge interactions between vendors and customers that would not take place because of the high level of information asymmetry.

It seems clearer now that it would be dangerous and actually disruptive to eliminate IPR. The introduction of non-exclusive intellectual property rights seems, instead, the right way to proceed. Non-exclusive IPR combine the positive effects of patents in terms of effective alternatives to secrecy and effective tools able to implement trade in knowledge and the associated knowledge interactions between parties that can rely upon each other without their negative effects in terms of the possibility of excluding for a substantial stretch of time potential users from access to the new knowledge available.

In the new approach the critical levels of the exclusivity of intellectual property rights emerge as the key issue that may solve the intrinsic contradiction of the knowledge trade-off (Antonelli, 2007).

4. Generalized compulsory licensing as an institutional innovation

Generalized compulsory licensing-cum-royalties is a major institutional innovation that is being used by a growing number of countries. It is the result of the recombination of the copyright regime with the patent regime. It can be regarded as a new mechanism of knowledge governance that combines the property rule with the liability rule. As such it seems to enable a better allocation of property rights and hence a reduction of social costs (Coase, 1960).

Compulsory licensing has been practiced for quite a long time, since the Paris Convention of 1883. It was regarded as a technical specificity originating in the copyright regime that might be applied to the patent legislation in special circumstances beyond the limits of the Berne Convention for the Protection of Literary and Artistic Works (Merges, 2004).

Its application is now spreading especially under the pressure of the debates about TRIPs (Trade Related Intellectual Property Rights). Compulsory licensing is emerging in the international arena stirred by the globalizing economy as the result of a spontaneous and collective bottom-up process of social governance of knowledge commons based upon the implementation of the grafting of the copyright tradition onto patent law, making possible a new and superior allocation of intellectual property rights. Its first applications were found in pharmaceuticals and health care products.[4] It is now spreading in biotechnologies and information and communication technologies. From this viewpoint it shares the characteristics of an emerging and collective process similar to FLOSS with the specific characteristic that, here, actors are not individual software developers but many small industrializing countries that try to participate in the generation of new technological knowledge (Ostrom, 1990).

Generalized compulsory licensing combines a reduction of the exclusivity of the patent regime with the identification of a royalty for the use of proprietary knowledge. Intellectual property rights on new knowledge are recognized at the same time; however, the use of proprietary knowledge can take place by third parties without authorization, but after registration and the payment of a royalty. Generalized compulsory licensing is a hybrid form in between the property and the liability rules. The property rule applies although in a reduced form that no longer includes any exclusivity. The property rule applies because patentees have the right to command an economic benefit from the use of their patents, although they cannot limit the conditions of use in terms of their number and the scope of their action, i.e. whether the patent is used to produce other goods or other knowledge. The liability rule applies to users who are obliged to register and pay a royalty (Reichman, 2000; Reichman and Maskus, 2005).

Table 13.1 makes clear how compulsory licensing makes possible the combination of the enforcement of the property rule and the application of the liability rule. A reduction of the exclusivity of intellectual property rights seems useful to reduce the negative effects upon the use of technological knowledge as an input into the generation of new technological knowledge and yet preserving the key role of intellectual property rights to favor the dissemination and social availability of existing technological knowledge. The reduction of exclusivity needs to be balanced by the royalties that the users of patented knowledge should pay to inventors. Royalties are necessary to provide inventors with a reward for undertaking risky research, development and learning activities and in general to cope with all the costs that are associated with the introduction of technological innovations.

Compulsory licensing differs sharply from generalized compulsory licensing-cum-royalties. In the former framework knowledge holders are deprived of all economic rights and cannot contest the free use of their proprietary knowledge by third parties. In the latter framework the

Table 13.1 The combination of property and liability rules

	Property rule	Liability rule
Knowledge producers	Exclusive intellectual property rights	Mandated licensing to any registered user
Knowledge users	Users can purchase and use patents provided the exclusive owners agree	Users can use patented knowledge with no permission but must identify themselves and pay a royalty

users of the patented knowledge are expected to inform the patentee that they are going to use the knowledge and are willing to pay the royalties. Patentees that discover a user that did not declare itself and did not pay the royalties can claim that an infringement has been taking place and ask the judiciary power to act against the clandestine user. In contrast, the patent holder cannot refuse the prospective user the right to access the patented knowledge and can only ask for the payment of the royalty.

The introduction of generalized compulsory licensing-cum-royalties can be regarded as a major institutional innovation that is able to reconcile, knowledge trade-offs favoring not only competition in the product markets, but also the generation of new technological knowledge.

From this specific viewpoint it seems clear that the negative consequences of exclusive intellectual property rights are all the stronger the larger the scope of application of technological knowledge. Barriers and delays to the use of technological knowledge that has a limited scope of application have smaller negative consequences than barriers and delays to the use of technological knowledge that has a wide scope of application. In the latter case in fact intellectual property rights with high levels of exclusivity slow down and may actually impede the advances of a large portion of the scientific and technological frontier (Antonelli, 2007).

The introduction of generalized compulsory licensing-cum-royalties seems most promising for general-purpose technologies and technological knowledge with high levels of fungibility. The negative effects of the exclusivity of intellectual property rights are all the stronger the wider their scope of application. The new understanding of the mechanisms underlying the generation of technological knowledge enable us to grasp that the reduced availability of existing knowledge has negative consequences that are stronger the larger the range of products and derivative advances in technological knowledge that rest upon its unlimited imitation and use as an intermediary input into the generation of new technological knowledge (Reitzig, 2004; Hagiu and Yoffie, 2013).

Generalized compulsory licensing-cum-royalties should combine the positive effects of the rewards of the generation of technological knowledge and the introduction of technological innovations with the positive effects of the reduction of monopolistic power in product markets and of access to and actual use of technological knowledge once generated. Generalized compulsory licensing-cum-royalties deprives inventors of their exclusive property right so that they can no longer impede the imitation of innovations and the use of technological knowledge but entitles them to royalties based upon the actual use of their new technological knowledge and the related innovation (Barton, 2000; Penin, 2005).

5. The economics of compulsory licensing in product markets

The economics of compulsory licensing, so far, has focused exclusively on the effects on both users and producers of technological knowledge in the markets for the products that embody technological knowledge (Tandon, 1982).

The modeling exercises, based upon the analysis of the downstream product markets, try to show how the introduction of compulsory licensing-cum-royalties can reduce the levels of exclusivity of intellectual property rights with positive effects in the markets for products that embody new technological innovations in terms of a reduction of monopolistic power in product markets that is compatible with the identification of the rewards for inventors that are necessary to avoid the use of secrecy.

Figure 13.2 helps us grasp the point. Let us assume that C_1 are the costs of a good sold in a monopolistic market at price P_1. Before innovation the equilibrium quantity is Q_A.

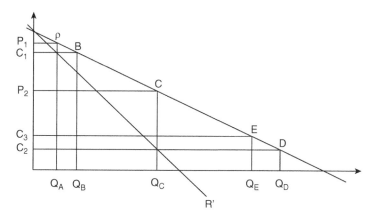

Figure 13.2 Compulsory licensing in product markets

The introduction of an innovation reduces the costs to C_2. These new costs include the innovation costs but no rewards for the innovator. In a monopoly the new price would be P_2 and the new equilibrium quantity Q_C. In a competitive market the price would coincide with C_2 and the new equilibrium quantity would be Q_D.

An inspection of Figure 13.2 confirms that in monopolistic product markets the consumer surplus is lower than in the competitive market, but in the competitive market there are no profits. Yet the competitive market enables the maximization of the social surplus defined as the sum of profits and consumer surplus. From the social viewpoint the competitive market is clearly superior, but there are no rewards for the innovator and hence the incentives to innovate are completely missing. The economic system risks a dramatic undersupply of the technological knowledge that is necessary to introduce the innovation that enables the reduction of the costs from C_1 to C_2.

From an ex-post perspective, assuming that the profits stemming from the introduction of an innovation do incentivize their introduction, it seems clear that competitive markets are superior in terms of static efficiency, but absolutely inferior in terms of dynamic efficiency (Schumpeter, 1942).

Let us now consider the case that compulsory licensing is introduced with royalties that are fixed at the level R. Royalties are a cost for the producer and a revenue for producers of the technological knowledge that is necessary for the introduction of innovations. Hence costs increase from C_2 to C_3. C_3 include both the costs of the product after the innovation and the rewards for the activities that have made possible the generation of technological change and the introduction of the innovation. Compulsory licensing implies that there are no barriers to entry to imitators: competitive markets can substitute monopolies. In a competitive market, where all firms can use the new technology, the price would coincide with the new costs. The new equilibrium is found in E and the system would produce the quantity Q_E.

The equilibrium in E combines royalties with consumer surplus. Royalties indeed provide incentives to innovate. The key question concerns their correct levels: too high royalties create static inefficiency while too low ones end up in dynamic inefficiency.

In solution E the consumer surplus is larger than in the monopolistic solution identified by point C. As a result the social surplus of compulsory licensing with royalties is larger than in the monopolistic product markets and yet provides the appropriability that is necessary to yield incentives. Compulsory licensing enables the combination of the benefits of incentives for 'inventors' and hence for innovators with the social goal of increasing as much as possible the social surplus stemming from the generation of technological knowledge and the ensuing introduction of innovations. The E solution, however, does not provide any hint that the future consumers' surplus is actually maximized by the current levels of royalties.

The E solution has been selected with a rule of thumb procedure that does not necessarily lead to the maximization of dynamic efficiency. The maximum levels of dynamic efficiency would be actually identified only if it were possible to select the 'correct' amount of royalties that combine the optimum incentive to introduce innovations with the maximum levels of consumers' surplus at time t and in the following periods.

The analysis has focused on the markets for the products that embody new technological knowledge in the attempt to identify the correct level of royalties starting from the analysis of their characteristics. The levels of royalties affect at least three categories of agents: the holders of patents or the innovators, the users of the patents or the imitators and finally the customers of the products that have been produced with the innovation.

Scherer (1977), with a path-breaking empirical study on the propensity of firms to fund R&D activities after compulsory licensing and to innovate, found that the consequences were negative but only to a limited extent. This result is important but does not shed any light on the actual optimum levels of the royalties. More recently Moser and Voena (2012) provide interesting evidence on the effects of compulsory licensing on the users of knowledge. The effects were absolutely positive, with an increase in innovation activities for users estimated around 20 percent. In this case however compulsory licensing was enforced without royalties as a part of the Trading with the Enemy Act enforced in 1917 by the US against German patents. The positive effects on US users should be contrasted with the negative effects on patent holders in order to assess the general effects of compulsory licensing (Moser, 2013).

The main result of this approach consists in the identification of the characteristics of the markets for the products such as the price and revenue elasticity of the demand, the type of rivalry on the supply side, and the extent to which barriers to entry prevent imitation that affects the conduct of both innovators and imitators. This approach however has not provided any clear-cut definition of the optimum level of royalties that are associated with compulsory licensing (Lanjouw and Lerner, 1997).

So far the identification of the correct level of royalties remains unsettled. The limits of this approach are more and more evident with: a) the failure of patent pools where the literature has not been able to elaborate a coherent methodology for the identification of the levels of royalties, undermining their practical application (Lerner and Tirole, 2004; Lerner et al., 2007); b) the spreading of patent thicketing as a strategic tool to reduce the risks of non-appropriability and the increasing limits to the use of technological knowledge to generate new technological knowledge (Shapiro, 2001; Lerner, 2009); c) the increasing levels of litigation and legal costs (Hall, 2007); and d) the spreading of 'trolls' that try to maximize the benefits stemming from knowledge indivisibility in terms of complementarity among patents (Chien, 2008 and 2011). The lack of a correct methodological approach to identify the correct levels of royalties limits the application of compulsory licensing to the field of drugs and medical products, typically in developing countries (Chien, 2003).

The identification of the correct level of royalties is crucial (Scherer and Watal, 2002). Non-exclusive property rights with no rules about the correct level of royalties would give patentees the right to ask huge royalties that would deprive the content of non-exclusivity with the well-known negative effects that are all the stronger when innovation is cumulative (Shapiro, 2001 and 2010; Llobet, 2002).

A step forward is necessary towards the identification and implementation of a methodology to identify the correct level of royalties to which all parties involved in non-exclusive property rights – sellers and customers – should stick. This implies a shift of intellectual property rights away from the property rule towards the liability rule. The distinction is important as with an entitlement protected by property rule a collective decision can be made with respect to the content of an entitlement, but not upon the value of the entitlement. An entitlement protected by a liability rule, instead, involves a collective decision on the value of the entitlement (Calabresi and Melamed, 1972).

The analysis of the upstream generation of knowledge as a good per se that is not yet embodied in new products but is strictly necessary to introduce product or process innovations seems to offer a promising opportunity to solve the problem.

6. Optimum royalties in the generation of knowledge

The economics of knowledge by now provides a large set of analytical tools and ammunitions to try to identify the correct level of royalties. Knowledge is the result of a recombinant and collective activity that uses existing knowledge as a necessary input for the generation of new knowledge as an output (Antonelli, 2011). This background enables the direct analysis of the knowledge generation activity rather than of the markets for products that embody new technological knowledge.

More specifically the rich literature of the economics of knowledge shows that each firm can generate new knowledge as long as it can rely upon the knowledge activity implemented at each point in time by all the other firms with which it can interact. External knowledge is acquired by means of transactions enriched by interactions. The mix of transactions-cum-interactions is made necessary by the tacit component of knowledge. At the same time external knowledge cannot be considered as a stock. Knowledge exists as long it consists of an ongoing activity. External knowledge is always and necessarily a flow of competences practiced by other agents in the system.

The analysis of the knowledge generation function, as distinct from the knowledge production function that includes knowledge as an input, enables us to make an important step forward. Following Griliches (1979) the knowledge production function applies to all the other goods and includes explicitly knowledge as an input, next to the traditional inputs such as capital and labor. The knowledge generation function applies only to the upstream activities that make it possible to generate new knowledge (Nelson, 1982).

Building upon Weitzman (1996 and 1998) the generation of knowledge can be considered as the result of a recombination activity of all existing knowledge available at each point in time. The diverse knowledge items that exist at each point in time are dispersed in a myriad of possessors and used in a variety of activities. The stock of knowledge does not exist independently of the learning activity of the agents that possess and use it. A bit of knowledge that is not used is lost. External knowledge is the basic indispensable and non-disposable input that feeds the eventual generation of new knowledge. The knowledge possessed by all the other agents is external to each agent and yet is a crucial input into the recombinant generation of new knowledge. Research and development activities together with learning processes enable us to recombine the existing knowledge items into new knowledge. No generation of new knowledge is possible without the access to and the use of existing knowledge.

The access to external knowledge by each agent requires a complex set of transactions-cum-interactions. Because of the tacit component of knowledge, perfect, impersonal, spot transactions are not sufficient to transfer knowledge. Dedicated, personal interactions are necessary. The price of knowledge plays an important although not exhaustive role in the actual acquisition of external knowledge and its effective use in the recombinant generation of new knowledge.

The specification of a knowledge generation function and the appreciation of the dual role of knowledge as both an input and an output provide the opportunity to identify the correct price for knowledge. The identification of the correct levels of royalties is in fact possible as soon as we consider jointly their positive and negative effects on the economics of the generation of technological knowledge. High levels of royalties engender high revenues for the knowledge producer as well as higher costs. Technological knowledge, in fact, is both an output and an input, more specifically, a necessary and indispensable input for the production of new technological knowledge. Hence technological knowledge is found twice in the generation function of the inventor, on both the revenue and the cost sides.

This frame enables us to identify an optimum level of royalties. Let us assume that, at the system level, the amount of new knowledge Y that the system is willing to use is generated with the following Cobb-Douglas production function:

$$F(R\&D, K_n) = R\&D^\alpha K_n^{1-\alpha} \tag{1}$$

where $0 < \alpha < 1$.

In particular, F(R&D, K_n) represents the additional level of knowledge produced, Y, given the two productive factors employed: research and development (R&D) and initial quantity of knowledge (K_n). As in the standard Cobb-Douglas we assume that the two productive factors are complements with a certain degree of substitutability. In other words, the production of knowledge requires a minimum amount of the productive factors R&D and K_n, so that even if royalties are very large, the production cannot rely exclusively on the factor R&D, and some minimum amount of K_n must be used in any case. Let us call this minimum amount $K_{n\,min}$. Let us call $R\&D_{max}$ the corresponding level of R&D, where, from (1), $R\&D_{max} = Y^{-\alpha} K_n^{(\alpha-1)/\alpha}{}_{min}$. Figure 13.3 identifies the substitutability range and the combination $K_{n\,min}$, $R\&D_{max}$ of productive factors on the upper boundary of this range.

Assuming linear costs g of R&D and K_n, and a price for the royalties R, the profit function is the following:

$$\Pi(R\&D, K_n) = R\,F(R\&D, K_n) - g\,R\&D - RK_n \tag{2}$$

In the range of substitutability, the firm chooses the level of R&D that maximizes its profits:

$$\frac{d\Pi}{dR\&D} = 0 \Rightarrow R \cdot \alpha \cdot R\&D^{\alpha-1}K_n^{1-\alpha} - g = 0 \Rightarrow R\&D* = \left(\frac{\alpha R}{g}\right)^{\frac{1}{1-\alpha}} K_n^* \tag{3}$$

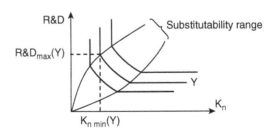

Figure 13.3 Substitutability range for a given level of Y

Similarly, the level of K_n that maximizes the firm's profits is

$$\frac{d\Pi}{dK_n} = 0 \Rightarrow R \cdot (1-\alpha) \cdot R \& D^\alpha K_n^{-\alpha} - R = 0 \Rightarrow K_n^* = (1-\alpha)^{\frac{1}{\alpha}} R \& D * \tag{4}$$

Considering that $Y = R \& D^\alpha K_n^{1-\alpha}$,

$$Y = \left(\frac{\alpha R}{g}\right)^{\frac{\alpha}{1-\alpha}} K_n^{*\alpha} K_n^{*(1-\alpha)} = \left(\frac{\alpha R}{g}\right)^{\frac{\alpha}{1-\alpha}} K_n^* \Rightarrow K_n^* = Y \left(\frac{g}{\alpha R}\right)^{\frac{\alpha}{1-\alpha}} \tag{5}$$

and, by substituting (5) in (3)

$$R \& D * = Y \left(\frac{\alpha R}{g}\right) \tag{6}$$

The revenue function is:

$$RV(R) = R \cdot Y \tag{7}$$

From expression (7), the revenue function is linear with respect to R as shown in Figure 13.4 with the bold straight line increasing from the origin.

The total costs are the sum of the cost component related to R&D and the cost component related to K_n:

$$C = C_{R\&D} + C_{K_n}. \tag{8}$$

In the substitutability range both cost components depend on R, as expressed by (5) and (6). The cost components in the substitutability range are then:

$$C_{R\&D}(R) = g \cdot R \& D * = g \cdot Y \cdot \left(\frac{\alpha R}{g}\right) = \alpha \cdot Y \cdot R \tag{9}$$

and

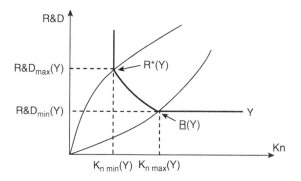

Figure 13.4   R* and optimal combination of productive factors

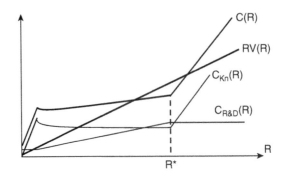

Figure 13.5 Cost and revenue function for $\alpha > \frac{1}{2}$ and complementary productive factors, with $Y < K_n$

$$C_{K_n}(R) = RK_n^* = R \cdot Y \left(\frac{g}{\alpha R} \right)^{\frac{\alpha}{1-\alpha}} = Y \cdot \left(\frac{g}{\alpha} \right)^{\frac{\alpha}{1-\alpha}} \cdot R^{\frac{1-2\alpha}{1-\alpha}} \qquad (10)$$

In the substitutability range, the quantity of productive factors used depends on R. Indeed, if R increases, the production of Y relies more on R&D and less on K_n. In particular, from the expressions above, we see that the component of cost related to R&D is linear with respect to R, while the convexity with respect to R of the cost component related to K_n depends on the value of α. In particular, if $\dfrac{1-2\alpha}{1-\alpha} < 0$, namely if $\alpha > \frac{1}{2}$, the component of cost related to K_n, C_{Kn}, has the form of a hyperbole.

This case is shown in Figure 13.5, where the productive factors are substitutes for $\underline{R} < R < R*$. In this interval, the thin hyperbole represents C_{Kn} and the thin line represents $C_{R\&D}$. Their sum is shown by the bold curve C(R).

When R increases beyond a certain value (that we denote R*), K_n cannot further decrease and the combination and amount of productive factors remains constant at $K*_{n\,min}(R*)$ and $R\&D*_{max}(R*)$. Symmetrically, when R decreases beyond a certain level (that we denote $\underline{R}$), K_n cannot further increase and the combination and amount of productive factors remains constant at $K*_{n\,max}(\underline{R})$ and $R\&D*_{min}(\underline{R})$. These situations are represented in Figure 13.4.

This implies that for $R > R*$ (namely, out of the substitutability range) the component of cost related to R&D remains constant with respect to R, while the component of costs related to K_n increases linearly with R:

$$C = g \cdot R \& D_{max}^* + RK_{n\,min}^* \qquad (11)$$

We thus have that, out of the substitutability range, for $R > R*$, revenues increase linearly (with the multiplicative factor being the given level of Y), and costs increase linearly (with the multiplicative factor being $K_{n\,min}$). The situation is represented in Figure 13.5 for values of $R > R*$. $C_{R\&D}$ is the thin horizontal line, while C_{Kn} is the thin increasing line. Their sum is shown by the bold increasing line for $R > R*$.

Assuming that the slope of the revenue curve (Y) is lower than the slope of the cost curve (K_n) (namely, that the quantity of additional knowledge produced is lower than the initial level of knowledge used), it is evident from Figure 13.5 that an optimal level of R exists, where profits are maximized. This level corresponds to R*. The model has shown the strict interdependence between active and passive royalties when the stock of technological knowledge is considered as an input into the production of new technological knowledge.

In the following we show the relationship between R* and Y. Let the complementarity ratio on the upper boundary be:

$$R \& D_{max} = xK_{n\,min}^{\beta},$$ (12)

with $x > 0$ and $\beta < 1$.

Notice that the profit maximizing R* corresponds to the level of R at which the optimal combination of productive factors is $K_{n\,min}$, $R\&D_{max}$, lies on the upper substitutability boundary. Hence, the value of R* for a given level of Y can be obtained by solving a system in which one equation identifies the optimal level of R&D given R, and is thus given by (6), and the other expresses the upper substitutability boundary,[5] and is thus represented by (12):

$$\begin{cases} R \& D_{max}^{*} = Y\left(\dfrac{\alpha R^{*}}{g}\right) \\[2mm] R \& D_{max}^{*} = xK_{n\,min}^{*\beta} \end{cases}$$ (13)

Using (5), the previous system becomes

$$Y\left(\frac{\alpha R^{*}}{g}\right) = xY^{\beta}\left(\frac{g}{\alpha R^{*}}\right)^{\frac{\alpha\beta}{1-\alpha}}$$ (14)

We can thus obtain the value of R* such that, given a level of Y, the optimal solution lies on the upper boundary:

$$R^{*} = \frac{g}{\alpha}x^{\eta}Y^{-(1-\beta)\eta},$$ (15)

where $\eta = \dfrac{1-\alpha}{1-\alpha+\alpha\beta}$.

The value of R* expressed in (15) represents the value of the profit maximizing R such that the optimal combination of K_n and R&D lies on the upper boundary of the imperfect substitutability range between the two factors.

To see how R* is affected by variations of Y, we compute the derivative of (15):

$$\frac{dR^{*}}{dY} = \frac{g}{\alpha}x^{\eta}\left(-(1-\beta)\eta\right)Y^{-(1-\beta)\eta-1}.$$ (16)

As both η, x and $(1-\beta)$ are positive, we obtain that $\dfrac{dR^{*}}{dY} \leq 0$: as the amount of new knowledge produced increases, the profit maximizing royalty does not increase.

The model provides an analytical framework that builds upon the central role of existing knowledge in the generation of new knowledge according to which it is indeed possible to identify an optimum level of royalties. This procedure enables us to overcome the many limitations and inconsistencies in the attempts to identify the optimum level of royalties upon the analysis of the markets for the products that embody the new knowledge.

Cristiano Antonelli

7. A Tentative framework for practical implementation

The identification of an optimum level of royalties and its stability with respect to the amount of knowledge generated in the system is important from a theoretical viewpoint. Its implementation in the real world is difficult as information on the stock of the existing knowledge is missing.

From a regulatory viewpoint the implications of this analysis are straightforward and consist of the application and extension of the existing regulatory body on essential physical facilities such as telecommunications, energy, transportation. Existing knowledge can be considered as an essential facility. Non-exclusive property rules apply on physical essential facilities: the owners of the networks cannot discriminate against the users, limit or condition their uses. Users however must pay a 'fair' fee that regulatory agencies are expected to identify effectively.

The implementation of the current regime of intellectual property rights with the reduction of exclusive property rules can be based upon the generalized compulsory licensing that makes it possible to apply the notion of mandated interconnection. The unlimited use and access by third parties to the new intangible essential facility represented by the stock of existing knowledge can take place with a new intellectual property right regime that respects the property rule of the current regime and hence the right of patented inventors to benefit from the application and uses of their proprietary knowledge and shift upon users the obligation to pay a royalty. Users are now submitted to the liability rule that implies a collective decision valid *erga omnes* on their value and access conditions (Antonelli, 2007; Choi, 2010).

In order to identify a workable level of royalties that is able to approximate the criteria at which an optimum level can be found, applications for patents should be integrated by the identification of the research costs that have been expensed to generate the new technological knowledge. The declaration of the costs incurred should be supported by appropriate accounting evidence. Patent offices are expected to acquire the competence that is necessary to assess the congruence of the cost declaration so as to limit the drawbacks of inefficiency in knowledge generation and/or opportunistic behavior in declaration. Moreover, in order to counterweight the creation of spurious incentives to opportunistic behavior of inefficient inventors, renewal fees will be calculated as a share of the costs that have been admitted by the patent office. Once the patent is granted, compulsory licensing applies and the use of patents by third parties cannot be impeded or limited, provided the request for license is registered and royalties are paid.

The royalties will be calculated as a share of the costs. Because the costs incurred for the generation of new technological knowledge are fixed, the average costs of patents with a wide application will decrease over time favoring the increase of the profits.

On the demand side knowledge generators will try to identify the best mix of knowledge inputs according to their content and their costs. On the supply side the generation of technological knowledge can became a specialized industry where firms compete in the generation of useful knowledge that can be patented and used with no exclusivity by third parties. The identification of mark-ups can help foster the entry of new competitors in specific domains. Inventors of minor inventions will barely cover costs. Inventors of radical inventions will gain major profits stemming from the difference between the fixed royalty and the declining average costs of the patent.[6] Entry into the knowledge generation industry however is open as there are no barriers to entry determined by exclusive intellectual property rights. High profits in specific domains are likely to attract the entry of new competitors while inventors might want to exit from scientific and technological domains with low demand for licenses.[7]

226

Because of generalized compulsory licensing and the consequent right to use the existing knowledge although at a price paid to the possessor of its patent we can assume that Schumpeterian competition takes place in both product and knowledge markets with a plurality of firms both upstream and downstream that enter and exit. Many firms try to generate new technological knowledge using the stock of existing knowledge as much as many firms try to introduce technological innovations in the product markets.

A Marshallian selection process based on entry and exit with the failure of less attractive innovations and firms is likely to take place. At each point in time a plurality and variety of innovations are being introduced. The Marshallian selection process applies to both firms and innovations and leads to the social optimum in terms of the amount of new technological knowledge identified by the maximum difference between the consumer surplus and the cost of generating new technological knowledge and introducing technological innovations.

Compulsory licensing bears direct effects on patent design and especially on their breadth and duration. Compulsory licensing reduces the relevance of both scope and duration since their implications on the exclusivity of property rights are deprived of content from the right to use a patent provided that a fee is paid (Ayres and Klemperer, 1999).

The systematic application of compulsory licensing-cum-royalties opens new opportunities for knowledge exploitation, favoring the direct valorization of knowledge as a commodity embodied neither in goods nor in knowledge intensive property rights, becoming an alternative both to vertical integration in the direct application of new knowledge in the production of other goods and to venture capitalism (Coriat and Weinstein, 2012).

Generalized compulsory licensing-cum-royalties makes possible the working of the markets for knowledge favoring the meeting of the demand and the supply for knowledge. Moreover they can help stir the interaction between knowledge producers and knowledge users. Knowledge users have a clear interest in purchasing technical assistance and support from knowledge producers. At the same time knowledge producers have an interest in assisting prospective knowledge users and adding to the royalties the revenue stemming from their assistance. Generalized compulsory licensing becomes an incentive to the growth of markets for knowledge transfer services that become strictly adjacent and complementary to the markets for knowledge. From this viewpoint compulsory licensing favors the actual consolidation of a knowledge economy (Arora et al., 2012; Shavell and Van Ypersele, 2001).

8. Conclusions

The generation of new technological knowledge is possible only if the stock of existing knowledge can be used as an input. All barriers and delays in access to existing knowledge risk reducing the capability to generate new technological knowledge. Intellectual property right regimes based upon exclusivity may increase the incentives to generate new technological knowledge but reduce the efficiency and the actual viability of the knowledge generation process. This risk is all the more relevant when the levels of knowledge fungibility are high. The costs of all barriers to the access to existing knowledge are larger the larger the scope of application of new technology. Compulsory licensing for technological knowledge, especially if it exhibits high levels of fungibility, can increase substantially the rate of generation of new technological knowledge.

Knowledge is characterized by the idiosyncratic characteristics of limited natural appropriability, non-exhaustibility, indivisibility and hence cumulability and complementarity. Its efficient generation requires at the same time its unconditioned use as an input and its full exploitation as an output. With too little appropriation, knowledge externalities are very high as well as the efficiency of the knowledge generation process, but the exploitation conditions are so bad and the incentives so low that nobody is willing to engage in the generation of knowledge. Too much appropriation reduces the uncontrolled leakage of knowledge spillovers, limits knowledge externalities and improves exploitation conditions but reduces the viability and the efficiency of the generation process.

In this context intellectual property rights play a central role. Intellectual property rights are necessary to enable the appropriability of technological knowledge, to favor its dissemination in the economic system and to prevent the systematic use of secrecy. The tuning of their characteristics is also necessary in order to reduce their negative consequences both in the product markets and in the knowledge markets. The exclusivity of intellectual property rights and specifically of patents is a crucial characteristic that deserves much attention and analysis. The reduction of the exclusivity of patents by means of the systematic use of compulsory licensing seems to yield positive effects both in product and in knowledge markets.

Generalized compulsory licensing enables a solution to the Arrovian paradox according to which it is at the same time true that the social surplus of innovation is larger in competitive markets than in monopolistic ones, but the incentives to innovate are stronger in the latter than in the former. The identification of the correct levels of royalties however is crucial to substantiate the effective use of this important institutional innovation.

Generalized compulsory licensing-cum-fair-royalties enables a combination of the need to secure the rewards to innovators with the goal of increasing as much as possible the social surplus stemming from the introduction of innovations. The analysis of the pay-off of the levels of royalties on the economics of knowledge generation enables an identification of the correct levels of royalties.

The identification of the dual role of technological knowledge as both the output of a generation process and an essential input into the recombinant generation of new technological knowledge makes it possible to make important progress towards the identification of the correct price for knowledge.

The fine tuning of intellectual property right regimes with their recombination and based upon the reduction of the exclusivity of patent legislation with the enforcement of royalty rights can become a major institutional innovation. The advantages of dynamic efficiency are maximized under the constraints of the appropriate conditions for the implementation of static efficiency. Generalized compulsory licensing gives a new functionality to the patent system as it becomes an essential tool for increasing the dissemination of technological knowledge and hence increasing its repeated use as an intermediary input and, at the same time, a mechanism that favors the working of the markets for knowledge securing appropriate rents to innovators and inventors.

Notes

1 This project has received funding from the European Union's Seventh Framework Programme for research, technological development and demonstration under grant agreement no. 266959. The author acknowledges also the institutional support of the Collegio Carlo Alberto and the University of Torino. This chapter elaborates and implements in a broader context some of the findings published in Antonelli (2013).

2 The quote is often attributed to Sir Isaac Newton. John of Salisbury in his *Metalogicon*, however, a few centuries before had attributed quite the same sentence to Bernard of Chartres: '*Dicebat Bernardus Carnotensis nos esse quasi nanos, gigantium humeris insidentes, ut possimus plura eis et remotiora videre,*

non-utique proprii visus acumine, aut eminentia corporis, sed quia in altum subvenimur et extollimur magnitudine gigantea.' (Salisbury, 1159: 167). It seems clear that Sir Isaac was actually standing on the shoulders of a giant.

3 The economies of density engendered by exclusive intellectual property rights have the consequence that the slope of the long-term cost curve for the generation of technological knowledge is negative for patent holders and positive for non-patent holders obliged to invent around (see Antonelli, 2007).

4 See Regulation (EC) No. 816/2006 of the European Parliament and of the Council of 17 May 2006 on compulsory licensing of patents relating to the manufacture of pharmaceutical products for export to countries with public health problems. See Chien (2003) and Scherer and Watal (2002).

5 Notice that the value of $R^\star$ is always on the upper substitutability boundary, while the combinations of K_n and R&D lying on the lower substitutability boundary are a suboptimal solution.

6 Patent offices might be given regulatory powers that enable them to reduce the unit royalty for patents that register very high levels of licenses.

7 To increase the levels of actual competition in the markets for products, the direct exploitation of a patent by the inventor with the creation of a firm should be impeded. The inventor however can retain the right to use the knowledge generated and patented to generate new knowledge. Clearly the inventor has the incentive to acknowledge the royalties paid to its own knowledge generating activity.

References

Antonelli, C. (1999), *The microdynamics of technological change*, Routledge, London.

Antonelli, C. (2005), Models of knowledge and systems of governance, *Journal of Institutional Economics* 1, 51–73.

Antonelli, C. (2007), Knowledge as an essential facility, *Journal of Evolutionary Economics* 17, 451–471.

Antonelli, C. (2011), The economic complexity of technological change: Knowledge interactions and path dependence, in Antonelli, C. (ed.) *Handbook on the economic complexity of technological change*, Edward Elgar, Cheltenham, pp. 1–62.

Antonelli, C. (2013), Compulsory licensing: The foundations of an institutional innovation, *WIPO Journal* 4, 157–174.

Antonelli, C. and Teubal, M. (2012), From the corporation to venture capitalism: New surrogate markets for knowledge and innovation-led economic growth, in Dietricht, M. and Krafft, J. (eds.), *Handbook on the economics and theory of the firm*, Edward Elgar, Cheltenham, pp. 545–560

Antonelli, C., Crespi, F., and Scellato, G. (2012), Inside innovation persistence: New evidence from Italian micro-data, *Structural Change and Economic Dynamics* 23, 341–353.

Arora, A., Fosfuri, A., and Roende, T. (2012), *Managing licensing in a market for technology*, NBER Working Papers, 18203.

Arrow, K.J. (1962), Economic welfare and the allocation of resources for invention, in Nelson, R. R. (ed.) *The rate and direction of inventive activity: Economic and social factors*, Princeton University Press for NBER, Princeton, pp. 609–625.

Arrow, K.J. (1969), Classificatory notes on the production and transmission of technical knowledge, *American Economic Review* 59, 29–35.

Arthur, W.B. (2009), *The nature of technology. What it is and how it evolves*, Free Press, New York.

Arundel, A. (2001), The relative effectiveness of patents and secrecy for appropriation, *Research Policy* 30, 611–624.

Ayres, I. and Klemperer, P. (1999), Limiting patentees' market power without reducing innovation incentives: The perverse benefits of uncertainty and non-injunctive remedies, *Michigan Law Review* 97, 986–1033.

Barton, J. (2000), Reforming the patent system, *Science* 287, 1933–1934.

Bessen, J. (2005), Patents and the diffusion of technical information, *Economics Letters* 86, 121–128.

Bessen, J. and Maskin, E. (2009), Sequential innovation patents and imitation, *RAND Journal of Economics* 40(4), 611–635.

Boldrin, M. and Levine, D.K. (2002), The case against intellectual property rights, *American Economic Review* 92, 209–212.

Boldrin, M. and Levine, D.K. (2013), The case against patents, *Journal of Economic Perspectives* 27, 1–22.

Buzzacchi, L. and Scellato, G. (2008), Patent litigation insurance and R&D incentives, *International Review of Law and Economics* 28, 272–286.

Calabresi, G. and Melamed, A.D. (1972), Property rules, liability rules and inalienability: One view of the Cathedral, *Harvard Law Review* 85, 1089–1128.

Chien, C. (2003), Cheap drugs at what price to innovation: Does the compulsory licensing of pharmaceuticals hurt innovation? *Berkeley Technology Law Journal* 18(3), 859–907.

Chien, C. (2008), Of trolls, Davids, Goliaths, and kings: Narratives and evidence in the litigation of high-tech patents, Santa Clara Law Digital Commons Faculty Publications.

Chien, C. (2011), Predicting patent litigation, *Texas Law Review* 90, 283–329.

Choi, J.P. (2010), Compulsory licensing as an antitrust remedy, *WIPO Journal* 1, 75–80.

Coase, R.H. (1960), The problem of social cost, *Journal of Law and Economics* 3, 1–44.

Cohen, W.M., Nelson, R.R., and Walsh, J.P. (2000), Protecting their intellectual assets: Appropriability conditions and why U.S. manufacturing firms patent (or not), NBER Working Paper W7552, http://www.nber.org/papers/w7552.pdf, accessed July 8, 2014.

Corbel, P. and Le Bas, C. (eds.) (2011), *Les nouvelles fonctions du brevet*, Economica, Paris.

Coriat, B. and Weinstein, B. (2012), Patent regimes and the commodification of knowledge, *Socio-Economic Review* 10, 267–292.

Cugno, F. and Ottoz, E. (2006), Trade secrets vs. broad patent: The role of licensing, *Review of Law and Economics* 2, 209–220.

Cugno, F. and Ottoz, E. (2011), Choosing the scope of trade secret law when secrets complement patents, *International Review of Law and Economics* 31, 219–227.

Dalle, J.M., David, P.A., den Besten, M., and Steinmueller, W. E. (2008), Empirical issues in open source software, *Information Economics and Policy* 20, 301–304.

David, P.A. (1993), Knowledge property and the system dynamics of technological change, *Proceedings of the World Bank Annual Conference on Development Economics*, The World Bank, Washington.

David, P.A. (2010), Mitigating 'anticommons' harms to research in science and technology: New moves in 'legal jujitsu' against unintended adverse consequences of the exploitation of intellectual property rights on results of publicly and privately funded research, *WIPO Journal* 1, 58–73.

Gilbert, R. and Shapiro, C. (1990), Optimal patent length and breadth, *RAND Journal of Economics* 21, 106–112.

Griliches, Z. (1979), Issues in assessing the contribution of research and development to productivity growth, *Bell Journal of Economics* 10, 92–116.

Griliches, Z. (1992), The search for R&D spillovers, *Scandinavian Journal of Economics* 94, 29–47.

Hagiu, A. and Yoffie, D.B. (2013), The new patent intermediaries: Platforms, defensive aggregators and super-aggregators, *Journal of Economic Perspectives* 27, 45–67.

Hall, B.H. (2007), Patents and patents policy, *Oxford Review of Economic Policy* 23, 568–587.

Heller, M.A. and Eisenberg, R. (1998), Can patents deter innovation? The anticommons in biomedical research, *Science* 280 (5364), 698–701.

Jaffe, A.B. and Lerner, J. (2004), *Innovation and its discontent: How our broken patent system is endangering innovation and progress and what can be done about it*, Princeton University Press, Princeton.

Lanjouw, J. and Lerner, J. (1997), The enforcement of intellectual property rights: A survey of the empirical literature, NBER Working Paper 6296.

Lerner, J. (2009), The empirical impact of intellectual property rights on innovation: Puzzles and clues, *American Economic Review* 99, 343–348.

Lerner, J. and Tirole, J. (2004), Efficient patent pools, *American Economic Review* 94, 691–711.

Lerner, J., Strojwas, M., and Tirole, J. (2007), The design of patent pools: The determinants of licensing rules, *RAND Journal of Economics* 38, 3, 610–625.

Llobet, G. (2002), Patent litigation when innovation is cumulative, *International Journal of Industrial Organization* 21, 1135–1157.

Machlup, F. and Penrose, E. (1950), The patent controversy in the nineteenth century, *Journal of Economic History* 10, 1–20.

Merges, R.P. (2004), Compulsory licensing vs. the three 'golden ladies' property rights, contracts and markets, *Policy Analysis* 508, 1–15.

Mokyr, J. (1990), *The lever of riches. Technological creativity and economic progress*, Oxford University Press, Oxford.

Mokyr, J. (2002), *The gifts of Athena: Historical origins of the knowledge economy*, Princeton University Press, Princeton.

Moser, P. (2013), Patents and innovation: Evidence from economic history, *Journal of Economic Perspectives* 27, 23–44.

Moser, P. and Voena, A. (2012), Compulsory licensing: Evidence from trading with the enemy, *American Economic Review* 102, 396–427.

Nelson, R.R. (1959), The simple economics of basic scientific research, *Journal of Political Economy* 67, 297–306.

Nelson, R.R. (1982), The role of knowledge in R&D efficiency, *Quarterly Journal of Economics* 97, 453–470.

Ostrom, E. (1990), *Governing the commons: The evolution of institutions for collective action*, Cambridge University Press, Cambridge.

Penin, J. (2005), Patents versus ex-post rewards: A new look, *Research Policy* 34, 641–656.

Reichman, J. (2000), 'Of green tulips and legal kudzu': Repackaging rights in subpatentable invention, *Vanderbilt Law Review* 53, 17–43. Reprinted in Dreyfuss, R. and Zimmerman, D. (eds.), *Expanding the boundaries of intellectual property*, Oxford University Press (2001), Oxford, pp. 23–54.

Reichman, J. and Maskus, K. (eds.) (2005), *International public goods and transfer of technology under a globalized intellectual property regime*, Cambridge University Press, Cambridge.

Reitzig, M. (2004), The private value of 'thickets' and 'fences', *Economics of Innovation and New Technology* 13, 443–456.

Romer, P.M. (1994), The origins of endogenous growth, *Journal of Economic Perspectives* 8, 3–22.

Salisbury, J. of (1159), *Metalogicon* (*The Metalogicon of Salisbury*), University of California Press, San Francisco (1955).

Scherer, F. M. (1977), *The economic effects of compulsory patent licensing*, New York University Monograph Series in Finance and Economics, New York.

Scherer, M. and Watal, J. (2002), Post-TRIPS options for access to patented medicines in developing nations, *Journal of International Economics and Law* 5, 913–939.

Schumpeter, J.A. (1942), *Capitalism, socialism and democracy*, Harper and Brothers, New York.

Scotchmer, S. (1991), Standing on the shoulders of giants: Cumulative research and the patent law, *Journal of Economic Perspective* 5 (1), 29–41.

Shapiro, C. (2001), Navigating the patent thicket: Cross licenses, patent pools, and standard setting, *Innovation Policy and the Economy* 1, 119–150.

Shapiro, C. (2010), Injunctions hold-up and patent royalties, *American Law and Economics Review* 12, 280–318.

Shavell, S. and Van Ypersele, T. (2001), Rewards versus intellectual property rights, *Journal of Law and Economics* 44, 525–547.

Stallman, R.M. (1998), *The GNU project*, O'Reilly, Sebastopol.

Tandon, P. (1982), Optimal patents with compulsory licensing, *Journal of Political Economy* 90, 470–486.

Trajtenberg, M. (1990), A penny for your quotes: Patent citation and the value of innovations, *RAND Journal of Economics* 21, 172–187.

Weitzman, M.L. (1996), Hybridizing growth theory, *American Economic Review* 86, 207–212.

Weitzman, M.L. (1998), Recombinant growth, *Quarterly Journal of Economics* 113, 331–360.

14

The dynamics of knowledge governance

Cristiano Antonelli

1. Introduction

The quality and the efficiency of the mechanisms that make possible the generation and the use of knowledge in the economic system are determinants that define its static and dynamic efficiency. Markets and hierarchies are unable to provide economic systems with the generation and use of the correct amount of technological knowledge because of its idiosyncratic characteristics as both an economic good and an economic activity with strong systemic and dynamic features. Knowledge governance is necessary in order to overcome these limits.

Knowledge governance consists of an array of institutional settings that combine and integrate market transactions, personal interactions and communication, ex-ante and ex-post coordination both among firms in the economic system and between them and the academic system. Knowledge governance is intrinsically dynamic. Its ingredients and mechanisms keep changing with the continual introduction of new modes. These dynamics exhibit the typical traits of an emergence process whereby the identification of limits and failures engenders a creative reaction that eventually leads to the articulation of a new mode.

In the rest of the chapter, Section 2 summarizes the idiosyncratic characteristics of knowledge from the viewpoint of economic theory, highlighting the risks of both market and government failure in the generation and dissemination of knowledge viewed as an emergent property of the system. Section 3 frames the analysis of knowledge governance and explores the intrinsic variety and dynamics of the changing modes of knowledge governance. The conclusions summarize the results of the study.

2. The generation and use of knowledge as a systemic economic activity

2.1 Beyond market failures

The economics of knowledge has made significant progress in the recent years. Four steps can be identified. Since the beginning, and for a long time, the economics of knowledge has focused attention on the identification of the limits of knowledge as an economic good such as limited appropriability, divisibility, and excludability, limited rivalry in use, low levels of exhaustibility, and intrinsic information asymmetries. High levels of risk and in some circumstances radical uncertainty seem to characterize both its generation and exploitation. Its generation can be anticipated only to a limited extent: both its timing and its content can be predicted up to a point. Its exploitation is affected by systematic information asymmetries: customers have major problems in assessing its actual economic value without the full disclosure that vendors are reluctant to provide because of the increasing risks of reducing appropriability.

As a consequence markets are unable to perform their classical function of selection and coordination of economic activities. The benefits stemming from knowledge's generation and the exchanges in the market place are at risk, together with their advantages in terms of division of labor and specialization, and the incentives for the allocation of resources to generate knowledge are missing. These characteristics account for substantial market failure and major risks of undersupply. Because markets are unable to allocate the correct amount of resources into the generation of technological knowledge, public intervention is necessary. The buildup of a huge public research system has found in this analysis its founding argument (Nelson, 1959; Arrow, 1962 and 1969).

This approach has been partly reconsidered when, in a second wave of analysis, instead of focusing upon the negative aspects – in terms of missing incentives – stemming from knowledge non-appropriability, attention has been directed upon the positive effects of the uncontrolled spillover of knowledge from 'inventors' to third parties. Technological knowledge generated by each firm displays relevant positive effects, as a 'non-paid external' production factor, on the production function of all the other firms. Technological knowledge, spilling in the atmosphere, becomes an externality and hence a resource for prospective recipients. Limited appropriability has both negative and positive effects (Griliches, 1979 and 1992; Adams, 1990; Link and Siegel, 2007).

Building upon the notion of technological spillovers, Griliches introduces the technology production function where technological knowledge enters as a production factor next to the traditional capital and labor. The technology production function exhibits increasing returns at the system level, but not at the firm level. The critical part of the output elasticity of technological knowledge that, added to the output elasticity of capital and labor, exceeds unity, benefits the system but not the individual firm because of the limited appropriability of the benefits of technological knowledge. In this approach external knowledge is an output-augmenting factor, not a necessary input. The new growth theory has built an array of growth models based upon the knowledge production function and the notion of free spillover, impinging upon the notion of knowledge externalities as if they were automatic and homogeneous across the system and agents could access and use freely with no cost the knowledge spilling from third parties (Romer, 1990 and 1994).

The growing empirical evidence provided by the applied economics of knowledge has progressively highlighted the limits of the new growth theory and made clear that the use of knowledge spillovers indeed exerts positive effects on the total factor productivity of other firms that, however, are far from being homogenous across time sectors and regions, and free. Heterogeneity across countries, regions, industries and agents in the benefits of spillovers is explained by the relevant costs of the dedicated activities that are necessary to actually access and use external knowledge. Knowledge does not fall from heaven to passive recipients and does not spill freely in the atmosphere, either. The prospective users of technological spillovers need to act intentionally in order to take advantage of them and be ready to bear specific costs of imitation and absorption (Mansfield, Schwartz and Wagner, 1981; Cohen and Levinthal, 1989 and 1990).

In this context the systems of innovation approach has stressed the crucial role of the structural characteristics of the system in which firms are located in the effective dissemination and actual use conditions of technological knowledge. At each point in time, each system is endowed with a given amount of technological knowledge characterized by high levels of heterogeneity and diversity, both with respect to its epistemic content and location. Moreover it is possessed by the myriad of agents that generated it and are generating it. As such the stock of existing technological knowledge is not only heterogeneous but also dispersed and fragmented: much technological knowledge is external to each agent. Relevant efforts are necessary to screen, identify, access and use it in the generation of new knowledge (Nelson, 1993). The structural characteristics of the system in terms of industrial and regional composition, the features of intermediary markets, the availability of research centers, both public and private, and the institutional context in which the division of labor and the exchanges that are necessary for the generation and the use of technological knowledge take place affect the actual amount of external knowledge that each firm can actually access. The structure of the innovation system qualifies and specifies the workings of knowledge pecuniary externalities. Technological change is localized by the context in which knowledge externalities make the necessary generation of technological knowledge possible (Antonelli, 2008c).

A third major step has been made with the change in focus of the analysis away from the characteristics of knowledge as a good, with the exploration of the knowledge generation process. The attention is now drawn to identifying the characteristics of the activities that lead to the generation of knowledge. The generation and use of new technological knowledge by each firm consists in the recombination of existing modules of knowledge that entails specific and dedicated activities and impinges upon high levels of complementarity with the knowledge generating activities in place in other firms and research centers, and cumulability with the existing stock of knowledge. Technological knowledge is at the same time an output and an input of the recombinant generation of new technological knowledge. Next to the stock of knowledge internal to each organization – because nobody can command all the existing knowledge – external knowledge is an essential – indispensable – input. Eventually knowledge enters the production function of all goods, as such it is twice an input: an input into the generation of new technological knowledge and an input into the generation of all the other goods. The firm is primarily a knowledge integrator able to bundle different sources of knowledge in order to generate new knowledge (David, 1993; Weitzman, 1996 and 1998; Saviotti, 2007).

In this context it became clear that external knowledge is strictly necessary to generate new technological knowledge. The generation of knowledge within firms is based upon recombination processes that are able to combine internal sources of knowledge with external ones, as well as codified knowledge with tacit competence acquired by means of learning processes. In this process existing knowledge is an essential input into the generation of new knowledge. No new knowledge can be generated without the use of existing knowledge (Langlois, 1999).

External knowledge is not supplementary – as in the Griliches approach – but complementary as it is strictly necessary. Its access and use are not free, but require dedicated activities that entail costs. More specifically, external knowledge that can be accessed either via market transactions or by spilling from its possessors can be used by third parties only after dedicated interactions have been implemented and structured. Hence relevant search and absorption costs are necessary to acquire and use it.

The acquisition of external knowledge from other firms entails absorption costs. The access and use of scientific knowledge generated by universities entails exploitation costs. The new understanding about the costs of external knowledge as a necessary input in the recombinant generation of new knowledge makes clear that knowledge externalities are pecuniary rather than pure. The actual levels of pecuniary knowledge externalities, i.e. the actual difference between the absorption and access costs to external knowledge and its reproduction costs, depend upon the quality of mechanisms that enable the access and use of existing knowledge, i.e. knowledge governance (Antonelli, 2008b and 2013).

A new chapter in this evolutionary sequence of analytical achievements is now in progress with the discovery of the irreducible tacit content of technological knowledge. Knowledge is characterized by its strong tacit content: agents know more than they can articulate. The tacit component may be eventually articulated and made partly explicit so as to decrease over time but cannot be eliminated (Polanyi, 1966). The identification of the key role of tacit knowledge and the consequent understanding of the central role of user–producer interactions in the access of users to the knowledge generated by third parties make clear that both knowledge cumulability and complementarity require the active participation of prospective users to access external knowledge and to use it in the generation of new technological knowledge (Von Hippel, 1988, 1994 and 1998).

Knowledge tacitness implies that dedicated interactions among agents are necessary to make its use possible not only when spillovers are concerned but also when transactions in knowledge markets and in knowledge intensive products are involved, as well as in the crucial interface between the scientific knowledge generated by the public research system and its recombinant transformation into technological knowledge. This is due to the fact that knowledge is characterized by a strong and irreducible tacit content such that it can be shared and disseminated only by means of personal relations. Knowledge is dispersed in a myriad of highly idiosyncratic local contexts of application with high levels of irreducible tacit content. Moreover it is codified in a variety of non-trivial codes and possessed by a myriad of heterogeneous agents with their own idiosyncratic characteristics and routines. Because of knowledge tacitness personal interactions are necessary to implement the division of labor and the related exchanges. This implies that existing external technological knowledge can be used in the recombinant generation of new technological knowledge only after dedicated resources have been invested to identify, retrieve and extract it from its original context, learn it and adapt it to a specific context of application. Most importantly it becomes clear that the use of external knowledge requires, occasionally, transactions, but always and mainly, dedicated and intentional interactions with the actual possessors (Cassiman and Veugelers, 2006).

In this context the grafting of recent advances in communication studies onto the new economics of knowledge makes it possible to analyze how knowledge governance and specifically knowledge externalities work with the tools of communication processes and hence to identify three distinct factors, i.e. the characteristics of a) emissaries, b) the recipients and c) the context in their successful use. Within this framework, the spillovers, which carry knowledge externalities, can be thought of as signals that reach their destination according to the characteristics of their sources, the context in which they take place, and the features of their possible recipients.

This framework makes it possible to articulate the view that the actual levels of effective knowledge externalities and their actual effects on the generation of new technological knowledge and the eventual introduction of technological innovations with its positive effects in terms of the increase of total factor productivity depend on the characteristics of a) the emissaries of knowledge spillovers, b) the recipients and prospective users and c) the context in which the use of external knowledge carried by spillovers takes place (Rochet and Tirole, 2003).

The grafting of the tools of communication studies helps to investigate the mechanisms of knowledge governance. Four basic issues can be identified. First, it is clear that the quality of communication channels and the context in which user–producer interactions take place exert a key role. The institutional context, in which knowledge interactions take place, can be characterized by high levels of transaction and communication costs that add on to knowledge absorption costs and reduce the levels of pecuniary knowledge externalities. Other contexts may ease the access to external knowledge for the high quality/low cost of knowledge interactions and transactions, perhaps thanks to high levels of trust and low levels of information asymmetries (Arrow, 1969).

Second, the characteristics of the users of external knowledge spilling in the context play a key role. Some recipients are more apt than others to take advantage of some types of techno-logical knowledge. Some recipients may be more able than others to interact with the emissar-ies of knowledge spillovers and/or to take advantage of the characteristics of the institutional context in which the emission and eventual absorption of knowledge take place (Graf, 2011).

Third, the characteristics of knowledge need to be taken into account. Knowledge is not all alike. Knowledge items differ in terms of appropriability, excludability, cumulability and fungi-bility. Knowledge items also differ in terms of their tacitness. Some knowledge items are more codified than others and as such increase the viability of the actual transmission and secondary use by new recipients for the generation of new technological knowledge. The characteristics of the knowledge generation process matter. Some kinds of technological knowledge have a strong content of generic knowledge acquired through pure research and are based upon deductive processes of generalization. The variety of knowledge items that contributes to the generation of new knowledge also differs: in some cases new knowledge uses a limited knowledge base, in others recombination includes a wide variety of knowledge items. The larger the variety is, the more relevant the quality of the context and the heterogeneity of actors participating in the process are (Saviotti, 2007).

Finally, the characteristics of emissaries are crucial. The characteristics of the knowledge spill-ing, once generated, its actual effects on the generation of new technological knowledge, and eventually its impact on productivity growth are influenced by the strategies of the firms in terms of intellectual property right regimes. The industrial sector of activity of the emissaries has important implications whether it is upstream or downstream. In the former case technological knowledge has a wider scope of possible application.

The organization of the production process of the emissaries plays a central role. Firms char-acterized by tight vertical integration are less likely to favor the emission of spillovers ready for use by new recipients. In contrast, firms that rely on a variety of other firms at different levels of the production process for specialized tasks and use platform types of industrial organization are more likely to spill technological knowledge that can be readily used by third parties. Systematic user–producer interactions qualify their production organization.

Research strategies of large corporations typically have a long-term horizon and as such their research projects are characterized by higher shares of pure research. For this reason, large firms are more likely to be the emissaries of technological knowledge with high levels of fungibil-ity and hence to affect the generation of new technological knowledge by third parties more directly because of the high levels of diversification. The intrinsic serendipity of the knowledge generation process of large corporations leads to niche innovations that are less likely to be directly developed and may instead actually be introduced by smaller firms that are part of the platform (Antonelli and Patrucco, 2014).

Most importantly, emissaries differ substantially in terms of sheer fungibility of the knowl-edge generated. Large firms fund and perform large research projects that rely on systematic interactions with the academic system and large public research centers (Howells *et al.*, 2012). Large research centers of large corporations have high levels of institutional and cultural proxim-ity with academic research. Academic scientists are likely to work for such organizations. Their academic career often started from research activities carried out in the large research laborato-ries of such corporations. Professional interactions based on repeated short-term consultancies characterize their academic life. Knowledge spilling from such firms has a much wider scope of application than knowledge spilling from focused research activities carried out by specialized firms with a narrow technological field of activity and high levels of specialization in applied and development research.

As much as communication takes place when the emission of signals is strong and clear, the context through which it is disseminated does not obstruct it and the recipients are equipped to actually receive it, knowledge spillovers do take place and make the generation of new technological knowledge possible and hence pecuniary knowledge externalities are found and make total factor productivity growth stronger, when the combination of characteristics of technological knowledge spilling and the features of emissaries of technological knowledge are favorable.

The appreciation of the role of technological knowledge as a complementary – i.e. necessary and indispensable – input into the generation of new technological knowledge changes the traditional framework of the market failure hypothesis. Because of the crucial role of knowledge as an indispensable input into the generation of new knowledge, its timely dissemination and access are in fact necessary to generate new technological knowledge. Hence the conditions for knowledge generation and knowledge exploitation are intrinsically in conflict. Because of the inefficient allocation of property rights, resources and incentives that is intrinsic to the twin nature of technological knowledge as an output and a necessary input into the generation of further knowledge, the system risks experiencing either the tragedies of knowledge commons in which opportunistic behavior leads to undersupply or the opposite tragedies of the knowledge anticommons where excessive exclusivity of intellectual property rights endangers the generation of new knowledge (Buchanan and Yoon 2000; Patrucco, 2014).

The characteristics of the knowledge generation process add on to the analysis of knowledge as a good and push to go beyond the notion of market failure so as to articulate a framework where the structural characteristics of the system and the interaction mechanisms among learning agents play a crucial role in supporting the generation and use of technological knowledge.

The new combined understanding of the complementary – as opposed to supplementary – role of external knowledge in the generation of new technological knowledge and hence in the introduction of technological innovations solicits the application of the tools provided by the Schumpeterian legacy articulated by Schumpeter (1947), with the notion of innovation as the outcome of a creative reaction – of agents caught in out-of-equilibrium product and factor markets conditions – conditional to the actual availability of knowledge externalities (Antonelli, 2015).

This new appreciation of the crucial role of the characteristics of the system in which the efforts to generate and use technological knowledge take place enables us to frame technological knowledge – and technological innovation – as an emergent property of a system. The amount of efforts of the individual agents involved in the generation of new technological knowledge plays a crucial role. The efforts of the learning agents, however, are not the single factor. For given levels of individual efforts, in fact, the amount of technological knowledge that can be generated at each point in time depends on the structure of the knowledge interactions and transactions within the system that make it possible to access and use the existing stock of knowledge as well as the current efforts of all other learning agents as indispensable inputs into the generation of new technological knowledge. Technological knowledge is an emergent property because its generation stems from the quality of interactions between the individual efforts and the structure of the system that makes knowledge externalities possible (Antonelli, 2009 and 2011; Martin and Sunley, 2012).

Here the quality of the governance mechanisms that implement the levels of compatibility between the necessary levels of appropriation and incentives with the necessary levels of accessibility of existing knowledge is crucial. From this viewpoint the amount of technological knowledge a system is able to generate and use effectively depends upon both the amount of individual efforts and the characteristics of the system, including its knowledge governance mechanisms.

In this context the structure of the knowledge interactions, communication and transactions and their governance mechanisms that shape the amount of technological knowledge being generated at each point in time is itself both an endogenous product and an endogenous factor of change. The generation of technological change, in fact, is the result of the amount of individual efforts, of the interaction between the learning efforts of the agents and among them and the structure of system and the cause of structural changes that affect the architecture of knowledge interactions and transactions. The notion of third order emergence accommodates nicely this dynamic. According to Martin and Sunley:

> third order emergence is an 'emergent phenomena and systems characterized by memory' where an amplification of high-order influences on parts is combined with a selective sampling of these influences which reintroduces the parts into different realizations of the system over time, imparting both continuity with and divergence from prior states of the system.
>
> *(Martin and Sunley, 2012: 341)*

The new appreciation of technological knowledge as a high-power emergent system property and of the pervasive role of the intertwined nest of transactions, interactions and communication in the generation, dissemination and use of knowledge raises new questions about not only the working of the markets but also the real effects of the direct participation of the State in the provision and dissemination of knowledge to the system. The failure of the market place has called for the direct intervention of the State in the supply of knowledge to the economic system that has led to the creation of a large academic system dedicated to the generation and dissemination of knowledge to firms. The new understanding of technological knowledge as an emergent property of the system puts under scrutiny the working of the academic system.

Table 14.1 summarizes the steps in the debate from which the notion of knowledge governance has gradually emerged.

2.2 Government failures in the academic generation of knowledge

In the Arrovian tradition of analysis the public research system based upon universities and public research laboratories is the basic remedy to the market failures of knowledge stemming from the limits of knowledge as an economic good. The new achievements of the economics of knowledge and the identification of the crucial role of knowledge externalities raise substantial concern about the possibility of a government failure, on the one hand, and about its actual role within the new systemic approach to understanding the dynamics of knowledge generation as an emergent system property, on the other. The enquiry about the conditions that are necessary to make the public research system effective parallels the enquiry about the limits of the market system in the generation of technological knowledge.

Universities receive public subsidies from the business sector, channeled by the state, to create incentives for talented people to specialize in the generation and publication of knowledge products. Academic chairs are the incentive to specialize in the generation and publication of knowledge. Scholars are willing to disseminate their knowledge by means of publications in order to get a chair. This elegant system design is functional as long as the loss of revenue by the business sector, in terms of levies paid to the state, is compensated by the amount of useful knowledge made available by means of publications and dissemination of human capital, including doctors able to support the dissemination and use of scientific advances by the business sector. The public system can remedy the failure of markets only if firms can actually access the advances in scientific knowledge made possible by the incentive mechanism called 'university' and use them to introduce innovations (Feller, 1990; Feldman, 1994; Geuna, 1999).

In the frame elaborated by Partha Dasgupta and Paul David the university becomes a triangular mechanism that integrates and in extreme cases substitutes the missing markets for knowledge.

Table 14.1 From knowledge spillovers to knowledge interactions

Key characteristics of knowledge	Assumptions about the role of external knowledge	Economic tools	Economic frame	Economic theory
Limited appropriability	External knowledge is a supplementary input in the generation of other goods	Technical knowledge externalities	Technology production function	New growth theory
Knowledge differs from information: screening, searching, absorption and learning are necessary to use it	Absorption costs are necessary in order to benefit from external knowledge as a supplementary input in the generation of knowledge	Pecuniary knowledge externalities	Innovation systems	Evolutionary approaches blending Marshall and Schumpeter
Knowledge generation as a recombinant process	External knowledge as a necessary and strictly complementary input in the generation of new knowledge	Network analysis to grasp the flows of external knowledge	Knowledge generation function	Knowledge as a systemic activity
The tacit component of technological knowledge is irreducible	Knowledge transactions-cum-interactions	Use–producer interactions and communication	The economics of knowledge governance and localized technological change	Knowledge as an emergent property

The public university system could be viewed as an institution that attempts to reconcile the conflicting incentives necessary to fund and perform the generation of knowledge with the incentives that are necessary to secure its timely dissemination and unlimited use as an input into the generation of further technological knowledge. This result is made possible by the role of the State as an intermediary that collects taxes from economic agents and proves funds to the university. The university in turn provides incentives to researchers to generate and disseminate knowledge (Dasgupta and David, 1987 and 1994).

Together with the creation of human capital embedded with frontier competences in advanced scientific fields, the publication is the key device that makes the mechanism work. The allocation of tenures and salaries in general by universities is based upon the proofs of the scientific capabilities of the researchers, as documented by authored publications in scientific journals that are able to screen and assess whether the contribution is actually relevant and original and as such able to increase the stock of knowledge. Publications perform the twin crucial role of carriers of the proof of the scientific capabilities and vectors of the new knowledge in the dissemination process. As soon as a scientific advance is published in a scientific journal it is also made publicly available to all possible users.

The institutional combination of publication-cum-taxation embedded into the university makes it possible to reconcile the conflicting incentives. On the on hand the prospect for the wages and eventually the tenure allocated by the university provides sufficient incentive to researchers to publish. The disclosure of the secret is compensated by the wages paid by the university. On the other hand economic agents are ready to accept the reduction in their income engendered by the dedicated taxation necessary to support the university as long as they are compensated by the economic value that can be extracted by the free access to the new knowledge generated by the scholars organized within the academic system.

In this frame the academic system is expected not only to make an efficient use of the public resources, but also to be able to provide useful knowledge to the rest of the system. Much attention has been paid to the issue of the internal efficiency of the public academic system: whether it was able to avoid internal inefficiencies stemming from inaccurate selection of the personnel or low levels of efforts by scholars. Little attention, instead, has been paid to the typology of knowledge being produced: whether it is actually useful for the pursuit of economic growth.

The issue of the disciplinary allocation of the resources made available by the State to the academic system becomes crucial. The public provision of resources to the academic system cannot be justified if the scientific knowledge generated by the academic system is of little use to and/or poorly used by the economic system. This may happen when and if the academic system allocates the public resources to scientific domains that are not clearly relevant for the economic system, or the communication from the academic system is not able to convey relevant scientific knowledge to the economic system, and of course when the economic system is not able to make the correct use of the relevant scientific knowledge made available by the academic system. The actual interaction between the academic and the economic system is clearly a major issue that has led to the implementation of different coordination and communication mechanisms (Cave and Weale, 1992; Antonelli and Fassio, 2014c; Antonelli et al., 2013).

The role of teaching activities traditionally associated with the academic institution requires further investigation. Tuition and creation of human capital are supposed to contribute economic activity as scientific knowledge is directly embodied in human beings that are expected to have higher levels of efficiency. The analysis of the exploitation conditions of scientific knowledge is crucial to grasp the problem of the matching between types of scientific knowledge and the needs of the business sector in terms of inputs into the generation of technological knowledge (Aghion et al., 2009).

The enquiry about the efficiency of the academic system, within this mode of knowledge governance, if it is directed mainly, if not exclusively, towards the assessment of its internal efficiency, as distinct from its general, or external efficiency, is not sufficient. Much effort, in fact, has been directed to identifying new metrics so as to assess the quantity and quality of scientific knowledge generated, in order to establish appropriate measures of the relationship between the amount of economic resources transferred to the academic system and the amount of scientific knowledge generated, but fail to identify the actual amount of technological knowledge that could be generated with it (Auranen and Nieminen, 2010).

From an economic viewpoint, however, it is not sufficient to assess the internal efficiency of the academic system in terms of the relationship between economic inputs and knowledge outputs. It seems in fact even more important to assess whether the amount of knowledge – efficiently – generated by the academic system is actually useful to support the generation of technological knowledge and hence economic growth (Jaffe, 1989).

Following this line of analysis it is clear that a major problem of coordination and composition may take place. The State provides subsidies to implement a public academic system as a remedy to the – possible – undersupply of knowledge, but the academic system insists on the generation of knowledge that is not useful for economic growth. The mismatch between the objectives of public policy and its effects may become gradually evident and the consensus for a public academic system would decline, even if the academic system were able to generate efficiently large amounts of knowledge with a limited amount of public economic resources.

As long as knowledge is regarded as a heterogeneous intermediary input, the effects of the efficiency in its generation are relevant not only internally but also externally. The exploration of the composition of the knowledge generated by the public academic system and the actual assessment of its external efficiency become necessary. Only when the levels of both internal and external efficiency are high is it possible to support the hypothesis that the supply of knowledge generated by the public academic system is actually able to match efficiently the 'correct' levels of the derived demand for knowledge by the rest of the economic system.

The two notions of internal and external efficiency would coincide only if knowledge were a homogenous good. As soon as we appreciate that knowledge is a composite bundle of a variety of different kinds of knowledge, the problem of the composition of the bundle becomes crucial. The academic system may generate too much of one kind of knowledge and too little of another. The system would suffer both from the undersupply of the relevant knowledge and the oversupply of knowledge that is not directly useful to support growth.

In order to assess whether the public academic system is actually working as a complementary mechanism able to compensate for the undersupply of knowledge by the private sector, it is in fact necessary to assess what the relationship is between the amount of public subsidies paid to the academic system and its revenue measured by the effects of knowledge externalities spilling from the academic system in terms of additional economic output.

In the market place prices signal the relative scarcity and abundance of goods and enable suppliers to modify their production. The indirect supply of knowledge to firms by the academic system via the spillover mechanisms suffers from the lack of signaling mechanisms that make it possible to gauge the relative abundance of some kinds of goods and the relative scarcity of others. As a consequence the academic system may keep producing types of knowledge that the economic system is not able to use and may not provide adequate supplies of knowledge that are necessary for economic growth.

The academic mechanism can work effectively as long as the basic functions of the market place in terms of selection of less efficient producers and allocation of activities across producers is efficiently mimicked. This requires that two conditions be fulfilled. First, the academic system is able to transform efficiently the resources transferred by the State into advances in scientific knowledge. The academic system in other words is able to cope with the pressure to use efficiently the resources made available by the taxpayer. Second, and most important, the bundle of knowledge activities that are performed by the academic system matches the needs of the business sector. As soon as we realize that knowledge can no longer be regarded as a homogeneous activity, but rather as a bundle of differentiated types of knowledge activities and specific knowledge items with highly idiosyncratic and peculiar characteristics, the problem of the matching becomes relevant (Antonelli, 2008a).

Scientific knowledge cannot be directly used as such for economic purposes: it requires dedicated efforts to obtain specific applications that yield an actual transformation. Technological knowledge consists in the application of scientific knowledge to economic purposes. The transformation of scientific knowledge into technological knowledge requires dedicated resources and entails costs. Profit-seeking agents are willing to bear the costs of the transformation of scientific knowledge into technological knowledge only if and when its exploitation conditions are viable (Mansfield, 1991 and 1995; Mansfield and Lee, 1996).

The transformation of scientific knowledge into technological knowledge is all the more difficult when the locus of generation differs from the locus of application. Scientific knowledge generated within the R&D laboratories of a corporation can be transformed into technological knowledge more directly. As a matter of fact technological knowledge generated for economic purposes reveals scientific contents as it consists of general laws that are valid also in other contexts different from the original ones. The transformation of scientific knowledge into technological knowledge useful for economic purposes is more complicated when the latter is generated for the sake of scientific advances in academia. A crucial issue of communication and interaction emerges (Dasgupta and David, 1987 and 1994; David, 1993).

The costs of the resources that are necessary to transform the new scientific knowledge into a technological one are subject to scrutiny and attentive examination by firms. As a consequence not all knowledge generated for the sake of scientific progress, spilling in the atmosphere, is actually perceived, appreciated and transformed by firms into technological knowledge. The notion of absorption costs – not only among firms but also and mainly between the academic and the economic system – plays once more a crucial role and acts as a strategic interface that must be taken into account when considering the possible effects of scientific knowledge upon economic progress (Stephan, 1996 and 2011).

It is no longer possible to believe that a large academic system generously funded by the State is sufficient to overcome the failure of markets in the correct generation and use of technological knowledge. The analysis of the relations between the academic and the economic systems in the generation and use of technological knowledge becomes as important and problematic as that of the knowledge relations among firms. The case for a government failure in generating and disseminating technological knowledge acquires growing consensus.

3. Knowledge governance

3.1. Ingredients and mechanisms

The new assessment of technological knowledge as an emergent system property stemming from the appreciation of the crucial role of external knowledge as a complementary – rather than supplementary – input into the generation of new knowledge and of its strong tacit content suggests that: a) a systemic approach to understanding the context in which technological knowledge is generated and used is necessary; b) the systems are defined in structural terms: their

structure, the types of relations among firms, and the relations of the public research infrastructure with the business sector matter in assessing the actual availability and the cost of secondary
use of existing knowledge; c) the connectivity of the system is crucial to grasp its capability
to make external knowledge accessible; and d) the systems keep changing over time. They are
not given once forever. Moreover their change is endogenous, as it is determined by the very
dynamics of the generation of technological change and its eventual use for the introduction of
technological innovations.

As soon as it becomes evident that knowledge, Jefferson's candle, can lighten wide spaces, provided a wise architecture of reflecting glasses is implemented, the role of the organization of the
system in which knowledge is generated, disseminated and used again and again and its analysis
acquire a new relevance. The levels of pecuniary knowledge externalities are strongly influenced
by the knowledge governance mechanisms that are at work between and among firms, house-
holds and institutions, within industries, regions and countries.

In the new context shaped by the analysis of the limits of knowledge as both an economic
good and a standard economic activity, the new understanding of the crucial role of the access
to external knowledge as an indispensable input into the generation of new knowledge, and
the new awareness about the limits of the public supply of knowledge, it becomes necessary to
elaborate the knowledge governance approach, i.e. a systemic and institutional approach aimed
at understanding – and possibly implementing – the mechanisms that organize the flows of
knowledge transactions-cum-interactions that enable agents to generate, disseminate and use
technological knowledge.

The working of an economic system requires that crucial functions such as the coordination,
selection, and the creation of incentives and rewards be performed. Perfect markets apply when
spot transactions among independent parties are able to identify the correct levels of prices
and quantities. In such circumstances market mechanisms provide: a) prices that convey all the
relevant information, b) full coordination among producers and consumers; c) correct levels of
incentives that are able to identify the appropriate number and size of producers; and d) fair
selection of the agents with the identification of the most efficient technologies and firms' strategies. Pure hierarchies are based on interactions and the organization takes all the responsibility
and undertakes the decision making that is able to provide the necessary coordination, selection
and reward of the agents that are part of it. Within pure hierarchies there are no transactions.
The notion of governance applies when and where both perfect markets and pure hierarchies
cannot be used. Governance applies where neither pure transactions nor pure interactions are
sufficient to convey all the information that is necessary for efficient decision making at the firm
level and effective coordination and selection at the system level. Governance mechanisms apply
when transactions are necessarily intertwined with interactions and neither one can be separated
and isolated without the loss of substantial information. Governance mechanisms apply to a
variety of circumstances where trust and cooperation integrate pure transactions and decentralized selection mechanisms that take into account the actual performances of agents integrate the
working of pure interactions.

Knowledge governance consists in the set of rules, procedures, modes and protocols that
organize the generation, dissemination and use of knowledge in an economic system, including the conditions that make possible the actual use for economic purposes of the scientific
knowledge supplied by the State by means of its direct support to the academic system. It
includes the variety of ex-post and ex-ante coordination mechanisms and types of relations
among economic agents comprising the extremes of pure transactions and pure interactions,
both among firms in the economic system and between them and the academic system created
by the State, with special attention to the wide spectrum of transactions-cum-interactions, that

qualify the knowledge connectivity of the system (Antonelli, 2006; Ostrom and Hess, 2006; Foss and Michailova, 2009).

Knowledge governance is intrinsically dynamic and endogenous. Its ingredients and mechanisms keep changing with the continual introduction of new modes as the result of collective processes aimed at complementing the inefficient working of the markets and overcoming the limits of the direct intervention of the State in the supply, dissemination and use of knowledge. This endogenous dynamic exhibits the typical traits of an emergence process whereby the identification of limits and failures engenders a creative reaction at the institutional level that eventually leads to the articulation of new governance modes (Ostrom, 2010).

Knowledge governance lies in between perfect markets and hierarchies and consists of different combinations among markets and hierarchies that include the working of the public research system. In order to implement the analysis of this variety of hybrid forms between markets and hierarchies – both in academic and the business systems – it is necessary to appreciate the distinction between: interactions, transactions, and ex-post and ex-ante coordination. Hierarchies are based upon pure interactions. Pure impersonal transactions take place in perfect, impersonal, spot markets. Coordination within hierarchies takes place ex-ante by means of managerial action ex-ante. Coordination in the market place takes place ex-post by means of selective inclusion and exclusion. When interactions prevail, coordination is typically ex-ante. When transactions prevail coordination takes place ex-post.

In between the two extremes it is possible to gauge a variety of hybrid forms based upon the mix between transactions and interactions that are placed in a continuum between pure transactions and pure interactions that combine ex-post and ex-ante coordination. The overlapping between interactions and transactions, and ex-post and ex-ante coordination identifies the crucial area of governance where the two forms of organizing the division of labor complement each other. This framework includes both the analysis of the relations among firms in the business system and between them and the academic system. This is an important step. So far the literature, in fact, has separated the analysis of the knowledge governance among firms and the knowledge governance of the relations between the academic and the economic systems. Both types of knowledge governance can be successfully analyzed with the same tools implemented in this analysis. In our analytical frame the relations of the academic system – including universities and other public research centers – with the rest of the system play a crucial role. It is in fact important to see whether the provision of public subsidies to the academic system is actually an effective tool to combat the undersupply of knowledge.

Knowledge governance can be regarded as a crucial component of the emergence of technological knowledge within an economic system. It is the result of self-organizing processes based upon feedbacks as well as trial and error processes by means of which a variety of heterogeneous agents discover new ways to organize the generation and dissemination of scientific and technological knowledge. In these processes agents are not alike: some actors may occasionally play a central role and become the pillars of the governance mode. Knowledge governance mechanisms are intrinsically dynamic and new modes emerge around key figures that alternate in assuming the role of pillars.

Knowledge governance does not have a single and static recipe. On the contrary it keeps changing the architecture or modes of integrating the different ingredients and mechanisms in a process that highlights the limits and failures of the existing mode and identifies new possible organizations of its ingredients and mechanisms. Its changing ingredients and mechanisms and its evolving architectures are fully endogenous as they are determined by the interactions of the agents that are part of the collective endeavor of the organization of the generation, dissemination and use of scientific and technological knowledge, both within institutions and in the market place.

Knowledge governance is a key component of the national systems of innovations as it plays a central role in assessing their actual capability to support the introduction of technological innovations. As a component of the emergence process that makes the reaction of firms creative and is part of the generation of technological knowledge, however, it is intrinsically dynamic and endogenous to the national systems. It keeps changing and adjusting to the dynamics of interactions and feedbacks that take place within the system among agents and between them and the institutions (Ostrom, 2010).

This approach enables us to elaborate an analytical framework that makes it possible to gauge the crucial elements of the different modes of knowledge governance observed diachronically in economic history and synchronically across countries and sectors:

A)   the public mode,
B)   the corporate mode,
C)   the new markets for knowledge,
D)   technological districts,
E)   venture capitalism,
F)   platforms.

These modes of knowledge governance rely upon different combinations of hybrid forms of transactions-cum-interactions and ex-post and ex-ante coordination that qualify the emergence of the different modes of governance that enable the generation and the use of knowledge in an economic system. Table 14.2 provides the general framework that can be identified when the two analytical dimensions of ex-post and ex-ante coordination are crossed with the corresponding combinations of transactions and interactions. The different modes of knowledge governance can be identified by the changing mix of coordination mechanisms and types of relations among the innovative efforts of agents and between them and the academic system.

In between the extremes of pure transactions based upon ex-ante coordination and interactions based upon ex-post coordination, the division of labor can take place by means of a variety of hybrid forms that are found at the crossing. These hybrid forms take place when transactions among partners take place in a context that is complemented by weak hierarchies and, alternatively, interactions are structured by means of transactions and ex-post sanctions. Transactions-cum-interactions are typically found within centered networks and especially structured platforms. In these hybrid forms the coordination that is necessary to achieve and integrate an efficient division of labor is defined ex-ante and implemented by managers and hierarchical control. Transactions-cum-interactions enable the parties to complement the specification of their obligations, including the prices and the quantities in the exchanges, with the inclusion of information based upon ex-post outcomes.

Table 14.2 Ingredients and mechanisms of the variety of knowledge governance modes

	Ex-ante coordination	*Ex-post coordination*
Interactions	Schumpeterian corporation	University–industry in the public mode
Transactions-cum-interactions	- academic outsourcing - long-term contracts - platforms - bankers as shareholders	- technological districts - networks - incomplete contracts - venture capitalism
Transactions	- credit financing - non-exclusivity of academic labor contracts	- KIPR (knowledge intensive property rights) - KIBS (knowledge intensive business services) - markets for knowledge

The use of scientific knowledge, generated by the academic system, by entrepreneurs to generate in turn technological knowledge and eventually introduce technological innovations embodied in new firms does not rely only upon the standard dissemination of new scientific knowledge by means of publications and training activities. Two important hybrid forms support the access to scientific knowledge by firms: a) the participation of scholars as consultants in knowledge transactions, and b) the participation of universities as institutions in the markets for knowledge. In both cases transactions-cum-interactions within the framework of long-term contracts make ex-ante and ex-post coordination compatible. While the first mechanism has received very little attention by the literature, the second is much studied. Let us consider them in detail.

The active participation of scholars in the professional markets for consultancy is an important mechanism for the dissemination of scientific knowledge and its use for the generation of technological knowledge. Here the non-exclusivity of academic labor contracts enables scholars to act as both employees of their academic institutions responding to ex-ante coordination mechanisms and independent consultants responding to ex-post ones. The dissemination of scientific knowledge is not left to publications, but is enforced by the private undertaking of scholars who are able to combine personal interactions with actual transactions in the markets for knowledge services. The non-exclusivity of academic labor contracts has been often regarded as a privilege. As such it is not allowed or has been reduced in some systems. Yet the evidence suggests that it is an effective mechanism to help the actual use of scientific knowledge by the economic system. It is not clear, however, to what extent the consultant-scholars are able to help directing the selection of academic work according to the results of their professional activities.

The identification of academic outsourcing is the result of a typical institutional branching. In this new context universities enter the markets for research services that firms can purchase. Academic outsourcing enables firms to substitute the intramuros performance of research activities with the purchase of qualified services provided on a contractual base by the academic system with positive effects in terms of selection and exploitation of selected skills and competencies. Academic outsourcing enables the academic system to integrate the public funding with additional funds. Most importantly, however, academic outsourcing enables the identification of the types of knowledge and the specific resources in terms of personnel that are actually more directly useful to the economic system. The market mechanism integrates the ex-post relations based upon the reading of journal articles and the hiring of trained personnel.

This analytical framework enables us to accommodate the crucial distinction between credit and equity financing and articulate the hybrid forms of finance for innovation. On the one hand, credit financing of innovation takes place in a typical ex-ante context. The banker cannot participate in the positive results of the new undertakings. The relationship between the banker and the entrepreneur takes place in an ex-ante context. On the other hand, equity financing is characterized by ex-post coordination. Equity owners can fully participate in the ex-post outcome of the new undertaking with their share of the profits. In between these extreme forms we can identify two hybrid forms of provision of funds to new innovative undertakings such as the evolution of bankers into shareholders that characterized Italian 'mixed banks' at the end of the nineteenth century (Gerschenkron, 1962), and venture capitalism where specialized firms combine the provision of equity together with systematic interactions based upon the provision of management and tight scrutiny of the conduct of the new firms (Antonelli and Teubal, 2008, 2010 and 2012). In both cases the provider of funds integrates transactions with interactions. Both the Italian 'mixed bank' and venture capitalists participated in the management of the start-up.

Transactions-cum-interactions associated with ex-post coordination are found in the 'spontaneous networks' that characterize cooperation within technological districts. Proximity within districts favors the emergence of tacit forms of cooperation based upon reciprocity procedures.

Here firms agree to share their knowledge on the basis of tacit reciprocity agreements such as in the case of the mobility of personnel where each firm believes that the losses associated with the exit of skilled personnel to other firms will be balanced by the entry of new skilled technicians coming from other firms, or in user–producer interactions that follow and integrate market transactions of capital and intermediary goods where downstream users are ready to support upstream producers and vice versa in the common undertaking of knowledge generation. Firms that do not comply with the tacit reciprocity agreements are progressively excluded from the flows of communication and interactions. Coordination takes place ex-post.

Transactions-cum-interactions associated with ex-ante coordination are typically found when knowledge transactions take place in the context of long-term and incomplete contracts: transactions are no longer impersonal and no longer take place in spot markets. In the long term, partners in trade are personally identified as transactions are repeated over time with the possibility of accommodating the emergence of new conditions and rectifying the specifications of the contracts. The platform is a knowledge governance mechanism that allows long-term coordination among partners that participate in a common innovative venture, contributing with their own specialization. Platforms are typically based upon incomplete contracts where the obligations of the parties involved concern the procedures rather than tangible goods. Renegotiation of the obligations is crucial to make the platform viable: the parties agree ex-ante to renegotiate their obligations according to a variety of possible outcomes. Coordination within networks, instead, is ex-post. Exclusion, according to the actual contribution of each partner, is always possible. The actual participation of each agent in the common pools of knowledge is not implemented centrally.

The hybrid forms so far identified are the basic tools elaborated to remedy the failures of both the markets and the hierarchy to organize viable knowledge governance. Knowledge governance shares all the characteristics of an emergent property of a system. Its changing ingredients and mechanisms and its evolving architectures within different modes are the endogenous result of systemic changes that are determined by the interactions of the agents that participate in the collective endeavor of the organization of the generation, dissemination and use of scientific and technological knowledge, both within institutions and in the market place.

The working of knowledge governance mechanisms, at each point in time, within each economic system, can be seen as the spontaneous result of a systemic process of polycentric governance where the interaction between a myriad of actors is able to implement the emergence of structured and viable modes of coordination that are able to complement or substitute the imperfect allocation of property rights. Knowledge governance mechanisms change across time as the architecture of their elements is the object of different forces that act in diverse relations and reflect the changing weights within the system. A variety of localized paths to organizing and managing at the system level the use of the existing technological knowledge as an input into the recombinant generation of new technological knowledge and the consequent introduction of total factor productivity enhancing technological change can emerge and consolidate, according to the institutional setting of each system and its path dependent characteristics (Antonelli, 2011).

3.2 The changing modes of knowledge governance

Economic history documents the emergence and implementation of different forms of knowledge governance. These different knowledge governance mechanisms can be considered alternative institutional solutions that have emerged through historic time by means of recursive processes of interactions and structural changes to better organize the complexity of knowledge interactions and support the creation and exploitation of knowledge externalities according to the changing knowledge infrastructure of the system.

The notion of emergence applies nicely to understand the dynamics of governance mechanisms. Agents experience the limits of the existing governance mechanisms and try and react with a variety of attempts and efforts in different directions. A typical selection process of the different institutional devices elaborated in the process takes place. Occasionally, some complementarity among the different undertakings is identified. Agents act so as to reinforce the coherence and consistence of their attempts activating a convergence of partial solutions. Specific components of the previous governance mode contribute to the new one in a different institutional architecture. Eventually the 'dominant design' of a new governance mode consolidates and provides the new architectural and institutional framework. In this collective process some agents play a central role and are able to fix the interface standards and the institutional procedures that manage the interactions among the agents and make them more effective with respect to the previous governance modes. As a consequence it is clear that, at each point in time, a variety of governance mechanisms is at work in parallel in different contexts, and different governance modes emerge in different countries.

The public mode

The pillar of the public mode of knowledge governance is the public research system implemented by the State. The public research system is articulated in an academic system complemented by an array of specialized public research centers. The mission of the university is basic research and teaching. The activity of the specialized public research centers is mainly concentrated on applied research and technology transfer. The generation of scientific and technological knowledge, in this governance mode, is almost completely implemented by public agencies. The public research system provides knowledge externalities by means of publications and skilled personnel with a specific competence in conducting research. The knowledge generated by the public research system is crucial for firms as it is the basic input for their generation of technological knowledge. Firms are active in the development stage and rely upon the public research system for both pure and applied research.

A major source of strength of the public mode of knowledge governance is provided by the peculiar role of scholars who are active both in the generation of scientific knowledge and – as private consultants – in its dissemination and actual application in the generation of technological knowledge. The non-exclusivity of most academic labor contracts allows the entry of scholars into the markets for professional services aimed at guiding the exploitation of the scientific knowledge generated in academia by private firms. Knowledge transfer between the public research and the business systems is made effective by the direct participation of scholars as service providers that assist in the selection and use of the new scientific knowledge as a source for the generation of technological knowledge conducted by firms. The activity of scholars as consultants secures the rapid transformation of relevant scientific knowledge into new technological opportunities. The lack of an institutional framework, however, limits the capability of the academic system to benefit from the feedbacks of the business sector as a guidance mechanism to direct the allocation of public resources across disciplinary fields.

The coordination between the generation of scientific knowledge by the academic system and its use by entrepreneurs as an externality to generate technological knowledge, however, takes place ex-post. The academic system is fully and exclusively responsible for the choice of the fields of activity. The allocation of resources among the many possible fields of investigation is decided exclusively by the academic community. The research is performed in the fields that have been decided by the academic community and the results are eventually disseminated and possibly used by firms. In this mode of knowledge governance there is a clear sequence with very little room for the working of feedbacks. The academic system may insist on the generation of scientific knowledge that is little used by firms to generate technological knowledge.

Next to the public research system, this mode relies upon the combination of two basic ingredients: the entrepreneur and the innovative banker. In the public mode of knowledge governance the size of firms is typically small. Natality, entry and innovation are closely intertwined. Entrepreneurs spot new ideas and enter the product markets by means of innovations. The creation of the new firm takes place after the generation of new knowledge. The entry of new firms relies heavily on the provision of credit by the banking system. Ownership and management overlap. A clear division of labor takes place between the entrepreneur and the new firm: the first performs the generation of new knowledge while the second is responsible for its economic exploitation.

Small innovative bankers play a crucial role in providing entrepreneurs with the indispensable financial resources that are necessary to fund the new ventures. The banker suffers from the intrinsic asymmetry of credit financing to risky ventures: he can participate only in the failures, but not the successes. As a matter of fact the innovative banker can play a central role in the entrepreneurial mode only when the levels of risks associated with new ventures are low.

The provision of credit to entrepreneurs in fact is made especially difficult by the intrinsic asymmetry by which the banker cannot participate in the extra profits of new risky ventures while is fully exposed to their failures. The consequent increase of interest rates necessary to compensate for the failures risks in turn increasing the rate of failures and hence the losses of the banker. The intrinsic asymmetry of the innovative banker who can only participate in the losses and cannot participate in the profits of the entrepreneurs that have received the credit is all the more dangerous when the innovative banker is not able to reduce major inclusion errors: the larger share of 'lemons', the higher the negative consequences of the credit asymmetry.

The evidence about the working of credit supplied by the innovative banker suggests that the chances to fund radical innovations are large and hence the risks of major omission errors are low as innovative bankers can rely upon an extended network of talented experts that are able to provide reliable suggestions and advice about the actual quality of the technological knowledge that lies at the heart of the new ventures. Innovative bankers able to implement systematic interactions with a wide spectrum of reliable experts are able to spot the opening of new technological fields and hence are better able to fund new radical innovations.

The combination of credit and equity typical of the 'mixed bank' enables bankers to better monitor the new undertakings and to participate not only in their possible losses but also in their profits, but risks reducing their ability to scrutinize the evolution of the new firm. Because of the dynamics of sunk costs associated with equity, the mixed bank risks becoming a prisoner of its own commitments reducing its capability to stop providing additional credit and to exit a failing undertaking in time.

The historic implementation of the public mode of knowledge governance exhibits a major weakness in the poor assessment of the actual levels of efficiency of the public research system. As soon as it becomes apparent that knowledge is not a homogenous bundle of standardized items it also becomes clear that its heterogeneity risks undermining the working of the elegant Arrovian mechanism and raises a major problem of coordination between the supply of knowledge by the academic system, its implementation by the public research centers and the actual content of the derived demand expressed by the rest of the economic system (Rosenberg and Nelson, 1994).

In this mode of knowledge governance the actual provision of effective knowledge externalities works if the firms are able to implement dedicated strategies aimed at benefitting from the academic spillovers flowing from the public research system. The business sector is expected to make the necessary efforts to enhance the complementarity between the internal research strategies and the academic spillovers, organizing an actual division of labor between the public sources of knowledge and its internal applications. The academic system is not expected to try to direct the generation of scientific knowledge towards the fields that are most likely to engender the eventual transformation into technological knowledge at that time and in that specific context (Etzkowitz and Leydesdorff, 2000).

The public mode of knowledge governance suffers from four main limits: a) the academic community enjoys a full and unconstrained freedom to direct the use of the public funds in the fields that are considered more appealing for the pursuit of the generation of scientific knowledge without any accountability; b) the innovative banker cannot participate in the success of the new undertakings while is exposed to their failures; and c) the size of firms is too small to perform efficiently the generation and exploitation of technological knowledge.

The public mode of knowledge governance is quite effective in newly industrializing countries able to use an advanced public research system as a tool to absorb scientific and technological knowledge from abroad. The direction of the research activity is in fact well guided by the current advances of the scientific and technological frontier worldwide.

The public mode of knowledge governance can be very effective when the State is able to act as an entrepreneur, targeting new emerging technologies and coordinating the activity of various public institutions towards a common goal (Mazzucato, 2013). Public procurement plays an important role in this mode of knowledge governance. The emphasis on the direct supply of knowledge via the public research system is coupled with the intentional use of public procurement as a dedicated tool able to organize sophisticated platforms of innovative suppliers. The competent demand for advanced products becomes an effective tool to promote the generation, dissemination and use of technological knowledge. Public agencies participate directly in promoting, sponsoring and guiding the creation of organized groups of firms that cooperate in the provision of new, advanced products. Ex-ante coordination is combined with ex-post assessment of the results. Transactions within the groups are systematically implemented, with repeated interactions implemented by means of long-term open contracts (Edquist and Zabala-Iturriagagoiti, 2012).

The corporate mode

The corporate model of knowledge governance, as the major institutional innovation introduced in the US in the twentieth century, can be considered the result of a radical attempt to overcome the limits of the public mode of knowledge governance. It was first identified by Joseph Schumpeter (1942).

The corporate mode is characterized by large corporations being able to rely upon internal financial markets and hierarchical interactions in the generation of new technological knowledge. Corporations were able to engage in the systematic performance of research activities with the creation and active implementation of intramuros research and development laboratories, hiring skilled scientists and implementing long-term research programs. The strength of the corporate model lies in the capability to: a) generate efficiently new knowledge, building upon the accumulation of competence based upon learning processes and its recombination with formal research activities, b) valorize internally stocks of existing knowledge with systematic strategies of knowledge exploitation based upon diversification, c) rely upon the internal availability of funds, and d) acquire competences to screen the different research avenues.

Diversification provided, at the same time, the opportunities to increase the scope of application and to increase the breadth and diversity of knowledge units that could enter the recombinant generation of new knowledge processes. The corporate model appeared for quite long time especially effective in the organization of internal financial markets where extra profits stemming from the previous generation of knowledge and the related introduction of innovation could overcome the serious problems of financial markets and, specifically, the banking system in the provision of credit to fund the generation of new knowledge and the introduction of innovations. The effective intramuros management of the interactions between production, marketing, internal finance and research seemed for quite a long time the best way to secure the correct allocation and direction of resources for the generation and use of appropriate quantities of knowledge. The success of the corporate model of knowledge governance put the university aside, pushing it towards specialization in the performance of didactic activities, on the one hand, and basic science, on the other. The bulk of applied research was mainly implemented by corporations, intramuros.

Research strategies of large corporations have typically a long-term horizon with high levels of serendipity. For this reason, large firms are more likely to be especially successful in the generation and exploitation of technological knowledge with high levels of fungibility because of the high levels of diversification. Diversification makes it possible to take advantage of the intrinsic serendipity of the knowledge generation process. The exploitation of the 'unexpected' results of long-term R&D activities would be much more difficult for small companies (March, 1991).

In the corporate mode of knowledge governance the academic system plays much a weaker role with respect to the public mode. Corporations play a central role in the generation of both technological and scientific knowledge. In the public mode of knowledge governance the generation of technological knowledge is made by the entrepreneur able to take advantage of the scientific knowledge provided by the public academic system and the firm is eventually created to exploit it. In the corporate mode, generation and exploitation are integrated within the corporation. The coordination between the generation of scientific and technological knowledge takes place in parallel.

Large firms fund and perform large research projects that are characterized by large shares of pure research that rely on systematic interactions with the academic system and the large public research centers. Large research centers of large corporations have high levels of institutional and cultural proximity with academic research. Academic scientists are likely to work for such organizations. Their academic career often started from research activities carried out in the large research laboratories of such corporations. Professional interactions based on repeated short-term consultancies characterize their academic life. Knowledge spilling from such firms has a much wider scope of application than knowledge spilling from focused research activities carried out by specialized firms with a narrow technological field of activity and high levels of specialization in applied and development research.

The higher level of coordination between the generation of scientific and technological knowledge is one of the elements of strength of the corporate model. In this mode the corporation participates directly in selecting the fields of investigation for the generation of scientific knowledge that are more likely to benefit the eventual generation of scientific knowledge. The inefficiency of the ex-post coordination of the public mode is limited. Intramuros the interactions between scientific and managerial personnel are much stronger and systematic with much higher levels of dissemination, scrutiny and feedback (Mowery, 2010).

The working of internal financial markets is the second element of strength of the corporate mode. Corporations fund directly the generation of scientific and technological knowledge and its exploitation. In so doing they can participate directly not only in failures but also in all the economic benefits of the successful ventures. The extra profits of the innovations that survive the selection can compensate for the losses of the failures and actually feed further investments in R&D activities. Equity is not affected by the intrinsic asymmetry of credit.

The limits of the corporate mode of knowledge governance, however, become evident as soon as two new factors are identified. Corporations indeed are able to minimize commission errors but are exposed to severe omission ones. Omission errors stem from the 'not invented here syndrome' and take place because of the limited span of competence that can be found within the internal corporate markets. Corporate experts are better able to screen and select incremental innovations rather than new areas of technological knowledge that emerge in unrelated fields that are far away from the competence acquired by means of learning processes. Omission errors are all the more frequent when a discontinuity in the knowledge generation processes takes place.

The new understanding of the 'burden of knowledge' helps in grasping another major limitation of the corporation. As it is well known since the much cited sentence of Sir Isaac Newton according to which to generate science it is necessary to stand on giants' shoulders, knowledge indivisibility and cumulability make it necessary to command the stock of existing knowledge in order to generate new knowledge. After much appreciation of the positive effects of the repeated use as an input of the knowledge generated as an output in terms of long-term increasing returns, the negative effects in terms of the burden of knowledge are acknowledged. The purchasing cost of skilled labor able to command the increasing stock of knowledge increases more than proportionately. Increasing returns with increasing input costs identify a maximum size. The Arrovian limits of organizations apply to corporations also in the generation of technological knowledge (Arrow, 1974; Jones, 2009).

The discontinuity brought about by the introduction of the new flood of information and communication technologies and later of biotechnologies brought attention to the limitations of the corporate model. The corporate model seemed more and more unable to grasp the new technological opportunities. The main limitation of the corporate model was found in the resistance and lack of interest with respect to the external sources of technological knowledge. The corporation appeared to be afflicted by the not-invented-here syndrome and the high costs of absorption of external knowledge. The corporate model excelled in directing technological change towards incremental advances, but failed in taking advantage of new radical scientific and technological breakthroughs. When the direction of technological knowledge exhibits significant discontinuities and sudden changes in direction, the corporate model can suffer dramatically. The main weakness of the corporate model can be identified in the high risk of errors of exclusion. Corporate managers are better able to select incremental innovations that build upon internal knowledge cumulability, avoiding the inclusion of 'lemons', but less ready to grasp new opportunities that emerge in scientific fields that are far away from their competence that is based too much upon experience acquired by means of internal learning processes (Chandler, 1977).

The decline of the corporate model as the core of an effective knowledge governance mechanism and the need to extend the scope of the search process so as to include new emerging opportunities have provided the push to try to implement alternative modes of knowledge governance, including the return to a public mode strengthened by the active role of the State with a competent procurement (Mowery, 2009).

In the US after the ICT revolution an array of distributed modes viable for science based technologies have been consolidating. The European evidence suggests that the new mode also applies successfully to skill intensive manufacturing activities concentrated geographically within technological districts (Chesbrough, 2003; Chesbrough et al., 2006). This mode builds upon a variety of complementary mechanisms: a) the new role of the markets for knowledge; b) regional proximity as a mechanism of systematic implementation of structured procedures of transactions-cum-interactions among the main players; c) the role of scientific entrepreneurship coupled with financial markets; and d) the emergence of platforms. Let us analyze them in turn.

The new markets for knowledge

The appreciation of the tacit and sticky aspects of technological knowledge favors the creation of new markets for knowledge embodied in knowledge intensive business services (KIBS).

In this mode KIBS makes the commodification of knowledge easier and easier because knowledge is sold and bought as a dedicated service. KIBS specialize in the storage of knowledge and in its continual application to a variety of specific conditions. Tight user–producer interactions parallel market exchanges of services between specialized producers upstream and downstream users in manufacturing industries. KIBS become the institutional setting for the actual implementation of the knowledge generation function as distinct from the knowledge production function. The generation of new knowledge takes place upstream in the new KIBS industries. Its application takes place within the technology production function of downstream manufacturers. The growth of knowledge intensive business services can lead to the emergence of a knowledge industry (Probert *et al.*, 2013).

Intellectual property right regimes play a crucial role in the implementation of this model of knowledge governance. The clear definition of property rights is, in fact, necessary for the indirect exchange of the existing units of technological knowledge (Gallouj and Windrum, 2009).

Since the late twentieth century the new specialization of advanced countries is more and more based on the large array of KIBS industries that provide their services to the global markets. Their competitive advantage stems from the large stock of technological knowledge they can command and implement, building upon the close interactions with the users of their technologies (Antonelli and Fassio, 2011, 2014a and 2014b).

In this context the relations between the business sector and the university are increasingly characterized by academic outsourcing. Academic outsourcing is based upon transactions-cum-interactions that lead to the private and selective funding of academic research. Academic outsourcing within the framework of long-term contracts is used more and more as an effective tool to better identify and valorize the actual relevance of the academic output and to shorten the time lags between inventions and innovations. By means of academic outsourcing firms can take advantage of the existing academic infrastructure to perform research projects that in the corporate mode of knowledge governance used to be realized intramuros. By means of academic outsourcing firms can select the best scholars in each field and hire their research capabilities for a limited period of time. Systematic transactions-cum-interactions between the business sector and the academic system enable coordination to take place ex-ante rather than ex-post (Etzkowitz and Leydesdorff, 2000; Antonelli *et al.*, 2010).

Academic outsourcing makes possible the ex-post coordination of the generation of scientific and technological knowledge. This increases the effective transfer of dedicated scientific knowledge from the academic to the economic system with clear advantages in terms of better division of labor, reduction of redundancies and better exploitations of talents and skills.

The enhancement of the direct relations between scholars as individuals, universities as institutions, firms and in general the new academic outsourcing based upon transactions-cum-interactions between university and industry may help directing the scientific work towards the pursuit of specific goals favoring more effective ex-ante coordination, but may risk inhibiting the necessary freedom of scholars to explore wider and potentially more useful areas of investigation. It is clear that the excess reliance of academic activity on rent-seeking funding may compromise the central role of the university in the pursuit of knowledge advancement in unknown directions, the dissemination of advanced knowledge and the provision of knowledge spillovers to the rest of the system.

The technological district

The emergence of the technological district can be identified in southern Europe, including Italy and Spain in the second part of the twentieth century. The geographic agglomeration of small firms specializing in complementary activities became a viable alternative to the corporation. The geographical concentration of firms specializing in different layers of the same value chain is the prerequisite for the emergence of the technological district. The vertical complementarity strengthened by proximity enhances the dissemination of tacit knowledge and its generation along the vertical relations within the value chains between users and producers.

Geographical proximity helps reinforcing trust and favors personal interactions among firms. Firms are specialized in a narrow range of products. In this mode of knowledge governance, high levels of agglomeration within technological and industrial districts favor the dissemination of knowledge among firms. Proximity favors the recurrence of interactions, because it reduces the risks of opportunistic behavior and increases the opportunities for reciprocity. Proximity helps structuring informal cooperation within 'democratic' networks with low levels of hierarchical stratification. Proximity within technological districts favors the mobility of skilled personnel from one firm to another increasing the speed of dissemination of new technological knowledge and its scope of application to an array of complementary activities (Özman, 2009).

Repeated interactions based upon co-localization between the producers of capital and intermediary inputs and their users provide the opportunity to enhance mutual learning based upon the bilateral communication of problems experienced by the users and the continual introduction of improvements and innovations. Users challenge producers to solve problems and to take opportunities from their own learning processes. Systematic user–producer interactions within localized value chains make it possible to generate knowledge upstream by means of the recombination of upstream codified knowledge with the tacit knowledge accumulated in downstream activities. More generally, systematic and localized user–producer interactions make it possible to combine learning-by-doing in upstream activities with learning-by-using in downstream ones (Antonelli et al., 2011).

Technological districts differ from the traditional Marshallian districts. Marshallian districts are characterized by high levels of homogeneous specialization within a single industry. Technological districts on the other hand are characterized by the co-localization of different industries that are tightly related by vertical complementarity. Technological districts are often the result of a historic evolution of Marshallian districts after the entry of new upstream producers. In technological districts user–producer transactions-cum-interactions along value chains play a crucial role in providing the opportunity for the entry of new innovative firms in the emerging intermediary markets that stem from the increasing levels of division of labor. User–producer interactions enable us, in fact, to identify new specialized activities that increase the roundaboutness of the production process and qualify the market transactions that take place in new layers of the vertically integrated sectors (Von Hippel, 1988, 1994 and 1998).

Proximity plays a crucial role not only with respect to the dissemination of and access to tacit knowledge but also with respect to the access to financial resources for innovation. In the technological mode the provision of funds for innovative undertakings of both incumbent and newcomers rests on credit. The small size of firms and the lack of a financial market limit the use of both internal funds and equity to finance innovative activities. The innovative banker is strictly necessary to fund new ventures and new investment. Proximity helps by increasing transparency and reducing information asymmetries and the risks of opportunistic behavior. Proximity helps by strengthening the personal interactions between bankers and investors. Local bankers know personally the business community and are an integral part of it. The local banker can perform the crucial role of 'innovative banker' because of the trust and information symmetries built upon proximity and co-localization within the district. The provision of credit to innovators takes again the peculiar form of a transaction-cum-innovation. The provision of the credit – a financial transaction – could not take place without the support of systematic interactions between creditors and debtors. The centrality of local banks in this mode of knowledge governance has important consequences for the structure of the banking industry. Excess concentration with the creation of large financial corporations reduces the autonomy and competence of the local banker and puts at risk the effective selection and implementation of new viable entrepreneurship and the access to credit of small incumbents.

Advanced technological districts are more and more able to stretch their value chains beyond the limits of the manufacturing industry and exhibit a clear trend towards the active inclusion and participation of knowledge intensive business services (KIBS). Their inclusion in the local value chains represents a major step in the evolution of technological districts. Local value chains were originally formed within the manufacturing sectors, with the producers of machinery and capital goods upstream and the producers of final goods downstream. The growth of KIBS provides technological districts with the opportunity to stretch the value chains further upstream to service industries that are able to produce knowledge intensive activities for downstream users. Local KIBS in turn have the opportunity to take advantage of knowledge interactions with co-localized users. This evolution of the KIBS industries, within technological districts, favors their geographic concentration, but contrasts with their industrial concentration. In countries and regions where the technological districts are able to evolve towards the inclusion in their localized value chains of knowledge intensive services, the new service industries exhibit the typical traits of the district such as the small size of the firms and their geographic dissemination. Small KIBS firms fail to grow beyond the borders of their own districts while large KIBS firms often record unsuccessful entries in existing technological districts. Once more the crucial role of personal interactions supported by proximity is at the same time the base and the constraint on their success.

In the original technological districts mode of knowledge governance, academics play an important role as private consultants that favor the dissemination of new scientific breakthroughs and their use in implementing new technological knowledge. The universities and the research centers, as institutions, experience low levels of exchange with the business community. Hence the contribution of the public research infrastructure is indirect and concerns the dissemination more than the generation of new knowledge. In the new updated organization of the technological district mode local universities are more and more active in the direct and institutional provision of knowledge services to the firms co-localized. In this case universities try to solicit demand for their services with the creation of local interface structures that help the small firms of the district to interact with the academic system.

The coordination among the innovative undertakings of different firms, however, takes place ex-post. Within technological districts there is no a central agency that plans the complementarity between the research agenda of the different innovative agents: coordination may fail or succeed.

Venture capitalism

In the new distributed mode venture capitalism plays a central role. Venture capitalism has changed the structure of interactions and transactions in financial markets with important effects upon the capability to fund, select and exploit new technological knowledge. Venture capitalism itself is a major institutional and organizational innovation that has activated a new mechanism for the governance of technological knowledge. Venture capitalism, as well, is the result of systemic dynamics where a variety of complementary and localized innovations introduced by heterogeneous agents aligned and converged towards a collective platform. The new mechanism favors the creation of new science based start-ups and has led to the creation of new, dedicated financial markets. These new financial markets, specialized in the transactions of knowledge intensive property rights, combine the advantages of polyarchic decision making in screening and sorting radical innovations with the direct participation in the profits of new outperforming science-based start-ups typical of the corporate model (Antonelli and Teubal, 2008, 2010 and 2012).

In the new mode of distributed knowledge governance the role of the new equity based finance, however, marks a major difference. So far the provision of funds for the exploitation of scientific knowledge was based either on the credit provided by banks or on the internal funds made available by extra profits within corporations. In the new model, exploitation is based upon equity provided by venture capitalism and, eventually, by means of mergers and acquisitions of the start-ups publicly traded in the stock exchange markets by corporations. This difference has major implications in terms of the viability of the screening process. The university provides a large and differentiated supply of new possible avenues for extracting technological knowledge from a variety of scientific advances. The structured provision of equity, organized on venture capitalist companies and sequentially on the working of the stock exchanges, increases the chances of a polycentric inclusion of the most promising areas for technological exploitation. The crucial difference with respect to the two previous funding systems – credit and corporate equity – is found in the capability of venture capitalism to combine the benefits of both increasing the chances of inclusion of radical innovations – typical of the credit system – and yet avoiding the asymmetries of creditors which can only participate in losses with no tools to share the profits of the successful ventures, with the advantages of corporate equity that bears the risk of the losses but can cash the profits (Stiglitz and Weiss, 1981).

Besides the clear differences with respect to the funding mechanisms, the new distributed model of knowledge governance puts again the university–industry relations at the center of the generation of new knowledge. This mode recognizes the central role of universities as the main locus for generation of both scientific and technological knowledge, specifically for its wide range of search directions that can be implemented and assessed. Countries and regions with a strong academic and scientific infrastructure have an advantage in the introduction of science-based technologies especially when and where the start-up–venture capitalism mechanism can complement the academic generation of knowledge as an effective tool for its economic exploitation and further dissemination (Chesbrough, 2003).

Scientific entrepreneurship becomes a complementary communication mechanism between university and industry. Academic entrepreneurship supported by the screening assistance and financial participation of venture capitalism maximizes the capillarity of the search for relevant units of existing knowledge. Knowledge dispersed and fragmented in a myriad of possessors can be actively searched and accessed by a myriad of academic entrepreneurs endowed with the distinctive capability to screen and appreciate the scope of application and recombination of the existing knowledge.

The return to the centrality of the academic system within the new mode of knowledge governance takes place with considerable changes with respect to the public mode. Increasing attention has been paid to improving the dissemination of academic knowledge based upon traditional tools such as the publication of scientific papers and the enrollment of PhDs in productive activities in the economic system, strengthening direct transactions-cum-interactions between the academic system and the business sector.

In the distributed mode of knowledge governance the generation and exploitation of technological knowledge split, again, as in the public mode. The academic system is, again, the main locus of generation. Corporations and start-ups specialize in the exploitation. The distributed mode, however, is characterized by a new complementarity between corporations and start-ups: the take over of start-ups that have survived and become public with initial public offerings to the stock exchange enables corporations to acquire new technological knowledge that exhibits high levels of economic viability. Financial takeovers of start-ups that entered financial markets and their eventual delisting and merger become alternative modes to acquire technological knowledge and substitute R&D expenditures of corporations. The trade of knowledge intensive property rights (KIPR) in financial markets provides a surrogate for the trade of disembodied knowledge. Technological knowledge in fact is embodied in the stock of the high-tech start-ups. Financial markets integrate both the direct knowledge interactions of the public mode and the knowledge transactions-cum-interactions of the corporate mode (Kenney, 2011).

Platforms

Finally transactions-cum-interactions are systematically implemented by the introduction of the platform, a new organizational form, based upon incomplete contracts, that makes it possible to combine ex-ante with ex-post coordination among independent firms. The complementarity between the research projects of different firms is enhanced by the creation of platforms of cooperating firms that try to implement the division of innovative labor favoring the convergence of complementary research activities within a central framework that is typically mastered by a large corporation. Platforms are based upon a nexus of incomplete contracts where the parties agree upon the procedures to validate their performances as they agree that they are not able to specify ex-ante all the possible states of the world. The content of the contract shifts away from the specific identification of tangible obligations that are substituted by agreement upon the procedures that will be implemented according to different possible occurrences with multiple stages of renegotiation (Hart and Moore, 1988).

Incomplete contracts make it possible to complement the ex-ante coordination where the parties agree to cooperate on a common project with the ex-post coordination based upon the actual outcomes of the collaboration. The differences among platforms with respect to their location within technological districts is sharp. Platforms are created to bring together in a single framework the complementary competences of diverse firms that can be activated to cooperate in the realization of a common innovative project where the competences of each are identified ex-ante together with the implementation of a convergent strategy of knowledge generation and exploitation that is verified ex-post (Patrucco, 2011; Consoli and Patrucco, 2008 and 2011).

4. Conclusions

Knowledge is essential for the efficiency of an economic system. The increase in efficiency of an economic system can only take place as a result of the increase in the amount of knowledge used as intermediary input for the production of all other goods. Knowledge is a very special economic good characterized by an array of highly idiosyncratic characteristics such as non-exhaustibility, non-appropriability, non-divisibility and hence cumulability, complementarity and fungibility. Moreover the recombinant generation of new knowledge necessarily impinges upon the use of existing knowledge as an intermediary input. Hence knowledge is at the same time an output and an input. The appreciation of the crucial role of external knowledge as a necessary, indispensable and strictly complementary input into the generation of new knowledge marks a major step in the analysis of the generation of technological knowledge, after the Arrovian concern about market failure and the discovery by Griliches of knowledge spillover as a supplementary production factor.

The frame elaborated by the new growth theory upon Griliches' contributions exhibits all its limitations with the new understanding of the working of knowledge externalities and of the mechanisms that make the generation of new knowledge possible. The analysis of knowledge externalities has shown that external knowledge does not fall from heaven. Knowledge externalities are pecuniary rather than technical because the access and use of external knowledge requires dedicated activities that entail specific costs. The identification of the generation of knowledge as a specific activity into which existing knowledge, including external, is not a supplementary input that helps to increase output levels and hence total factor productivity growth, but quite a complementary and indispensable production factor, without which the generation of technological knowledge cannot take place, has important implications.

First, the limitations stemming from exclusive intellectual property rights to the dissemination and use of new knowledge may increase the incentives for its generation but do have direct negative consequences not only on the efficiency of the generation of new technological knowledge, but on its actual viability. Redundant duplications of effort reduce efficiency and in some cases knowledge rationing caused by exclusive intellectual property rights may actually block the generation of new knowledge. The search for new intellectual property rights regimes based upon compulsory-patenting-cum-royalties that allow the combination of the necessary remuneration of knowledge together with its dissemination becomes even more necessary.

Second, the appreciation of the crucial role of knowledge interactions, transactions and communication in the recombinant generation, dissemination, use and exploitation of technological knowledge opens a new chapter. The standard understanding of the working of both the market mechanism and the public research system needs to accommodate a new broader framework that is able to integrate the working of knowledge interactions. Because of the poor understanding of the knowledge communication mechanisms, the institutional setting elaborated to cope with the failure of markets, based upon exclusive intellectual property right regimes and the large public research system, risks the systematic misallocation of the generous resources provided by the State. A public failure adds to the private one.

In this context, the tools of complexity economics enable us to frame the analysis of the generation of knowledge governance procedures and of technological knowledge – and the eventual introduction of technological innovations – as emergent properties of an economic system that is able to provide, with organized architectures of network relations, access to the external knowledge that supports the creative reaction of firms that try to innovate in response to unexpected changes in their economic environment. The identification of the mechanisms that are necessary to accommodate and integrate the pervasive role of external knowledge brings the notion of knowledge governance to the center of the analysis. Knowledge governance is necessary to coordinate the array of institutional surrogates that reduce the risks of undersupply and misallocation of resources of both pure markets and public bodies.

Knowledge governance mechanisms make it possible to coordinate the flows of knowledge transactions, interactions and communication within the wide spectrum of transactions-cum-interactions so as to enable the access and use of knowledge as an indispensable input into the recombinant generation of new knowledge. The inclusion in this single, integrated frame of knowledge governance, of both the analysis of the relations among firms in the business system and between them and the academic system, enables us to implement the assessment of their viability in terms of actual amount of useful knowledge made available to the economic system.

This chapter has shown that knowledge governance is an emergent property of an economic and institutional system. Its changing ingredients and mechanisms and its evolving architectures are fully endogenous as they are determined by the interactions of the agents that are part of the collective endeavor of the organization of the generation, dissemination and use of scientific and technological knowledge, both within institutions and in the market place.

Knowledge governance is a key component of the national systems of innovation as it plays a central role in assessing their actual capability to support the introduction of technological innovations. As a crucial component of an emergent property, however, it is intrinsically dynamic and endogenous to the national systems. It keeps changing and adjusting to the dynamics of interactions and feedbacks that take place within the system among agents and between them and the institutions.

Knowledge governance is itself an emergent property of an economic system that makes the generation of technological knowledge and the introduction of innovation – as emergent systemic property – possible. Knowledge governance, in fact, is the result of self-organizing processes based upon feedbacks as well as trial and error processes by means of which a variety of heterogeneous agents discover new ways to organize the generation, dissemination and exploitation of scientific and technological knowledge. Such self-organizing processes are occasionally centered and guided by changing key figures that take the role of beams of a new governance mode. The evidence suggests that knowledge governance takes place with many alternative mechanisms, ingredients and architectural modes. The dynamics of the modes of knowledge governance lead to a variety that reflects the differences across economic systems in terms of industrial, institutional, regional and technological structure.

As such the dynamic variety of modes of knowledge governance can be considered a distinctive aspect of the variety of capitalism. These different knowledge governance mechanisms and modes can be considered alternative institutional solutions designed and implemented to organize the complexity of knowledge interactions that are specific to each economic system in supporting the creation and exploitation of the pecuniary knowledge externalities that are at the origin of the increase of total factor productivity and hence of economic growth (Hall and Soskice, 2001).

Only economic systems able to organize their complexity and implement effective knowledge governance mechanisms can sustain their growth of output by means of the systematic increase of total factor productivity. The continual recreation of pecuniary knowledge externalities is crucial for the process to keep momentum in its dynamic path. Pecuniary knowledge externalities are not bound to increase steadily, on the contrary, their levels can decline and reduce the opportunities for the successful generation of new technological knowledge and the eventual introduction of productivity enhancing technological innovations. Dynamic increasing returns stemming from sustained growth of total factor productivity can take place as long as the system is able to sustain appropriate levels of pecuniary knowledge externalities. Congestion and opportunistic behavior may easily increase. The dynamic maintenance of knowledge governance mechanisms is crucial for the sustainability of dynamic increasing returns.

Acknowledgements

This project has received funding from the European Union's Seventh Framework Programme for research, technological development and demonstration under grant agreement no. 266959. The author acknowledges also the institutional support of the Collegio Carlo Alberto and the University of Torino.

References

Adams, J.D. (1990), Fundamental stocks of knowledge and productivity growth, *Journal of Political Economy* 98, 673–702.

Aghion, P., Dewatripont, M., Hoxby, C.M., Mas-Colell, A., and Sapir, A. (2009), The governance and performance of research universities: Evidence from Europe and the U.S., NBER Working Paper 14851.

Antonelli, C. (2006), The governance of localized knowledge. An information economics approach to the economics of knowledge, *Industry and Innovation* 13, 227–261.

Antonelli, C. (2008a), The new economics of the university: A knowledge governance approach, *Journal of Technology Transfer* 33, 1–22.

Antonelli, C. (2008b), Pecuniary knowledge externalities: The convergence of directed technological change and the emergence of innovation systems, *Industrial and Corporate Change* 17, 1049–1070.

Antonelli, C. (2008c), *Localized Technological Change. Towards the Economics of Complexity*, Routledge, London.

Antonelli, C. (2009), The economics of innovation: From the classical legacies to the economics of complexity, *Economics of Innovation and New Technology* 18, 611–646.

Antonelli, C. (2011), The economic complexity of technological change: Knowledge interactions and path dependence, in Antonelli, C. (ed.) *Handbook on the Economic Complexity of Technological Change*, Edward Elgar, Cheltenham, pp. 1–62.

Antonelli, C. (2013), Knowledge governance, pecuniary knowledge externalities and total factor productivity growth, *Economic Development Quarterly* 27, 62–70.

Antonelli, C. and Fassio, C. (2011), Globalization and innovation in advanced economies, in Libecap, G. (ed.) *Advances in the Study of Entrepreneurship, Innovation and Economic Growth*, Volume 22, Emerald Publishing, Cambridge, pp. 21–46.

Antonelli, C. and Fassio, C. (2014a), The economics of the light economy. Globalization, skill biased technological change and slow growth, *Technological Forecasting and Social Change*, forthcoming.

Antonelli, C. and Fassio, C. (2014b), Globalization and the emergence of the knowledge economy, *Economic Development Quarterly* 87, 89–107.

Antonelli, C. and Fassio, C. (2014c), The heterogeneity of knowledge and the academic mode of knowledge governance: Italian evidence in the first part of the xx century, *Science and Public Policy* 41, 15–28.

Antonelli, C. and Patrucco, P.P. (2014), Organizational innovations, ICTs and knowledge governance: The case of platforms, in Bauer, J. M. and Latzer, M. (eds.), *Handbook on the Economics of the Internet*, Edward Elgar, Cheltenham, forthcoming.

Antonelli, C. and Teubal, M. (2008), Knowledge intensive property rights and the evolution of venture capitalism, *Journal of Institutional Economics* 4, 163–182.

Antonelli, C. and Teubal, M. (2010), Venture capital as a mechanism for knowledge governance in Viale, R. and Etzkowitz, H. (eds.), *The Capitalization of Knowledge*, Edward Elgar, Cheltenham, pp. 98–120.

Antonelli, C. and Teubal, M. (2012), From the corporation to venture capitalism: New surrogate markets for knowledge and innovation-led economic growth, in Dietricht, M. and Krafft, J. (eds.), *Handbook on the Economics and Theory of the Firm*, Edward Elgar, Cheltenham, pp. 545–560.

Antonelli, C., Patrucco, P.P., and Rossi, F. (2010), The economics of knowledge interaction and the changing role of universities, in Gallouj, F. and Djellai, F. (eds.), *Handbook of Innovation and Services*, Edward Elgar, Cheltenham, pp. 153–177.

Antonelli, C., Crepax, N., and Fassio, C. (2013), The cliometrics of academic chairs. Scientific knowledge and economic growth, the evidence across Italian regions 1900–1959, *Journal of Technology Transfer* 38, 537–564.

Arrow, K. J. (1962), Economic welfare and the allocation of resources for invention, in Nelson, R. R. (ed.), *The Rate and Direction of Inventive Activity: Economic and Social Factors*, Princeton University Press for NBER, Princeton, pp. 609–625.

Arrow, K. J. (1969), Classificatory notes on the production and transmission of technical knowledge, *American Economic Review* 59, 29–35.

Arrow, K. J. (1974), *The Limits of Organization*, W.W. Norton, New York.

Auranen, O. and Nieminen, M. (2010), University research funding and publication performance. An international comparison, *Research Policy* 39, 822–834.

Buchanan, J. and Yoon, Y. (2000), Symmetric tragedies: Commons and anticommons, *Journal of Law and Economics* 43, 1–13.

Cassiman, B. and Veugelers, R. (2006), In search of complementarity in innovation strategy: Internal R&D, cooperation in R&D and external technology acquisition, *Management Science* 52, 68–82.

Cave, M. and Weale, M. (1992), The assessment of higher education: The state of play, *Oxford Review of Economic Policy* 8, 1–18.

Chandler, A. D. (1977), *The Visible Hand: The Managerial Revolution in American Business*, The Belknap Press of Harvard University Press, Cambridge.

Chesbrough, H. (2003), *Open Innovation. The New Imperative for Creating and Profiting from Technology*, Harvard Business School Press, Boston.

Chesbrough, H., Vanhaverbeke, W., and West, J. (eds.) (2006), *Open Innovation: Researching a New Paradigm*, Oxford University Press, Oxford.

Cohen, W.M. and Levinthal, D.A. (1989), Innovation and learning: The two faces of R&D, *Economic Journal* 99, 569–596.

Cohen, W.M. and Levinthal, D.A. (1990), Absorptive capacity: A new perspective on learning and innovation, *Administrative Science Quarterly* 35, 128–152.

Consoli, D. and Patrucco, P.P. (2008), Innovation platforms and the governance of knowledge: Evidence from Italy and the UK, *Economics of Innovation and New Technology* 17 (7), 701–718.

Consoli, D. and Patrucco, P.P. (2011), Complexity and the coordination of technological knowledge: The case of innovation platforms, in Antonelli, C. (ed.), *Handbook on the Economic Complexity of Technological Change*, Edward Elgar, Cheltenham, pp. 201–220.

Dasgupta, P. and David, P.A. (1987), Information disclosure and the economics of science and technology, Chapter 16, in Feiwel, G. (ed.), *Arrow and the Ascent of Modern Economic Theory*, New York University Press, New York.

Dasgupta, P. and David, P.A. (1994), Toward a new economics of science, *Research Policy* 23, 487–521.

David, P. (1993), Knowledge, property and the system dynamics of technological change, in Summers, L.S. and Shah, S. (eds.), *Proceedings of the World Bank Annual Conference on Development Economics* (published as a supplement to the World Bank Economic Review), International Bank for Reconstruction and Development, Washington D.C., pp. 215–248.

Edquist, C. and Zabala-Iturriagagoiti, J.M. (2012), Public procurement for innovation as mission oriented innovation policy, *Research Policy* 41, 1757–1769.

Etzkowitz, H. and Leydesdorff, L. (2000), The dynamics of innovation: from National Systems and 'Mode 2' to a Triple Helix of university–industry–government relations, *Research Policy* 29, 109–123.

Feldman, M. (1994), The university and economic development: The case of Johns Hopkins University and Baltimore, *Economic Development Quarterly* 8(1), 67–76.

Feller, I. (1990), Universities as engines of R&D-based economic growth: they think they can, *Research Policy* 19, 335–348.

Foss, N.J. and Michailova, S. (2009), *Knowledge Governance: Processes and Perspectives*, Oxford University Press, Oxford.

Gallouj, F. and Windrum, P. (2009), Services and services innovation, *Journal of Evolutionary Economics* 19 141–148.

Gerschenkron, A. (1962), *Economic Backwardness in Historical Perspective. A Book of Essays*, Belknap Press of Harvard University Press, Cambridge.

Geuna, A. (1999), *The Economics of Knowledge Production: Funding and the Structure of University Research*, Edward Elgar, Cheltenham.

Graf, H. (2011), Gatekeepers in regional networks of innovators, *Cambridge Journal of Economics* 35, 173–198.

Griliches, Z. (1979), Issues in assessing the contribution of Research and Development to productivity growth, *Bell Journal of Econometrics* 10, 1, 92–116.

Griliches, Z. (1992), The search for R&D spillovers, *Scandinavian Journal of Economics* 94, Supplement: 29–47.

Hall, P.A. and Soskice, D. (eds.) (2001), *Varieties of Capitalism: The Institutional Foundations of Comparative Advantage*, Oxford University Press, Oxford.

Hart, O. and Moore, J. (1988), Incomplete contracts and renegotiation, *Econometrica* 56, 755–785.

Howells, J., Ramlogan, R., and Cheng, S.-L. (2012), Innovation and university collaboration: Paradox and complexity within the knowledge economy, *Cambridge Journal of Economics* 36, 703–721.

Jaffe, A. (1989), The real effect of academic research, *American Economic Review* 88, 957–979.

Jones, F.B. (2009), The burden of knowledge and the death of the Renaissance man: Is innovation getting harder? *Review of Economics and Statistics* 76, 283–317.

Kenney, M. (2011), How venture capital became a component of the US national system of innovation, *Industrial and Corporate Change* 20, 1677–1723.

Langlois, R.N. (1999), Scale, scope and the reuse of knowledge, in Dow, Sheila C. and Earl, P.E. (eds.), *Economic Organization and Economic Knowledge: Essays in Honour of Brian J. Loasby*, Edward Elgar, Cheltenham, pp. 239–254.

Link, A. and Siegel, D. (2007), *Innovation, Entrepreneurship, and Technological Change*, Oxford University Press, Oxford.

Mansfield, E. (1991), Academic research and industrial innovation, *Research Policy* 20, 1–12.

Mansfield, E. (1995), Academic research underlying industrial innovations: Sources, characteristics, and financing, *Review of Economics and Statistics* LXXVII, 55–65.

Mansfield, E. and Lee, J.Y. (1996), The modern university: Contributor to industrial innovation and recipient of industrial R&D support, *Research Policy* 25, 1047–1058.

Mansfield, E., Schwartz, M., and Wagner, S. (1981), Imitation costs and patents: An empirical study, *Economic Journal* 91, 907–918.

March, J.C. (1991), Exploration and exploitation in organizing learning, *Organization Science* 2, 71–87.

Martin, R. and Sunley, P. (2012), Forms of emergence and the evolution of economic landscapes, *Journal of Economic Behavior and Organization* 82, 338–351.

Mazzucato, M. (2013), *The Entrepreneurial State: Debunking Public vs. Private Sector Myths*, Anthem Press, London.

Mowery, D. (2009), Plus ça change: Industrial R&D in the 'third industrial revolution', *Industrial and Corporate Change* 18, 1–50.

Mowery, D.C. (2010), Alfred Chandler and knowledge management within the firm, *Industrial and Corporate Change* 19, 483–507.

Nelson, R.R. (1959), The simple economics of basic scientific research, *Journal of Political Economy* 67, 297–306.

Nelson, R.R. (ed.) (1993), *National Innovation System: A Comparative Analysis*, Oxford University Press, Oxford.

Ostrom, E. (2010), Beyond markets and states: Polycentric governance of complex economic systems, *American Economic Review* 100, 641–672.

Ostrom, E. and Hess, C. (eds.) (2006), *Understanding Knowledge as a Commons: From Theory to Practice*, MIT Press, Cambridge.

Özman, M. (2009). Interfirm networks and innovation: A survey of the literature, *Economics of Innovation and New Technology* 18, 39–67.

Patrucco, P.P. (2011), Changing network structure in the organization of knowledge: The innovation platform in the evidence of the automobile system in Turin, *Economics of Innovation and New Technology* 20 (5), 477–493.

Patrucco, P.P. (2014), The economics of innovation and knowledge interactions: Toward a systemic approach, in Patrucco, P.P. (ed.), *The Economics of Knowledge Generation and Distribution: The Role of Interactions in the System Dynamics of Innovation and Growth*, Routledge, London.

Polanyi, M. (1966) *The Tacit Dimension*, Anchor Books, New York.

Probert, J., Connell, D., and Mina, A. (2013), R&D service firms: The hidden engine of high-tech economy? *Research Policy* 42, 1274–1285.

Rochet, J.C. and Tirole, J. (2003), Platform competition in two-sided markets, *Journal of the European Economic Association* 1(4), 990–1029.

Romer, P.M. (1990), Endogenous technological change, *Journal of Political Economy* 98, S71–102.

Romer, P.M. (1994), The origins of endogenous growth, *Journal of Economic Perspectives* 8, 3–22.

Rosenberg, N. and Nelson, R. R. (1994), American universities and technical advance in industry, *Research Policy* 23(3), 323–348.

Saviotti, P.P. (2007), On the dynamics of generation and utilization of knowledge: The local character of knowledge, *Structural Change and Economic Dynamics* 18, 387–408.

Schumpeter, J.A. (1942), *Capitalism, Socialism and Democracy*, Harper and Brothers, New York.

Schumpeter, J.A. (1947), The creative response in economic history, *Journal of Economic History* 7, 149–159.

Stephan, P.E. (1996), The economics of science, *Journal of Economic Literature* 34, 199–235.

Stephan, P.E. (2011), *How Economics Shapes Science*, Harvard University Press, Cambridge.

Stiglitz, J.E. and Weiss, A. (1981), Credit rationing in markets with imperfect information, *American Economic Review* 71, 393–410.

Von Hippel, E. (1988), *The Sources of Innovation*, Oxford University Press, Oxford.

Von Hippel, E. (1994), Sticky information and the locus of problem-solving: Implications for innovation, *Management Science* 40, 429–439.

Von Hippel, E. (1998), Economics of product development by users: The impact of sticky local information, *Management Science* 44, 629–644.

Weitzman, M.L. (1996), Hybridizing growth theory, *American Economic Review* 86, 207–212.

Weitzman, M.L. (1998), Recombinant growth, *Quarterly Journal of Economics* 113, 331–360.

Index

263

For Product Safety Concerns and Information please contact our EU
representative GPSR@taylorandfrancis.com Taylor & Francis Verlag GmbH,
Kaufingerstraße 24, 80331 München, Germany

Printed and bound by CPI Group (UK) Ltd, Croydon, CR0 4YY
08/05/2025
01864358-0007